Women Philosophers on Economics, Technology, Environment, and Gender History

Women Philosophers on Economics, Technology, Environment, and Gender History

—

Shaping the Future, Rethinking the Past

Edited by
Ruth Edith Hagengruber

DE GRUYTER

ISBN 978-3-11-221500-5
e-ISBN (PDF) 978-3-11-105180-2
e-ISBN (EPUB) 978-3-11-105226-7

Library of Congress Control Number: 2023934078

Bibliographic information published by the Deutsche Nationalbibliothek
The Deutsche Nationalbibliothek lists this publication in the Deutsche Nationalbibliografie; detailed bibliographic data are available on the internet at http://dnb.dnb.de.

© 2025 Walter de Gruyter GmbH, Berlin/Boston
This volume is text- and page-identical with the hardback published in 2023.
Cover image: Ruth Edith Hagengruber
Printing and binding: CPI books GmbH, Leck

www.degruyter.com

Preface

In times of current crisis, the voice of women is needed more than ever. The accumulation of war and environmental catastrophes teaches us that exploitation of people and nature through violent appropriation and enrichment for the sake of short-term self-interest exacts its price.

There can be no new perspective on the future if we do not reconsider the past. This collection of texts is an expression of that opinion, and I thank all those who have agreed to work together to reshape the future, by reflecting on the past.

At the symposium organized by Xiao Wei at Tshingua University in Beijing, I was entrusted to host the 18th symposium of the International Association of Women Philosophers. I am grateful for having been given this opportunity. Far more than five hundred participants attended the hybrid conference and about 140 lectures were offered. Due to the covid epidemic, the symposium had to be postponed for one year and was held in hybrid form in 2021. Thirty essays are presented in this volume, dedicated to the topics of economy, environment and technology, and to a new reading of the history of philosophy, from western and non-western tradition.

My warm thanks go to all the contributors and participants. I am grateful to the German Research Foundation for the funding of the conference. In particular, I thank my team at the Center for the History of Women Philosophers and that from the EcoTechGender Teaching and Research area, Shari Wölker, Rebekka Schubert, Felix Grewe and Violeta Milicevic.

In this volume world renowned philosophers as well as up-and-coming philosophers from all over the world sketch out in a constructive and in a critical take what must be changed, and how a world that takes women's concern into account will look like. Together we define the future and we re-interpret the past.

Paderborn, 31.01.2023   Ruth Edith Hagengruber

Table of Contents

Abbreviations —— XI

Part I: Introduction

Ruth Edith Hagengruber
Women Philosophers on Economics, Technology, Environment and Gender History. Shaping the Future – Rethinking the Past. —— 3

Herta Nagl-Docekal
The Beginnings: A Retrospective View by a Former Board Member of the IAPh —— 13

Part II: Economics, Technology, Environment

Julie A. Nelson
Economic Theory and Moral Imagination —— 23

Federica Giardini
Ecology and Economy. Feminist Perspectives —— 35

Andrea Günter
Towards a Feminist Theory of Money. Patriarchal Economic Structures, the Aristotelian Concept of Justice and the Intermediacy of Money —— 45

Kateryna Karpenko
Gender Justice and Ecological Issues —— 57

Shalini Attri and Priyanka Singh
***Sultana's Dream:* Eco[U]topian and Feminist Intersections** —— 69

Anne Sauka
Ontogenealogies of Body-Environments: Perspectives for an Experiential Ontological Shift —— 81

Corinna Casi
Women, Nature and Neocolonial Struggles: Different Perspectives on Indigenous Women's Position —— 97

Emma Baizabal
From Cyberfeminism and Technofeminism to an Ontological and Feminist Technology —— 109

Ruth Edith Hagengruber
The Third Knowledge Dimension: From a Binary System to a Three-limbed Epistemology —— 119

Sabine Thürmel
Social Machines in a Data-driven World —— 129

Laura Roberts
Smart Feminist Cities: The Case of Barcelona en Comú —— 137

Tatiana Kolomeitceva
User Experience as Enlightenment: User Experience for Women Philosophers' Presentation —— 147

Talya Ucaryilmaz Deibel and Eric Deibel
Artificial Intelligence in Ancient Rome: Classical Roman Philosophy on Legal Subjectivity —— 157

Part III: History (Non-Western and Western)

Priyanka Jha
Pursuits of Global Gendered Intellectual History: Stories from India —— 171

Toyomi Iwawaki-Riebel
Yosano Akiko's Philosophy and Poetry – Modernization of Japan and Women's Liberation —— 191

Timothy DeGriselles
A Philosophical Defense of Self-Defense: Examining Sor Juana Inés de la Cruz' *Reply to Sor Filotea* —— 203

Demin XU
Le rôle des œuvres de Rousseau dans les mouvements féministes en Chine moderne —— 217

Pedro Falcão Pricladnitzky
Mind of Nature: Cavendish's Argument for Panpsychism —— 235

Sarah Bonfim
First Principles: The Path to Women's Emancipation in Wollstonecraft's *Rights of Woman* —— 249

Annabelle Bonnet
Women's Access to French Philosophy: A Forgotten History (1880–1924) —— 261

Andrea Pérez-Fernández
Hannah Höch: Notes on Violence and Vulnerability —— 271

Part IV: Gender Issues and Feminist Concepts

Cristina Sánchez
Feminist Philosophy and Democracy: The Case of Spain —— 285

Diana María Acevedo-Zapata and María Lucía Rivera-Sanín
Gender Equality in Colombia's Philosophy Programs: Faculty Participation —— 295

Tzitzi Janik Rojas Torres
Teaching Islamic Feminisms in the History of Philosophy in Mexico: A Decolonial and Feminist Effort —— 323

Ingrid Alloni
From Self-awareness to Political and Social Improvement: A Feminist Identitarian Path —— 335

Ariadni Polychroniou
"*Je me* révolte, donc *nous* sommes": Reconceptualizing Contemporary Refugee Resistances through the Butlerian Reconstruction of Hannah Arendt's Public Sphere —— 347

Rosaura Martínez Ruiz
Covid-19 and "Stay at Home": A Contrast Dye That Highlights Gender Violence and the Violence of Inequity —— 361

Valentina Gaudiano
A New-old Topos for the Future. Rethinking and Rediscovering Oneself as Human —— 371

Contributors to This Volume —— 381

Index of Names —— 389

Index of Subjects —— 393

Abbreviations

Abbreviations for Works Quoted in This Volume

GNP Margret Cavendish, *Grounds of Natural Philosophy*
Ins. Gaius, *Institutiones*
NE Aristotle, *Nicomachean Ethics*
OEP Margret Cavendish, *Observations Upon Experimental Philosophy*
PL Margret Cavendish, *Philosophical Letters*

Other Abbreviations

AAP Australian Association of Philosophy
ADHUC Research Center for Theory, Gender, Sexuality at Barcelona University
AI Artificial Intelligence
APA American Philosophical Association
BEC Barcelona en Comú
BPS Bhagat Phool Singh
BPSMV Bhagat Phool Singh Mahila Vishwavidyalaya
CEDAW Convention on the Elimination of All Forms of Discrimination against Women
CEO Chief Executive Officer
CPA Canadian Philosophical Association
CT Computed Tomography
CV Curriculum Vitae
CWDS Centre for Women's Development Studies
DHE Department of Higher Education, Haryana
EHESS École des Hautes Études en Sciences Sociales
ERDF European Regional Development Fund
EU Europoean Union
FAPESP São Paulo Research Foundation
FISP International Federation of Philosophical Societies
GDP Gross Domestic Product
GIH Gendered Intellectual History
HEI Higher Education Institutions
HELSUS Helsinki Institute of Sustainability Science
HIPA Haryana Institue of Public Administration
HWPS History of Women Philosophers and Scientists, Paderborn University
IAPh International Association of Women Philosophers
ICT Information and communications technology
IFRIS Institut Francilien Recherche Innovation Société
JIWS Journal of International Women's Studies

JMIT	Seth Jai Parkash Mukand Lal Institute of Engineering and Technology
LGBTI	Lesbian, gay, bisexual, transgender, and intersex
LGBTQ+	Lesbian, gay, bisexual, transgender, and queer (or questioning), plus other sexual and gender identities
LGTB	Lesbian, gay, bisexual, and transgender
MEN	National Education Department of Colombia
PNAAM	Protocols for Native American Archival Materials
POLIS	Department of Politics and International Studies, University of Cambridge
RAF	Red Army Faction
SNEEJ	Southwest Network for Environmental and Economic Justice
SNIES	National Information System of Higher Education
STEM	Science Technology Engineering Mathematics
STN	Strategic Research Council, Academy of Finland
STS	Science and Technology Studies
SWIP	Society of Women in Philosophy
TEK	Traditional Ecological Knowledge
TUM	Technical University of Munich
UFRGS	University of Rio Grande do Sul
UNAM	Autonomous National University of Mexico
UNESCO	United Nations Educational, Scientific and Cultural Organization
WCP	World Congress of Philosophy
WED	Women, Environment and Sustainable Development
WWII	World War II
YHYS	Finnish Society for Environmental Social Science

Part I: **Introduction**

Ruth Edith Hagengruber
Women Philosophers on Economics, Technology, Environment and Gender History. Shaping the Future – Rethinking the Past.

In times of current crisis, the voices of women are needed more than ever. The accumulation of war and environmental catastrophes teaches us that exploitation of people and nature through violent appropriation and enrichment for the sake of short-term self-interest exacts its price.

This book presents contributions on the most relevant and currently most urgent issues: The reshaping of the economy, environmental problems, technology. In addition, history from the non-Western and Western tradition is re-read. With an outlook into the problems of class, race and gender in its intersectional framing, the collection offers a unique overview of current research in these fields and contributes to the renewal and contemporary presentation of feminist thought from concrete perspectives and with regard to factual issues.

Though many things have changed for women in the last 40–50 years and mile steps have been taken to understand that women's concern is one of human concern, that impacts everyone. The United Nation supported the advancement of gender equality through landmark agreements such as the Beijing Declaration, the Platform for Action and the Convention on the Elimination of All Forms of Discrimination against Women (CEDAW). However, although themselves half of humanity and with the offspring under their responsibility, women make up more than 75% of the world's population, still they have little say in shaping the future and even less when we look into the past. Neither are women equally represented nor is it clear how the future should look like to enhance the change. *Shaping the Future, Rethinking the Past* is intended to fill this gap. In this volume world renowned philosophers as well as up-and-coming philosophers from all over the world sketch out in a constructive and in a critical take what must be changed, and how a world that takes into account women's concern will look like. Together we shape the future and we re-interpret the past.

The book starts by recalling the founding of the Assoziation von Philosophinnen in Deutschland in the year 1974. The paper written by Herta Nagl-Docecal addresses the difficulties the Association encountered in its first decade, while it is now one of the most influential organizations of women philosophers.

The second part of the volume is dedicated to the most pressing topics of the present, economics, environment and technology. While women have yet to play a significant role in any of these fields and it is not clear how they will change the landmarks, this collection presents key texts on these topics to showcase the visions of established and new voices from women researchers. Fifteen papers are dedicated to the topics economics, environment, technology.

Economic Theory and Moral Imagination contributed by Julie A. Nelson, Boston University, US argues that economists have, for more than a century, portrayed economics as a physics-like discipline concerned with explaining the underlying mechanics of an amoral market system, presumed to be driven by self-interest and competition. Drawing on feminist work in economics, she examines the binary, hierarchical gender metaphors underlying these claims. Nelson explores the damage these biased beliefs have done to the creation of knowledge and to our ability to deal with issues such as climate change, and suggests alternatives. Federica Giardini is deeply rooted into the Italian feminist tradition. In *Ecology and Economy. Feminist Perspectives* she takes a perspective that refers economies with the other disciplines questioning the forms of knowledge that aggravate the hierarchy of economics to the point of autonomy: to proceed to formalization and to explain reality by datafication. She criticizes that economic science thus no longer consists in representing, and not even in producing, reality, but rather in a formalization – a sort of updated version of the 17th-century "Calculemus!", that returns loaded with ideology. Giardini asks how an alternative perception of the feminine body will change the framework of economics and the links between economics and ecology. In doing so, she starts to reconstruct a feminist and genealogical perspective with the reconceptualization of the term "value". Value is in fact a hybrid term that connects morality and economics, and thus allows us to identify the interactions between ideology and mathematical calculation, in short, it allows us to trace the interaction between domination and exploitation. Andrea Günter, Freiburg University, Germany presents in her paper *Towards a Feminist Theory of Money* a critique of patriarchal economic structures, going back to the Aristotelian concept of justice and the intermediacy of money. Her demand to develop a feminist critique of money economics relates to a statement that denies the neutrality of money, much more she claims that its appearance within the different realms of social life, in its material and legal substance, and its social structure framed by reciprocity and justice, should be investigated for reconstructing its implicit patriarchal traditions. Kateryna Karpenko from National Medical University Kharkiv, Ukraine connects questions of *Gender Justice and Ecological Issues*. Karpenko argues that the environmental and economic problems are strongly connected to the distribution of roles in society between men and women. Now, as we are all facing the issue of survival this topic is receiving new interest. However, she adds a further argument, which is the neglect of a philosophical perspective. The philosophical discourse suffers from all sides as it neglects philosophical tasks, such as to come up to universalist stances. The mechanism of formation of research approaches has become pluralistic and highly dynamic, but the reference to universal principles should not be ignored. In *Sultana's Dream: Eco[U]topian and Feminist Intersections*, Shalini Attri and Priyanka Singh, from BPS Women's University, India present a broad scope tackling with Earth's geology, anthropogenic climate change, the notion of capitalism, and the destruction of ecological resources. All these subjects are compelling for scholars to deal with the question of sustainability in the 21st century. A possible access to handle and to analyze this question is found in Begum Rokeya Sakhawat Hossain's *Sultana's Dream*, a narrative of ecotopia that dissolves the logocentric and essentialist notions centered on women and men offering a revolutionary combination to handle the ecological crisis successfully by investigating the harmful environmental impacts. Contributor Anne Sauka, from the University of Latvia, presents with *Ontogenealogies of Body-Environments* an onto-genealogical approach to the analysis of the lived, experienced materiality of the body-environment assemblage. In particular, she explores the tie between the bio(il)logical and biopolitical, characterizing this tie as a twofold onto-genealogical linkage that both a) reflects the genealogical character of life itself, as well as b) invites a critical analysis of the prevailing ontologies as co-constructive of lived materialities. It highlights the potential of considering local onto-genealogies that reflect alternative ontologies and run parallel to the dominant paradigm of the Global North. Corinna Casi, from Helsinki Institute of Sustainability Science HELSUS, Finland discusses *Different Perspectives on Indigenous Women's Position* in her *Women, Nature and Neocolonial Struggles* and situates the gender inequality debate within the relation between nature and women, conceptualized academically in 1970s in the philosophical field of ecofeminism. The paper also discusses the limitation of the women-nature link and then moves to the field of Indigenous feminism keeping the focus of the relation between nature and women and observing how this has influenced the condition of women within Indigenous communities such as the Igbo people in Nigeria, the Kahnawa:kev people in Canada and the Sami people living in Sapmi.

The following six articles deal with questions of technology and computer science. The authors span the arc from technology critique, technology as an opportunity for social and physical support, to technology as an enhancement of social interaction but also in its critical and historical dimension, as is shown in the paper on the meaning of technology in the period of Roman technology. Emma Baizabal, from University of Mexico, Mexico discusses in *From Cyberfeminism and Technofeminism to an Ontological and Feminist Technology*, the difference of the meaning of practical and theoretical concerns with technology. She holds that while practical requests and needs impose regulations and restrictions to the production, distribution and consumption of technical objects – what she calls an instrumental perspective focused primarily on the uses and misuses of some utensils – the feminist perspective is not yet part of such kind of deliberations. She presents a Feminist analysis that describes the access of women to the production, distribution and use of technical objects. Power relations, especially patriarchal and capitalist ones are also embedded into those objects perpetuating a gender role from its design and fabrication, but have not yet succeeded to become a constructive part of a regulative practice. In my paper on the *Third Knowledge Dimension. From a Binary System to a Three-limbed Epistemology* I argue that a new kind of epistemology evolves from the use of artificial intelligence. The path it takes changes our understanding of the world, of human values and also of science and it will be irreversible. The paper sets out what the cornerstones of change will be and what consequences this will have for our ontology of things. Through this new dimension of knowledge, we will also liquefy the binary understanding of gender as this form of intelligence influences our knowledge structure. Sabine Thürmel from Technical University, Munich, Germany turns to *Social Machines in a Data-driven World.* She focuses on the impact of robots in medicine and pharmacy. Algorithmic innovations in Big Data based on analytics and machine learning result in less influence for the human collaborators and more power for these machines. This becomes most evident for examples from medicine and pharmacy. Big Data analytics promises to provide not just insights but foresight: predictive analytics is used for optimizing the discovery path in drug discovery and decision processes in medical environments. The anticipatory governance in medical early warning systems and preventive healthcare systems allows medical decision processes to be supported or even automated. In her paper *Smart Feminist Cities: The Case of Barcelona en Comú*, Laura Roberts, University of Queensland, Australia uses a feminist philosophical framework to consider the case of Barcelona en Comú, an explicitly feminist political platform running in Barcelona, to illustrate how thinking through the lens of feminist philosophy enables us to appreciate how Barcelona en Comú is reimagining a 'smart city' – as an ethical, feminist and anti-racist city. It harnesses technology for the common good of all citizens rather than for profit of private capital and the elites. This work takes seriously our relations with technology and in framing these goals within feminist philosophy and political activism, imagines of technology emerge as a force for social change (Noble 2018). Tatiana Kolomeitceva, Moskow/Essen, Russia/Germany reflects in *User Experience as Enlightenment* about media anthropology and develops some thoughts on the epistemological critique of user experience theory. She highlights the importance of changing the work of user experience specialists to become an "'intra-active' network of 'becoming with'", using a notion developed by

Waltraud Ernst researching the process of communication of people using tools. Talya Ucaryilmaz Deibel from Max Planck Institute, Hamburg and Eric Deibel discuss in *Artificial Intelligence in Ancient Rome*, the claim that conceiving of technology in its relation to society in terms of power imbalances dates back to antiquity. Particularly the understanding that there are 'instruments' of 'instruments' has its roots in the Aristotelian conception of slavery as a morally unacceptable institution both historically and today. In antiquity, slaves were seen as tools in symbioses: The prosthetic extensions of others, simultaneously persons and things. When we conceive of digital technology as a communicative artefact that is an extension of technological reason we face the same dilemma today. The paper draws historical connections between cybernetics and slavery around the general question: will AI technology result in a new type of slavery? As such it requires us to rethink the intricate concepts of humanness and subjectivity in Roman philosophy in order to apply it to the contemporary questions on artificial agents and digitization of technology.

Eight papers are dedicated to reconstruct a new understanding of our history of philosophy, where the history of the Western and non-Western philosophy is at stake. It is not possible to shape a future if the past is not fundamentally re-reflected. For this reason, critical reflection on history should make an important contribution to finding new ways of thinking. Re-constructing the history of women philosophers means to support the process of rediscovering women's voices in history, to reconstruct their way to see and to understand the world and to give meaning to it. This third part of the volume tackles topics presented from women philosophers from European history and it re-discovers the voices from women philosophers around the world as well as the mutual influence.

Priyanka Jha, Hindu University, New Dehli, India discusses in *Pursuits of Global Gendered Intellectual History: Stories from India* the history of ideas as a field is continually shifting towards being global and that this is welcome, as we engage with ideas from cultures and contexts distinct from their original standpoint. She criticizes however that it is not taken into regard whether and to what extent this global history of ideas is gendered, given the fact that there is no equal attention given to women thinkers. Global intellectual history of ideas has failed to bring in the corpus of women writings and thinking. Despite gender equality being a given fact in the normative frameworks, the lacunae of being non-gendered mark the way the history of ideas is undertaken. There has been a failure in terms of engagement with women thinkers in the same way and with equal rigor in the ways it engages with the male thinkers. The list of thinkers as part of the syllabuses and pedagogies across the various universities around the world is inherently male. Consequentially, intellectual history is lopsided and male-oriented. This trouble is accentuated in the non-Western world, mostly in post-colonial societies. The paper reflects on the topic starting from the experiences of India, tracing how the shift towards gendering intellectual history was undertaken, with the contributions from multiple feminist interventions in sites of knowledge and the larger consequences it had. In *Yosano Akiko's Philosophy and Poetry – Modernization of Japan and Women's Liberation* contributed by Toyomi Iwawaki-Riebel, University of Applied Sciences Würzburg-Schweinfurt, women's liberation theory in the thoughts of Yosano Akiko (1878–1942) serves as the background to reconstruct the processes of modernization and internationalization in Japan in the (Post-)Meiji era (1868–1912). Akiko is also known for her anti-war poem, *Thou Shalt Not Die* (1904), which related to her brother who served in the Russo-Japanese War (1904–1905). She argued about the issue of women's liberation, refuting "the protection of mothers by the nation", and expanding the cultural criticisms on political, educational, and social issues. In Akiko's thoughts, the issue of "the protection of mothers by the nation" was conscious and opposed to women activists such as Hiratsuka Raichō (1886–1971), basing her firm female philosophy on the pride of her motherhood. Despite the problems of feudal and ultra-nationalist propaganda of women's education as "good wives and wise mothers" in the Post-Meiji era, Akiko defined the free and cultural way of women and mothers toward the future. Timothy DeGriselles, Toledo, US in *A Philosophical Defense of Self-Defense* examines Sor Juana Inés de la Cruz' Reply to Sor Filotea to defend herself from accusations from powerful church leaders at her time. Sor Juana compares her struggles to others such as Jesus Christ and Socrates. This essay examines the similarities between the persecution and the defense of Sor Juana to that of Socrates' self-defense found in Plato's Apology. Sor Juana uses similar arguments in *The Reply* that shows that her studies and beliefs in no way hinder Sor Juana's relationship with God but proves that her studies and writings improve her relationship. In the end, Socrates and Sor Juana are persecuted in similar ways and defend themselves by proving their superior, divinely inspired minds to that of their accusers. Demin Xu, University Paris VIII, France, presents *Le rôle des œuvres de Rousseau dans les mouvements féministes en Chine moderne.* Unlike the feminist movements of Western countries, where women have often played a central role, the feminist movement in modern China was originally – between the end of the 19th century and the very beginning of the 20th century – mainly led by intellectual men who called for gender equality and women's empowerment. Among them were Liang Qichao (1873–1929), Ma Junwu (1881–1940) and Jin Tianhe (1873–1947), promoters of Rousseau's thought, and intellectuals of the May Fourth Movement such as Chen Duxiu (1879–1942), Hu Shi (1891–1962) and Lu Xun (1881–1936). Huang Zunxian (1848–1905) was probably the first reader of the Chinese version of Rousseau's *The Social Contract*, due to the Japanese thinker Nakae Chomin (1847–1901) in 1882. In a letter to Liang Qichao, he shared his thoughts and urged the diffusion of the work in China. Even though the feminist thoughts of Liang, Ma and Jin are distinct, these three contemporaries reached an agreement: women are not inherently weak and they should have the opportunity to receive an education and hold a job for the same rights as men. "Man was born free": Rousseau, since his introduction in China, sowed the seeds of the revolution of mores in Chinese society, and opened the discussion on the "New woman" in the late Qing dynasty (1644–1911) and the early Republic of China (1912–1949).

Five papers address Western women philosophers as great thinkers in their own right. Margret Cavendish's panpyschism is presented by Pedro Falcão Pricladnitzky, Universidade Estadual de Maringa in *Mind of Nature.* Cavendish's main reasoning for the thesis is that nature, that is all individuals that make up nature, have mental properties, that is, consciousness, perception and cognitive capacity. Cavendish offered many arguments to show that matter has the capacity to think, but her central argument for the position is drawn from an observation that, for her, is evident and unquestionable: the bodies, or the parts of matter that make up nature, behave in an orderly and variable way and this is only possible if they have sensitivity and rationality. Cavendish's position is not just that matter has the capacity to think or that the assumption that some material being, by the very nature of matter, thinks is compatible with its nature. Her view that intends to explain the phenomena of nature rests on a stronger thesis: all matter, by its very nature, thinks. Sarah Bonfim and Matos Nunes, Universidade Estadual de Campinas, Brasil reflect on the *First Principles [...] in Wollstonecraft's "Rights of Woman"*. They present this text as a strategic resource and an argumentative basis for the emancipation project envisioned by Mary Wollstonecraft. Using *Vindication of the Rights of Woman* as a standpoint, this paper presents the *First Principles*, as set out in her 1792 work, with the aim of contributing to the historical location and debate on women's rights. The *First Principles* are conceptions of reason, virtue and knowledge that work in an interconnected way to demonstrate that women are as much a part of humanity as men. Divided into four sections, this paper presents each of these conceptions, starting from a general plan, that is, presenting how Wollstonecraft recognizes these conceptions, to a more specific plan for the case of women and their impacts.

In *Women's Access to French Philosophy: A Forgotten History (1880–1924)* Annabelle Bonnet, Center for Sociological and Political Studies Raymond Aron at the EHESS, Paris, France investigates the difficulties for women in France to get access to philosophy and putting in question the narrative that, before the period of the second half of 20th century women would hardly be present in the history of French philosophy. The dominant historiography is therefore structured in such a way as to suggest that women showed little or no interest in philosophy until recently. The article rebuts this assumption and prejudice and points out that the

1880–1924 period constitutes a blind spot. It is necessary to get the blindness out of the silence as this brings to light to the contradiction between the advent of liberal democracy in France and the official prohibition of philosophy for women by the French State, especially in the field of education. Andrea Pérez-Fernández, ADHUC – Research Center for Theory, Gender, Sexuality at Barcelona University, presents an analysis of alternative presentations of female thought in *Hannah Höch's (1889–1978) practice of photomontage*. Höch is a German artist mostly known for her pioneering role in the development of Dadaist inter-war photomontage and the only woman that took part in this movement in Berlin. Her work is notable for its use of irony and biting criticism through the technique of montage. Höch's way of describing the world through her theorization and practice of photomontage is presented in the light of Höch's experience of violence.

The final part of this collection is dedicated to gender issues and feminist concern. It presents voices from feminist scholars around the world to analyze the social and political practices from a current perspective. The focus lies on questions of parity, in state and institutions. Politics, society, colonialist and race issues are at stake, questions about religion are addressed as well as those about identitarian politics. Given that the Covid pandemic changed women's social status gravely, thinkers also address this issue. An important focus is set here on the Spanish-speaking world. We start with reflections on the situation of women in Spain. Cristina Sánchez, Autonomous University of Madrid, Spain, discusses in *Feminist Philosophy and Democracy: The Case of Spain* how Spain integrated feminist philosophy in its democracy. She discusses what role feminist philosophy can play in the creation and consolidation of democracy and demands women's participation in it. Recurring to its enlightened origins, when feminist philosophy posed the incompleteness of democracy if women were not included as political subjects, the 20th century authors such as Carole Pateman or Anne Phillips question the theoretical framework of democracy and citizenship. Impacts of the sexual contract, the disorder of the private sphere and the importance of a politics of presence need further analysis to consolidate democracy in Spain. Spanish feminist philosophers in the 1980s highlighted the necessary interdependence between gender equality, modernity, and democracy. Diana María Acevedo-Zapata and María Lucía Rivera-Sanín from Universidad Pedagogogica Nacional en Bogota, Colombia present the results of *Gender Equality in Colombia's Philosophy Programs: Faculty Participation*. This study offers a descriptive analysis of women's participation in philosophy programs in Colombia, showing that we are still a long way from gender equality in the field. The main objective is to contribute to an understanding of gender inequality in higher education in Philosophy in Colombia, in terms of teaching positions occupied by women. Tzitzi Janik Rojas Torres, Sorbonne Paris III, France raises questions on decolonial and feminist efforts in her paper on

Teaching Islamic Feminisms in the History of Philosophy in Mexico. The institutional teaching of philosophy in Mexico has traditionally been historicist and Eurocentric: for the most part, philosophy has been taught and thought in chronological order and articulated around European intellectual movements and philosophers. This implies that non-Eurocentric othernesses is invisible: the intellectual wealth of peripheral cultures and peoples does not appear in the universal history of philosophy taught in Mexico, in an example of "epistemicide": the systematic extermination of the systems of knowledge of certain communities. Faced with this restrictive conception of philosophy, decolonialism and feminism provide methodological and theoretical tools to deconstruct the paradigm of philosophy and eliminate epistemic and social injustices. Ingrid Alloni, Milan, Italy discusses the feminist identitarian path in her contribution *From Self-awareness to Political and Social Improvement*, connecting the theme of identity from feminist Western tradition and in Black thought. It is argued that identity can be claimed as an instrument of emancipation both from the recognition of personal history and biographical bearing, but also as a request for affirmation of the self in collective political and social struggles. Both sides must be considered: the feminist subject and the colonial subject are products of systems of domination, oppression and lack of recognition.

The part concludes with references to actual problems, the refugee crisis and the Covid pandemic, presenting two very different aspects from that catastrophe. With *"Je me révolte, donc nous sommes"* Ariadni Polychroniou, National and Kapodistrian Universitsity of Athens, Greece reconceptualizes the contemporary refugee resistances through the Butlerian reconstruction of Hannah Arendt's public sphere. Seeking for nuanced philosophical responses to the juridico-political aporia of modern refugee resistances, Judith Butler's feminist reconstruction of the Arendtian public sphere serves as a potentially productive reconceptualization of refugees' plural and heterogeneous political mobilizations. Judith Butler's ambivalent dialectic with the Arendtian oeuvre provides the context of the authors perspective also on contemporary collective struggles, finally supporting that the drastic Butlerian reconstruction of the Arendtian public sphere provides a more coherent epistemological, theoretical and methodological framework for the critical illustration of contemporary refugee political struggles in terms of embodied collective performances emerging in the heart of the political. Rosaura Martínez Ruiz, Universidad Nacional Autónoma de Mexico, Mexico highlights gender violence and the violence of inequity in *Covid-19 and "Stay at Home"*. The Covid-19 pandemic has been a sort of magnifying glass or perhaps a contrast dye that renders already glaring inequities even more visible by shedding light on their pressing consequences, now showcased in all their cruelty and immediacy. The "Stay at home" Mexican social distancing campaign had glaring blind spots, such as the foreseeable increase in domestic violence against women and children, as well as the lack of decent or sufficient shelters for migrants, homeless and sexual dissidents expelled from home. The author argues that "woman" is always a category that encompasses bodies already crossed by any number of forms and means of oppression as well as of privilege: ethnicity, citizenship, social class, sexual preference. Feminism therefore is here understood to fight a battle against inequity in a broad sense. A different voice is provided by Valentina Gaudiano, Sophia University Institute, Italy, as she uses the pandemic as *A New-old Topos for the Future* to *Rethinking and Rediscovering Oneself as Human.* This author claims that never before the degree of coexistence and interdependence among people had reached levels as in that period , made visible and to be experienced in the break out during the pandemic, Cov-Sars-19. For her this is a vivid example of how we made the same experiences of disease, suffering and death together with the deprivation of those common bodily expressions that enrich personal and community life and lived at a global level and at the same time. We experienced the physical limitation of proximity and the impossibility to express affections and emotions with our whole body. Rethinking the human under the aspect of love and proximity would trace a new-old *topos* for the future, something as the relationship expressed through the image of the embrace who welcomes and holds in her/his arms another person and doing so says: I love you, you belong to me, I'm *with* you, I'm *by* you, *I'm you.* So this book closes with this emphatic tribute of love and mutual recognition that thus saves itself from the disaster of the pandemic.

Authors from India to Brazil, from Finland to Ukraine have contributed to this volume. As different as the analysis and as different as the topics presented are, there is also a comprehensive unity in the will to reshape our world, or more precisely, to reshape our economic, environmental and technically designed living conditions. To this extent and in this diversity, it may be a first attempt to describe this as a common path. What is certain is that we seek a new path. We are willing to shape a different future based on a new reading of the past. Troubled times lie ahead of us. At the time of the book's completion, new wars have caught up with us.

Herta Nagl-Docekal
The Beginnings: A Retrospective View by a Former Board Member of the IAPh

Abstract: The paper provides some key elements of the early phase of the development of the IAPh, beginning with the founding of the "Assoziation von Philosophinnen in Deutschland" in 1974. It recalls the central aims, the enormous difficulties the Association encountered in the 1970s, and the outstanding commitment of Elfriede Walescha Tielsch and Brigitte Weisshaupt. It further focuses on the continuous process of internationalization, paired with an increasing diversification of philosophical approaches. Additional emphasis is given to the relations of the IAPh to SWIP (USA), to the "General Society for Philosophy in Germany", and to the FISP World Congresses of Philosophy.

It is obvious that a comprehensive history of the beginnings of the International Association of Women Philosophers (IAPh) could only be elaborated in a cooperative manner. Thus, the following account merely provides some fragments with gaps that need to be filled by contributions containing the memories of other women philosophers involved. The perspective on the first phase is limited specifically by the fact that I was not among the founding members but joined the IAPh only later.

In May 1974 an association called "Assoziation von Philosophinnen in Deutschland" (Association of Women Philosophers in Germany) was established. The founding members included Elfriede Walesca Tielsch – elected to be the first chairperson –, Brigitte Weisshaupt, Ruth-Eva Schulz-Seitz and Irma Tetter.[1] Important motivation had come from the American philosopher Linda López McAlister, who was in Germany at that time on the basis of a Fulbright scholarship.[2] In an essay on those early stages, Elfriede Walesca Tielsch recalls that Linda's report on the founding of SWIP (Society of Women in Philosophy, USA) in the year 1972 provided inspiration to her German-speaking colleagues (see Tielsch 1983, 245). The first report on the founding of the Assoziation appeared in the same year in the *Zeitschrift für philosophische Forschung* (see Tielsch 1974). The following year did, however, bring a nearly complete collapse: most of the students who had been interested early on encountered, on the part of their professors, such

---

1 Irma Tretter passed away very soon, on 8 December 1976.
2 Linda López McAlister passed away in November 2021.

strong reservations about any form of feminist research that they feared they would be unable to obtain their degrees. (It is important to consider that, in those years, there were only very few women among the professors at philosophy departments in Germany; in Austria there were none.) When the first public general assembly of the Assoziation von Philosophinnen was held on 10 October 1975, in the context of the congress of the Allgemeine Gesellschaft für Philosophie in Deutschland (General Society of Philosophy in Germany), just about four students attended. To my mind, it is important today to re-read Elfriede Walesca Tielsch's report on the frequent setbacks and painful experiences of humiliation that she and her colleagues had to endure. It was only thanks to the unwavering dedication of the first board members that a renewed beginning was made possible: at a meeting in Würzburg on 30–31 October 1976, the official act of founding the Assoziation von Philosophinnen in Deutschland as a registered society took place. That Brigitte Weisshaupt (Zurich) was entrusted with the function of deputy chair proved most important from the perspective that it secured essential support from a foreign country.

The Assoziation was defined as an "association of women academics working in the field of philosophy both at universities and schools and in extramural contexts who share the intention to promote women's studies (Frauenforschung) in philosophy and who seek the inclusion of this research in the curricula". More pointedly expressed, the Assoziation aimed at "establishing research that lays bare the discrimination against women in the male dominated sphere of philosophy, and that re-discovers hitherto unacknowledged contributions by women philosophers to the overall history of philosophy".[3]

A few years after the official act of founding an alteration to the name of the Assoziation proved advisable. This is what happened: when the first full symposium, to be held at the University of Würzburg in October 1980, was organized, it turned out that women philosophers in socialist Eastern European countries were denied the necessary visa because of the politically contested term "Deutschland" in the name of the Assoziation. Therefore, the members attending that Würzburg symposium opted for the new name: Internationale Assoziation von Philosophinnen. As we all know, the term "international" proved to be a driving force in the further development of the IAPh. First relations to women philosophers outside the German-speaking area had already been established in the late 1970s, in particular with the professors Ija Lazari-Pawlowska in Lodz (Poland) and Junko

---

[3] This definition is provided in Menzer (1981). Ursula Menzer passed away on 2 July 2021. She will always be remembered with gratitude as a leading contributor to the beginnings of the Association.

Hamada in Tokyo, who both were to give papers at IAPh conferences later on. At the Würzburg symposium in 1980 about 40 women from Germany and Switzerland attended. Among them was Elfriede Huber-Abrahamowicz, who had to flee from Vienna, Austria, when the Nazis took over, and who later taught feminist philosophy at the TU Zurich, while writing literary works expressing her terrible experiences – poems and short stories for which she received several awards in Switzerland.[4] The second symposium convened at the University of Zurich in 1982, with speakers from five countries and with the first talks in English (given by philosophers from the USA).

One further crucial step was the decision to publish the proceedings of the IAPh symposia in dedicated volumes – a decision that initiated a truly impressive series that has been continued to this very day. The first volume documents the meetings held in Würzburg in the 1970s: *Philosophinnen. Von Wegen ins dritte Jahrtausend* (Women Philosophers. On Their Way into the Third Millennium), edited by Ursula Menzer and Manon Maren-Grisebach (see Maren-Grisebach and Menzer 1982) (who, by the way, turned 90 in January 2021); the papers of the symposia in Würzburg (1980) and Zurich (1982) were published in the volume *Was Philosophinnen denken. Eine Dokumentation* (What Women Philosophers Think. A Documentation), edited by Halina Bendkowski and Brigitte Weisshaupt in 1983 (see Bendkowski and Weisshaupt 1983). The following book, *Was Philosophinnen denken II* (see Andreas-Grisebach and Weisshaupt 1986), which assembles the papers of the symposium at the University of Heidelberg in 1984, includes contributions from France (Monique David-Ménard), Italy (Constanze Peres), The Netherlands (Maija Pellikaan-Engel), and also the first from Austria: Elisabeth List (who soon was to become a board member of IAPh),[5] Gerda Ambros and Birge Krondorfer (who were to bring the IAPh symposium to the University of Klagenfurt in the year 1986).

The invaluable importance of these books lies in the fact that they allow us to understand the great variety of approaches and contested issues that shaped the early debates among IAPh members, in relation to the international discourse of that time. The essays represent multifaceted processes of exploring different fields of theory so as to achieve adequate accounts of the cause of women philosophers. The – often hotly disputed – issues include the idea of a specific "women's philosophy", the dichotomy "reason vs. sensuality", views associating "reason", "logic", and "science" with masculinity, notions of "the feminine", the relation between philosophy and mythology, feminist social criticism, and discourse ethics. Cornelia

---

4 Elfriede Huber-Abrahamowicz passed away on 15 July 2001, in Zurich.
5 Elisabeth List passed away on 21 August 2018, in Graz. See Nagl-Docekal and Nagl (2020).

Klinger found particular resonance, as she examined parallel shortcomings in the conceptions of emancipation discussed in the women's movement and in anti-colonialist theories, for instance in Leopold Senghor's notion of "négritude" (see Klinger 1986).[6] In terms of schools of philosophy some papers discuss the relevance of Marxism, Foucault, Irigaray, and analytic philosophy (to cite but a few examples), while others turn to the history of philosophy, examining authors from Socrates and Plato through Hildegard von Bingen to Fichte and Max Weber. Analyzing Otto Weininger, Hannelore Schröder addressed the linkage between anti-feminism and anti-Semitism (see Schröder 1986). The focus of the IAPh was also on key political issues of the time, for instance, on the panel at the Heidelberg symposium (1984) that took up the dispute over violent vs. non-violent forms of resistance, against the backdrop of the RAF terrorism.[7]

It is significant that the early phase of IAPh debates, which had been marked by a plurality of uncoordinated topics, was brought to an end in 1986 with the Klagenfurt symposium, which was the first with a conceptual conference title: "Jenseits von Herrschaft. Feministische Perspektiven praktischer Philosophie" (Beyond domination. Feminist perspectives on practical philosophy). The main organizers of that symposium were the IAPh board members Cornelia Klinger (Vienna) and Elisabeth List (Graz), in cooperation with the hosts Birge Krondorfer and Gerda Ambros at the University of Klagenfurt (see the report Di Maddalena 1986).[8] One specific focus was on inviting colleagues from (what was then) Yugoslavia. Incidentally, this was the first IAPh event that I attended, although I had become a member in 1983.[9] What I have appreciated in particular, from the early days until now, is IAPh's potential for preventing women philosophers from reflecting on their continuous unstable positioning in the academic sphere in an isolated manner, and for achieving increasingly elaborate categories of analysis and concerted action.

Much public attention was attracted by the fifth IAPh symposium, hosted by TU Berlin, 6–9 April 1989, which marked the bicentennial of the French Revolution under the title *"1789/1989. Die Revolution hat nicht stattgefunden (The Revolution Has Not Taken Place)"*. The papers presented, edited by Astrid Deuber-Mankowski, Ulrike Ramming and Elfriede Walesca Tielsch, were published in the same year, dedicated to Elfriede Walesca Tielsch for her eightieth birthday (see Deuber-Man-

---

6 Klinger served as a board member of IAPh in the 1980s.
7 The Abbreviation RAF designates the Rote Armee Fraktion (Red Army Faction).
8 It so happened that, on the train to Klagenfurt, I first met Herlinde Pauer-Studer (affiliated with the University of Graz at that time), with whom I was to cooperate in the fields of feminist ethics and political theory for many xears, publishing several books and organizing international symposia.
9 I was to serve as spokesperson of the IAPh from 1989–1996.

kowski, Ramming and Tielsch 1989). It is worth noting that this volume was the last to contain contributions exclusively in German.[10] A big leap forward in terms of internationalization was taken with the sixth symposium, which took place at the Free University Amsterdam in 1992, with the title Against Patriarchal Thinking. A Future Without Discrimination? It was organized by Maija Pellikaan-Engel, Hannelore Schröder and Mariette Willemsen; the proceedings were edited by Maija Pellikaan-Engel and published in the same year (see Pellikaan-Engel 1992),[11] with an annex that comprises a number of political statements concerning the economic and sexual exploitation of women, and a petition under the heading "Women Around the World Petition the United Nations to Recognize Women's Human Rights" (Pellikaan-Engel 1992, 379–394).

The process of internationalization received a decisive enhancement through the contacts with FISP (International Federation of Philosophical Societies), the organizer of the World Congresses of Philosophy. As early as 1978, when the XVI World Congress of Philosophy was held in Düsseldorf, Elfriede Walesca Tielsch and Brigitte Weisshaupt introduced the IAPh in an informal event within the framework of that congress. In 1982 the IAPh became a regular FISP member society; from then on its society meetings were included in the programs of the World Congresses. Brigitte Weisshaupt and I organized such meetings, with the aim of sharing information on the IAPh with a global audience, at the World Congresses in Montreal (1983) and Brighton (1988).[12] The World Congress in Boston (1998) brought two important innovations: firstly, the regular IAPh symposium was held in Boston on the days before the World Congress – a constellation that has been continued up to the present, allowing the IAPh to establish cooperation with women philosophers, for instance, in South Korea and China. Secondly, the IAPh successfully nominated me when the members of the Steering Committee of FISP were elected. This function allowed me to find support for the plan that congress sections on gender issues and feminist philosophy should become a regular part of the World Congresses. Later on, I suggested establishing a specially endowed plenary lecture – the "Simone de Beauvoir Lecture" – which was first held by Judith Butler at the WCP in Beijing in 2018. Furthermore, the permanent FISP Gender Committee was founded, the chairperson of which is currently a board

---

10 An additional option for publishing essays on feminist issues in German was created in the year 1990, when the Journal *Die Philosophin* was founded. See Deuber-Mankowski and Konnertz 1990. The two editors as well as the 11 members of the Advisory Board were members of the IAPh.
11 Maija Pellikaan-Engel has passed away in March 2018. Her last feminist text – "Calypso's Oath" – was read by me (due to her illness) at the FISP World Congress of Philosophy in Athens, 2013.
12 Later on, Brigitte Weisshaupt and I also cooperated when we were both members of the "Erweiterter Vorstand der Allgemeinen Gesellschaft für Philosophie in Deutschland" in the 1990s.

member of the IAPh: Sigridur Thorgeirsdottir, who is a participant at this conference in Paderborn.[13]

In terms of one key conception of this volume *Women Philosophers on Economics, Technology, Environment and Gender History*, I would like to suggest to the current board members the establishment of some kind of permanent archive, including a collection of photos to which many of us might be able to contribute. This would be a worthwhile project in preparation for the FISP World Congress of Philosophy to be held in Rome in 2024, as that year will coincide with the fiftieth anniversary of the IAPh (1974–2024).

As regards future perspectives, I would like to express my confidence that the IAPh will continue with its commitment across the globe – there is so much more to do in challenging the asymmetries women philosophers face! I am convinced that the IAPh will be moving further along interesting paths, on its "Wegen ins dritte Jahrtausend".

References

Andreas-Grisebach, M. and Weisshaupt, B. (Eds.) (1986). *Was Philosophinnen denken II*. Zurich: Amman.
Bendkowski, H. and Weisshaupt, B. (Eds.) (1983). *Was Philosophinnen denken. Eine Dokumentation*. Zurich: Amman.
Deuber-Mankowski, A. and Konnertz, U. (Eds.) (1990). *Die Philosophin. Forum für feministische Theorie und Philosophie*. Tübingen: edition diskord.
Deuber-Mankowski, A., Ramming, U. and Tielsch, E. W. (Eds.) (1989). *1789/1989 – Die Revolution hat nicht stattgefunden. Dokumentation des V. Symposiums der Internationalen Assoziation von Philosophinnen*. Tübingen: edition diskord.
Di Maddalena, A. (1986). "Femminismo: Al di là del dominio. Convegnio di filosofe a Klagenfurt". *Il manifesto*, 8 October, 11.
Klinger, C. (1986). "Modernisierungsorientiertes oder traditionsorientiertes Emanzipationskonzept? Zwei Befreiungsbewegungen – ein Dilemma". In Andreas-Grisebach, M. and Weisshaupt, B. (Eds.) (1986), *Was Philosophinnen denken II*. Zurich: Amman, 71–96.
Maren-Grisebach, M. and Menzer, U. (Eds.) (1982). *Philosophinnen. Von Wegen ins dritte Jahrtausend*. Mainz: Tamagnini.

---

13 These are the cities where IAPh symposia have been held to date: 1. Würzburg, Federal Republic of Germany, 1980 / 2. Zurich, Switzerland, 1983 / 3. Heidelberg, Federal Republic of Germany, 1984 / 4. Klagenfurt, Austria, 1986 / 5. Berlin, Federal Republic of Germany, 1989 / 6. Amsterdam, The Netherlands, 1992 / 7. Vienna, Austria, 1995 / 8. Boston, USA, 1998 / 9. Zurich, Switzerland, 2000 / 10. Barcelona, Spain, 2002/ 11. Gothenburg, Sweden, 2004 / 12. Rome, Italy, 2006 / 13. Seoul, South Korea, 2008 / 14. London, Ontario, Canada, 2012 / 15. Alcalà de Henares, Spain, 2014 / 16. Melbourne, Australia, 2016 / 17. Beijing, China, 2018 / 18. Paderborn, Germany, 2021. My thanks to Birge Krondorfer and Bettina Schmitz for providing this list.

Menzer, U. (1981). "1. Philosophinnen Symposion veranstaltet von der Internationalen Assoziation von Philosophinnen (IAPh), Würzburg, 17.–19.10.1980". *Das Argument* 125, 102–103.

Nagl-Docekal, H. and Nagl, L. (2020). "Nachruf Elisabeth List (1945–2019)". *Zeitschrift für Didaktik der Philosophie und Ethik* 2, 119.

Pellikaan-Engel, M. (Ed.) (1992). *Against Patriarchal Thinking. A Future Without Discrimination?* Amsterdam: VU University Press.

Schröder, H. (1986). "Zur Neuauflage von faschistischem Antifeminismus und Antisemitismus, oder: Vor Weininger wird gewarnt". In Andreas-Grisebach, M. and Weisshaupt, B. (Eds.), *Was Philosophinnen denken II*. Zurich: Amman, 134–156.

Tielsch, E. W. (1974). "Bericht über das Symposion der 'Assoziation von Philosophinnen in Deutschland', Würzburg 25./26.5.1974". *Zeitschrift für Philosophische Forschung* 28, 464–465.

Tielsch, E. W. (1983). "Geschichte der Internationalen Assoziation von Philosophinnen e. V." In: Bendkowski, H. and Weisshaupt, B. (Eds.), *Was Philosophinnen denken. Eine Dokumentation*. Zurich: Amman, 244–249.

Part II: **Economics, Technology, Environment**

Julie A. Nelson
Economic Theory and Moral Imagination

Abstract: Economists have, for more than a century, portrayed economics as a physics-like discipline concerned with explaining the underlying mechanics of an amoral market system, presumed to be driven by self-interest and competition. Drawing on feminist work in economics, this paper will examine the binary, hierarchical gender metaphors underlying these claims. It will then explore the damage these biased beliefs have done to the creation of knowledge and to our ability to deal with issues such as climate change and will suggest alternatives.

Introduction

In my paper I want to discuss economic theory and moral imagination. Since I am a feminist economist, you are probably not too surprised to hear that I find that standard economics is a bit lacking in several departments, one of which is its relationship to ethics. But I am going to challenge you a little bit further. I am going to argue that dominant economic theory has not only limited *economists'* thinking, it has actually poisoned the well for the way that people across the academic disciplines think about the economy and ethics.

Mainstream Economics

When I speak to groups of non-economists, sometimes there are people who have the impression that those who train in economics sit around and discuss Adam Smith and Karl Marx. Or maybe the economics grad student goes out in the world and spends some time in some businesses or government agencies to find out how they really run. Not at all. Economics graduate education is all about math. The typical theory section of a paper will read something like "Since both B and W lines are monotonically nonincreasing in Y1 and Y2, it is sufficient to show that W is steeper... From Lemma 1 we have that $\partial W/\partial Y2 < \partial B/\partial Y2 = 0...$" There is usually a lot of calculus. This mainstream approach – made up of neoclassical orthodox economic theory, plus a few additions such as game theory and behavioral economics – is what is taught at universities around the world, and certainly in any prestigious graduate department. So that is what we learned as theory. Our typical approach to empirical analysis is to go gather a big bunch of numeric data and use highly sophisticated (although unfortunately too often very poorly understood) econometric techniques – such as *IV* (instrumental variables), *FE* (fixed effects) and *discrete time hazard* models – to try to test hypotheses. This is all very scientific sounding.

If you read economics textbooks or hang around economists long enough, you realize that there are some key things that define what is economics and what is not economics.

Mainstream economics is usually defined either as being about markets where goods and services are exchanged for money, or as being about individual self-interested rational choice. Behavioral economics has recognized that maybe we are not always entirely rational, but rational choice is still the base model. The goal is always to find the most efficient solution – one that achieves the highest-valued output from given resources. The methodology is all about formal mathematics. There is a very strong belief among economists that this approach gives us objective knowledge: I mean, you can't argue with math! Right? Of course, that is incredibly naïve from an epistemological perspective, but economists think of philosophers as those soft folks doing that mushy stuff over there, and themselves as scientists. Sometimes, this is referred to as physics envy. We also head for the most general and abstract knowledge we can find and look down our noses at those who get enmeshed in detail such as data collection. The general sense is that the economy is a machine, with drives and certain kinds of energy sources, and that our goal is to find out how to control this mechanical system well.

What Is Left Out?

Back at the beginnings of feminist economics – there were a few brave pioneers before this but in the late 1980s and early 1990s, things stared to coalesce – some of us started to ask what was left out of this picture. Are there things that characterize the real economy that we live in that somehow did not make it into this economic science? We drew on the work of philosophers and historians of science such as Evelyn Fox Keller, Sandra Harding, Susan Bordo, and Helen Longino. Sandra and Helen came to some of our conferences early on.

We had a great time together because a lot of their critique – a lot of Enlightenment Era science was really based on prioritizing the masculine and getting rid of anything culturally associated with femininity – fits economics especially well. While, of course, more recent feminist work has gone beyond Western views and the idea of gender as binary, the Western Enlightenment view of science is still hegemonic, especially in my field. So, as awkward and partial as it may seem to many of you, my paper will still discuss my field in these terms.

So, when I looked for what was left out in terms of the definition of economics as a field, I came out with contrasts like those shown in Table 1. It was pretty clear that a focus on markets left out social life and family. Mental choice left out bodily experience. You might be surprised to know that economists never talk about physical needs: Because some people fast voluntarily, economists primarily regard eating as just another choice. "Development" economists spend some time on poverty, but it is not a core theme in the discipline. In focusing on choice behavior by individuals, we forgot about our relatedness – our interrelations and interdependencies. The focus on self-interest neglects that we sometimes do consider effects on other people. The emphasis on a reason means we deny emotion even when addressing things like stock market panics. You would think that emotional contagion would play some role here, but it gets ignored in the discipline. The focus on efficiency rules out a couple of things. It rules out both a focus on fairness (or equity), and it also deflects our attention from the need for resilience. Resilient systems often have a lot of redundancy in the form of backup systems. Well, backup systems that might never get used look terribly inefficient! All those resources just wasted on things like flood walls!

Table 1: Masculinist Bias in the Definition of Economics

"Economics"	"Not Economics"
Markets	Social life (and family)
Mental choice	Bodily experience
Individuality	Relatedness
Self-interest	Other-interest
Reason	Emotion
Efficiency	Equity, resilience
(Masculinity)	(Femininity)

If you look at the cultural connotations of these things, you can see that everything on the left is culturally associated with masculinity, and on the right, with femininity. Psychologists and others have, in fact, noticed that we tend to categorize a lot of the information we receive by gender. This even shows up in brain scans. I call it "cognitive gendering". This is not *at all* about saying that the items in the table actually reflect some presumed "essence" of masculinity or femininity – for example, that women are somehow more embodied than men – and *even less* about saying that men and women think differently. These are internalized cultural associations that may affect the thinking and behavior of all of us, even if we are not conscious of such influence.

Table 2 shows the same kind of contrasts, but concerning the methodology of economics rather than the definition. Economists feel that our use of math makes us positive and objective, and disparage qualitative, verbal, intuitive work which we believe is soft and merely subjective. We leave out ethics, because ethics are a topic that people argue about, while economists want to be hard scientists that come up with unassailable objective truth; reliable knowledge would be the more sensible goal. Economists do not do so well with the particular and the unexpected, such as the thousand-year flooding going on in parts of Germany as I write this paper. Fortuna, in mythology, is a female figure. We imagine a world in which things work with predictable regularity, such that we can control them.

Table 2: Masculinist Bias in the Methodology of Economics

"Economics"	"Not Economics"
Quantitative	Qualitative
Formal	Verbal or intuitive
Positive	Normative
Objective	Subjective
General	Particular
Control	The unexpected
(Masculinity)	(Femininity)

Now there are various ways you may go forward, once you recognize the truth in these tables. Most economists would say that of course the left-hand sides are better and harder and more rigorous and good, and the right-hand sides are squishy. So, we are just going to keep on doing what we have been doing. Another interpretation that I sometimes hear is that the economics profession is dominated by men and men do the left-hand sides, while women who enter the field do the right-hand sides – because we know that women are more emotional... I think that is hooey. I actually do the math quite fine, thank you very much! A third way I find is, unfortunately, common among many who (like me) have very serious concerns about the way our contemporary economies are going in terms of sustainability. These folks say that the sort of thinking reflected on the left-hand sides has created and exacerbated poverty, inequality, ecological disaster, racial strife. Since that is to be lamented, we need to flip over to the right-hand side, abandoning the use of math as an evil tool and setting aside rationality in favor of emotion. I think that is playing with half a deck – that is, like trying to play a card game with only 26 (of the required 52) cards.

I think *all* of the things listed are part of our economic life. The definition of economics I like is that economics is about the way that societies organize themselves for the survival and flourishing of life. That involves all of these things – it certainly involves family, since kids would not survive if just left out there in the marketplace, right? And good methodology includes a variety of approaches. Sometimes, qualitative methods are appropriate, sometimes quantitative, and sometimes both in combination. I would like us to be playing with a *full* deck.

Playing with a Full Deck

I invented something I called a "gender value compass" a while back. The usual interpretation of that sort of contrasts in Tables 1 and 2 is that one of each pair is good and the other one is bad. So, the masculine side is the good side. We focus on individual choice because otherwise everything is just a big mishmash. The negative contrast to that is "soluble" – that is, like salt dissolving in water, a pure merger, as shown in Figure 1.

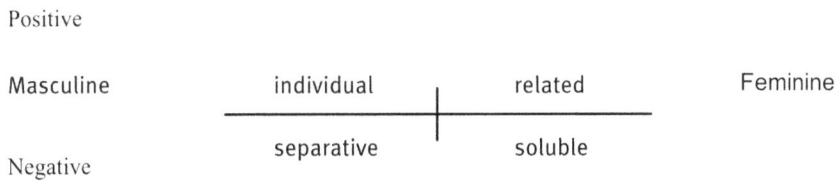

Figure 1: A Gender Value Compass for Individuality and Relation.

We feminist economists took this vocabulary of *separate* and *soluble* selves from theologian Catherine Keller. A separative self cannot actually live in the world, because they need to be fed and clothed by somebody and that traditionally has been a *soluble self* – a wife who is considered simply a support person. The same myth crops in business, e. g., when we think of a firm as simply a profit-maximizing entity, we turn all its employees *soluble* – we imagine that they have no room for independent action. To play with a full deck, we need to recognize ourselves as individuals-in-relation. Much feminist philosophy has been written about the dynamic tension that results when both relationality and individuality are kept in balance.

We can also get a lot further in terms of methodology if we open up options in a similar manner, as illustrated in Figure 2. Math is very precise and elegant, but if you just look at the math it can be very thin and unrealistic. A lot of economic theory does not have anything to do with any economy in the real world – it has to do with "the economy" that exists in a mental space that never touches down to earth. Economists do not like language because they consider it imprecise and vague. But sometimes that is the only way to get towards a rich and realistic investigation. So what if we could aim to get the best of both of these, that is, be as elegant and as realistic as we can?

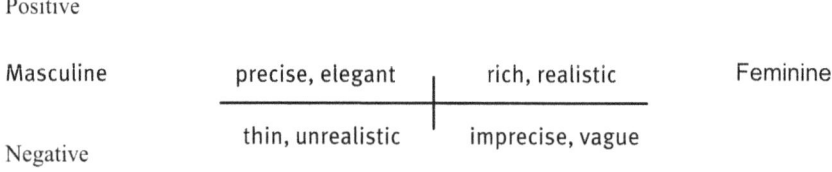

Figure 2: A Gender Value Compass for Methodology.

So that is what I mean about playing with a full deck – not buying into either one side or the other of this dualism as being the right way and the other ways being the wrong way. And certainly not buying into the idea that men do it one way and women do it the other.

Economists have a hard time seeing this, since they are very locked into this idea that math gives you objectivity. The truth is that at best math gives you internal consistency. There is nothing that says it is going to be correct about what's going on in the world.

Poisoning the Well

What I see more as I have traveled around to different disciplines, such as sociology and philosophy, over the years, is that people – including the critics of current economic systems – have believed economists *much* too much. Economic theory has essentially poisoned the well from which people all across the academic and political spectra draw their images of how economies work. And, particularly, it has poisoned the way that everybody thinks about ethics and economics.

Some common beliefs I have encountered about what is going on in economies include:
- People are purely self-interested in their commercial and business dealings.
- Businesses are all about making profits.
- The laws of markets are inexorable, like the laws of physics.
- Social and ethical aspects of humanity belong to a realm separate from business and markets.

Economists talk about the "law of demand" and "law of supply" as though economies run by forces directly analogous with those of physics. The image is that businesses and markets are part of a mechanical realm. Competition is said to drive out anybody who does not strictly profit maximize. The social and ethical aspects of humanity would seem to belong to a realm separate from business and markets. It would seem that if we want to be real full human beings with real full social and moral lives, that has to take place somewhere else. It does not happen in the economy.

You see a lot of critics of the discipline, and of contemporary economies, accepting those as facts, essentially saying,

> Economists say this, and so we say okay, yeah that's the way people *are* in economies. So we have to completely switch to the opposite: Instead of competition we have to entirely cooperation, instead of individuals we need solidarity and community, instead of global stuff we need everything local. We just have to completely turn the tables.

Well, that sort of dualistic thinking comes from believing economists that the economies really are that way.

Other critics propose "limits to markets", such as philosophers Michael Sandel, Virginia Held, and Jürgen Habermas. Essentially, they say that markets and businesses are fine if what is being bought and sold is umbrellas, but if it is education or healthcare we need to draw the line. That is not bad as far as it goes, but why does it still allow huge areas of human life to go on being amoral or immoral? It does that because the argument takes it for granted that the market-business-economy sphere is just as mechanical as economists say.

For example, Habermas distinguishes between *lifeworld* and *system*. He characterizes the economic *system* as this kind of masculine macho image of the economy as mechanical and objectified. He claims that it is driven by forces that come in from outside, like money, and a certain kind of strategic rationality. The *lifeworld* is where we get to be social and human and moral. And there is this (evil) process of *colonization* in which *system* takes over *lifeworld*. I have written about why this is just factually *wrong*. Money is actually entirely a social construction: A currency maintains value only as long as people *believe* it does. This idea that it is some kind of outside force just does not hold water.

And if you think that Marxist views go beyond these traps, go back and read Marx himself. He fell into the same trap of thinking of economies as mechanical. He tried to put everything together with equations – for example, the "falling rate of profit" and such. People who think of Marx primarily in terms of economic justice are using Marx' thought many times removed. I agree with the economic justice parts, but the mechanical model – not so much!

These beliefs about economies being mechanical did not come from economists going out and examining the economy. They were actually *invented* by economists. That is, these ideas about firms having to maximize profits, everybody is self-interested, everybody is an autonomous individual, etc. were *made up*.

John Stuart Mill, who did lots of interesting and broad and feminist things, also wrote a very badly taken article in the early 1800s where he actually set out the beginning of what is called *homo economicus* or *rational economic man*. Let us assume, he wrote, that we have got an individual who is only interested in wealth and knows rationally how to get there. He argued that that should be the basis of a "science" he called Political Economy. Mill also claimed that nobody would ever be foolish enough to try to apply Political Economy without also looking at ethics and social life and everything else. Unfortunately, many people *were* foolish enough to do that.

That is how we ended up with economics in the form it took in the late 1800s. Economists of the "Neoclassical" school realized that they could formalize this idea of one person rationally finding their way to the highest wealth using calculus. So that is where we got these cute little graphs that show up in Principles of Economics textbooks, that purport to show the essential function of a business in terms of mathematical profit, cost, and revenue functions. Apparently, a firm does not have management problems, personnel problems, supply problems, etc. – a firm to an economist is just a simple graph. How convenient! We can analyze firms while sitting at our desks using calculus, with no need to go out and actually find out what firms are doing.

And this led to one of the great moral failures of our age: With this kind of thinking, it is unimaginable that someone who is purely self-interested could run a company in the best interest of even the shareholders, much less the community or the environment in mind. Right? Because we have just assumed that they are only interested in themselves. Therefore, economists concluded, you have to *incentivize* CEOs. This is why the top one percent in the U. S. in wealth took off away from everybody else: stock bonuses given out as incentives. So one of the big moral failings of our age came straight out of economists, and the fact that economists have been believed by the business press, other academics

– and everyone, really. When everyone believes economists when they say that this is just a mechanical ethics-free realm, that helps immoral behavior keep going.

If you actually go out and investigate economies you find out that the opportunistic profit-only ethos is *destroying* companies and economies. There are many business leaders out there actually saying that the short-termism, that is, the drive for quarterly profit, is just destroying business. Not to mention that in the U. S. we are clearly also destroying the environment around us. We are destroying the basis for life.

But firms and economies are social organizations with inherent ethical dimensions. They are not in some mechanical sphere out there somewhere else. They are part of society, socially and politically organized. They involve cooperation as well as competition. Cooperation often has this good, nice connotation while competition is thought of as angry and mean. But this is not necessarily the case. For example, cooperation may be between the leaders of large corporate businesses and the government regulators who are supposed to be limiting them. That kind of cooperation on the golf course or wherever it takes place can end up hurting everyone else. But economists tend not to look at cooperation. The key model is still about competition. Neoliberal capitalism, which is the monopoly corporate capitalism that we have right now, has huge problems. But it is not Capitalism with a capital C. It is one form. If you look at the history of capitalism, or you look at it across countries, there are many different varieties.

Finally, the work of caring for people and the planet is at the core of sustainable economies. If we really want our economies to last, we have got to take care of people and we have got to take care of the planet we live on. Now, that word "care" has not come up before. Caring is very much on that feminine and other-interested side, very much a "not economics" word. You also do not see so much of it in traditional philosophy. But I was quite amused when I was reading Hans Jonas's *The Imperative of Responsibility*, a philosophical take on environmental ethics. It goes through all of the big names in philosophy. But after he reasons through all of that, he finds he has a lot of good philosophical theories but no answer to the questions: Why should you even *care* if you have the right philosophical theory? Why should you *care* about anything at all? When it comes down to the nub, he writes, that the "[T]he always acute, unequivocal, and choiceless responsibility which the newborn claims for itself creates the ought-to-do of the subject who, in virtue of their power, is called to its care" (see Jonas 1985, 134). The fundamental responsibility for caring for people and the planet comes from realizing human weakness.

Freeing Our Moral Imagination

There is a problem with the way we usually look at these things. If you do a Google image search on the word "economy", you get photos of stock market tickers or coins. If you do the same for "care" you usually end up with a mother and baby – often white both in race and clothing. If you have ever had a baby, you know how dangerous it is to do anything in white! If those are our mental images of care and economics, how would you ever get those two together? They are totally night and day.

I am going to appeal to your moral imagination to finish up with a couple of images I have been thinking about. First, if our image of care is mother-and-baby, then it seems like men would have to become mothers in order to care – they would have to become feminine. I wanted to combat that and say that care is *everyone's* responsibility. So, I have tried to revitalize the idea of "diligent husbandry". Husbandry is a good old English word that, to the extent it is still around, tends to refer to animal husbandry, that is, the care of animals, usually as part of a business. You are raising cattle for meat or you are raising sheep for wool or something like that. But "husbandry" has this connotation of *taking care of* the animals or taking care of your crops – keeping a close eye on the weather, paying attention to the details, paying attention to their health. So, it has both these productive connotations and these caring connotations. The shepherd is concerned with the health of the sheep and that is both productive and a form of care. I argue that women can also be diligent "husbands" of sheep or of businesses. The CEO, as a human being, may not be interested only in money, but may also be a full human being – may also recognize some responsibilities and seek to husband that business (whether that business leader is male or female).

But in case you want a somewhat more female-oriented image, let me suggest one of powerful care. Care is very weak if it depends on mom staying home with baby while all the resources to support this come in from somewhere else. And it is very limited if it never gets out of the home. So, we have in the U. S. an iconic WWII poster of a working woman flexing her biceps, with the title "Yes, We Can!" A contemporary representation of powerful care might swap former U. S. First Lady Michelle Obama into that image.

Conclusion

Care has to be powerful, too. We have to get out there, men and women both, and use our strength to move this economy around. We need to make it into something that actually supports people and the planet. So, I will leave you with those images.

References

Jonas, H. (1985). *The Imperative of Responsibility: In Search of an Ethics for the Technological Age.* Chicago: University of Chicago Press.
Nelson, J. A. (2009). "Between a Rock and Soft Place: Ecological and Feminist Economics". *Ecological Economics* 69, 1–8.
Nelson, J. A. (2016a). "Husbandry: A (Feminist) Reclamation of Masculine Responsibility for Care". *Cambridge Journal of Economics* 40(1), 1–15.
Nelson, J. A. (2016b). "Poisoning the Well, or How Economic Theory Damages Moral Imagination". In DeMartino, G. and McCloskey, D. (Eds.), *The Oxford Handbook of Professional Economic Ethics.* Oxford: Oxford University Press, 184–199.
Nelson, J. A. (2018). *Economics for Humans.* 2nd ed. Chicago: University of Chicago Press.

Federica Giardini
Ecology and Economy. Feminist Perspectives

Abstract: Addressing the question of the relationship between economics and ecology is an opportunity to redefine what a feminist approach consists of. In this text, taking on the established authority of feminist theoretical production, the possibility of a genealogical approach to the philosophical canon is explored – returning to the classics to identify conceptual tools suitable for analyzing the present times.

Preliminary Points on Feminist Method/Practices in Philosophy and Political Philosophy

To articulate the relationship between ecology and economy, I would first like to illustrate what it means to do so from a feminist perspective – for me. It is a way of showing how problems and answers take shape, during a research that has to be seen in its embodied and material constitution.

A first point is to consider feminism as a positioning – a cut, an approach – that is not resolved in taking on themes that can be characterized as feminist or as concerning women. Regarding this I have in mind Simone de Beauvoir's harsh if not ungenerous judgment of women writers. In *The Second Sex*, she states:

> [W]omen writers are doing the cause of women a great service; but – usually without realizing it – they are still too concerned with serving this cause to assume the disinterested attitude towards the universe that opens the widest horizons […]. When they have removed the veils of illusion and deception, they think they have done enough […] It is all very well not to be duped, but at that point all else begins. (Beauvoir 2013 [1949], 669)

Well, also in contrast – as I will say – with the neoliberal ideology, which hides contexts and conditions of our actions, at this point of my activity I propose a feminist approach in its specific capacity to make explicit, to question and to propose other contexts and conditions, other criteria so to intervene on the epistemological level – Beauvoir's "widest horizons". This approach implies reopening the relationship with the philosophical canon but on the condition of passing it through the scrutiny of a feminist epistemology, and not for the sake of interpretation but by using the authors for the questions to be addressed. Of course, I still work with feminist authors and women philosophers, but today I would like to present this other practice I am facing in my research. In this text I will try to give a brief example of what I mean.

The second point concerns my training, the formation of my research. In my development, the thought of sexual difference between Italy and France had to do with this stand – questioning, for example, equality as the only theoretical frame of women's liberation. And yet today I must also come to terms with the entropy that affects even the most radical openings. Nowadays, difference no longer captures contexts, conflicts, openings, as we need to handle them in the present times. To put it with Rosi Braidotti, often difference that reaches the mainstream is a "reified difference" (Braidotti 2013, 58) that has itself become a resource for profit. In my research path, this entropy of the criterion of difference has led to question the sufficiency of the analysis focused on domination – and on the order of discourse, on the "symbolic" – as a privileged way of critics and transformation. It has also meant investigating the interconnection between domination and exploitation; and it has therefore meant bringing together the legacy of two Italian feminist genealogies of the 1970s, which were divided and which have fought over precisely this issue – the thought of sexual difference (from Luce Irigaray and Carla Lonzi to Luisa Muraro and the philosophical community of Diotima) and the feminist thought revising Marxism (the Padua group – Alisa Del Re, Silvia Federici, Maria Rosa Dalla Costa, Leopoldina Fortunati) – which revealed exploitation on the invisible activities of reproduction (Giardini 2015).

A third and final point concerns doing philosophy, thus considering it as a situated practice. To hold an autonomous position in the interlocution with the canon, the knowledge produced *outside* the academy is relevant. This outside doesn't mean exclusion but rather recognition that the university is only one among the places where knowledge is produced. In short, transfeminist activism constitutes the distance from the situatedness of academic knowledge; the tension and the circular exchange between knowledge produced by mobilizations and conflicts and knowledge produced by academic study and research make philosophy a space in which to construct tools to open the possible within reality (Giardini 2017a).

Dealing with the Canon. The Neoliberal Paradox: "Calculemus!" and the Return of Ideology

I now turn to the specific issue about how to conceive the relations between economy and ecology. The first question I want to address is how economy establishes the connection with a specific conception of the human being; moreover, how economy is constituted through the feedback with an anthropological presupposition. The canon, mainly in modern times, but we could also think of Aristotle, makes this connection explicit – Adam Smith is the author of *The Wealth of Nations* as much as of the *Theory of Moral Sentiments.* Not so explicit, however, is the connection between neoliberal economics and the related anthropological conception, where according to the neoclassical, marginalist approach, economics is conceived as an articulation of the mathematical disciplines. Milonakis and Fine have formulated this transformation as the turn from political economy to economics (Milonakis and Fine 2009).

The eternal laws of economics are those of mathematics, of the calculus of probabilities and of Brownian motion (cf. Gallino 2013) – processed through computers. And the *metaphysical* assumption is that human reality – where all reality is anthropized or can be gradually anthropized – can be traced back to the formalization of mathematically calculable data. We could say, with Marc Fisher (2009), that we are living in an epoch of the return of metaphysical realism established according to the mathematical laws of economics.

In this perspective, the relationship with the other disciplines and forms of knowledge aggravates the hierarchy to the point of autonomy: to proceed to formalization, economics does not need any other material that does not come from the datafication of reality. The becoming of economic science no longer consists in representing, and not even in producing, reality, but rather in an undetermined task of formalization – a sort of updated version of the 17th-century "Calculemus!".

It is at this point that feminist incredulity and scrutiny intervenes and helps in questioning the theoretical background of this issue: beyond the claim of being a formal science, economics do use and enact an anthropological conception, that is consubstantial to economics: it works not only as the final objective of application of the results of the laws of calculation, but also as a presupposition of them. On the one hand, in fact, we have witnessed an increasingly accelerated configuration of an ideology of the human being that has its fulcrum in the individual. We know about the many critiques of the modern idea of the individual – within the feminist critique of the liberal tradition, the main and classical reference is Carole Pateman (1988) – but today we must take onboard a specific aspect of this anthropology of the individual: the individual is endowed with a rationality that consists in the exercise of choice, and this choice is presented in terms of a cost-benefit calculation. And this is precisely the point of the isomorphism between the claims of mathematical economics and its anthropological presupposition: the individual calculates, just as economics is a matter of calculation. Economics acts on the more general level of laws, but these are the ones functioning in individual rationality. On the other hand, individual anthropology is precisely what allows the metaphysical presuppositions of such analyses to go undeclared: the individual is an unencumbered self, exercising their own reason, their own choices by calculation, without contexts and conditions being considered (or, if considered, they are as variables of a choice themselves). This is the terrain in which the production and impact of the ideology that aspires to become a self-fulfilling prophecy is exercised (Laval 2007).

Indeed, the claim of marginalist economics to be part of the exact sciences can be defined with the oxymoron of an *operational metaphysics* that, through a retroactive dynamic, configures human behavior according to an assumed and undeclared model. We can find several examples of this peculiar short-circuit between what was considered, in our philosophical tradition, the transcendent dimension of the very theoretical assumptions, and the contingent dimension of human action. The first that comes in mind, relating to the governance of Covid-19 pandemics, is the declaration made by Stella Kyriakides, European Commissioner for Health and Food Safety, on the issue of the safety of the Astrazeneca vaccine. The objective of that declaration was properly political – assuming the institutional task of restoring public confidence – and yet the reasons of reassurance were made in terms of a "positive risk-benefit" ratio, that is of statistical *evidence* (e. g. Kyriakides 2021). A few months later, it is possible to assess the extent of the short-circuit between a metaphysics of the calculating individual and the economic governance of the pandemic – the institutions themselves have produced the ground for disbelief and distrust; indeed, political discourse achieves no effect if it pretends to legitimize itself through *formal*, that is mathematical, reasons.

Another example concerns a situation that is common to us here in Europe, the sectors established by the European Research Council, on the basis of which our research projects are evaluated and have, or do not have, funding. Well, our disciplines are assigned to the macro-sector of "Social Sciences and Humanities" (SH), whose first and most general specification is: "Individuals, institutions, and markets" (SH1). Perhaps this example makes the short-circuit in question more intuitive: the economics of research organizes the field of research itself – individuals, institutions, and markets – which in turn is called upon to confirm the epistemological thesis underlying the articulation of research fields and, at the same time, is rewarded or sanctioned on the basis of its compliance with that thesis.

If the 2008 financial crisis has shown that the economic claim of formalization as a form of exhaustive and predictive knowledge is false, nevertheless this denial has not served to decree the fall from grace of the related anthropological conception. There has been no reflection on the forces that transcend the human capacity for calculation, prediction, and control; instead, there has been continued hegemony for a transcendent idea of the human being, that is, of a being endowed with reason, out of conditions and context, and capable of controlling reality.

A traumatic variation of this perspective has recently appeared through the global phenomena of the pandemic and the generalized acquisition of the notion of the Anthropocene, as an era in which humans have developed forces that produce effects on a geological scale (Lewis and Maslin 2015). Pandemic and Anthropocene are two forms of re-immanentization of human action; the pandemic relocates us not at the top but within the food chain, while the Anthropocene shows how it is our own becoming that leads us to face equal and opposite forces of scale (Latour 2017). But even here, it would seem that – instead of concluding that a paradigm shift is necessary – the political response is to increase the pressure of ideology so to achieve what is assumed by economic formalization, this time resorting to state "*force de loi*" (Derrida 199) – according to the Foucauldian lexicon this development is more properly defined not as neoliberal but rather as "ordoliberal governamentality" (Foucault 2004, 135).

Feminist Perspectives. Shaping the Future, Rethinking the Past

As for the opening of alternative perspectives, I will concentrate on the very concept of the individual, without assuming alternative epistemologies and ontologies, as in the case, for instance, of authors such as Haraway, Latour, Braidotti. If we think in terms of the individuals that we should be, then our own inalienable functions – breathing, eating, drinking… – make us *environmental knots*. Not the body, but the dynamic that is our body must be thought about. A body that is no longer that of the mechanical *res extensa* of modern science; a body that cannot be considered as bounded and inert (e. g. Mbembe 2020) – not even when we sleep does this active relationship cease.

How can this alternative perception of the body be used to question the links between economics and ecology? The question in fact requires us to investigate a field that does indeed connect economics and ecology, but according to possibilities unexplored by hegemonic narratives.

From a feminist and genealogical perspective, firstly the ground for analysis and critique of undeclared metaphysical claims of economics on individuals concerned the reconceptualization of the term "value" (Giardini 2019). Value is in fact a hybrid term that connects morality and economics, and thus allows us to identify the interactions between ideology and mathematical calculation, in short, it allows us to trace the interaction between domination and exploitation (Giardini 2017b). In fact, it is precisely from the interaction of the two genealogies of Italian feminism in the 1970s that it became possible to see how the order of discourse – that which establishes a society's self-perception with respect to its needs, to what is essential, to what is desirable – attributes (or not) a value to human activities and, above all, organizes the regime of restitution of this value, in monetary and non-monetary terms.

An example, coming from the economic-political debate in Italy during the pandemic, will help to clarify this point: the work done at home, especially by women, in ensuring, for example, the continuity of their children's education, has been defined as "uncountable", "unpayable", or "essential"; at the same time, a very high rate of women have been leaving their jobs to face these new household activities, and very little has been done by public policies in response to the situation. Irigaray, in *Speculum*, gives us the clues about how the moral appreciation can be a form of devaluation or how the essential role attributed to the feminine must be balanced by their cancellation – women's divinity is displaced both at the lower origin and at the more distant transcendence (Irigaray 1974). The example shows how a body, however individual, is constituted and regenerated by activities and relations that go beyond both will and mastery and the criterion of maximizing individual utility; this body exceeds individual boundaries. Moreover, the example highlights a peculiar connection between economic regimes and regimes of public morality, which we might call negative complementarity – maximum moral appreciation corresponds to damage in strictly economic and quantitative terms.

In fact, initially I had thought of replacing exchange, that is trade – as the form of the relationship of the neoliberal individual that is subject to cost-benefit assessment and thus to the calculation of what is valuable and priceable –, with the complexity of the relationship itself, as it is resistant to formalization and to a proceduralist approach. Similar arguments are made in the field of reproductive relationships and activities, which are considered quantifiable in terms of salary only for the simplest, repetitive part, but not for the more complex part of affective relationships (Del Re 2012; Picchio 2020; Mellor 2017). However, today, starting from the acquisitions of theories on human and non-human reproduction, I think that the more appropriate term, which replaces trade as the hegemonic form of relationship between individuals, is the concept of "metabolism". Ariel Salleh, within a feminist approach to Marxian theory of value, proposes to assume the "metabolic value" (Salleh 2010), in order to investigate the relations and interactions between economy and ecology. In fact, compared to the economic demand for mathematical formalization, this perspective introduces, on the one hand, dynamism and circularity in the interaction between the human and the non-human, and on the other hand, it gives account on how value is constituted along a moving line which defines each time the zone where what is valuable and what is not is identified, at the crossroads between moral and economics, between ideology and calculation.

Addressing the philosophical canon with this question and urgency in relation to the present reveals unforeseen resources. It is in the 17th century that the idea of the individual became hegemonic, and that was also the period in which the idea of a possible mathematization of all reality predominated. Leibniz is the author who – besides the formulation of the concept of the monad – foresaw that in a not-too-distant future the republic of the cultured would open its assemblies with the invitation, not to discuss, but to calculate together – "calculemus!" (Leibniz 1688, 913). All of reality would finally be mathematized. And yet, if we look at his texts from the urgencies and sensitivities of the present, we can see how monads are not at all seats of calculation, rather they are environmental knots, where there is no ontological partition between reason, perception and sensibility and where universal connections deploy (e. g. Deleuze's (1988) reading of Leibniz). In this perspective, Leibniz inherits a humanistic and Renaissance sensibility for cross-references and connections between inanimate and animate entities – I am thinking of Raimon Lull but also of the allegorical connections that we find in authors such as Pico della Mirandola. Maybe this could be also identified as the genealogy lying behind the use of Greimas, and of his redefinition of subjects as "actants", by Haraway (1992). Could "calculemus" then stand for a knowledge that takes into account the semiotic texture between living, non-living and human?

Getting to Know about Economy and Ecology, Again

Which research perspective can unfold according to this approach? A feminist research perspective on the connections between economics and ecology unfolds at the intersection of the above: a materialist approach, which considers the conditions within which the problems to be addressed emerge; a knowledge that interacts with the non-academic knowledge produced by transfeminist conflicts and mobilizations; and a genealogical relationship with the disciplinary canon, which reopens texts to new possible uses. I will articulate these diverse possibilities as separate issues.

- *Crisis.* The economic and socioecological crisis should be understood as a loss of effectiveness – De Martino (1977, 632) expresses it as a "crisis of the presence" – of the schemes for intelligibility and interaction within human reality. This means the opening of a space for thinking radically new cultural, practical, and conceptual habits (Giardini 2017c). In respect of the previous approaches, crisis must be intended not as a solely human loss of orientation, but rather as a multiverse and assembled situation. From this point of view, it is interesting to note the, not yet hegemonic, use of the concept of "syndemics" (Singer 2009), which allows us to go beyond the human society-nature dualism.

- *Oikos.* It is possible to recover the common etymological root of the terms economy and ecology, without reducing it to a gimmick for some philosophy of origins. The *oikos*, in the societies of ancient Greece, is a space of reproductive activities and relations, which also produce their own and autonomous regularities – the *oikos* is a necessary element of the *polis* but is placed in a kind of internal exteriority. These regularities introduce a substantial idea of measure, distinct from monetary measure (which is rather the object of chrematistics) – it is this distinction that begins to decline with modern political economy until its definitive superimposition in contemporary marginalist economics. Therefore, the connection between economy and ecology poses the problem of which interactions and activities allow the reproduction and regeneration of the entities involved, as well as the question of how to see/signify such exchanges (Picchio 2020). Moreover, economics returns in a peculiar and updated way to being a social science – this time the social considered by economy concerns a society that is no longer only human but rather is the sphere of human and non-human agency and interactions.
- *Measure.* Economy can be reconsidered as the field in which to find measures of relationships, activities, and interactions. The challenge is not abandoning political economy for politics or setting quality against quantity or real economy against finance; rather it is rethinking what measure is and what it is about (Mellor 2017). Measure is to be considered as the result of social and collective conflict on what is identified as need and on what happens in interactions (e. g. Gibson-Graham 2006). Measure is both symbolic and material, thus it takes over and makes explicit the ambiguity of the term value. In this sense, we have recently been working in a project of creation of a free and feminist space for research and we have come to redefine what income is: not just a monetary measure, but above all a measure of restitution – the Italian word for income, *reddito*, comes from Latin *reddere* – giving back. If we really want to think in terms of exchange, then the question is not what we do, not what we get, but what is returned to us, to others, to all that is implied, in order to regenerate (to reproduce) the context and conditions of our qualified living.
- *Allegory.* A final development of the research concerns the forms of knowledge that are appropriate to these new problems. We know that some proposals, coming for example from object-oriented theory, concern the impossibility of perceiving "hyperobjects" such as climate change (Morton 2013). However, the feminist approach has introduced the notion of situated knowledge

which, in this context, must be understood as the refusal to reformulate and solve theoretical problems by canceling one's specific position. Furthermore, it is precisely the genealogical approach to the canon that allows us to draw on forms of knowledge and signification suited to the complex and multi-layered nature of contemporary phenomena. Indeed, allegory has recently been used in relation to the Anthropocene, as a literary form capable of accounting for the relationships between humans and non-humans in post-colonial literature (DeLoughrey 2019). Our research will move on a double field: on the one hand, it will return to some pre-modern authors, looking for a different conception and signification of the interaction between "human" and "nature"; on the other hand, partially following the indications of Spivak (2015) and Chakrabarty (2019), it will redefine allegory as a form of theoretical account of the interactions between the human need of sense and orientation (*world*), the formalized codifications constituting the objects of experience (*globe)* and the alterity of non-human activities and of the outer space dimension (*planet*).

References

Beauvoir, S. (2013 [1949]). *The Second Sex*. London: Vintage.
Braidotti, R. (2013). *The Posthuman*. Cambridge: Polity Press.
Chakrabarty, D. (2019). "The Planet: An Emergent Humanist Category". *Critical Inquiry* 46(1), 1–31.
De Martino, E. (1297). *La fine del mondo. Contributo all'analisi delle apocalissi culturali*. Turin: Einaudi.
Del Re, A. (2012). "Questioni di genere. Alcune riflessioni sul rapporto produzione/riproduzione nella definizione del comune". *About Gender* 1, 151–170.
Deleuze, G. (1988). *Le Pli. Leibniz et le Baroque*. Paris: Minuit.
DeLoughrey, E. M. (2019). *Allegories of the Anthropocene*. Durham and London: Duke University Press.
Derrida, J. (1994). *Force de loi: Le "Fondement mystique de l'autorité"*. Paris: Gallimard.
Fisher, M. (2009). *Capitalist Realism: Is There No Alternative?* London: Zero.
Foucault, M. (2004). *La naissance de la biopolitique. Cours au Collège de France (1978–1979)*. Paris: Seuil.
Gallino, L. (2013). *Finanzcapitalismo. La civiltà del denaro in crisi*. Turin: Einaudi.
Giardini, F. (2015). "Le symbolique, la production et la reproduction. Eléments pour une nouvelle économie politique". In Laval, C., Paltrinieri, L. and Taylan, F. (Eds.), *Marx & Foucault. Lectures, usages, confrontations*. Paris: La Découverte, 259–271.
Giardini, F. (2017a). "Concepire la trasformazione. Tra pensiero affermativo e vita concettuale". *Politica & Società* 2, 215–236.
Giardini, F. (2017b). "Dominio e sfruttamento. Un ritorno neomaterialista sull'economia". In: Finelli, R. and Bertollini, A. (Eds.), *Soglie del linguaggio. Corpi, mondi, società*. Rome: Roma Tre University Press, 69–80.
Giardini, F. (2017c). *I nomi della crisi. Antropologia e politica*. Milan: Kluwer.
Giardini, F. (2019). "Valore. Topologia e dinamica della misura". In EcoPol (Eds.), *Bodymetrics. La misura dei corpi. Tre quaderni su eco/nomia/logia transfemminista*, vol. 2. Rome: IaphItalia, 28–38.

Gibson-Graham, J. K. (2006). *The End of Capitalism (As We Knew It). A Feminist Critique of Political Economy:* Minneapolis: University of Minnesota Press.
Haraway, D. J. (1992) "The Promises of Monsters". In Grossberg, L., Nelson, C. and Treichler, P. (Eds.), *Cultural Studies.* New York: Routledge, 295–337.
Irigaray, L. (1974). *Speculum. De l'autre femme.* Paris: Minuit.
Kiriakides, S. (2021). "Letter to European Medicine Agency on vaxzevria, April 28, 2021". URL: https://www.ema.europa.eu/en/documents/referral/letter-commissioner-kyriakides-asking-ema-follow-vaxzevria-opinion-after-council-discussion_en.pdf (last accessed 17 November 2022).
Latour, B. (2017). *Facing Gaia. Eight Lectures on the New Climatic Regime.* Cambridge: Polity Press.
Laval, C. (2007). *L'homme économique. Essai sur les racines du néo-libéralisme.* Paris: Gallimard.
Leibinz, G. W. (1688). "De arte characteristica ad perficiendas scientias ratione nitentes". In *Sämtliche Schriften und Briefe,* ed. Berlin-Brandenburgische Akademie der Wissenschaften. Vol. VI/4, 912–913.
Lewis, S. and Maslin, M. A. (2015). "Defining the Antropocene". *Nature* 519, 171–180.
Mbembe, A. (2020). "Le droit universel à la respiration". *AOC media – Analyse Opinion Critique.* URL: https://aoc.media/opinion/2020/04/05/le-droit-universel-a-la-respiration/ (last accessed 17 November 2022).
Mellor, M. (2017). "Ecofeminist Political Economy. A Green and Feminist Agenda". In MacGregor, S. (Ed.), *Routledge Handbook of Gender and Environment.* London and New York: Routledge, 86–100.
Milonakis, D. and Fine, B. (2009). *From Political Economy to Economics Method. The Social and the Historical in the Evolution of Economic Theory.* London and New York: Routledge.
Morton, T. (2013). *Hyperobjects.* Minneapolis: University of Minnesota Press.
Pateman, C. (1988). *The Sexual Contract.* Cambridge: Polity Press.
Picchio, A. (2020). "A Partire dal lavoro non pagato". In Giardini, F., Pierallini, S. and Tomasello, F. (Eds.), *La natura dell'economia. Femminismo, economia politica, ecologia.* Rome: DeriveApprodi, 29–48.
Salleh, A. (2010). "From Metabolic Rift to 'Metabolic Value': Reflections on Environmental Sociology and the Alternative Globalization Movement". *Organization & Environment* 23(2), 205–219.
Singer, M. (2009). *Introduction to Syndemics: A Systems Approach to Public and Community Health.* San Francisco, CA: Jossey-Bass.
Spivak, G. C. (2015). "Planetarity". *Paragraph* 38(2), 290–292.

Andrea Günter
Towards a Feminist Theory of Money. Patriarchal Economic Structures, the Aristotelian Concept of Justice and the Intermediacy of Money

Abstract: People's lives are regulated more and more by money economy. It is therefore important to develop a feminist critique of the phenomenon of money. Such a criticism must form the basis of feminist economic criticism. Money is not a neutral intermediary. Money consists in a material and in a legal substance, it is also structured by reciprocity and justice. For reconstructing these aspects and its patriarchal traditions, it is worth taking a look at Aristotle's *Nicomachean Ethics*.

Why a Feminist Theory of Money?

Not only since the global financial crisis (which reached its first peak in 2007) has it become obvious that the banking and financial sector is one of the most influential areas of society that produces greatest injustice.

All over the world, people's lives are increasingly organized in the form of money economy. Money forms a sphere of its own that increasingly determines all areas of life. For defining the future, a feminist examination of this phenomenon is inevitable. Money is never neutral, as the representatives of neoclassical economic theory like to claim (cf. Busch 2004, 141). Money is a medium. Understanding its mediality precisely is the prerequisite for using it more justly in the future.

According to Aristotle, the structure of a mediate phenomenon such as money consists in the fact that it is at the same time "intermediate, relative and equal" (NE 1131a14–17). As a relative, money regulates sets of relationships. It must fit in with concrete situations, persons, and their dependencies. Accordingly, the equal and intermediary produce is relative: tied back to real relational structures. "Equality" as an intermediary factor is dependent on the concrete relationships from which it comes and which it is at the same time supposed to connect anew. As an intermedium, money transforms. But what does it transform in which manner? And how does it transform gender relations?

Due to its intermediary structure, money is based in many ways on social relations – and consequently on gender relations. Reconstructing this connection allows us to understand how gender relations are at work *in* money (cf. Günter et al. 2018, 250–276; Günter 2019).

Because of the increasing importance of money economy, the feminist Swiss economist and long-time member of *Aktion Finanzplatz Schweiz*,[1] Mascha Madörin, called for the development of a feminist theory of money. Actually, it should have been self-evident: a feminist critique of economics without addressing the phenomenon of "money" ignores a central aspect of economics. This leads to inadequate analyses, so that feminist economic goals become misleading. The critique of capitalist structures alone, for example, is often reduced to that of the relations between "capitalists" and those who they exploit. Furthermore, reconstructing gender relations of labor along the lines of "care" without taking into account money economy (consisting in material and legal dependencies, payment habits and future opportunities) as a supplementing complex that structures wages more and more, hardly hits the mark. "Care" as a gendered division of being paid is economically not simply based on the division of labor.

Thus, the demand for "equal pay for equal work" does not do justice to the complexity of women's connections with financial matters, nor to the historical changes in women's economic lives.[2] As long as money is not understood in its categoriality, as a relative and intermedium, but is conceived as a substance (money is a "God"), the search is on for a coincidence between money, objects of exchange and subjects or relations of exchange that does not exist. A "tautological incommensurability" (Krondorfer 2000, 71–89) comes to light, generating false ideas about money as well as false ideas about exchange, the market and gender relations.

Wages are practiced in money structures; they must be perceived in their monetary structure. The fact that wages of care workers (can) depend on returns for shareholders, i. e. that they can be regarded as a pure monetary value, reveals the financial mediality of money in wages. It is always inherent in wages that they can be declared in the form of money as a factor *independent* of (the complexity of) their generation.

The fact that wages must not be defined by gender identities, but also not merely by equivalent wage-ratio work performance, because a wage is always also in relation to the prices to be paid, is revealed in the fact that women have to pay the same rents, the same prices for towels or cars as men (Soo-Hyun 2006, 11–13; 163–165). Equal prices are as little equal prices as equal wages are

---

[1] www.aktionfinanzplatz.ch (last accessed 13 December 2022).
[2] Housework has changed over the last 50 years, observable in the fact that lunches are increasingly organized by inns, restaurants and school lunch. Everyday meals are practiced differently in terms of money management.

equal wages. In order to correct such inequality factors, diversified tax and social contribution payments are assessed more and more. This diversification process, however, is less and less sufficient. Overall, it makes visible the following: the financial aspect of economy is defined by rights (here: marriage law and tax law). In general, money consists not simply in a mathematical (Günter 2020, 173–190), but in a legal function, especially its capital character is a purely legal construction (Pistor 2019, 1–23). The connections between money, wages, prices, capital and law have to become discussed in more detail. Unjust "wages" are a symptom of an unjust overall economic situation. "Equal pay for equal work" is not an aim, it is a "regulatory idea" (Kant).

The special mediality of money makes it possible to segment interfaces of the economic, such as labor relations, money, wages, capital, tax payments and price. Thus, it seems absurd to distinguish between "paid" and "unpaid" work in a monetary economy and to raise wages to the crunch question (cf. Madörin 2014, 178–187; Madörin 2012, 14; Günter et al. 2018, 218–223). Rather, direct and indirect remuneration, direct and indirect exchange relations have to be distinguished together with the diversity that can be inherent in monetary transactions (their relativity).

Wages represent a social contract. Depending on the contract, different relations of exploitation or justice are inscribed in "money" (Günter 2013, 63–79). Towards which direction they lean also depends on which aspect of the money economy they represent. This may well turn out to be ambivalent: When a caregiver uses her inferior wage (wage-money economy) to buy shares of the nursing home (financial economy) where she works, she is both, subject and object of money. Her exchange situation elevates her to a subject of the enterprise "nursing home" and the wage she rents there, above subjugates her in a particularly perfidious way.

Dealing with the connection between money and gender relations broadens the perspective on the economic situation of women. Looking at poverty does not go far enough (cf. Günter 2016, 66–78). The deficit perspective prevents distinguishing the different participation of women in the economy, argue Regnath and Rudolf (2008, 9–10). Women are not merely recipients (of wages). This focus leaves them in the patriarchal logic of the breadwinner and the female situation of lack. Moreover, what women receive is not identical with what they have. The discussion of wages says nothing about how women deal with money or what they do for their financial security (Wrede 2003, 8–10). The monetary subject "woman" is multi-layered. The economic situation of women proves to be an effect of the complexity of economic structures.[3]

---

[3] The few publications on "women and money" include Annecke 1985; Dackweiler and Hornung

Patriarchy, Law and Economy

How are money and gender relations connected? If we look back in the past, we discover that Aristotle is one of the first introducing that connection in the Fifth Book of the *Nicomachean Ethics*. Here, he describes money as something that belongs to right and justice.

First, it must be noted that in the Aristotelian conception of justice, we find a connection between patriarchy and money that arises from the splitting of politics and economics in his political theory. This dynamic historically predates the economic developments we commonly call capitalism. To put it bluntly: Concepts of law and justice are as little neutral and objective as capitalism. On the contrary, without the Aristotelian split between economics and politics, the development of economics would probably have been different from the complex we now identify as capitalism.

Aristotle inscribes the master-servant/man-woman/household-political dualism not only in Western political and economic history, but also in the history of justice and law by explicitly installing the master-servant/man-woman dualism for distinguishing between domestic and political justice. On top of that, this division corresponds to the different legal positions of women and men in the Attic *legal system*, in which there is a master's right, a parental right, and a marriage right.

Furthermore, one could accuse Aristotle of androcentrism on the basis of the examples he gives (builder, cobbler, doctor). But this criticism falls short. If, like Plato, he would have referred to female milliners, bakers, midwives, market women and female merchants, his house-polis-rights scheme would be undermined. He uses his examples to place the legal schema above the reality of labor and exchange structures of men *and* women in his time. This allows him to absolutize the legal tripartite structure.

The real economic situation thus becomes irrelevant. It becomes historically invisible when only Aristotle is read and his remarks on economics and politics are treated as a historical reality. Those who follow his scheme affirmatively, but also those who follow it as a template for a critique of gender relations, fall for this example selection strategy. (Examining the selection of examples is an impor-

---

2003; Wrede 2003; Regnath and Rudolf 2008; above all, the fundamental writings of Madörin (1991; 2000; 2012; 2013; 2014). Due to global economic-financial developments, however, cultural scholars and philosophers have recently also increasingly been addressing the phenomenon of money, cf. Hörisch 1996; Hörisch 2004; Busch 2004; Hènaff 2002; Graeber 2011; Sahr 2017.

tant feminist methodology, because examples implement the relation of a theory to reality, other examples can lead to different economic, political, justice theories.)

Money and Justice

To explain that money is an aspect of law and justice, Aristotle cites the etymological relationship between the Greek "nomisma" – "money" – and "nomos" – " law". What money is, how it is practiced, what has what value, defines the "right".

According to Aristotle, the etymological context indicates that money does not exist because of nature, but because of law. If it were a natural (or else a divine or religious) phenomenon, it would be a phenomenon independent of men and their social conditions. But because it is a function of law, money is man-made and consequently depends on what men make. People can change its function, experience it as inexpedient, or even declare it as useless.

> ... and this is why it has the name 'money' (nomisma) – because it exists not by nature but by law (nomos) and it is in our power to change it and make it useless. (NE 1133 a 29–30)

The connection between law, justice and money is based on the fact that law and justice need an intermediary equal. Justice needs such a thing in order to establish a common denominator between different things for creating an exchange and ultimately a medium that is at once equal, intermediate, and relative.

> ... for [money] measures all things, and therefore the excess and the defect-how many shoes are equal to a house or to a given amount of food. The number of shoes exchanged for a house (or for a given amount of food) must therefore correspond to the ratio of builder to shoemaker. (NE 1133 a 19)

Aristotle draws on the proportionality formula a:b = c:d to demonstrate how such equality works. He describes that in this process men are identified with things. Women, children, slaves are understood as parts of patriarchal manhood, therefore men cannot do them wrong. As a consequence, justice in the household can be distinguished from justice in the polis.

Due to that character of such an abstraction, money as a medium de-personalizes persons and de-objectifies things on the one hand, while on the other hand it simultaneously objectifies the persons of exchange and personalizes the intermediary: Money becomes the subject of the process by constituting the equal sign. To this end, Aristotle identifies the structure of persons that forms a household, and thus produces and earns, as a property of the male subject of exchange, while no injustice can occur to the persons of the household because their interests are safeguarded (Günter 2022, chap. VI). – The deficits that arise from the fact that essential aspects of economic relationality are lost, Aristotle subsequently attempts to reintegrate, he confesses how difficult the undertaking of commensurability is and finally declares justice to be a transcendent factor.

If we now note that for the conception of justice both the household-polis distinction and the function of money are necessary, we can state that economics is indeed present in Aristotle's conception in *two* ways: as the *distinction* "economic-political" and as the *medium* "money". Without the factor of "justice", neither the economic nor money or the financial can be thought. Whoever tries to leave this connection out of the equation understands nothing of economics or deliberately torpedoes the justice factor in every economical act. On the other hand, if justice is the structure of every exchange, a concrete exchange must be examined to see how it realizes justice.

Consequently, the question of "equal pay for equal work" can be approached from two perspectives. First, as usual, one can look from the equality of labor to the difference in being paid. Secondly, the gender bias of money concepts can be analyzed. Their deconstruction can be used as a prerequisite for rethinking work and wages, and activating the justice structure in a new way.

In order to understand this constellation anew, it can furthermore be taken into account that women have been fully recognized as economic legal subjects since 1976 and that "unpaid" female domestic work is at the same time increasingly transformed into direct payment, taxes, insurances etc. Such a transformation is only possible due to the abstract character of money and indicates its shaping by legal history and its transformation of gender relations.

At the same time, it is precisely this double structure that allows us to see separate spheres in economy and politics and at the same time their interconnectedness. Economical patriarchalism means managing the separation and its abstraction practices absolute. To make separation absolute is possible in patriarchal relations in which children, women, and slaves are abstracted into manhood. Patriarchalism thus grounds capitalism. To overcome economic patriarchalism means to work through the simultaneity of the different spheres and their respective interdependencies again and again according to the situation (cf. Günter 2013, 63–79).

Working through the economic *and* monetary situation of women subsequently constitutes an essential moment for overcoming the maleness of money practices (Boesenberger 2003, 32–45; Irigaray 1976; Irigaray 1979, esp. 177–197). This is a procedure that is also proposed by the critical, not directly feminist social theorist Carl Friedrich von Weizsäcker.

> [...] it is also about the question of how to get out of the approach prevailing in the "mainstream" of allowing only the decisions of individuals in the market to be valid as an expres-

sion of their ways of satisfying meaningful needs without, on the other hand, lapsing into a paternalism that is certainly not forward-looking. Perhaps it is precisely the role of women in the economy to find a non-paternalistic way here. (Weizsäcker 2004, 366–367, Translation AG)

The male-individualized and *abstracted* subject *in the market* and the *role of* women in the *economy:* in this distinction, economic patriarchalism is observable as the basic figure of capitalism. This division can not only reinforce the understanding of money as an abstracting economic medium and the market as the effect of an absolute abstraction process. Since money rather makes the mediality of "the market" possible in the first place, "the role of women" in economy must be understood as an opposition to market events, decisively as its condition: as its house and hearth.

To consciously overcome the patriarchalism of economy, market *and* money will only be possible if the role of women in the economy is changed. At the same time, the reverse is true: changing the roles of women in the economy will only be possible if the patriarchal way of using money is overcome. As a consequence, it is possible to understand anew what satisfying meaningful needs, what exchange, and what "market" is.[4]

Money, Equality and Reciprocity

Through exchange, money becomes a mode of representing demands, Aristotle continues. In the context of justice, however, it is not a matter of what needs an individual has and how the market satisfies them. Demands, on the contrary, straightforwardly connect people. In the search for a (just) exchange, money primarily indicates the need, whether two people need and want an exchange or not.

> Now this unit is in truth demand, which holds all things together (for if men did not need one another's goods at all, or did not need them equally, there would be either no exchange or not the same exchange); but money has become by convention a sort of representative of demand. (NE 1133 a 26–28)

An exchange is therefore fundamentally based on the mutual demand for an exchange. This need leads to the desire to form an entity and to establish or recognize a medium such as money. Money is one of the means of satisfying *this* demand. It

---

[4] Irigaray and her successors spoke of money being "masculine" and identifying women as the object of economics (Irigaray, Madörin, Krondorfer). Here, a different view is elaborated. Money is not "masculine", it is organized "patriarchally". This means that money is dependent on legal systems.

structures reciprocity – that is, not through an individual, but through at least two individuals.

Money is thus clearly determined as a socio-political entity, as a socio-political phenomenon in which the conventions of the intersubjective are simultaneously inscribed. Observable and future money relations must consequently be understood as expressions of the need for reciprocity, intermediality and justice. Therefore, money undeniably represents gender relations. It reproduces established gender relations; traditional gender relations are implemented in the measurement of an amount. The discussion about "care" does take up this dimension, but at the expense of bringing the factor of "the reciprocity of the demand for exchange" into play.

Let us therefore take a closer look at whom Aristotle might mean as subjects of this reciprocity. Do "men" really mean men and women? Or only men? Perhaps even only free men? This ambiguity can be used to shed light on the connection between reciprocity and gender relations. For this purpose, an experiment can be carried out. What meaning emerges if one "gendered" the relational structure of exchange demands? Then one can create the following statement:

> Now this unit is in truth demand, which holds all things together (for if *men and women* did not need one another's goods at all, or did not need them equally, there would be either no exchange or not the same exchange); but money has become by convention a sort of representative of demand.

This exploration makes it clear that there can be an exchange of money between the sexes, in the case *where they both need each other*. The extent to which there is reciprocity, and therefore justice and equality, between the sexes is determined by how the *demand for exchange* between them is carried out. Thus, it is not (gender-specific) differences in the needs of women and men that lead to economic-financial inequality, but the difference in having the need to exchange with others of the opposite sex.

Exchange justice between the sexes is as reciprocal as the existing gender relations are and these define how women and men need each other. However, reciprocity cannot exist in the situation of patriarchal house-polis/man-woman-rights-dualization. It sets up the man as the head of the household, in which the woman is included as a part of himself. Men, consequently, do not need women in the same way that women need men; women are, after all, a part of them. Women, in turn, do not need the same goods as men in this order, nor do they have the same needs, nor the same need for exchange.

Thus, exchange with women is not a demand for men because women are a part of their selves. So, there is no reciprocity between women and men. As a consequence, there is also no need for justice and, in this way, equality and relationality between them. No pay – for housework – or unequal pay would consequently be just. Similarly, Simone de Beauvoir criticizes that only women are considered dependent on men. Although men are equally dependent on women, their dependence is ignored. This leads to the fact that women cannot be socially (and economically, we can add) liberated. Recognition of the mutuality of dependency relationships, on the other hand, opens up spaces of freedom. For this to happen, dependencies – the *demand for* exchange – must be managed differently (cf. Beauvoir 1976, 22–23).

Even if the economic conditions are currently more complex, and women themselves are engaged in (the same) gainful employment, they do not need neither the "equal" nor an intermedium as long as it is true that they are more dependent on men than men are on them, and they need men more than men need them. It turns out that gender relations are structured not by how the market satisfies their needs, but rather by how the need for exchange between the sexes is constructed. At the same time, it becomes clear that "the market" can only be something like "free" when there is real reciprocity between the sexes.

The Materiality of the Intermediate Same

Money, however, does not represent the only possible intermediary equal that Aristotle finds in exchange practices. Looking at the other items he addresses as intermediaries, one finds land, houses, food, and shoes. Since money forms one element of this series, it becomes clear that money is not simply a formal object such as a number that can simply be "added up", but must be a very material product. So instead of pushing the idealization of money because it abstracts and dematerializes, the opposite step must be taken in our times. Money must be treated like food in order to make the "household" visible in money.

Money must be produced like bread, shoes and houses. It can be cultivable or barren like land. The intermediate objects are produced or cultivated by someone. This obviously happens in the sphere of the household. An intermediate does not come from nothing, nor does it consist of nothing. The household's labor and cultural achievements are its material origin.

But what happens to the producers of the intermediary when it is exchanged? What happens, therefore, when it is a question of an exchange of men who, while equally dependent on each other, and at the same time remain dependent on those who are subordinate to them, who, while they produce the materiality of money, are not granted the *same demand of exchange?* Are such men free because these spheres are arbitrarily separated and the materiality of money is suppressed?

The unequal dependency relations guarantee the existence of the intermedia, but these relations become ignorable because of their detachability from the household and its legal-political situation.

Reciprocity, which is limited to subjects of exchange in a space of abstraction, systematically misses reciprocity for the producers. What remains is an exchange structure based on exploitation because the producers of the intermediary are not taken into account as a third partner. But only if the position of the producers of the intermediary means is taken into account can we really speak of reciprocity. Otherwise, it is reciprocity without reciprocity.

If one measures the demand for the intermediary to be produced, the exchange that arises from demands that do not estimate this proves to be an illusion. To this end, the position of the third partner as the one who provides the intermediary, that is, as someone who also has his demands for an exchange (and who brings additional inequalities into play, such as the social and cultural circumstances under which he produces), must be taken into account. While Aristotle does introduce a third function for the measurement of a (just) amount, namely the judge, he systematically defines the producer of the intermediary out of the exchange structure.

As far as equal pay between women and men is concerned, it is necessary to ask what actual reciprocity must look like and how it can come about. It implies that situations must be created that allow us to perceive that men demand for and depend on the exchange with women just as complexly as women demand the exchange with men, and to invent new practices and rituals accordingly.

Following Jean Piaget's understanding of reciprocity, formal and real respect must be distinguished. *Real reciprocity* involves the willingness to affirm one's dependence on others and to form *a structure of mutual subordination*. It is the very function of the law, to embody mutual subordination.

Money, therefore, does not liberate from dependency relations by abstraction. Rather, it subordinates again by reciprocity – each person and in all directions. Recognizing these practices of subordination presupposes including all those who have an equal claim to the moment of exchange, and thus transforming their dependence into a real mutual subordination – among at least three. This is the condition for a right money reciprocity (Piaget 1975, 76–94; Günter 2017, 167–176; Günter et al. 2018, 303–314). Ultimately, we have to imagine that women's history is legal history, is monetary history, and justice history is monetary history, is women's history (cf. Regnath and Rudolf 2008, 11–17).

References

Annecke, U. (1985). Geld oder Leben. *Beiträge zur feministischen Theorie und Praxis* 15/16. Köln: Eigenverl. des Vereins Sozialwiss. Forschung und Praxis für Frauen

Aristoteles (2009). *Nicomachean Ethics*. URL: http://classics.mit.edu/Aristotle/nicomachaen.5.v.html (last accessed 17 November 2022).

Aristoteles (1990). *Politik*. Hamburg.

Beauvoir, S. de (1976). *Le deuxième sexe I*. Paris.

Boesenberger, E. (2004). "Männlichkeit als Kapital. Geld und Geschlecht in der US-amerikanischen Kultur". In Wrede, B. (Ed.), *Geld und Geschlecht. Tabus, Paradoxien, Ideologien*. Opladen, 32–45.

Busch, U. (2004). "Alternative Geldtheorien und linker Geldfetischismus". *Utopie kreativ* 160, 137–149.

Dackweiler, R. and Hornung, U. (Eds.) (2003). *Frauen, Macht, Geld*. Münster.

Filli, H. et. al. (1994). *Weiberwirtschaft. Frauen – Ökonomie – Ethik*. Luzern.

Graeber, D. (2011). *Debt – Updated and Expanded. The First 5,000 Years*. London and New York.

Günter, A. (2013). *Die Kultur des Ökonomischen. Gerechtigkeit, Geschlechterverhältnisse und das Primat der Politik*. Sulzbach/Ts.

Günter, A. (2016). "Can an Ethics of Justice Have Its Starting Point in a Situation of Lack? Decentering Richness along with Plato's *Politeia*". In Masaeli, M. (Ed.), *Globality, Unequal Development, and Ethics of Duty*. Cambridge, 66–78.

Günter, A. (2017). *Wertekulturen, Fundamentalismus und Autorität. Zur Ethik des Politischen*. Vienna.

Günter, A. (2019). "Feministische Geldtheorie. Eine philosophische Kriterienklärung". *Journal Netzwerk Frauen- und Geschlechterforschung NRW* 45, 41–44.

Günter, A. (2020). "Über die Intermedialität von Ethik und Algorithmus. Ein Beitrag zur mathematisch-philosophischen Kontur der Algorithmenethik". In Köberer, N., Prinzing, M. and Debatin, W. (Eds.), *Kommunikations- und Medienethik – reloaded? Orientierungssuche im Digitalen zwischen Innovationsdruck, Postfaktizität und sich auflösenden Kommunikations- und Wahrnehmungsgewissheiten*. Baden-Baden, 173–190.

Günter, A. (2022). *Philosophie und Geschlechterdifferenz. Auf dem Weg eines genealogischen Geschlechterdiskurses*. Opladen.

Günter, A. et. al. (2018). *Denkwerkstatt Gerechtigkeit. Gerechtigkeit rekonstruieren, Geschlechterverhältnisse neu diskutieren*. Roßdorf.

Hènaff, M. (2002). *Le prix de la vérité. Le don, l'argent, la philosophie*. Paris.

Hörisch, J. (1996). *Kopf oder Zahl. Die Poesie des Geldes*. Frankfurt/M.

Hörisch, J. (2004). *Gott, Geld, Medien. Studien zu den Medien, die die Welt im Innersten zusammenhalten*. Frankfurt/M.

Irigaray, L. (1976). *Waren, Körper, Sprache. Der ver-rückte Diskurs der Frauen*. Berlin.

Irigaray, L. (1979). *Das Geschlecht, das nicht eins ist*. Berlin.

Krondorfer, B. (2000). "Das Geld hat k/ein Geschlecht". In Krondorfer, B. and Mostböck, C. (Ed.), *Frauen und Ökonomie oder: Geld essen Kritik auf. Kritische Versuche feministischer Zumutungen*. Vienna, 71–89.

Madörin, M. (1991). "Männliche Ökonomie – Ökonomie der Männlichkeit, Wirtschaft, Wirtschaftstheorie und phallokratische Ordnung". In *Forum* 153, 3–5.

Madörin, M. (2000). "Der Finanzsektor und die Macht, Sachzwänge zu schaffen". In Krondorfer, B. and Mostböck, C. (Eds.), *Frauen und Ökonomie oder: Geld essen Kritik auf. Kritische Versuche feministischer Zumutungen*. Vienna, 119–131.

Madörin, M. (2011). "Wirtschaftliche Zukunftsfragen aus der Sicht der Care Ökonomie". In Bundesministerin für Frauen und Öffentlichen Dienst (Ed.), *Arbeit. Neu. Denken, Dokumentation der Frauenenquete Oktober 2011*. Vienna, 8–44.

Madörin, M. (2013). "Bezahlte, schlecht bezahlte, unbezahlte Arbeit: eine gigantische Umverteilungsmaschine zuungunsten der Frauen". *Arbeitsblätter von Wide Switzerland* 6–8 https://wide-switzerland.ch/de/ (last accessed 2 January 2023).

Madörin, M. (2014). "Kommentar zu Donaths Artikel aus der Sicht einer feministischen Politökonomin". In: *Denknetz Jahrbuch* 2014, 178–187.

Mun, S.-H. (2006). *Wie viel Geld für wie viel Leistung? Weichenstellungen in der Frauenlohnfrage in Westdeutschland nach 1945*. Münster.

Piaget, J. (1975). *The Moral Judgment of the Child*. London.

Pistor, K. (2019). *The Code of Capital. How the Law Creates Wealth and Inequality*. Princeton and Oxford.

Regnath, R. J. and Rudolf, C. (Eds.) (2008). *Frauen und Geld. Wider die ökonomische Unsichtbarkeit von Frauen*. Königstein.

Sahr, A. (2017). *Das Versprechen des Geldes. Eine Praxistheorie des Kredits*. Hamburg.

Weizsäcker, C. C. v. (2004). "Gerechtigkeit als Voraussetzung für effizientes Wirtschaften. Zum Jahrbuch 'Normative und institutionelle Grundfragen der Ökonomik'". *ORDO. Jahrbuch für die Ordnung von Wirtschaft und Gesellschaft* 55, 364–367.

Wrede, B. (Ed.) (2003). *Geld und Geschlecht. Tabus, Paradoxien, Ideologien*. Opladen.

Kateryna Karpenko
Gender Justice and Ecological Issues

Abstract: Contemporaneity has posed many questions to people, forcing them to look at the world in a new way. Among them, environmental and economic problems, the distribution of roles in society between men and women, and the issue of survival are perhaps the most acute. The purpose of this paper is the interaction between gender justice and ecological issues. Its achievement includes three main tasks: to clarify the meaning of the concepts of "gender justice" and "ecological issues"; to investigate the relevance of the methodological foundations of the study of gender and ecological justice; and to outline the prospects for the impact of sustainable gender equality on environmental issues and vice versa – environmental justice on gender equality.

In clarifying the basic concepts of this paper, it is worth noting the depth and variety of approaches to the gender problem. According to Judith Butler, gender identities can never be securely pinned down. They must be seen as fundamentally contingent, stabilized only through the performative acts that attempt, unsteadily, to fix them as integral markings of our existence (Butler 1990b). In regard to the shifts and re-positioning in Butler's creativity Lynne Segal notices: "Nevertheless, identity concepts remain pivotal to our ways of perceiving the world, positioning ourselves, and asserting differing forms of agency within it" (Segal 2017). In the last years, Butler has solidified with various social groups concerning specific political goals, although she does not abandon her criticality in methodology.

Even the current crisis of gender theory indicates the degree of its depth as a theory, the adoption of which involves a change of values and revision of established ideas. In an interview with Alona Ferber, Butler expressed regret that the belief that gender should be determined by sex has become more acceptable in society. In her opinion, it is even more regrettable that the evangelical and right-wing Catholic effort to purge education and public policy from "gender" accords with the trans-exclusionary radical feminists return to biological essentialism. She concluded: "It is a sad day when some feminists promote the anti-gender ideology position of the most reactionary forces in our society" (Ferber 2020).

Recently, Judith Butler has been rethinking equality in terms of interdependence, including a wide range of socio-political and environmental interactions, thus broadening the horizons of understanding gender justice. In the above-mentioned interview, she described the main methodological setting of her recent book *The Force of Nonviolence:*

> We tend to say that one person should be treated the same as another, and we measure whether or not equality has been achieved by comparing individual cases. But what if the individual – and individualism – is part of the problem? It makes a difference to understand ourselves as living in a world in which we are fundamentally dependent on others, on institutions, on the Earth, and to see that this life depends on a sustaining organization for various forms of life. If no one escapes that interdependency, then we are equal in a different sense. We are equally dependent, that is, equally social and ecological, and that means we cease to understand ourselves only as demarcated individuals. If trans-exclusionary radical feminists understood themselves as sharing a world with trans-people, in a common struggle for equality, freedom from violence, and for social recognition, there would be no more trans-exclusionary radical feminists. But feminism would surely survive as a coalitional practice and vision of solidarity. (Ferber 2020)

Nowadays, gender issues have become relevant in interdisciplinary research. Raising the issues of gender justice and ecological issues, the methodology of modern ecofeminism is a confirmation of this. When the view of external nature and human nature becomes a central issue of feminist critique, and not limited to the problem of gender, a fundamentally new point of view is formed on the theoretical understanding of patriarchy. For American philosopher Karen Warren, ecofeminism is a critique of normative dualism that authorizes dominance through the privileges of one side of the binary opposition over the other, especially culture over nature (Warren 1997). In *Feminism and Ecology*, she emphasizes that the standard version of feminism does not focus on the relationship between nature and women, and therefore does not serve as a theoretical basis for ecofeminist discourse.

> If eco-feminism is to be taken seriously, then a transformative feminism is needed that will move us beyond the four familiar feminist frameworks and make an eco-feminist perspective central to feminist theory and practice. (Warren 1987)

However, the tasks posed by the first ecofeminist theorists are not very easy to solve. After a decade of lull, there has been a resurgence of interest in ecofeminist methodology (Power 2020; Wickström 2021).

The research trends that have emerged in the last decades at the crossroads of gender inequality, economics, and ecology have been comprehensively and convincingly analyzed by Julie A. Nelson and Marilyn Power (Nelson 2018; Power 2004).

> We have explored the many dimensions of care, delved into its implications for economic methodology, and advocated for appropriate support for our work activities, especially those directed toward the young, very old, and ill. Yet many also understand – in a time of crises such as climate change, species extinction, and access to water – that we, as a global

society, have also sorely neglected to "care about" and "care for" the natural environment. (Nelson 2018, 80)

Indeed, in the face of extreme economic pressure on the current environmental situation and back-lash trends in gender issues, recognizing care as a factor of the scientific study at the intersection of economy, ecology, and the pursuit of gender justice is fruitful and on time in each of these scientific discourses.

In the context of gender justice as a social value, it makes sense to clarify some concepts of ecology, environmentalism, and economics, which are often regarded as synonyms. Still, their specific correlations have their definite characteristics. There is a lot in common between environmentalist economics and ecological economics, environmentalist ethics, and ecological ethics. But some differences between them are also essential to understand.

In modern philosophy, the field of ethics which studies the ethical aspects of the relationship between nature and society is usually called environmental ethics. However, J. Baird Callicott (1997) and Holmes Rolston (1988), as the most recognized experts in this field, also admit the use of the concept of ecological ethics. In modern philosophical texts, it is gradually taking the leading place. Environmental economics was distinguished from ecological economics as being more theoretical upon preserving nature. Accordingly, environmental ethics has a component of mainstream economics. Ecological Economics regards the economy as a subsystem of the ecosystem with its focus directed much towards the understanding of general duties and values attributed to nature. But it has not developed the resources to address the diverse and often unique practical concerns of ecological researchers and managers in the field, lab, and conservation facility.

Thus, ecological ethics is a practical or applied scientific ethic that not only forms a system of universal environmental values, but also offers an approach to the ethical dilemmas of environmentalists and environmental managers (Collins 2008). In the context of gender justice and ecological issues, the concepts of ecological economics and ecological ethics are used to emphasize the socio-economic and socio-political components of this problem.

After clarifying the content of the concepts of gender justice and ecological issues, it is necessary to define *methodological approaches* to explain their relationship. This article presupposes a combination of the methodology of communicative philosophy with phenomenological and existentialist methodological approaches based on the fact that the subjects of ecological communication are not only subjects of speech. They also are the subjects of conscious existence, existential subjects not devoid of gender differences in contrast to Kant's transcendental subject.

The phenomenological approach, addressing the interrelated problems of economics, ecology, gender inequality, morality, becomes a kind of *research strategy* that creates a contextually working model of their awareness and identification of prospects for their solution. Of course, this research strategy should be based on experts' most profound, reasoned, and convincing conclusions in each of the studied problems. The main task is to correctly identify coherent ideas that reinforce each other and not lead to new contradictions.

At the beginning of the article, it was noted that the mechanism for the formation of research approaches to contemporary problems has become pluralistic and highly dynamic. For this reason, a contextual study of gender justice and ecological issues should not ignore their relationship to universal principles. Karl-Otto Apel's Discursive Ethics meets this requirement as much as possible. It is important to emphasize that the philosopher sought to reconcile his research method with opposing approaches to the problem. Thus, he emphasizes that solving the fateful global problems of humankind, including environmental ones, requires a universal social basis of ethics of justice, solidarity, and shared responsibility (Apel 2000).

At the same time, Apel says,

> On the other hand, however, we are told by some, or even the majority, of our most sophisticated philosophers, that no rational foundation of universally valid ethics is possible. Such is the creed of thinkers who went through the linguistic-pragmatic-hermeneutic turn of contemporary philosophy after Wittgenstein and Heidegger, and also of those so-called "communitarians" who rightly recognized that the liberalistic tradition of methodical solipsism and individualism (especially that of Hobbes) cannot provide a basis for solidarity and coresponsibilities. (Apel 1993, 18)

Representatives of the ecological economy usually claim that the contemporary ecological situation is primarily a consequence of productive consumer activity (Floro 2021; Raworth 2017). In this context, it makes sense to turn to gender analysis, which rejects homogenization, averaging, and inequality in the distribution of natural resources as a cause of gender injustice. Therefore, it is correct to say that the contemporary ecological situation is the result of the consumerism of the modern male-oriented Western civilization.

Thus, there is a need for a ratio of real and ideal communication. It reveals the methodological gap between the appropriate and the existing environmental situation. In this context, it makes sense to turn to gender analysis. Attempts to bridge this gap are present in Apel's "dual regulatory principle for the ethics of responsibility". Here, the categorical imperative of "act as if you are a member of an ideal communicative community" is complemented by the ontological imperative of "the necessity of human survival" (Apel 1993, 26).

Nature also needs protection outside the state and the economy. This aim is achievable in the social sphere, which is neither public nor private. Informal networks of stakeholders have challenged and continue to challenge the distribution of natural resources. They do so by referring to the intrinsic value of nature itself and separately consider the question of nature as a collective good. Here is a point where serious ethical issues arise. Suppose there is anything new in ethical-ecological discourse. In that case, it is the protection of the autonomous sphere that is necessary to uphold the value of nature as a collective good under conventional and post-conventional morality, which ensures mutual recognition of the claims of significance by participants in ecological communication.

Therefore, ideal ecological communication is, on the one hand, counterfactual, and therefore only formal. Its primary definition is the symmetrical relation of individuals in language-communicative acts concerning nature, and it acts as a regulatory principle, and on the other hand, it is realized only in real communication, which, to ensure the coincidence of the horizons of female and male attitudes to nature, should bring women's understanding of environmental issues from the realm of silence towards approximating the ideal communication community within the real one.

If we consider moral issues impartially by Apel, we must turn to the concept of the initial state of John Rawls, which provides that participants in the discourse can make rational decisions and are equal partners in the contract, regardless of their real social status.

Another issue is the concept of ideal adoption of the roles of George Herbert Mead. It requires for the subject of moral judgment to be concerned about the situation of all those who could be affected by the commission of problematic acts or the approval of questionable norms. Thus, the imaginary nature of the initial state acts as an artificial structure. At the same time, practical discourse can be defined as a process of understanding, which in its form motivates all participants at the same time to accept the ideality of roles.

In this context, Zigmund Baumann's research position could be critically taken into account. He notes that instead of thinking about morality as a mathematical formula that calculates the benefits of some abstract relationship, it is necessary to talk about morality in which "neither I nor the Other in this party is *replaceable*. It is precisely this *irreplaceability* which makes our togetherness moral, and the morality of our togetherness self-sustained and self-sufficient, needing no rules and law" (Bauman 1993, 112). Recognizing the irreplaceability of nature and man as a condition for human survival, this moral concept is becoming consistent with both ecofeminism and ecocentric views the justification and deployment of which is embodied in modern environmental discourse.

Discourse can serve as a method of analysis that suggests contextual meanings. It means a broader than usual understanding of language, which considers the designation of the final object and the expectation to see the object as such and not another, the intention to interact with the object, presented precisely in the systemic context of language.

The system context appears here as a set of desires, inclinations, and motives. In this case, it turns out that not the moments of truth, but the conditions of culture are involved in the convergence of specific values, which provide an idea of the ideal ecological communication.

Ideal language communication is characterized by four conditions: equal chances for the use of communicative language acts by participants in the discourse; equality of chances for thematization of opinions in discourse and criticism; freedom of self-expression, which prevents the formation of suppressed complexes; equality of chances for applying regulatory language acts, which ensures the reciprocity of relations between the participants of the discourse and excludes privileges – the rules of communication that fix the unilaterality of duty (Apel 1993).

But the situation is such that, as Luce Irigaray emphasizes, "He who governs discourse guides the definition of what is true" (Irigaray 2002, 145). And, of course, this process is dominated by men. The problem is not that women are not active enough in articulating their environmental demands and are unaware of women's participation in environmental issues. The need for this is fundamentally ignored because of the most common cultural settings and stereotypes.

Therefore, it is not enough to deny this situation when discussing the most critical issue. for the modern world remains fundamentally closed for women.

It is important to emphasize the transformation of Irigaray's postmodern feminist views into a more practical direction. She supported Jacques Lacan's assertion that the whole culture represents the patriarchal world. In Irigaray's opinion, a woman's physicality, especially her sexuality, is the only aspect of her existence that avoids male control. All that remains for a woman is her "pre-social self" (Irigaray 1985a, 16). It remains in her sexuality and sensual difference, in her enjoyment. For Irigaray, this means the triumph of female inferiority as an ontological state and the expression of female desire as "This sex that is not one"– that is, the multifaceted sexuality of the female as opposed to phallocentric masculinity (Irigaray 1985b).

However, femininity has limited possibilities in the mechanism of political action because it is, by definition, outside the phallocentric world. According to Lynne Segal, the manifestations of postmodernism and psychoanalytic thinking in feminism encourage idealistic and essentialist views on sexual differences. In her opinion, "to condemn only logical and symbolic reality means to silence the problems of the patriarchal socio-cultural system as a whole" (Segal 1987, 133). Thus, the role of women as conscious mediators between humans and nature provides an epistemological basis, which will be both a critique and a means of transforming phallocentric ideology and relevant social institutions.

Irigaray's later philosophy includes this kind of rethinking of the relationship between nature and culture. Her ideas can be reconciled with Judith Butler's performative concept of gender by rethinking gender differences in attitudes. In *The Way of Love* (2002) she writes "For the welcome to be real, it is important to step back behind one's one horizon, beyond the limit of what was until then proper to oneself in order, beyond the threshold, to question the unknown who comes" (Irigaray 2002, 77).

Is there a real cultural space in which women's claims to significance in discussing environmental issues could be articulated and heard? Unfortunately, the discourse of Jacques Lacan's "A woman does not exist" is still quite influential. It does not mean that she does not exist physically. It means that she does not exist as an equal cultural agent. Instead of an independent female position, there is often a projection of male expectations, which do not always have to be accused of open hostility toward nature and misogyny. But even a benevolent attitude is not equal to the voice of the woman herself. Therefore, it is vital to change the type of vision, the contextual understanding of the situation and, in general, change the discourse.

The ability of the participants of ecological discourse to explain their negative attitude towards projects harmful to the natural environment and understanding the irreplaceability of nature and humans should become a linguistic reality and testify to the moral and intellectual maturity of the subject. Proponents of Wittgensteinian ecofeminism Wendy Lee-Lampshire, Donna J. Haraway, and others draw attention to this feature of ecological discourse. However, they note that in real environmental communication, it is difficult to avoid repressive discursiveness. As soon as a woman becomes a subject of discourse, it happens that the supposed autonomy as a necessary condition for mutual criticism loses its force due to the existing traditions and stereotypes in society.

The historical paradox is that, as Lee-Lampshire points out, when women achieved political rights and asserted themselves in the political structures of society, the problem of the autonomous subject became obsolete in philosophy. Philosophers, primarily men (for example, Derrida), questioned the concept of "subject" (Lee-Lampshire 1995, 16). Without agreed ecological information, nothing will be achieved: no legitimating for environmental discourse, no mobilization of strategic action on the environment, no new patterns of rationality and behavioral patterns in the public sphere.

This statement is based on the assumption of the relationship between environmental conditions and ideas about them. The moralization of ecological problems through ethics and identity becomes a strategic element of ecological discourse as knowledge of the environment becomes more profound and broader.

Today, the challenge is to expand the content of identification from personal to ontological and ecological in the context of gender aspects of ethics of justice and ethics of care. Consideration should be given to how each and both should be rethought in the process of environmental identification. Some researchers argue that concern is a broader area where there should be room for justice, utility, and dignity. The American philosopher Virginia Held believes that "care is a basic moral value. Without the actual practice of care, human life cannot exist because people must survive ... although life can be without justice, it cannot be a life without a care, which is a value" (Held 1999, 302).

The opposite view is related to the belief that liberalism and egalitarianism create sufficient conditions for realizing concerns in the ethics of justice (Krebs 1999).

However, based on the discussion by Lawrence Kohlberg (Kohlberg 1981) and Carol Gilligan (Gilligan 1982), it is possible to substantiate the assumption that the result of expanded identification is the development of morality as integration of justice and care.

Gilligan calls the basis of the theory of femininity moral development based on the ethics of care. "Moral development for women reaches a higher level not in the realization of justice in itself, but in the realization that you and others are independent of each other, and that life has value in itself, and can become more sustainable through caring in relationships" (Gilligan 1982, 127).

The ethics of justice and care ethics emerged as two opposed concepts of morality and moral development. But we can say that they complement each other rather than conflict with each other.

At the highest level of abstraction, the ethics of justice as honesty asserts a universal duty to humanity. This duty is usually understood in terms of the universal requirement to respect the intrinsic dignity of all individuals. The ethics of care, for its part, recognizes that moral commitment is based on the specifics of the moral context. In this sense, the ethics of care seek the foundations of morality in associative ethics.

In other words, the ethics of care is based on reversibility (interdependence). Without the ability to put yourself in the place of another, it is impossible to take care of him/her. As mentioned above, the ethics of justice also cause reversibility. Kohlberg argues that it is impossible to be honest without compassion. If justice is a function of reflexive equilibrium, then it must, by definition, cause reciprocity.

Ironically, Gilligan's ideas were used to legitimize discrimination. Based on her research, certain circles have tried to dissuade women from many activities. The argument of these ideologues was as follows: since women and men are different, excluding women from specific fields of activity cannot be considered discrimination. On the contrary, it can be seen as a show of respect and respect for differences.

Gilligan was not late in responding to such a distortion of her thoughts.

> The title of my book was not accidental; it sounds like "another voice" instead of "female voice". In the introduction, I explain that this voice is not determined by gender but by the theme... Tracing human development, I note the interaction of these voices within each sex and suggest that their convergence indicates moments of crisis and change. (Gilligan 1986)

She also makes such clarifications in her subsequent works and interviews (Gilligan 2011).

Kohlberg's and Gilligan's orientations to justice and concern have many similar features that apply to Naess's ecosophy. All three directions are ontological. Morality is understood here not as an abstract set of rules but as a state of being. Morality here is not a set of principles to be obeyed but a way of being in the world that includes attitudes toward other people as much as attitudes toward nature.

Naess's notions of ecosophy and self-realization (Naess 1989) suggest that we can be friendly to nature and the earth by expanding our awareness of ourselves by recognizing ecological interdependence. Here our identification is ecological, and, in turn, our moral sensitivity expands to include the natural environment.

According to Gilligan, women's awareness of their rights restrains the self-destructive potential of sacrificial morality, and men's awareness of their responsibility to loved ones corrects the potential for indifference to the morality of justice and draws attention from the logic of moral choice to its real consequences (Gilligan 1982). This perspective represents moral development as progressing in the face of states of identification that expand, generating justice in terms of increasing respect for nature and respect for women.

The gender approach insists that the destruction and exploitation of nature are rooted in men's dominance over women. It is symptomatic that the attitude towards ecofeminism changes from criticism through silence to interest and recognition. Critical thinking is, in principle, very relevant today. Naturally, criticism of modern economics is not limited to gender methodology. Ecological ethics holds technology and industry responsible for the ecological crisis. But this does not deny the need for a gender discourse about the essence of technology and industry.

British economist Kate Raworth drew the economic model of Doughnut's Economics, where GDP is displaced from the core of economics. The doughnut's inner ring represents a social foundation of the minimum social standards such as food, health, political voice, and gender equality. The outer ring illustrates the ecological ceiling beyond nine planetary boundaries, tipping points, and unacceptable environmental degradation like climate change, land conversion, and biodiversity loss. The task is now to bring humanity into what Raworth calls the "doughnut's safe and just space" to prevent social shortfall and ecological overshoot (Raworth 2017).

The merits and demerits of technology depend on its application, accessibility for all people, and effect on social relations, including gender relations. Gender discourse about ecological justice improves the process of valuing environmental economics, disclosing the bias of the dualistic methodology in this field of economic theory. Thus, the prospects for sustainable gender justice are closely linked to ecological justice and overcoming the disregard for care in economic theory and practice. The movement in this direction provides a particular approximation of real ecological communication to the ideal one.

References

Apel, K.-O. (1993). "How to Ground a Universalistic Ethics of Co-responsibility for the Effects of Collective Actions and Activities?". *Philosophica* 52(2), 9–29. DOI: 10.21825/philosophica.82377.
Apel, K.-O. (2000). "Globalization and the Need for Universal Ethics". *European Journal of Social Theory* 3(2), 137–155.
Apel, K.-O. (2001). *The Response of Discourse Ethics to the Moral Challenge of the Human Situation as Such and Especially Today.* Brussels: Peeters.
Austin, K. and Banashek, C. (2018). *Gender Inequality and Environmental Well-Being: A Cross-National Investigation of Ecosystem Vitality and Environmental Health. Sustainability in Environment.* DOI: 3. 257. 10.22158/se.vse.v3n3p257.
Bauman, Z. (1993). *Postmodern Ethics.* Cambridge: Blackwell.
Butler, J. (1990a). *Gender Trouble: Feminism and the Subversion of Identity.* London: Routledge.
Butler, J. (1990b). "Performative Acts and Gender Constitution". In Case, S.-E. (Ed.), *Phenomenology and Feminist Theory. Performing Feminisms: Feminist Critical Theory and Theatre.* Baltimore: Johns Hopkins UP.
Butler, J. (1993). *Bodies that Matter: On the Discursive Limits of 'Sex'.* New York: Routledge.
Callicott, J. B. and Mumford, K. (1997). "Ecological Sustainability as a Conservation Concept". *Conservation Biology* 11, 32–40. URL: https://www.sierraforestlegacy.org/Resources/Community/Sustainability/SY_CallicottMumford1997.pdf (last accessed 17 November 2022).
Collins, J. P. and Minteer, B. A. (2008). "From Environmental to Ecological Ethics: Toward a Practical Ethics for Ecologists and Conservationists". *Science and Engineering Ethics* 14(4), 483–501.
Ferber, A. (2020). "Judith Butler on the Culture Wars, JK Rowling and Living in 'Anti-intellectual times'" URL: https://www.newstatesman.com/uncategorized/2020/09/judith-butler-culture-wars-jk-rowling-and-living-anti-intellectual-times (last accessed 30 November 2022).
Floro, M. and Reksten, N. (2021). "Feminist Ecological Economics: A Care-centered Approach to Sustainability". Sustainable Consumption and Production 1, 369–389.
Gilligan, C. (1982). *In a Different Voice: Psychological Theory and Women Development.* Cambridge, MA: Harvard University Press.

Gilligan, C. (1986). "Reply by Carol Gilligan". *Signs: Journal of Women in Culture and Society* 11(2), 324–333.

Gilligan, C. (2011). "Interview on June 21st." Ethics of Care. Sharing Views on Good Care. URL: https://ethicsofcare.org/carol-gilligan/ (last accessed 17 November 2022).

Held, V. (1999). "Liberalism and the Ethics of Care". In: Card, C. (Ed.), *On Feminist Ethics and Politics.* University Press of Kansas, 288–309.

Irigaray, L. (1985a). *Spectrum of the Other Woman.* Ithaca and New York: Cornell University Press.

Irigarey, L. (1985b). *This Sex Which Is Not One.* Ithaca and New York: Cornell University Press.

Irigaray, L. (2002). *The Way of Love.* London and New York: Continuum.

Kohlberg, L. (1981). *The Philosophy of Moral Development.* Cambridge, MA: Harvard University Press.

Krebs, A. (1999). *Ethics of Nature: A Map. With a Foreground by Bernard Williams.* Berlin and New York: De Gruyter.

Lee-Lampshire, W. (1995). "Women-animals-machines: A Grammar for a Wittgensteinian Ecofeminism". *The Journal of Value Inquiry* 29, 89–101. DOI: 10.1007/BF01079066.

Naess, A. (1989). *Ecology, Community and Lifestyle.* New York: Cambridge University Press.

Nelson, J. A. and Power, M. (2018). "Ecology, Sustainability, and Care: Developments in the Field". *Feminist Economics* 24(3), 80–88. DOI: 10.1080/13545701.2018.1473914.

Okin, S. M. (2003). "Poverty, Well-being, and Gender: What Counts, Who's Heard?" *Philosophy & Public Affairs* 31(3), 280–316.

Power, Ch. (2020). "Multispecies Ecofeminism: Ecofeminist Flourishing of the Twenty-First Century". *University of Victoria.* URL: https://base.socioeco.org/docs/power_chelsea_ma_2020.pdf (last accessed 30 November 2021).

Power, M. (2004). "Social Provisioning as a Starting Point for Feminist Economics". DOI: 10.1080/135457004200026760.

Raworth, K. (2017). *Doughnut Economics: Seven Ways to Think Like a 21st-Century Economist.* Vermont: Chelsea Green.

Rolston, H. (1988). *Environmental Ethics: Duties to and Values in the Natural World.* Philadelphia: Temple University Press.

Segal, L. (1987). *Is the Future Female?* London: Virago.

Segal, L. (2017). "Gender, Power, and Feminist Resistance". In Bolsø, A., Svendsen Bang, S. H. and Sørenson Øyslebø, S. (Eds.), *Bodies, Symbols and Organizational Practice.* London: Routledge.

Solomon, R. C. and Murphy, M. C. (Eds.) (2000). *What Is Justice? Classic and Contemporary Readings.* 2nd ed. Oxford: Oxford University Press.

UN Environment programme (2020). *Gender equality – a critical missing piece of the climate puzzle.* URL: https://www.unep.org/news-and-stories/story/gender-equality-critical-missing-piece-climate-puzzle (last accessed 2 January 2023).

Warren, K. (1987). "Feminism and Ecology: Making Connections". *Environmental Ethics* 9(1), 3–20.

Warren, K. (Ed.) (1997). *Ecofeminism: Women, Culture, Nature.* Bloomington: Indiana University Press.

Wickström, A., Lund, R. W. B., Meriläinen, S., Øyslebø Sørensen, S., Vachhani, S. J. and Pullen, A. (2021). "Feminist Solidarity: Practices, Politics and Possibilities". *Gender Work and Organization* 28(3), 857–863. URL: https://onlinelibrary.wiley.com/doi/10.1111/gwao.12689 (last accessed 30 November 2021).

Zahidia, S. (2021). "Preface". *Global Gender Gap Report 2021.* World Economic Forum. URL: https://www.weforum.org/reports/global-gender-gap-report-2021/in-full/ (last accessed 17 November 2022).

Shalini Attri and Priyanka Singh
Sultana's Dream: Eco[U]topian and Feminist Intersections

Abstract: Earth's geology, anthropogenic climate change, the notion of capitalism and the destruction of ecological resources are subjects of debate among scholars, environmentalists, and economists compelling them to anticipate the question of sustainability in the 21st century. The imaginative capacity of literature promises a vision of a future that is ecologically balanced. This essay analyzes Begum Rokeya Sakhawat Hossain's *Sultana's Dream*, a narrative of ecotopia that dissolves the logocentric and essentialist notions centered on women and men that offers a revolutionary combination to handle the ecological crisis successfully by investigating the harmful environmental impacts. The paper develops an argument that is based on the ecofeminist philosophy of Vandana Shiva, further theorizing upon deeper meanings of ecology, femininity, and 'Prakriti' (nature) with an emphasis on a humane approach creating a shift from the dominant 'scientific' paradigm to indigenous systems for a balanced ecotopian world.

Introduction

A unique quality of man is his imagination that has invariably guided him to constantly improve his position and amplified his aspiration to create and control. The rise of science, development, and the industrial revolution that laid the foundations of a patriarchal model of economic expansion in industrial capitalism are viewed as the main cause of obliteration of both nature and women. The scientific revolution in Europe (in modern times) is seen to transform nature from a *terra mater* into a machine and a source of raw material consequently removing all ethical and cognitive constraints against its violation and exploitation. The industrial revolution converted economics from the prudent management of resources for sustenance and basic-need satisfaction into a process of commodity production for profit maximization. Industrialization, as a resultant outcome, fashioned a limitless appetite for resource exploitation, and modern science provided the ethical and cognitive license to make such exploitation possible, acceptable, and desirable. The new relationship of man's domination and mastery over nature is, thus, associated with new patterns of authority and mastery over women, and their exclusion from participation as partners in both scientific appetite and development. Modern science is projected as a universal, value-free system of knowledge, which has displaced all other belief and knowledge systems by its universality and value neutrality, by the logic of its method to arrive at objective claims about nature. The last few years have seen feminist scholarship recognizing the dominant science system emerging as a liberating force not for humanity as a whole (though it legitimized itself in terms of universal betterment of the species), but for patriarchal ventures which essentially coerces both nature and women. Man has used narratives to create a social, cultural and economic reality to suit his ever increasing and expanding needs. The masculine accounts, as suggested by Stibbe (2015) in *Ecolinguistics: Language, Ecology and the Stories We Live By*, needs to be redefined to create a new reality that is unbiased to nature and women which have been coerced to satiate man's need to dominate, control and use. *Sultana's Dream* offers a new reality, a vision, that enables sustenance of producers, pro-generators, nurturers and protectors who, in absence of man's consumerist intentions have the capacity to sustain themselves. The short ecotopian narrative envisages the transformation of the world initiated by a woman suggesting an ecological-utopian feminist alternative and advocating a 'non-gendered science'. *Sultana's Dream* is framed around the feminist philosophy that nurtures earth's image as sustainable and stands in contrast to the masculine science that is based on developmental patterns and capitalism causing ecological crisis.

The Eco-Utopian Ideal

Published in Latin in 1516, Thomas Moore's *Utopia* propagates the design of an ideal society with perfect citizens. Hanallah and Faragallah, in "Ecotopia between Traditions and Technology", extended the idea further and defined utopia as "an ideal, imaginary state of social and political perfection" (Hanallah and Faragallah 2010, p.27). Ecological utopia, thus, provides a dialogue for a more sustainable society which can be achieved by the preservation of the wilderness – a key ecological issue. Devall and Sessions define wilderness as "a landscape or ecosystem that has been minimally disrupted by the intervention of humans" (Devall and Sessions 2007, p. 110). The term ecotopia referring to an ecologically utopian state is an idea based on Callenbach's novel *Ecotopia* that describes a society in which recycling is a way of life, gas powered cars are replaced by electric cars, and bicycles are placed in civic spaces. The 'leading edges' in the text forms the main ideas for ecological values and practices and describes patterns of actual social experimentation taking place in the American West. The utopian concept of a 'stable state' is constructed upon the idea that in *Ecotopia* the well-being of nature should not be disrupted or destroyed; everything should be reused and reprocessed. This notion advocates the desire to live in an ecologically, socially balanced society in perfect harmony with nature i. e., existing in a 'stable state', in equipoise (Coelho et al. 2016).

Ecotopia and Feminist Linkage

The emergence of a contemporary sustainable conscience is associated with Rachel Carson's seminal book *Silent Spring*, published in 1962. Carson's articulation and critique of scientific approaches in her work dominate the ecofeminist thought that raised the deliberations on ecocritical ethics around the ecosphere. Howard Odum's work *Environment, Power and Society* (1971) pioneered notions of ecological engineering, economics, and environmental accounting. Women's aspiration to live in balance with nature thereby waging a movement against mal-development, environmental degradation, global capitalization, and the need for indigenous cultures, economic values, and programs based on sustainability has found its voice in ecofeminism. Starhawk, a notable thinker on ecofeminism, challenges the idea of male dominated Western economies destroying nature and transforming the structures of power (in hands of males) while drawing parallels with nature and women as life giving forces thus placing them (women and nature) at the center. Ecofeminism theorizes upon the recognition of connections between the domination of nature and women across the patriarchal society further locating these two entities with racism, colonialism, neo-colonialism, and class exploitation. Hence, earth as a feminist space becomes the central category of analysis in this context that encounters the nature-culture dualism. The devastation of earth has made the ecofeminist to rethink and reconsider the antithetical viewpoint of capitalism and science that stands in sharp contrast to the 'green earth'. The green politics calls for structural changes in the society where feminist ethics binds together to create an ecotopia (Ecology + Utopia) – i. e., green is 'Utopia'. This formulation further leads to the interrogations and debates that further raise questions and concerns like:
1. Can nature, women, development, and science maintain a harmonious relation?
2. If science/technology and capitalism – a developmental necessity – are thought to be the major force causing the destruction of nature and women, how can an ecotopian world be created?

In an attempt to address these questions, the paper formulates the discussion on Vandana Shiva's ideas on ecocriticism, women and nature. Vandana Shiva, an Indian physicist and ecofeminist, founded the Research Foundation for Science, Technology and Natural Resource Policy that emphasizes on sustainable methods of agriculture. Shiva has articulated the complications caused by capitalist domination and provided adoptive measures and realistic solutions in *Globalization's New Wars: Seed, Water, and Life Forms* (2005) and *Earth Democracy: Justice, Sustainability, and Peace* (2005). As an ecofeminist, Shiva in her article, "Empowering Women" remarks that sustainable and productive methods to agronomy can be attained by restoring the system of agriculture in India that is women-centered (Shiva 2004, n. p.). Her arguments frame around ecological devastation and industrial calamities that threaten everyday life, thereby suggesting that safeguarding ecology is the prime responsibility of women.

Shiva co-authored *Ecofeminism* (1993) with German feminist sociologist Maria Mies that condenses Western and Southern feminism probing into environmental, technological, and feminist ideas. Both thinkers, while condemning science and technology, opine that capitalism connects with science to obtain maximum productivity and capital from nature or earth. This compels them to treat nature as a resource, thus, calling it 'reductionist'. Mies, particularly, portrays indigenous women and nature as targets of scientific domination. Shiva contends that development is the main reason for uprootedness and violently severing the sacred bonds between the people and the soil. In their article "Mies and Shiva's *Ecofeminism*: A New Testament?", Molyneux and Steinberg illustrate Shiva's notion of the pre-enlightened, pre-colonial and pre-modern cultures based on feminine principles. Such knowledge systems that express respect for nature were often women-centered and women-friendly (Molyneux and Steinberg 1992). Shiva criticizes capitalism and overproduction, further emphasizing the assumption that tribal women and peasant societies are unproductive. In fact, they are the alternative model of self-sustainability and their identification "with nature is organic and authentic" (Shiva 1988, p. vii). They provide an excellent example when they uncover the connection between ideologies of development, new technologies of reproduction, and approaches to nature. The indigenous scientific approach can be adopted to combat destructive science.

Another notable work by Shiva, *Staying Alive*, exports dominant culturalist tendencies in ecofeminist literature. She remarks:

> It is in managing the integrity of ecological cycles in forestry and agriculture that women's productivity has been most developed and evolved. Women transfer fertility. They transfer animal waste as fertilizer for crops and crop by-products to animals as fodder. They work with the forest to bring water to their fields and families. This partnership between women's and nature's work ensures the sustainability of sustenance ... (Shiva 1988, p.45)

The reason for ecological ruin according to her is:

> The forest is separated from the river, the field is separated from the forest, the animals are separated from the crops. Each is then separately developed and the delicate balance which ensures sustainability and equity is destroyed. The visibility of dramatic breaks and ruptures is posited as progress. (Shiva 1988, p.129)

Shiva argues that there exists a connection between commercialized technological science and masculine self-glorification which results in a certain development and that this development is not advantageous to women and nature.

Drawing on Indian mythology, Shiva introduces the notion of *Prakriti* as a feminine principle or life force, an alternative 'universal' basis for gender liberation. She focuses on the point of view of Indian cosmology that explains how the world is produced and renewed by the dialectical play of creation and destruction, cohesion, and disintegration. All existence arises from this primordial energy which is the substance of everything, pervading everything. The manifestation of this power, this energy, is called nature (*Prakriti*). Nature, both living and inorganic, is an expression of *Shakti* (dynamic energy) and is the feminine principle in the universe that stands in conjunction with the masculine principle (*Purusha*), and it is *Prakriti* that produces the world. Nature (*Prakriti*) is fundamentally active, a controlling, productive force in the dialectic of the creation, renewal, and sustenance of all life (Shiva 1988). *Prakriti* is a popular category, one through which ordinary women in rural India relate to nature. Nature, an indicator of the feminine principle, is categorized by: (a) creativity, activity, productivity; (b) diversity in form and aspect; (c) connectedness and inter-relationship of all beings, including man; (d) continuity between the human and natural; and (e) sanctity of life in nature (Shiva 1988). For women, whose productivity in the sustenance of life is based on nature's productivity, the death of *Prakriti* is the beginning of their marginalization, devaluation, displacement, and ultimate dispensability (Shiva 1988). The ecological catastrophe is the death of the feminine principle in the processes of survival and sustenance. These ecocritical and ecofeminist theoretical formulations of Shiva bring forth the role of nature and women that turn out to be an important stricture in looking at the text from an ecocritical or ecofeminist standpoint.

An Ecotopian Reading of *Sultana's Dream*

Sultana's Dream (1905) by Begum Rokeya Shakhawat Hossain (1880–1932) foregrounds the ecofeminist perspective and has been phenomenal as far as the feminist movement in the Indian sub-continent is concerned. It embodies the ecotopian forethought, thereby adopting a positive solution-based approach, and provides a *holistic* environmental philosophy that advocates nature-centered values, circularity, and the natural regeneration of ecosystems. Rokeya had aimed to inspire women from all walks of life and backgrounds into action since action is the quality of Nature (*Prakriti*). Her feminist dialogue is drawn on the need of women bound by a different culture, values, and geography and it is interesting to observe the ecofeminist tendencies in her work written as early as the 20th century (in 1905). *Sultana's Dream* is unique in the manner that the author proposes a feminist utopia where one witnesses a reversal of secluded enclosures in the form of '*mardana*' and a rejection of the capitalist model and consumerism. A scientific and environment-friendly approach is adopted to tackle the mess and problems created by men, whom Rokeya describes as complex creatures with predatory features in her short story *Sristi Tawtho* (Theory of Creation). Thus, science is not necessarily repressive to nature and women.

To understand Rokeya's ideology, her vision, and her inspiration one needs to have a quick look into her life that too has been challenging. A contemporary of Rabindranath Tagore, Rokeya's writing belongs to the early 20th century, a period when Bengal Renaissance-inspired writers had mobilized India's independence movement. Even while Bengal's social-political milieu was being influenced by modernization, industrialization, printing (thereby more and easy access to literature, scientific developments, and resources) Rokeya's exposure to education and open space was restricted. Rokeya, born as a daughter of one of the four wives of Zahiruddin Mohammad Abu Ali Saber, a well-educated landowner of Pariband (a village in Rangpur in British India), grew up in an environment where observance of the veil was strictly followed. Girls, as young as five years old had to keep themselves sequestered from not only men but from all strangers including women. Rokeya herself describes: "I had to observe purdah even from women from the age of five" (Joarder 1980, p.6). Women were educated in etiquettes and reciting Quran. Therefore, going out of the house for education was far from the question – not to mention the opportunities of employment, economic independence, and decision making. It was her elder brother Ibrahim Saber who home-tutored Rokeya in Bangla and English at night when everybody would go to sleep. Rokeya had seen her elder sisters' quest for education being crushed when she was found reading and being married off at the insistence of relatives. As she did not want to meet the same fate, she would take lessons from her brother at night. Later, her husband Sakhwat Hossain, a Deputy Magistrate in The Bengal Civil Service, also contributed to Rokeya's education and her writing pursuits (Hossain 1988). He persuaded Rokeya not to give up writing after she lost her children in infancy. Rokeya's inclination and visualization of possibilities of science-nature might have possibly evolved from her interactions with her husband who was a Bachelors in Agriculture and a member of the Royal Agricultural Society of England. Devastated after losing her husband in 1909, she utilized the money left by him to open a girl's school, Sakhawat Memorial Girl's School in Calcutta, for which she faced a lot of criticism and opposition from her in-laws – to such an extent that she had to sever ties with them. She also established the Bangali Muslim Women's Association, Anjum-e-Khawatin-e-Islam.

It is interesting to note that in Rokeya's school the curriculum included, besides language courses in Bangla, Urdu, English, Arabic, and Persian, subjects like home economics, gardening, physical education, cooking, handicrafts, sewing and nursing that could empower women in more than one way. With the publication of *Sultana's Dream* in 1905 in *The Indian Ladies Magazine* Rokeya drew attention. Her works laid bare the women's world under the spectrum of seclusion and *purdah* and conveyed her call for women's emancipation through education, scientific exploration, and participation in all spheres of activities.

Sultana's Dream as Ecotopia

The narrative of *Sultana's Dream* opens right away with the concern of the writer on the condition of Indian womanhood. The restriction on movement of women even within the boundary of the home is apparent when the narrator, Sultana, is invited by Sister Sara to have a look at the garden and thinks it is an appropriate time to go out as "the men-servant outside was fast asleep" (Hossain 2005). The presence of Sister Sara and her insistence to come out and take a look at the garden is a clever usage of the concept of 'Sisterhood' guiding Sultana from the darkness and restriction of the *zenanas* to the morning of hope and freedom and new thought.

Sultana is soon taken to the Lady-land that is free from sin and harm and where virtue reigns. The capacity and likeness of women's temperament to live in closeness with nature is apparent when Sultana informs the reader how she loved taking long walks with Sister Sara in the Botanical Garden. In the Ladyland the green grass carpeted the metal street: "… it was grand. I mistook a patch of green grass for a velvet cushion. Feeling as if I were walking on a soft carpet, I looked down and found the path covered with moss and flowers" (Hossain 2005, p. 4). One can hope of converting the city into a similar beautiful garden when Sister Sara proposes: "your Calcutta could become a nicer garden than this if only your countrymen wanted to make it so" (Hossain 2005, p. 4). But with Sultana's reply that, "They would think it useless to give so much attention to horticulture, while they have so many other things to do" (Hossain 2005, p.4), one comes to understand that both nature and women have been entrapped in the very artificial world created and dominated by men. The possibilities and capacities of nature and women have been veiled, ignored, and closed while other things have been termed as important more so because of the unwillingness of men whose profit-maximizing tendency has only led to creating a concrete jungle.

The concept of '*mardana*' (for men) similar to '*zenana*' (for women) is surprising as well as amusing for Sultana. Sister Sara elucidates the logic behind keeping men "in their proper places, where they ought to be", i. e., "shut [...] indoors" (Hossain 2005, pp.4-5). Sister Sara explains that just as lunatics that cause mischief to men and creatures are, under all circumstances, captivated and sent to an asylum, untrained men are capable of doing no end of mischief and cannot be trusted out of doors. "How can you trust those untrained men out of doors?", asks Sister Sara (Hossain 2005, p.5). One can see her linking man's mischief to the abuse of both nature and women, thereby restricting their nurturing and creative faculties and rendering them as mere objects concretized. Charlotte Perkins Gilman's *Herland* (1915) too advocates an all-female society entwined with masculine adventure tales and centers down upon the idea of mothering, natural cooperation and collectivism which is in contrast to the individual competitiveness of capitalism. But it also promotes the idea that motherly skills were not natural to women and that women require training in maternal skills and that the future generation was to be reared by professionals. Therefore, despite the capability of parthenogenesis in *Herland* child rearing is entrusted upon the elite. In fact, Gilman rejects the 19th-century-explorer scientist goal of conquering nature. The world created by men has now and then given birth to innumerable problems and ailments, epidemics and pandemics leading to the loss of precious lives, a loss that is incalculable. Contrastingly, Sultana discovers that in the Lady-land no one suffered even mosquito bites – leave aside epidemics as in man's commercialized world. The kitchen is an eco-friendly setup that has no sign of smoke, no chimney, no coal, no fire. Solar energy is most efficiently used for all tasks. Sister Sara owes all these innovative scientific enterprises to their Queen whose inclination towards science is phenomenal. She has ordered all women in her Kingdom to be educated and not be married until the age of 21. The women experiment with the extraction of water from the atmosphere thereby stopping untamed rain, storms, and destruction. An instrument is invented to collect solar heat and use it for cooking, locomotion, for providing warmth on cold days. On the other hand, these women are ridiculed for the scientific research and pursuits by men who term this a "a sentimental nightmare" (Hossain 2005, p.8). Menfolk of the Lady-land are seen engaging themselves in their primary interest of attaining power and desire of ruling the 'other', e. g., we see the Prime Minister dedicated himself to increasing military power and investing in warfare. However, the military expertise of menfolk fails to defend the Kingdom from the attack from a neighboring country whose King had declared war on the Lady-land. The impending doom on the country is evident. The Queen, however, asserts that women may not have sufficient training to use the armaments; they can at least try to counter the enemy by brainpower. Consequently, a plan is proposed. All men, being wounded and tired, willingly resign and retire to the '*zenana/ mardana*'. Sister Sara describes how women use concentrated sunlight and heat on the enemy which they are unable to respond to: "The heat and light were too much for them to bear. They all ran panic-stricken, not knowing how to counteract that scorching heat" (Hossain 2005, p.10). This is a weapon they did not know how to embark upon and they run away. Big guns and armaments left behind by the enemy are also burned using the same sun heat. Since then, tells Sister Sara, no one had dared to invade the Lady-land. It is significant and noteworthy what Sister Sara says:

> We do not covet other people's land, we do not fight for a piece of diamond though it may be a thousand-fold brighter than the *Koh-i-Noor*, nor do we grudge a ruler his Peacock Throne. We dive deep into the ocean of knowledge and try to find out the precious gems, which nature has kept in store for us. We enjoy nature's gifts as much as we can. (Hossain 2005, p.13)

The idea of self-sustenance and preservation of nature by controlling the wanton desires is loud and clear. It is also instrumental to note here that the armaments are symbols of destruction and the women destroy them rather than assembling them for use in the future even if it is for defense.

Christine de Pizan envisioned a more equal world anchored in acceptance and respect for women and their designated roles in society which according to her were more unique and distinct from men. Her book, *The Book of the City of Ladies* (1405), celebrates the capabilities and capacities of women because of whom "men have been brought out of ignorance and led to knowledge" (Pizan 1982 [1405], p. 78). Pointing at the massive "ingratitude of men ... who live off the goods of others [nature and women] without knowing their source and without thanking anyone" (Pizan 1982 [1405], p. 77), Pizan recognizes the capacity of women to learn, retain and discover new sciences themselves. For instance, the art of making nets for catching birds, fishes, rabbits and hares reflect upon the consumerist tendency. Also, she goes to the extent of saying that all those men have come from women, given by women, "custom of bearing armies, of dividing armies into battalions, and ... fighting in ordered ranks" (Pizan 1982 [1405], p. 80). This is in sharp contrast to the Indian ecofeminist philosophy of nurturing, protecting and anti-consumerist tendency of women that separates them from men and draws them close and in line to nature. Pizan also seems to be promoting consumerism and profit making as she talks of "useful and profitable sciences" (Pizan 1982 [1405], p.83). *Sultana's Dream* does advocate a useful and profitable science; however, the 'use & profit' is to achieve a utopian and egalitarian state. Like Callenbach's *Ecotopia* that embodies several principles of deep ecology, an innovative and visionary dream of a more sustainable society, *Sultana's Dream* conceptualizes several social, political, technological, and environmental solutions. In this ecotopian world, no land is consumed for a disparaging construction like roads and streets, and aerial conveyances run by electricity invented by women are used for transportation. Sister Sara remarks that physical strength is not required to do work in the fields: "Our fields are tilled by means of electricity, which supplies motive power for other hard work as well. And we employ it for our aerial conveyance too. We have no railroad nor any paved streets here" (Hossain 2005, p.11). Since the "water balloon" was set up, the people in Lady-land never suffered from want of water deriving from it as much water as required. It is not in the nature of women to engage in quarrel as they were never idle because they were "very busy making nature yield as much as she can... it is her [queen's] ambition to make the whole country into one grand garden" (Hossain 2005, p.12). The Lady-land, in a way, promotes a small-scale self-sufficient mini-city that is in tune with the bio-region and which embodies the ideal mix of modern science and sustained environment.

Conclusion

Following the theoretical discussion on *Ecotopia* and the analysis of Rokeya's *Sultana's Dream*, it can be concluded that *Sultana's Dream* raises the concern of preserving nature and its resources in totality as early as 1905. Even though it is an imaginary record it leaves behind curious readers who want to know the 'what and how' of the inventions talked about in the narrative, and it definitely proposes a concept and a vision of the possibilities encompassing the utopian world. It also contemplates the notion that women have the capacity and ability to conserve and best utilize what is given to them living in coordination with nature rather than having a desire to rule, command and abuse it.

Rokeya empowers women with education, scientific temperament, authority, and power, all in line with nature. The scientific temperament is not akin to the consumerist ideologue but with the eco-logue (refering to the term 'eco-logue' as a dialogue on the environment). Locking men in an enclosure called the *'mardana'* analogous to *'zenana'* where women are enclosed by menfolk should not be taken as an implacable act on part of Rokeya, but should be seen as a logical action taken to keep the world safe from the concretizing, commercial, hostile temperament and warlike insanity that man possesses.

Utopia can be established through the feminist space and the ecological world – hence creating an ecotopia. Pre-modern cultures have treated nature with respect and have legitimatized female power. Women's knowledge had been at the center regarding the mainstay of the dairy industry as well as the expertise in breeding and feeding farm animals and also in forestry. Women have been custodians of biodiversity; thus, they produce through biodiversity as stated by Shiva. *Sultana's Dream* deals with earth and sustainability and biodiversity where nature is treated with respect. The utopia of ecological, eco-centric science in *Sultana's Dream* delves into ecological feminisms that give an alternative form of women rulers and ecological conservation. Shiva's ecofeminist philosophy offers a view where science becomes peaceful, endures life, and is rampant to women in South Asian culture providing a firm ground on sustainability. The work demonstrates indigenous scientific methods developed by women and accordingly highlights the harmonious relation of women and nature. *Sultana's Dream* further suggests that science does not have to be a destructive enterprise, it is men who make science disparaging. It underlines the idea that nature, women, development, and science can collaborate to create a self-sufficient bio-region.

References

Callenbach, E. (1975). *Ecotopia*. Berkeley, CA: Banyan Tree Books.
Carson, R. (1962). *Silent Spring*. Greenwich: Crest Books.
Coelho, N. and Ecotopia team members (2016). *Ecotopia. A Sustainable Vision for a Better Future*. Porto: University of Porto.
Devall, B. and Sessions, G. (2007). *Deep Ecology*. Layton: Gibbs Smith.
Gilman, C. P. (1999 [1915]). *The Yellow Wall-Paper, Herland, and Selected Writings*. Intr. by K. Bolick. New York: Penguin.
Hanallah, G. and Faragallah, R. (2010). "Ecotopia between Traditions and Technology". *Traditional Dwellings and Settlements Review* 22(1), 27–28.
Hossain, R. S. (1988). *Sultana's Dream and Selections from The Secluded One's*. New York: Feminist Press.
Hossain, R. S. (2005). *Sultana's Dream* (1905). Trans. and Intro. by B. Bagchi. New Delhi: Penguin.
Joarder, H. (1980). *Begum Rokeya, the Emancipator*. Dacca: Nari Kalyan Sangstha.
Mies, M. and Shiva, M. (2014). *Ecofeminism*. London: Zed Books.
Molyneux, M. and Lynn Steinberg, D. (1995). "Mies and Shiva's *Ecofeminism:* A New Testament?" *Feminist Review* 49(1), 86–107. DOI: 10.1057/fr.1995.8.
Odum, H. T. (1971). *Environment, Power and Society*. New York: Columbia UP.
Pizan, Ch. de (1982 [1405]). *The Book of the City of Ladies*. Trans. by E. J. Richards. New York: Persea.
Shiva, V. (1988). *Staying Alive*. New Delhi: Kali for Women.
Shiva, V. (2004). "Empowering Women". URL: https://www.lkouniv.ac.in/site/writereaddata/site Content/202004150927005180nishi_Empowering_Women_1.pdf
Shiva, V. (2005a). *Earth Democracy: Justice, Sustainability, and Peace*. Cambridge, MA: Southend Press.

Shiva, V. (2005b). *Globalization's New Wars: Seed, Water, and Life Forms.* New Delhi: Women Unlimited.
Stibbe, A. (2015). *Ecolinguistics: Language, Ecology and the Stories We Live by.* London and New York: Routledge.

Anne Sauka
Ontogenealogies of Body-Environments: Perspectives for an Experiential Ontological Shift

Abstract: In this article, I invite an ontogenealogical approach to the analysis of the lived, experienced materiality of the body-environment assemblage. In particular, the article explores the tie between the bio(il)logical and biopolitical, characterizing this tie as a twofold ontogenealogical linkage that both a) reflects the genealogical character of life itself, as well as b) invites a critical analysis of the prevailing ontologies as co-constructive of lived materialities. The significance of the ontogenealogical approach is studied in context with the parallelism between the genealogies of the self and the environment, highlighting the need for elaborating a critique of the dominant imaginaries of the human self via the notions of the abject and body-environment processuality. The article highlights the potential of considering local ontogenealogies that reflect alternative ontologies and run parallel to the dominant paradigm of the Global North.

Introduction: Of Enfleshed Becomings

In scholarly practice Cartesian dualism has long been transgressed and today bodies have been further analyzed in feminist post-humanist and new materialist theorizations as materially embedded and transcorporeal (Alaimo 2019), porous (Neimanis 2017) and leaky transspecies assemblages (Radomska 2016). Several other conceptualizations such as *Leib* phenomenology (Waldenfels 2000; Böhme 2003, 2008, 2019), the 4E approach in cognitive sciences (Varela 2016; Noë 2009), processual philosophy of biology (Dupré 2012; Nicholson and Dupré 2018, Meincke and Dupré 2021) as well as Eugene Gendlin's processual model of the body (Gendlin 2017; Schoeller and Dunaetz 2018) and eco-phenomenological (Marder 2021) approaches in phenomenology and material affect theories (Bladow and Ladino 2018) also tackle the boundaries of the self and enfleshment.

Acknowledgments: This article was supported by the European Regional Development Fund (ERDF) Post-doctoral Research Support Program (project Nr 1.1.1.2/VIAA/1/16/001 research application Nr. 1.1.1.2./VIAA/4/20/613, project "Onto-genealogies: The Body and Environmental Ethics in Latvia").

https://doi.org/10.1515/9783111051802-010

All these accounts, although varied and often partially conflictual, highlight the notion that how (human) bodies are perceived and experienced also co-produces lived materialities, and thus, all the approaches that tackle dualism today, have an implied or outspoken ethico-political dimension that oftentimes argues for a shift in the dominating ontologies, praxes, and attitudes toward human enfleshment and the understanding of agency and subjectivity.

This ethico-political dimension is particularly born out of the fact that although dualist explanations of the body are scientifically outdated, they continue dominating the cultural imaginaries of the social field. Namely, the critique of dualist accounts of the self/other, mind/body, body/environment, and nature/culture dichotomies is connected with the ever-so-significant bio-/necro- and geontopower (Povinelli 2016) of the social field, that is continuously haunted by a Cartesian and humanist paradigm, that Deleuze conceptualizes in the notion of a "reactive nihilism" (Deleuze 2006, 148–151; Sauka 2020a). As a concept that ties together a critique of humanism, reductionism, capitalism, neo-Kantian transhumanisms,[1] and androcentrism of the Global North, the notion of reactive nihilism reflects theorizing with Nietzsche's diagnosis of the society via the idea of the death of God that sees the replacement of God by Man and the replacement of transcendental ideals by those same values, recaptured in a secular and material context. Ultimately, reactive nihilism ties together the entanglement of a cancerous orientation towards "having" (Fromm 1976) and stasis in both self-understanding as well as socio-ethical contexts in its connection with the humanist ontologies of the Global North. Supplemented by Walter Benjamin's and Agamben's (Agamben 2016) notion of capitalism as religion, the transhumanist secular world is demonstrated as an inverted and secularized version of the previous materiaphobic world of "negative nihilism" that delivers a reversed dualism with dreams of immortality to a secular level, by replacing immortality of the soul in a future beyond time with the fantasy

---

[1] With this term I here mean the forms of transhumanism that stem from humanism and emphasize a human-centric vision of "human enhancement", thus, leading to a "reversed dualism", where the body is still "stripped from spirit" and the focus is placed on a mechanical understanding of materiality, while still maintaining the dream of control over materiality as nature.) See Braidotti 2013 and Wolfe 2010, esp. "As Bostrom puts it in 'A History of Transhumanist Thought ', transhumanism combines Renaissance humanism 'with the influence of Isaac Newton, Thomas Hobbes, John Locke, Immanuel Kant, the Marquis de Condorcet, and others to form the basis for rational humanism, which emphasizes empirical science and critical reason—rather than revelation and religious authority—as ways of learning about the natural world and our place within it, and of providing a grounding for morality. Transhumanism has its roots in rational humanism'" (Bostrom 2005, cited by Wolfe 2010, xiii–xiv). In this form, transhumanism is a logical continuation of humanism and part and parcel of it, esp. in the context of reactive nihilism after the death of God.

of the immortality of an uploaded consciousness/brain or even a mechanically-extended body, in transhuman futurity.

In the last instance, the problems of the reactive nihilist lifeworld are connected to the substance ontologies (Meincke 2018) of the Global North that require the conceptual static nature of essence, and the prioritization of things over processes, which ultimately leads to the necessity of viewing selfhood as something that necessitates clear, delineable boundaries (such as the skin-line or, alternatively, "the mind") and an essential autonomy from all else. Namely, while the dichotomies may vary, the ultimate challenge for selfhood or a subject in the imaginaries of the Global North is the disposition of the self as autonomous from difference itself – in *sameness*, that is then conceptualized via otherness.[2] Thus, substance ontology problematizes the fragility and inconsistency of selfhood, urging the subject/object/abject triad, wherein, in the terms of philosophical psychoanalysis, "abject" (Kristeva 1982) functions as a third that negotiates the boundary of selfhood and otherness and allows the constitution of selfhood via the repetitive reconstitution of sameness through abjection. The plural and embedded interdependency of self-constitution that arrives from a body-environment entanglement (as the bio(il)logical[3] foundation for any subjectivity to become) is thus concealed by the triad of the subject, object, and abject that comes with the self-consciousness of the lived body. The prioritization of substances over processes creates theoretical problems such as the "mind-body problem" that complicate the analysis of enfleshed becoming with ontological questions that themselves already place focus upon *thingness* and thus endeavor an ontological account that leaks into the contemporary biopolitics via the social field and the situated contexts of science (see Rose 2007, Rose and Abi-Rached 2011).

Yet, the cognitive structure of a lived human subjectivity also necessarily leads to the recognition of the self as differentiable from the other (while simultaneously depending on the interdependency of body-environmental embeddedness) and thus facilitates the self-evidence of substance ontological accounts. Thus, while the critiques of the reactive nihilist paradigm and its co-production of lived mate-

---

[2] Here I should again stress that while I am aware of the various ways in which human-centered substance ontology is challenged in theoretical accounts, the problem that I here discuss is more connected to the possibility to challenge substance ontology on an experiential and sociopolitical level – are we able to "live" differently, reposition the "self" and build our lived genealogies upon different – processual ontologies?

[3] I use here the term bio(il)logical to refer to the genealogical character of life itself, highlighting that rather than refusing biology as part of the cultural self-disposition of humanity with regard to the disenchantment of life, biology itself should be re-enchanted and reinterpreted as naturecultured (Haraway 2016) site of creation, symbiosis and lived ontogenealogies.

rialities clearly delineate the entangled societal, ethico-political, and environmental problems caused by the Cartesian cultural imaginaries, reflecting how substance ontologies themselves take part in the way our material lifeworlds exist, i. e., in the *materialities we-live-by*, the question remains, how and if a potentially post-anthropocentric shift in the experiential ontological understanding of body-environments is possible. This question is reflected also in posthuman phenomenology. Astrida Neimanis states:

> While feminist phenomenologies help us articulate a phenomenology that is attentive to the ethical flows of difference, posthuman phenomenology must still surmount another problem: if bodies of water emerge through a description of embodiment as experienced in/as the life-world, how can we account for the limits of human perception and the many ways in which bodies of water seem to escape our directly sensed corporeality? (Neimanis 2018, 60).

This question can be reconsidered in this broader context of conceptualization vs. the experiential domain of shifting ontologies. Neimanis, along with Stacy Alaimo and Ulrich Beck (Neimanis 2018, 60–61) provides one viable solution in allowing scientific knowledge to form a "syncretic assemblage" (Alaimo 2010, 19) with phenomenology. While the acknowledgment of a syncretic assemblage of science and phenomenology can allow doing conceptual phenomenological work and change the perspectives towards embodiment, thus, in part, facilitating an ontological shift, the parallelism between how bodies are understood and the praxes and attitudes towards the environment necessitates a solution that not only allows conceptualizations beyond the I-conscious intentionality but also opens up the horizon for an affectual and experiential shift in ontologies, to change how bodies and environments are acted upon and how selfhood is experienced. Put shortly, are humans able to experience the self beyond a substance ontological understanding? And if, yes, then – how?

Since scientific knowledge does not develop in an empty place, and has its own genealogies of situated knowledges, resting upon already existing experiential ontological models that allow resistance of the dominating discourses, it seems plausible, that the recent theorizations already evidence the existence of alternate experiential knowledges and thus it is possible to look beyond the critique of existing knowledges to seek out these already present alternatives.

Here, I see two potential paths forward: either to discuss the phenomenological and first-person instances of environed embodiment (Åsberg and Braidotti 2018, 1) as endeavored by embodied critical thinking accounts (Gendlin 2017; Jóhannesdóttir and Thorgeirsdottir 2016; Schoeller and Dunaetz 2018; Schroeder 2008;

Sauka 2022a), or to seek out alternate genealogies that form the social field.[4] The shift of experiential dimension is thus seen as both a conceptual task of seeking alternate ontogenealogies in local contexts, as well as a phenomenological project for problematizing ontogenealogical production of meaningful materialities. While intentionality (with its cultural context) dominates the experiential field, promoting I-consciousness as a vehicle and origin of symbolic activity in humans, the lived-body embeddedness presents also alternate ontologies that form the experiential realm and the social field, and could thus be explored as a source of knowledge for promoting environmentally-minded thinking. Both potential research paths ultimately come together in the ontologies we-live-by, however, due to the scope and length of this article, I discuss only one of the potential paths here, arguing that one of the ways to capture alternative ontologies lies in the exploration of alternative worldings (Barad 2007) or "situated knowledges" (Haraway 1988, 1991) concealed by the dominant narratives of the Global North. This possibility is justified by the already existing biophilosophical and post-humanist alternative conceptualizations.

Genealogy of Life Itself

The reflection of the ontogenealogical embeddedness of body-environments thus begins with the reconsideration of the Foucauldian critical genealogy in a new materialist context. Genealogy in philosophy is usually understood as a methodological approach in the analysis of the history of the present, implemented by Michel Foucault (1977). Inspired by Friedrich Wilhelm Nietzsche (Sauka 2020b), Foucault's genealogy refrains from scientific monism (for a critique of monism see Dupré 2012, 22–39) and the search for a single *Ursprung*, arguing its impossibility (Foucault 1977). That allows building genealogy upon the broader paradigms of perspectivism and discontinuity and indeterminism in the generation of various phenomena.

The plausibility of an ontogenealogical view is inspired by Philipp Sarasin's "Darwin and Foucault: Genealogy and History in the Age of Biology" (Sarasin

---

4 Namely, two different approaches have proven to be especially important in reflecting ontogenealogical embeddedness of body-environments, i. e., 1) eco-phenomenology and embodied critical thinking, and 2) critical genealogy – both considered in a posthuman and new materialist context. Ontogenealogical inquiry via first-person science (i. e., embodied critical thinking and phenomenology), however, could not be sufficiently considered in this article due to its length and scope, despite being an important method for bringing experiential ontologies closer together with conceptual inquiries and eco-minded theorization.

2009). Sarasin considers Charles Darwin and Michel Foucault as genealogists, challenging the traditional interpretation of their contributions as contradictory perspectives of biologization and culturalism respectively. While still treating genealogy as a methodological approach, Sarasin demonstrates that this approach not only allows for the analysis of discontinuity but also illustrates the linking and overlapping of the spheres of biology and culture (Sarasin 2009, 313–325). His research thus invites a reevaluation of the distinction and repositioning of the processes of sense-making, indeterminism, and discontinuity *before* the human in the sphere of biology itself, which transforms the understanding of human enfleshment and demonstrates phylogenesis and natureculture as genealogical (Sauka 2020b).

Several of Nietzsche's ideas are significant for the development of a materially embedded genealogy:
1. The idea of the lived body as the "big mind" (Nietzsche 1999b, 39) that sees culturality before I-consciousness.
2. The idea of the world as an aesthetic phenomenon (Nietzsche 1999a, 17) that sees meaning beyond individual human accounts within immanent materiality.
3. The idea of historicity of the flesh/carnal body and the ingraining of history in the flesh (Nietzsche 1999c) enables the reconstitution of genealogy in an ontological context (discussed first in Sauka 2020b).

In line with these Nietzschean ideas that have inspired enfleshed yet non-essentialist approach to historicity beyond I-consciousness, I use the concept of ontogenealogy here to endeavor an analysis of the materiality of genealogical ties, upon the basis of a materiality cast as sense-forming and genealogical. Hence, resting on the embedding of critical, Foucaldian genealogy *in the flesh* (Foucault 1977), the ontogenealogical approach goes out from the premise of natureculture and a pluralist and processual understanding of the bio(il)logical materiality.

The question of experiential change of ontologies is set against the backdrop of body-environment as a relational and processual assemblage that allows for different points of departure.
a) Bodies and environments can be reflected through their material processuality, with concepts such as transcorporeality, body porosity, environmental embodiment, or even in the context of contemporary biosciences and the 4E cognitive science model, etc. In this sense, life itself is conceptualized as genealogical.
b) Bodies and environments can be reflected through the parallelism of cultural imaginaries relating to the understanding and genealogy of bodies and the environment, i. e., the concept of "nature".

c) Both dimensions merge in the reflection on the embodied environment, i. e., in the context of body-environment co-production through the cultural imaginaries related to their materialization.

The ontological and genealogical lines of research, in which processuality and the ontological and body-environment entanglement refer to the bio(il)logical context and the parallelism of cultural imaginaries relating to bodies and environments refers to the bio- and necro-political context, see their connection through a materially embedded critical genealogy, namely, ontogenealogy. Here the ontogenealogical approach considers a double entanglement, in which, on the one hand, bodies and environments are considered through a processual lens and, on the other hand, the patterns reflecting bodies and environments are analyzed in their co-constitution of materialities-we-live-by. In this way, ontogenealogy refers both to the genealogical character of the creation of meanings and their rootedness in the flesh, and to the genealogical character of life itself, and thus to the production and co-production of materialities by ontologies, and allows for the theorization of the entanglement of bio(il)logical and biopolitical factors, traditionally assigned to the material and symbolical realms respectively.[5]

The ontogenealogical approach thus endeavors to reflect the threefold codependency of genealogies, ontologies, and materialities. If natureculture and biology themselves are understood as genealogical (Sauka 2020b), embedding genealogy within materiality (1), the historicity, indeterminacy, and, the lived experience of constructed ontologies appears logically consequent: while separate ontologies are genealogically constructed (2), the genealogically constructed ontologies also co-construct lived materialities (3). For example, if one thinks of the man-machine metaphor (1) as the facilitator of an instrumentalizing understanding of the human being and the subsequent invention of computers as a human extension (2), the resultative technologies transform the lived ontologies in such a way that, while the baseline body-environment processuality remains, the calculative aspect of the *I-consciousness* is now expanded upon data-carriers, promoting an instrumentalist vision of the human mind and further – securing the appearance of dualism and ratio-centeredness that has now moved from metaphor to reality (3) via the ontogenealogical process. As a result, what was once a somewhat malfunctioning metaphor, is now a powerful material phenomenon to be reckoned with.

---

[5] On a broader scale, the ontogenealogical approach is thought to combine experiential first-person insights that recapture ontological sense-making, and conceptual alternatives that co-produce the materialities we-live-by, within and without the dominating thought patterns.

The lack of elasticity regarding a post-anthropocentric cultural shift is, thus, probably also connected to both bio(il)logical as well as genealogical and ontological factors that play into the problem but might also provide a solution. Two factors come to the foreground: 1) the pluralist and discontinuous character of the onto-ethical bind, inviting genealogical analysis and showing that no one ontogenealogy exhausts the material production and 2) the materiality itself as discontinuous and undetermined, inviting biophilosophical (Radomska 2016, 25–31; Thacker 2008) reconditioning the sphere of biology.

Namely, while the lifeworld is ontogenealogical in the sense that biology itself is naturecultured and thus should be viewed via a pluralist lens, accepting its ingraining through human and non-human naturecultured activity that also presumes the co-production of social sphere via materiality (Alaimo 2010, 6–11), this process is discursively layered and co-constituted by many different genealogies (vertical axis) and ontologies (horizontal axis) that invite philosophical reevaluation.

Both factors are materially embedded and lived, yet, what continues on a bio(il)logical level are the 'deep-seated' *ingraining in the flesh* that, although ultimately transformable and transformative, give precursors to what a human is genetically, evolutionary, and also socially. The line between 'deep-seated' and 'short-lived' ontogenealogies can only be thought of as blurred since it is ultimately history that determines, which biopolitical and social praxes will live on within us or form powerful technologies that transform us,[6] and which will fade away quickly. One of such deep-seated precursors is also the objectified image of a human body as something that one "has", rather than is.

Sense of Place and Process Ontology

Although there is no such *thing* as a distinguishable abstracted body, since bodies are not homogeneous and, in many ways, bodies and environments mix in such manifold ways that it may not even be recognizable whether a phenomenon is more to be considered a "place" or a "body" (a conundrum that could just as well apply to the human being as well as to The Humongous Fungus on the Malheur National Forest (Schmitt & Tatum, 2008; Sheldrake 2020)), it is useful to explore ontogenealogical parallelism between bodies and environments as parallel-

---

[6] Thus, some authors might already claim that today's digital natives are 'built differently' than previous generations – see Michel Serres, *Thumbelina*, for example (2015). A lot more research in genetic memory and epigenetics might be necessary to see the ties that are built within materiality via symbolic or behavioral processes (see Jablonka 2014 on the four pathways of evolution).

ism between the ontologies of embodied selfhoods (and their psychoanalytical contexts) and the ontologies of spatial places and environments, leading to congruent sociopolitical, ethical, and material worldings.

Most notably, this parallelism between bodies and environments is explored in feminist philosophy, as parallelism between the discourses of nature and femininity (Lloyd 1984; Merchant 1990), and these accounts allow the preliminary conclusion that the way to understand self-embodiment evidently pours out toward the way all embodied environment is experienced and understood in a broader sense (and *vice versa*). The self-constitution thus also importantly impacts lived environments either as embodied places or experienced ecological assemblages.

The parallelism between bodies and environments reveals another important conceptual dilemma of the dichotomy between deterritorialization and reterritorialization (Heise 2008, 51; Deleuze and Guattari 1977, 1978) that is to be considered in the context of the notion of "place" in at least two different contextual domains:

a) In the context of alternate ontogenealogies as situated knowledges that can be sought in the margins of the Global North or seep through the dominating discourses;
b) In the context of bodies and environments as themselves ecologies and places of worlding.

Moreover, the classic dichotomy of reterritorialization vs. deterritorialization in the case of seeking situated knowledges, is connected with the ontogenealogies of bodies and environments as lived and experiential places. On the one hand, a place-orientation in conceptualizations of body-environments can be problematic both in the context of a global application of local knowledges (Guha 2013) and in the ontological dimension as an anchoring of the self in a fixed symbolic field that attempts a new dichotomy between the self and the other. On the other hand, situated knowledge can also function as a subversive strategy not only for the benefit of ethics but also as a subversion of scholars' critical perspective, to alleviate the problem of strengthening dominant narratives through their critique.

As an example, Ramachandra Guha critiques "Radical American Environmentalism and Wilderness Preservation", and highlights the four "tenets of deep ecology" that function as the key thinking patterns underlying American environmentalism (Guha 2013, 410). Shortly they can be described as 1) a move from anthropocentrism to biocentrism, 2) the underscoring of the preservation of pristine wilderness, 3) an invocation that deep ecology is inspired by "Eastern spiritual traditions" (Guha 2013, 411), and 4) the belief that deep ecology is the highest achievable form of environmentalism.

In his critique Guha notes that the shift toward biocentrism fails to tackle the real problems that environmentalists today face, namely the "1) overconsumption by the industrialized world [...] and (2) growing militarization" (Guha 2013, 412). While this is a significant aspect, it is also important to mention that it is here rather a dichotomy between transhuman anthropocentrism and bioconservativism that is itself problematic and partaking in the maintenance of the factual problems of environmentalism. Namely, while Guha correctly identifies the strive for pristine wilderness as adequate to the situated ecologies of Americans who experience a dichotomy of vast "wilderness" areas and equally wild urban jungles, this dichotomy of wilderness/civilization itself is genealogically embedded and draws from the anthropocentric thought paradigm that dominates Northern genealogies of bodies, genders, environments, and pre-forms language and thinking. As such it is not only the application of local genealogies to global discourses but has been firstly the application of global or dominating narratives to materialities in particular places, that are then exported outwards. Thus, the dichotomy of local vs. global is in itself problematic and does not refer to the factual problem of a dialectic between bioconservative and neoliberal transhumanist outlooks.

In the context of the abovementioned, wilderness preservation thus opens up as an ideological construct that functions within the dominating dialectics of the Global North and is connected to both a) the formation of material surroundings and b) an activity that is enmeshed in the understanding of the human as alienated from the environment, and thus 1) objectifies and fragmentarizes nature and 2) denies the entanglement of human/non-human ecologies as well as conceals the factual multidimensionality of genealogies that occur simultaneously with the dominating narratives.

In her book *Reinventing Eden* (2003) Carolyn Merchant discusses the narratives of nature and states that:

> The first story is the traditional biblical narrative of the fall from the Garden of Eden from which humanity can be redeemed through Christianity. But the garden itself can also be recovered. By the time of the Scientific Revolution of the seventeenth century, the Christian narrative had merged with advances in science, technology, and capitalism to form the mainstream Recovery Narrative. (Merchant 2003, 11)

This quote illustrates how the bioconservative attitude has long endured a dialectic relationship with the anthropocentric one, mutually reinforcing each other. In particular, the human being is thought to be alienated from nature through original sin, which in the secular analysis can be seen as a cultural imaginary of the Western conceptualization of the atopicality of the human being, who is always poised between nature and culture because of consciousness. This alienation and abstraction of the human being (Williams 1980) thus sees the production of a dialectic between an idea of pristine nature, devoid of human beings, as a God-given garden of prosperity, and the idea of an imperfect nature, deformed by its materiality, to be perfected through the human mind. Both ideas work together in a non-contradictory discourse that simultaneously sees humanity as angelic and demonic. The idea of wilderness devoid of human beings, therefore, rests on anthropocentric grounds and is a type of inverted anthropocentrism that still evaluates human beings as exceptional (Barad 2017, 26; Braidotti 2013, 66, 86 et.al.) – only not because of their virtue, but because of their unfortunate toxic capacities.

What disrupts the dialectic of the *status quo* are therefore phenomena that reach a meta-level of disruption and are to some extent abject to the human self-constitution that is based on human exceptionality, such as today, for example, the return of wild animals to Europe – an example that I analyze more closely in an article reflecting on the genealogy of the self with the example of bears as abject disruptors of the dialectics of self and other (Sauka 2022b).

The main conflict in environmental discussions is thus not the conflict between local and global approaches, but rather the conflict between essentialism and pluralist processuality. Namely, essentialist attitudes endeavor a dialectics of local vs. global that either 1) envisions and materializes local thinking or needs as conflictual with global demands (as in Guha's example of India and tiger-conservation (2013, 423) or 2) universalizes local experiences as global demands. Both aspects demonstrate a paradox, where "thinking globally" foregoes the heterogeneous global scale, through "local approaches" that, however, also forego local embeddedness of communities. Thus, while it is dangerous to extrapolate local approaches to global discourses, it is also necessary to respect global contexts, and to do that – local, place-based assessment is needed. The terminology here seems lacking to encompass the spatial connectedness, which is why the dialectics of local vs. global lacks the potential for conceptualizing place-based solutions that adhere to global environmental problems.

In this context, the conceptualization of body-environments as genealogically embedded (and thus non-essentialist) ecologies and places of worlding allows critically reconsidering the dialectics of place-based vs. global accounts, via the reflection of the embodied self as a placed yet continuously transforming and transporting (displacing) process. Thus, the ontogenealogical approach strives to go beyond the dialectic of bodies and environments as places of dwelling that enable a sense of place or rootedness (Heise 2008, 29–49) *vs.* bodies and environments as globally enmeshed, non-discernable entanglements (see Marder 2021).

In the last instance, the dichotomy of place and displacement is possible only via a substance ontology of the self that necessitates the constitution of skin-line embodiment as an anchor of selfhood which then reverberates towards local environmental embeddedness via a static notion of home as a place of dwelling. If the self is contextualized via an enfleshed understanding of process ontology that acknowledges the significance of movement and transformation in the becoming self, a sense of place acquires the dimension of dynamic interaction, thus, enabling a non-essentialist approach to seeking out local genealogies. The notion of "nomadic subjectivity" instituted by Rosi Braidotti (1994) here could prove to be a fruitful concept that would not mean a displaced, atopical, homeless subjectivity, but rather a subjective disposition that exists in the interdependent, processual, non-essentialist entanglement and connects via place-oriented yet transformative processes that refrain from an essentialist confrontation of radical dichotomies.

Seeking Alternative Ontogenealogies

The consideration of local ontogenealogies, thus, follows from this conceptualization as an affirmative approach to environmental ethics that seeks to subvert the reinforcement of dominating dualist thought paradigms through their critique (Neimanis et.al. 2015) by acknowledging the manifold beginnings (genealogies) of materialities beyond the subject/object/abject triad. It is an ontological and genealogical endeavor to consider the alternate creeks and ripples of sense-making and worlding, while also problematizing the homogenization of the Global North under a unified matrix of explanation.

Many well-known authors[7] have successfully analyzed the dominant ontologies and genealogies of the Global North. What is similar in these accounts, however, is a tendency to cite a single substance ontology underlying the dominant genealogies, as I have also done here before. Thus, for instance, the discourse of physiologization can be successfully traced back to a substance ontology that ultimately establishes an autonomous, individualized but objectifiable body, etc. While the genealogical features of the meanings differ, the underlying problem remains the same and brings to light a seemingly universal materiaphobia of the Global North.

On the one hand, this dominating paradigm does, largely, constitute the materialities we live by, such as, for example, from issues with the ozone layer to the sixth extinction, and as far as one acknowledges the interconnectivity of attitudes and praxes and the underlaying ontological premises, invites criticism. On the other hand, the highlight of the dominating paradigm conceals the actual complexity of ontogenealogical processes and the ongoing processuality of the bio(il)logical

---

7 Namely, entire research directions such as critical theory, poststructuralism, several strands of phenomenology, as well as newer iterations of philosophy such as critical posthumanism, pay a great deal of attention to various critical accounts of the genealogies of the Global North, although the use of the concept of genealogy is used rarely.

sphere, and thus also possibly conceals viable alternate ontologies to live by in the future.

Three interconnected problems arise here: 1) universalization, 2) disregard of alternative models and their minor or major influence on global discussions, and 3) depoliticization of environmental issues and, thus, the major and minor resistances against universalized environmental ethical (justice/etc.) models. All three problems today are in part acknowledged in academia and the environmental humanities (Neimanis et.al. 2015; Hamilton and Neimanis 2018), and are also addressed, for example, since the interest in the Global South as a possible knowledge source has gained traction within the scholarly practice.

Although still lacking and incomplete, this interest is present, yet the search for possible knowledge sources as well as the analysis of possible conflictual and competitive ontologies largely surpasses the territories and cultures that are "too Nordic to be South and too Eastern to be West" as well as, repeats a dialectic of the self and the other.

In a recent article, "Thinking Food Like an East European: A Critical Reflection on the Framing of Food Systems " (Jehlička et al. 2020), the authors claim that:

> Whereas the West European (and North American) context is perceived as a source of universally valid knowledge claims, Eastern Europe is expected to be a mere recipient and testing ground for concepts and research agendas developed in the West. (Jehlička et al. 2020, 286)

Thus, in addition to being marginalized as the Other to its Western counterpart, the post-soviet space[8] is often doubly erased by drawing the line between the Global North and South that sees the vanishing of the 'Second World' as Other, instead of adding it as a province to the Northern discourse (Müller 2018, 3–4; Jehlička et al. 2020, 286–287), excluding the East from the "map of knowledge production" (Müller 2018, 3). The marginalization of the other within, thus, is reflected again in the marginalization of the Other without. The example of Eastern Europe allows a tentative proposal that the homogenization of the Global North, below the umbrella terms of the Global North, the West, Anglo-Saxon or European, and the like, dismisses the variability and genealogical differences between the many cultures that bear layers upon layers of histories from their pagan past to today's inclusion under the same homogenizing concepts and thus dismissing the complexity of the Global North itself even beyond such larger categories as Eastern and Western Europe.

---

[8] In continuation to the discussed necessity to mobilize situated knowledges, I discuss the postsocialist situated knowledges further in Sauka 2023.

In context with the endeavor to depoliticize environmental problems, this factor also leads to the undermining of possible competitive or conflictual ontogenealogies that might resist mainstream scientific or entrepreneurial solutions to environmental issues. What is more important, though, is that the possibility to search for alternatives in one's own cultural background, opens up the opportunity to find relatable, close-to-heart ontogenealogies that make up the fabric of becoming, which, thus, allows the ontological shift via both genealogical and phenomenological channels. Thus, it is important to note that, taking into account ontogenealogical heterogeneity, is important for at least two significant reasons – first to properly regard potential conflict situations and understand their ontogenealogical embeddedness but second – also as a possibility to trace alternative solutions within situated naturecultured praxes and attitudes.

Thus, also situated, locally produced knowledges as ontogenealogical models could inform, educate, and co-constitute materialities, as well as serve as alternative ethicalities. Moreover, these models could be implemented not only as sources of knowledge in global discussions but also as sources for introducing global initiatives in local contexts, as well as models for understanding particular societal conflicts and resistances. Additionally, investigating local ontogenealogies also promises a way to reconsider post-anthropocentric, processual models (thus the research movement here is thought to be is circular from model to study, and from study to the supplementation of the said model).

References

Agamben, G. (2016). "Capitalism as Religion". In McLoughlin, D. (Ed.), *Agamben and Radical Politics.* Edinburgh: Edinburgh University Press, 15–26.

Alaimo, S. (2010). *Bodily Natures: Science, Environment, and the Material Self.* Bloomington: Indiana University Press.

Åsberg, C. and Braidotti, R. (2018). "Feminist Posthumanities: An Introduction". In Åsberg, C. and Braidotti, R. (Eds.), *A Feminist Companion to the Posthumanities.* Cham: Springer, 1–22.

Barad, K. (2007). *Meeting the Universe Halfway.* Durham, NC: Duke University Press.

Bladow, K. and Ladino, J. (Eds.) (2018). *Affective Ecocriticism: Emotion, Embodiment, Environment.* Lincoln: University of Nebraska Press.

Bostrom, N. (2005). "A History of Transhumanist Thought". *Journal of Evolution and Technology* 14(1), 1–25.

Braidotti, R. (2008). "Of Poststructuralist Ethics and Nomadic Subjects". In: Düwell, M., Rehmann-Sutter, C. and Mieth, D. (Eds.), *The Contingent Nature of Life. Bioethics and the Limits of Human Existence.* Cham: Springer, 25–37.

Braidotti, R. (2013). *The Posthuman.* Cambridge: Polity Press.

Deleuze, G. and Guattari, F. (1977). *Anti-Oedipus: Capitalism and Schizophrenia.* Trans. by R. Hurley, H. R. Lane and M. Seem. New York: Viking.

Deleuze, G. and Guattari, F. (1987). *A Thousand Plateaus: Capitalism and Schizophrenia.* Trans. by B. Massumi. Minneapolis: University of Minnesota Press.
Dupré, J. (2012). *Processes of Life: Essays in Philosophy of Biology.* New York: Oxford University Press.
Foucault, M. (1977). "Nietzsche, Genealogy, History". In Bouchard, D. F. (Ed.), *Language, Counter-Memory, Practice: Selected Essays and Interviews.* Ithaca: Cornell University Press, 139–164.
Fromm, E. (1976). *To Have or to Be?* New York: Harper and Row.
Gendlin, E. T. (2017). *A Process Model.* Evanston: Northwestern University Press.
Guha, R. (2013). "Radical American Environmentalism and Wilderness Preservation: A Third World Critique". In Robin, L., Sörlin, S. and Warde, P. (Eds.), *The Future of Nature. Documents of Global Change.* New Haven: Yale University Press, 409–426.
Hamilton, J. M. and Neimanis, A. (2018). "Composting Feminisms and Environmental Humanities". *Environmental Humanities* 10(2), 501–527.
Haraway, D. J. (1988). "Situated Knowledges: The Science Question in Feminism and the Privilege of Partial Perspective". *Feminist Studies* 14(3), 575–599.
Haraway, D. J. (1991). *Simians, Cyborgs, and Women: The Reinvention of Nature.* New York: Routledge.
Haraway, D. J. (2016). "The Companion Species Manifesto". In Haraway, D., *Manifestly Haraway.* Minneapolis: University of Minnesota Press, 91–198.
Heise, U. (2008). *Sense of Place and Sense of Planet: The Environmental Imagination of the Global.* Oxford: Oxford University Press.
Jablonka, E. and Lamb, M. J. (2014). *Evolution in Four Dimensions: Genetic, Epigenetic, Behavioural, and Symbolic Variation in the History of Life.* Revised edition. Cambridge: MIT Press.
Jehlička, P., Grīviņš, M., Visser, O. and Balazs, B. (2020). "Thinking Food Like an East European: A Critical Reflection on the Framing of Food Systems". *Journal of Rural Studies* 76, 286–295. DOI: 10.1016/j.jrurstud.2020.04.015.
Jóhannesdóttir, G. and Thorgeirsdottir, S. (2016). "Reclaiming Nature by Reclaiming the Body". *Balkan Journal of Philosophy* 7(1), 39–48.
Kristeva, J. (1982). *Powers of Horror: An Essay on Abjection.* Trans. by L. S. Roudiez. New York: Columbia University Press.
Lloyd, G. (1984). *The Man of Reason: 'Male' and 'Female' in Western Philosophy.* London: Methuen.
Marder, M. (2021). *Dump Philosophy: A Phenomenology of Devastation.* London: Bloomsbury.
Meincke, A. S. (2018). "Persons as Biological Processes: A Bio-Processual Way Out of the Personal Identity Dilemma". In Nicholson, D. and Dupré, J. (Eds.), *Everything Flows: Towards a Processual Philosophy of Biology.* New York: Oxford University Press, 357–378.
Meincke, A. S. and Dupré, J. (Eds.) (2021). *Biological Identity: Perspectives from Metaphysics and the Philosophy of Biology.* London: Routledge.
Merchant, C. (1990). *The Death of Nature. Women, Ecology and the Scientific Revolution.* San Francisco: Harper and Row.
Merchant, C. (2003). *Reinventing Eden. The Fate of Nature in Western Culture.* New York: Routledge.
Müller, M. (2018). "In Search of the Global East: Thinking between North and South". *Geopolitics.* DOI: 10.1080/14650045.2018.1477757.
Neimanis, A. (2017). *Bodies of Water.* London: Bloomsbury.
Neimanis, A. (2018). *Posthuman Phenomenologies for Planetary Bodies of Water.* In Åsberg, C. and Braidotti, R. (Eds.), *A Feminist Companion to the Posthumanities.* Cham: Springer, 55–66.
Neimanis, A., Åsberg, C. and Hedrén, J. (2015). "Four Problems, Four Directions for Environmental Humanities: Toward Critical Posthumanities for the Anthropocene". *Ethics and the Environment* 20(1), 67–97. DOI: 10.2979/ethicsenviro.20.1.67.

Nicholson, D. J. and Dupré, J. (Eds.) (2018). *Everything Flows: Towards a Processual Philosophy of Biology.* New York: Oxford University Press. DOI: 10.1093/oso/9780198779636.001.0001.

Nietzsche, F. W. (1999a). "Die Geburt der Tragödie aus dem Geiste der Musik". In *Sämtliche Werke. Kritische Studienausgabe*, vol. 1. Ed. by G. Colli and M. Montinari. Munich and Berlin: Deutscher Taschenbuch Verlag and De Gruyter, 9–156.

Nietzsche, F. W. (1999b). "Also sprach Zarathustra". In *Sämtliche Werke. Kritische Studienausgabe*, vol. 4. Ed. by G. Colli and M. Montinari. Munich and Berlin: Deutscher Taschenbuch Verlag and De Gruyter.

Nietzsche, F. W. (1999c). "Zur Genealogie der Moral". In *Sämtliche Werke. Kritische Studienausgabe*, vol. 5. Ed. by G. Colli and M. Montinari. Munich and Berlin: Deutscher Taschenbuch Verlag and De Gruyter, 245–413.

Noë, A. (2009). *Out of Our Heads: Why You Are Not Your Brain and Other Lessons from the Biology of Consciousness.* New York: Hill and Wang.

Povinelli, E. A. (2016). *Geontologies: A Requiem to Late Liberalism.* Durham: Duke University Press.

Radomska, M. (2016). *Uncontainable Life: A Biophilosophy of Bioart* [Ph. D. dissertation]. Linköping: Linköping University Electronic Press.

Sauka, A. (2020a). "A Lack of Meaning? Reactive Nihilism and Processual Materiality". *Approaching Religion* 10(2), 125–140. DOI: 10.30664/ar.91788.

Sauka, A. (2020b). "The Nature of Our Becoming: Genealogical Perspectives". *Le foucaldien* 6(1), 1–30. DOI: 10.16995/lefou.71.

Sauka, A. (2022b). "Beyond the Skin Line: Tuning into the Body-Environment. A Venture into the Before of Conceptualizations". *The Polish Journal of Aesthetics* 64, 161–181. DOI: 10.19205/64.22.10. Selfhood in Question: The Ontogenealogies of Bear Encounters. Open Philosophy, 5(1), 532-550. https://doi.org/10.1515/opphil-2022-0211

Sauka, A. (2023). Breaching the Dialectic with Situated Knowledges: The Case of Postsocialist Naturecultures. The Polish Journal of Aesthetics, 68, 35-56. https://doi.org/10.19205/68.23.2

Schmitt, C. L., & Tatum, M. L. (2008). The Malheur National Forest: Location of the World's Largest Living Organism [The Humongous Fungus]. United States Department of Agriculture, Forest Service, Pacific Northwest Region. Retrieved from https://www.fs.usda.gov/Internet/FSE_DOCUMENTS/fsbdev3_033146.pdf

Sheldrake, M. (2020). *Entangled Life: How Fungi Make Our Worlds, Change Our Minds & Shape Our Futures.* New York: Random House.

Williams, R. (1980). "Ideas of Nature". *Problems in Materialism and Culture* 65, 67–85.

Wolfe, C. (2010). *What Is Posthumanism?* Minneapolis: University of Minnesota Press.

Corinna Casi
Women, Nature and Neocolonial Struggles: Different Perspectives on Indigenous Women's Position

Abstract: This article is situated within the gender inequality debate associated with the relation between nature and women, which began to be conceptualized academically in the 1970s in the philosophical field of ecofeminism. After presenting some ecofeminist perspectives highlighting the reasons of the women/nature connection, some criticism will be advanced challenging the invisibility of women's role and their work in society, showing as well the limitation of such approaches. The argument will then move to the field of Indigenous feminism, keeping the focus of the relation between nature and women, and observing how this has influenced the condition of women within Indigenous communities such as the Igbo people in Nigeria, the Kahnawa:kev people in Canada and the Sami people living in Sapmi, in the North of Europe and Northwest of Russia.

Introduction

The women's rights movement has come a long way since its beginning with the suffragette activist movement in London in the 19th century. In the history of women's struggle for political and civil rights, New Zealand was the first country in the world in 1893 to grant woman the right to vote, followed by Australia in 1902 and Finland in 1906 and then many more. Meanwhile, in 2020, we witnessed the New Zealand Parliament passing the Equal Pay Amendment Act. Even though this is not the first of its kind, there are still many other countries where the pay gap for job compensation between men and women is in place and is seriously rooted. Despite these achievements, inequality between men and women are still in evidence in many parts of the world and yet gender equality is one of the basic human rights (UN Women 2021). The implications of gender inequality extend to many areas of society and its consequences are not always visible and understandable by many. These are some of the reasons why research and debates on such matters as gender inequality are of vital significance even in the 21st century.

This article is situated within the gender inequality debate, associated in particular with the relation between nature and women. After taking a critical stand on the devaluation of women's work in societies due mainly to the invisibility of their work and by the division of the public and domestic sphere, I present ecofe-

https://doi.org/10.1515/9783111051802-011

minist viewpoints emphasizing on the contrary 'the productive role of women' due to their link with nature. The connection between nature and women started to be conceptualized at the academic level in the 1970s in the applied philosophical field of ecofeminism. After presenting some ecofeminist perspectives in order to criticize the invisibility of women's work in society, these viewpoints will be critically scrutinized to show some of their limitations. This will allow the move forward to a younger feminist field such as that of Indigenous feminism, keeping in focus the relation between nature and women and observing how this connection has influenced the condition of women within Indigenous communities.

A conceptual analysis of the relation between nature and women will be carried out in this article within the ecofeminist framework and beyond it, connecting it subsequently with Indigenous feminism and explaining the links and the diversities.

Women in Society: Devaluation of Intrahousehold Women's Work

In many cultures, as the Nobel Prize-winner Amartya Sen wrote, matters of gender inequality are associated with correctness. In some families and communities, for instance, unequal treatment between men and women, as well as between boys and girls, "are often accepted as 'natural' or appropriated" (Sen 1995, 260) although those behaviors and their consequences are not generally examined or talked over. Among other inequalities, this has serious implications since the family is the first and one of the most powerful learning schools for children, along with a model for children's moral development (Mill 1988 [1869]; Okin 1989; Okin 1995).

Considering the role of women in society, the separation between the public and the domestic spheres has brought significant consequences. For example, it has for a long time obscured intrahousehold women's work such as cooking, cleaning, caring for children, as well as for old and sick family members. The huge amount of intrahousehold work which women have been carrying out for centuries, without being acknowledged, has contributed in various ways to men's work and success as well as favoring men's ascending career in different fields of society.

The political philosopher and liberal feminist Susan Moller Okin (1995) argued that this picture, unfortunately depicting most human societies through time, lies on the one hand on the assumption that only paid work in the public domain counts as work. On the other hand, domestic household tasks, carried out mainly by women, are somehow invisible and considered not 'productive' (Okin 1995) in monetary terms, because they are unpaid and therefore judged 'of lesser worth'. Therefore, the view that intrahousehold women's work is unpaid and 'of lesser worth' contributes to the devaluation of women in the public and in both the domestic sphere. This is one way in which women are caught by a spiral of various forms of asymmetries, intersectionally I would add, from which it is not easy to escape (Okin 1995). Not to mention that it is often the case that women's access to paid jobs is affected by discrimination in the workplace itself (Fuchs 1988; Okin 1989; Okin 1995). Moreover, Nkiru Nzegwu, a Nigerian philosopher and professor with a specialization on African feminism, stresses that "in an environment where success is defined in economic terms many women, who have had to [...] subordinate ...] to their male partners do not realize that this is itself a form of oppression" (Nzegwu 1995, 451). This condition for a long time has been contributing to the devaluation of women and their work in the public and in the domestic sphere; the same devaluation is also reflected in the Condition of many Indigenous women, such as Sami women, presented in the last part of this paper.

Ecofeminism and the Relation between Women and Nature: Tradition and Criticism

Starting from the 1970s, in several parts of the world and from different perspectives, renewed attention has been given to the connection of women and nature. Concerning non-European perspectives, in India the initiative known as the Chipko movement was a non-violent movement from Uttarakhand, inspired by Mahatma Gandhi, which gained global attention. It was a grassroots initiative where local people, mostly women, started embracing trees to stop deforestation and to protect their forests (Knauss 2018). This movement took place at the same time as the 1972 UN conference on the Human Environment in Stockholm which marked the beginning of developing common environmental policies with a global perspective. The Chipko movement was an inspirational example for other initiatives in the Global South which stimulate bottom-up activities (Braidotti et al. 1997).

Another of these perspectives was ecofeminism, also called "ecological feminism", which is situated within the applied field of environmental ethics and underlines the significant link between women and nature, and the ways of acting upon it. The term "ecofeminism" was first coined in 1974 by Françoise d'Eaubonne and was initially "used for any view that merges environmental advocacy with feminist enquiry" (Brennan and Lo 2021). As I will attempt to show in this work, within ecofeminism there have been diverse and contrasting views. The Western Northern feminists, for instance, started to "draw parallels" between male control over nature and over women (Visvanathan et al. 1997, 24). However, according to Bina Agarwal (1997), ecofeminism seeks for an alternative view which looks more egalitarian and harmonious. Maria Mies (1986), for instance due to her Marxist and feminist influence, emphasizes childbearing and child-rearing regarding women's position in society and sees their reproductive role as a necessary and vital contribution for family survival. Women are nature because they give birth and bring up their children. This double role of women contributes to their closeness and better understanding of nature. Women and nature also share the process of growth that Maria Mies calls the 'production of life'. In this sense it is a paradox that women and nature are called 'unproductive' from a market and capital accumulation viewpoint since they are the ones who produce and help the growth of human lives.

According to Vandana Shiva (1989), the feminine principle, understood as women's essence, is embodied by the practical relations that women have with nature, for instance, in the context of Indian rural areas. The feminine principle supports a traditional Indian agricultural system, a tradition that started in pre-colonial times, in harmony with natural cycles. This ancient system promotes multicultural plantations in opposition to the nowadays dominant mode of development, which is Western and patriarchal, hence serving the unsustainable global market.

Braidotti et al. (1997) criticized Shiva for proposing a return to an idyllic past where there was an idealized harmony with nature that might never have existed. On the other hand, Shiva advanced a crucial point central to the criticism of the Eurocentric perspective. This point refers to the proposal that the Western development model might not be the only possible one, but other possibilities, which are fairer and more respectful to nature, exist.

In Mies and Shiva's viewpoints the interest of the environment becomes the interest of women due to their interconnections. In their view, women are seen as the answer to the environmental crisis, the ones who have the solutions due to their connections to nature. Braidotti and the Northern women's movement questioned and criticized the rhetoric of instrumentalizing women for environmental recovery. The woman's position as the unique knower and the most valuable resource for the sustainable use of resources, as well as to solve the environmental crisis, is rather questionable (Braidotti et al. 1997).

The line of arguments of the Northern women's movement starts from the different fundaments of the women/men relationship: while in the Global South during pre-colonial times this relation was rather equal, in the global North, since the Middle Ages, women have been subordinated to men. From this differentiation, it follows that women from the South can easily see the connection of women/nature as not discriminatory and use it in their arguments differently than Northern women do (Braidotti et al. 1997).

Bina Agarwal has a different view on the link between women and nature, asserting that this connection is culturally and socially constructed rather than biologically determined (Agarwal 1989). She criticizes ecofeminism, first for promoting the idea of women as a category and as a unity, ignoring the differences among race, religion, class, ethnicity, and the like. Ecofeminism has also been neglecting other forms of oppression, other than gender, that have influenced women as well (Agarwal 1997). This allowed, in such a way, the opening of debates from the Third World standpoint about gender and environment. Second, the ecofeminist argument is based mainly on an ideology which ignores the interconnected material origins of this oppression, such as economic advantage and political power. Third, ecofeminism does not spell out or give details about the social, economic and political structures in which these constructs are created, nor does it give the reasons for which certain groups are able to dominate. Ultimately this can be seen as adhering to essentialism[1] and to a sort of 'female essence' notion which opens the way for ecofeminism to be grounded in essentialist generalizations about the relation of women and nature (Agarwal 1997). In contrast to that, Agarwal highlights the significance of showing how the material realities in which women of different class, caste, or race live, might what they think of environmental exploitation.

Moreover, Agarwal, using the term "feminist environmentalism" instead of ecofeminism, suggests understanding the women/nature relationship via their material reality, within their interaction with the environment (Agarwal 1997). For instance, in the case of poor peasants and tribal women, the knowledge of nature is experiential, meaning that they acquire a special knowledge of natural species and natural cycle processes via their everyday interaction with nature. Based on their experiential knowledge, they can offer a special perspective (Agarwal 1997) and this is also more evident in the example of Indigenous women, presented in the last part of this paper.

Indigenous Feminism

Disagreement exists when discussing the role and the status of women within different Indigenous populations in precolonial times but surely "there is no ambigu-

---

1 Essentialism within feminist theory is the view that focuses on the existence of a sort of female 'essence' which is unchangeable and irreducible.

ity about the negative consequences of the views and actions of European missionaries, soldiers, and settlers" (Kahaleole Hall 2009, 15–16) on the role of Indigenous women. It is valuable to critically assess that Indigenous communities are nowadays still under several forms of oppression by dominant societies (Green 2001; Smith 1999; LaRoche 1996). Therefore, it is of the utmost importance to acknowledge that not only Indigenous women are under oppression, but entire Indigenous communities are in the same condition (Kuokkanen 2007). The Indigenous struggle to preserve their integrity cannot be separated from the culture of the dominant society, which is sexist, racist, violent and disrespectful of minorities. "Indigenous feminism grapples with the ways patriarchal colonialism has been internalized within indigenous communities, as well as analysing the sexual and gendered nature of the process of colonization" (Kahaleole Hall 2009, 16).

The Indigenous scholar and Associate Professor of Political Science Joyce Green describes Indigenous, or Aboriginal, feminism as dealing with issues of colonialism, sexism and racism, and the impacts these three violations of human rights have on each other (Green 2007). It also raises attention on decolonization and issues of gendered power in settlers and Indigenous communities (Green 2007). Indigenous feminists use the feminist theoretical approach as a tool to counteract racism, colonialism, and their consequences. They also attempt to unveil power structures in the dominant societies as well as within Indigenous communities. They offer a political and philosophical path "of conceptualizing, and of resisting, the oppression" (Green 2007, 30) that many Indigenous people are enduring.

Colonialism and Gender: Examples from Nigeria, Canada and Sapmi

The Case of the Igbo People in Nigeria

Traditions and materials from non-Western societies had been eroticized in Africa as ethnographic literature and, on the other hand the material of white-Western culture is 'naturalized' and proposed as natural and unproblematic (Nzegwu 1995, 444). Talking about colonialism in the African continent, especially in Nigeria in the land of Igbo Indigenous people, Njiru Nzegwu claimed that this was "an alienating historical condition that erased and silenced the voice of women" (Nzegwu 1995, 445) through the British policy of indirect rules. Precisely through the British policy of indirect rule, a sexist administrative and asymmetric political structure of power was put in place within that structure women were marginalized and robbed of their historical powers. In pre-colonial time, times Igbo society was based on a dual-sex symmetrical structure. This social structure was based on the one hand on the active participation of women in political life, for instance they had their own Governing Council which tackled specific women's affairs and needs. Men, on the other hand, "were used to see women in position of influence and power and had developed a respect for their administrative skills (Nzegwu 1995, 447). Women were publicly validated for their skills and their presence in the economic, juridical and political domains, so that women's independence was a fact during pre-colonial times. Additionally, Nzegwu (1995, 445) highlights the "enforced invisibility" in which women were denied education, employment and decisional power during the British domination period. Barbara Rogers (1980) was right to affirm that in pre-colonial cultures it was highly unlikely that men would objectify women as passive and inert. However, after many protests between 1925 and 1935, in 1929 there was the Women's War in which Igbo women among other indigenous woman sought some type of representation (Nzegwu 1995).

In the 1970s within the development program discourses, more attention was given to women's relationship with the natural environment, which was called Women, Environment and Sustainable Development (WED) (Braidotti et al. 1997) within which there have been several different perspectives. An economic approach, for instance, looks at WED from a women's work perspective. Historically the sexual division of labor between men and women led to a defined women's responsibility in dealing with natural resources, assigning them work with lower consideration and consequently men having higher a role in economic production. Nzegwu radically criticizes the foundational assumptions of gender inequalities upon which many development programs in Africa are built. The same development programs which were supposed to equally help the population in nigeria and be gender-neutral, in fact turned out to favor and benefit primarily men, while Nigerian women have mainly been excluded (Nzegwu 1995).

We can also notice a reference to Okin (1995)'s idea of invisible women's work considered of less worth because it does not produce a financial gain. Differently, an ecofeminist view focused on culture conceptualizes women's closeness to nature as a result of the sexual division of labor entitling women to have an essentially closer relation with nature. Due to this prerogative over the years, women accumulated detailed and practical knowledge concerning natural processes in respect to men. This viewpoint conceptualizes the relationship women/nature "as one of reciprocity, symbiosis, harmony" and mutual inter-relation due to women's dependence on nature for subsistence (Braidotti et al. 1997, 56).

Nigerian women subordinated to their male partners did not understand that this was also a form of oppression (Nzegwu 1995). Nigerian men profited profoundly by the sexism brought by the British colonizers shown in their willingness to collaborate with them while installing colonial rule. The consequences of this collaboration were: the denial of women's representation, the devaluation of women's work, the creation of politically passive female citizens as well as sexist authoritarian men (Nzegwu 1995).

The Case of the Kahnawa:ke Indigenous People in Canada

Some of the inequities that weigh upon Indigenous people are "embedded in the history of land dispossession [...] and destruction of their social systems (Delormier et al. 2018, 1). This is the case, for instance of the Kahnawa:ke Indigenous community in Quebec, Canada, where there are traditional gender roles which foster the harmony of the community- and gender-based division of labor, related to the food system (Delormier et al. 2018). From this situation, gender responsibilities are derived in such a way that they do not have a negative or devalued connotation. In fact, the crucial point in this type of societal structure is to keep the role complementary between men and women in order to resist the colonial concept of gender. The significance of gender complementarity was evident during crisis times, when people gave priority at working together for the well-being of the community.

Responsibilities of women are food preparing, child-caring and education, teaching the values of the Indigenous community such as love, compassion and care, especially care for the community. Women have a central role in modeling and teaching traditional values. Other than in Western perspectives, traditional Kahnawa:ke Indigenous women's responsibilities come from a spiritual connection with earth, moon and garden, which are all feminine entities (Delormier et al. 2018).

The Case of the Sami Women in Sapmi

The Sami are the Indigenous people of the North of Europe and part of Russia; their territory encompasses the North of Norway, Sweden, Finland and the Northwest of Russia. Even though the Sami are divided in to different communities with their own characteristics, they have all been through common struggles such as identity crises, mental disorders, psychological stress, violence, increased alcoholism and other types of issues (Kuokkanen 2007). Within Sami communities there exists a common and traditional view of strong Sami women as a sort of myth (Aikio 1998; Lukkari 1998; Kuokkanen 2007). Until the late 1980s, in order to distinguish Sami women from the non-Sami Nordic women, belonging to the dominant society, it was common to underline the image of strong Sami women and the Sami as a matriarchal society. According to Jorunn Eikjok (1992), a Sami feminist scholar, this artificial construction was operated to stress the difference from the patriarchal settler society, but it was rather based on the idealization of Sami women and their society, than on reality.

As in other Aboriginal and native populations, Sami Indigenous women historically enjoyed "a form of equality with men, characterized by a symmetrical complementary of domains, roles and tasks" (Kuokkanen 2007, 74). Sami women were independent, and had power and control over certain domains, but over the years, Christianity and Laestadianism, an evangelical movement within the Lutheran church, had a strong influence on the image of Sami women (Kuokkanen 2007).

Concerning the livelihood activities within the Sami community, Eikjok notices that reindeer herding is nowadays commonly identified as a male practice, despite the fact that women continue to help in most of the reindeer production (Eikjok 1992) but their work has been made invisible. Therefore, Sami women ended by abandoning reindeer herding and focusing for other livelihood practices (Eikjok 1992).

Concluding Reflections

Often women, and especially Indigenous women, are aware of their subordinate position but are unable to challenge their exclusion since they do not have the means for reacting and dealing with this sensitive and complex matter. The case of Igbo and Sami Indigenous women shows that women are not in a position to deeply argue for their own terms, due to oppression by Indigenous men as well as by colonizers and the contemporary structure of their communities. Hence, they need more empowerment and autonomy within their Indigenous communities. In this regard, the philosopher Martha Nussbaum (1997) talks about 'political poverty' as the lack of relevant political capabilities, compared to poverty as a lack of resources. Finally, agency does not only indicate moral agency or responsibility, but it rather refers to 'feeling capable of' political agency, of having a voice, a voice that can be heard by their communities first and by non-Indigenous societies second. As a concluding remark, I suggest raising awareness about subordinated positions and power structures within Indigenous communities as an encouragement to indigenize discourses on gender inequality by Indigenous women. Far from being the last word on this matter, this paper aims to start a conversation. Ultimately, within this context 'indigenize gender inequalities discourses' refers not only to discourses about gender injustices within the dominant Western white culture but also and especially within Indigenous communities.

References

Agarwal, B. (1989). Rural Women, Poverty and Natural Resources: Sustenance, Sustainability and Struggle for Change, Economic and Political Weekly 24(43), 46–65.

Agarwal, B. (1997). "The Gender and Environment Debate: Lessons from India". In Visvanathan, N., Duggan, L., Nisonoff, L. and Wiegersma, N. (Eds.), *The Women, Gender and Development reader*. London and Atlantic Highlands, NJ: Zed Books.

Aikio, I.-M. (1998). "I Write to Get Loads Off My Chest". In Helander, E. and Kailo, K. (Eds.), *No Beginning, No End. The Sami Speak Up*. Edmonton: Canadian Circumpolar Institute/Nordic Sami Institute.

Braidotti, R., Charkiewicz, E. Häusler, S. and Wieringa, S. (1997). "Women, the Environment and Sustainable Development". In Visvanathan, N., Duggan, L., Nisonoff, L. and Wiegersma, N. (Eds.), *The Women, Gender and Development Reader*. London and Atlantic Highlands, NJ: Zed Books.

Brennan, A. and Yeuk-Sze Lo (2021). "Environmental Ethics". In Zalta, E. N. (Ed.), *The Stanford Encyclopedia of Philosophy* (Winter 2021 Edition). Stanford University. URL: https://plato.stanford.edu/entries/ethics-environmental/ (last accessed 18 November 2022).

Delormier, T., Horn-Miller, K., McComber, A. M. and Marquis, K. (2018). "Reclaiming Food Security in the Mohawk Community of Kahnawà:ke through Haudeenosaunee Responsibilities". *Material and Child Nutrition*, Supplement S3, 13. DOI: 10.1111/mcn.12556.

Eikjok, J. (1992). "The Situation of Men and Women in the Reindeerheding Society". *Diehtogiisá* 1, 7–8.

Fuchs, Victor (1988). *Women's Quest for Economic Equality*. Cambridge, MA: Harvard University Press.

Green, J. (2001). "Canaries in the Mines of Citizenship: Indian Women in Canada". *Canadian Journal of Political Science* 34(4), 715–738.

Green, J. (Ed.) (2007). *Making Space for Indigenous Feminism*. Manitoba: Fernwood.

Kahaleole Hall, L. (2009). "Navigating Our Own 'Sea of Islands'. Remapping a Theoretical Space for Hawaiian Women and Indigenous Feminism". *Wicazo Sa Review* 24(2), 15–38.

Knauss, S. (2018). "Conceptualizing Human Stewardship in the Anthropocene: The Rights of Nature in Ecuador, New Zealand and India". *Journal of Agricultural and Environmental Ethics* 31, 703–722.

Kuokkanen, R. (2007). "Myth and Realities of Sami Women: A Post-colonial Feminist Analysis for the Decolonization and Transformation of Sami Society". In Green, J. (Ed.), *Making Space for Indigenous Feminism*. Manitoba: Fernwood Publishing.

LaRoche, E. (1996). "The Colonization of a Native Woman Scholar". In Miller, C., Churchryk, P., Marule, M. S., Manyfingers, B. and Deering, C. (Eds.), *Women of the First Nation: Power, Wisdom and Strength*. Winnipeg: University of Manitoba Press.

Lukkari, R. M. (1998). "Where Did the Laughter Go?" In Helander, E. and Kailo, K. (Eds.), *No Beginning, No End. The Sami Speak Up*. Edmonton: Canadian Circumpolar Institute/Nordic Sami Institute.

Mies, M. (1986). *Patriarchy and Accumulation on a World Scale: Women in the International Division of Labour*. Atlantic Heights, NJ.: Zed Books.

Mill, J.-S. (1988 [1869]). *The Subjection of Women*. Indianapolis, IN: Hackett.

Nussbaum, M. C. (1997). "Kant and Cosmopolitanism". In Bohman, J. and Lutz-Bachmann, M. (Eds.), *Perpetual Peace: Essays on Kant's Cosmopolitan Ideal*. Cambridge, MA: MIT Press, 25–57.

Nzegwu, N. (1995). "Recovering Igbo Traditions: A Case for Indigenous Women's Organizations". In Glover, J. and Nussbaum, M. C. (Eds.), *Women, Culture, and Development: A Study of Human Capabilities.* Oxford: Oxford University Press, 444–466.

Okin, S. M. (1989). *Justice, Gender, and the Family.* New York: Basic Books.

Okin, S. M. (1995). "Inequalities between the Sexes in Different Cultural Contexts". In Nussbaum, M. C. and Glover, J. (Eds.), *Women, Culture, and Development: A Study of Human Capabilities.* Oxford: Oxford University Press, 274–297. DOI: 10.1093/0198289642.003.0012.

Rogers, B. (1980). *The Domestication of Women: Discrimination in Developing Societies.* London: Kogan Page.

Sen, A. (1995). "Gender Inequality and Theories of Justice". In Glover, J. and Nussbaum, M. C. (Eds.), *Women, Culture, and Development: A Study of Human Capabilities.* Oxford: Oxford University Press, 259–273.

Shiva, V. (1989). Staying alive, London: Zed Books.

Shiva, V. (1997). "Women in Nature". In Visvanathan, N., Duggan, L., Nisonoff, L. and Wiegersma, N. (Eds.), *The Women, Gender, and Development Reader.* London and Atlantic Highlands, NJ: Zed Books.

Smith, L. T. (1999). *Decolonizing Methodologies. Research and Indigenous People.* London: Zed Books.

UN Women (2021). "Status of Women". United Nations Secretariat, New York, NY. URL: https://www.unwomen.org/en/about-us/about-un-women (last accessed 15 November 2021).

Visvanathan, N., Duggan, L., Nisonoff, L. and Wiegersma, N. (Eds.) (1997). The Women, Gender, and Development Reader. London and Atlantic Highlands, NJ: Zed Books.

Emma Baizabal
From Cyberfeminism and Technofeminism to an Ontological and Feminist Technology

Abstract: In this essay, I analyze some of the relationships that have been historically articulated between feminisms and technologies – specifically, the positions of cyberfeminism and technofeminism. I am interested in recognizing some of the instrumentalist and political assumptions about technology, where technology is understood in the sense of particular and discrete objects that have a specific political use, namely, to enslave or liberate. I articulate a critique of these assumptions from an ontological view of technology, which attends to the becoming of technical objects, recognizing in them their technological potencies and what this implies for a political, specifically feminist perspective.

Introduction

Every time we talk about technology we refer to categories such as instruments, tools, machines, etc., as if they were synonymous. Even in sociological and some philosophical discourses, technology is always thought as an aggregate of modern production of objects, inscribed in the big technoscience picture. The brief and Eurocentric history of philosophy of technology is outlined in an unbending antagonism between technophobes and technophiles. The former characterize technology as the main reason of alienation, loss of experience and mystification of life, as well as the mechanization of the body, territory, nature; in short, technology is equated with capitalism. The latter, on the other hand, deem technology as the dogmatic dream of freedom, emancipation, progress and an utopian future. This view of technology is also possible due to capitalism, but in a good-spirited nature.

Both approximations to the issue have some problems: 1) their starting point is a colonialist, masculinist bias characteristic of the state of production in the Global North, as if this were the only form of technological production. 2) the understanding of technology is reduced to dealing with specific objects produced from the industrial revolution onwards, which are also reduced to the category of utilities; as well as to the idea of means to an end. This can be encompassed in an instrumentalist notion were technology can only be enslaving or emancipatory and dependent of the good use or bad use of individuals. 3) they displace the problem of these instruments to the ideology that produces them as a particular form (capitalist, extractivist, dominant) that encloses them.

https://doi.org/10.1515/9783111051802-012

Cyber-techno-feminist Lineage

In order to confront these matters, several feminist theorists have done critical contributions about the epistemic and political conditions from which technical production unfolds. Whether it concerns the modification of life, bodily experience, in real or digital life, the relationship with nature and biology or the production of subjectivity of the gender named woman, technology, qua objects of interaction, has been intertwined with feminist concerns since well into the 70s. While it is possible to follow the interwoven thread of the feminist's waves of evolution and the transformations and bifurcations of the various critiques of technology, in order to understand how these movements and theories have affected each other, the interest of this paper is more modest. Here, I would like to map some of the ways in which these contributions have been made in order to recognize some implications bordering on the notion of technology itself.

It is well known that among socialist feminists, for example, the relations between women and technology runs through the acknowledgment of reproductive work, their role in the workplace and care work. Shulamith Firestone is one of the pioneer thinkers whose famous claim about the potential of modern technology, specifically embryology, to "freeing women from the tyranny of their reproductive biology" (Firestone 2003, 185) still resonates every time we deal with the problem of conceiving a feminist oriented technology. It is possible, however, that this condition of freedom or emancipation that wants to be imbued in technology is determined, as every well socialistic position, by the faith in the scientific knowledge of which technical objects are normally understood as an apex. According to Sarah Franklin, the reading of technology from Firestone runs through a dialectical perspective, where the interaction is understood not only between the abstract entities "society" and "technology" but even more between the internal tensions of each of these spheres (Franklin 2010, 33). This means that this vision of technology brings with itself the solution of every problem, as long as it is on the side of a just cause. What in today's rampant capitalism we would call the other end of the scale: cybernetic socialism, is undoubtedly one of the bets from which this type of proposal is nourished (Medina 2014; Paasonen 2010). Firestone's critique of the heteronormative, *bourgeois* family form tends to want to naturalize the use of reproductive technologies in order to deal with a biology contested by generic conformity (Lewis 2019, 16). This could be considered naïve in principle, precisely because it is increasingly evident that every technical solution that claims to be definitive brings with it a tensional movement. But it is also a reflection of the inauguration of a conflict that occurs in the political sphere between the difference between nature and culture or sex and gender. The conflict between nature and technique continues to object to the paradigm of feminisms that go through technology to create more critical exercises.

Donna Haraway's work as we all know is the paradigm from which many of the critiques of the nature-culture divide, from the 1990s to date, originate. The cyborg, or the material semiotic machine embody this relationship between nature and culture and the complexity of the relationship to the point of questioning both fervent optimism and constricting fear, are undoubtedly one of the richest conceptual experiences that have been the legacy of the articulated dimension between technology and feminisms. It is true that the cyborg imaginary has often been confused with the organology of an externalization mechanic capacity, reaching the prosthetic extreme as a symbol of its technical constitution, especially among those posthuman researches that took the cyborg metaphor not so much as a metaphor but as a material experiment over the body (Wolfe 2010). Nonetheless, and even away from the big shift that came to turn the *Cyborg Manifesto* (2004) into a more radical and surrounding *Companion species manifesto* (2003), the cyborg figurine takes into consideration not only the disembodied industrial production that connects a certain socialist feminism, *ad hoc* with the old command to take over the means of production to achieve the expectation of emancipation, but mainly the experience of the bodies that are traversed in the mechanisms of production both technical and knowledge (Haraway 1988).

This is an inheritance that takes into account technology not only understood as particular objects of production, as tools and implements that would have to have certain dispositions in order to be used in an emancipatory way to redeem the enslaving uses. Rather, it is a technology that considers the symbolic, linguistic and knowledge framework of its own production. This is not, contrary to what one would like to think, a mere constructivism, but a kind of synthesis that seeks to question technology from its institutional models, a technology much closer to the mechanisms of production in which situated experiences take place.

The cyberfeminisms of the 90s were born out of this concern and cover a wide spectrum of digital arts and practices, from representation and participation of the feminized bodies in digital spaces to the question about the makeup of these same bodies/practices in such spaces. We all are only too familiar with the pioneer collective VNS Matrix and the Old Boys Network's 100 anti-theses, from whom the new network technologies enable inexperienced forms of resistance that nowadays we find customary. With a reminiscence of the imaginaries of the cyborg farther away from the maquila and closer to the metaverses these experiences have traced a broad path for the expectation of art and technology in the feminist conceptions of a digital world.

The importance of digital spaces in these practices is that they are understood not as alien to day-to-day practices but as an extension that, in many instances, emancipates the inventive potential from recodification, reclaiming economic and artistic spaces (Plant 2020, 326). In these eccentric imaginaries, what is being sought is plasticity to catalyze experimental identities, even performative ones. An exacerbation of the modes of representation that still cannot come to terms with the political expectations of the collective autodetermination (Wajcman 2006). This is, at least, one of the criticisms that people want to make from the most contemporary fronts, forgetting that art, and even more so digital art, is also a space of dispute for subjects who are not identified in the social and political framework as techno-savvy men (Avanessian and Hester 2015).

Today, some of the cyberfeminist approaches from Latin-American contexts are more preoccupied by the political potency of the internet understood as the field of everyday battles against violence against women and girls. To this appropriation of the theories that came from the Global North, the most important things to elaborate on are mainly a critique of access to technology and the security of digital spaces (Torrano and Fischetti 2020, 62–63.)

Closer to Haraway than I would like to admit, and further away from the conceptions of technology that subscribe to the digital realm, are the contributions of Judy Wajcman who has developed an important analysis regarding the specific relations between gender and technology that picks those contributions and critiques of radical feminism that center around sexed bodies and the exercise of women's sexuality, as well as the reproductive condition attached to women's gender. This author's technofeminist proposal is based on a constructivist viewpoint of technology that recognizes the double implication and co-creation between technological materiality, understood as a network of artifacts, institutions, organizations, etc., and gender, where the relation between production/design and use/consumption is not only intimate but has to be de-constructed (Wacjman 2009). The most important distinction to be made regarding this emphasis in the prefix of techno, unlike the prefix cyber, reveals the amplification of the notion of technology. Although she declares herself an open constructivist – which for her means nothing other than that technology is not seen as an immovable monolith but also depends on valorization and cultural discourses – her amplification of technology seems to be situated only in relation to generic construction. This also places it much closer to those radical feminists for which the real axis of oppression is to be found in gender identification.

Another contemporary theoretical development, for example among xenofeminists (Laboria Cuboniks 2017) has followed a strand of analysis of technology that leads to the participation of the production of a "better quality of life" for everyone, where the gender term "women" wouldn't be a problem. In fact, this position collects and amplifies the positive appreciations of technology stemming from the socialist currents briefly outlined above, and positions itself as some political engaged extrapolation of the most experimental cyberfemism that yearns to avoid the techno-utopian ingenuity anchored to the decorporeization located on the internet.

The 2014 collective "Laboratoria Cuboniks" has made this interpretation of technology possible, which is embraced by philosophers like Lusiana Parisi (2017, 140) who seeks in this scaffolding document a facilitator of speculation. This manifest, refreshing as it is, engages with left accelerationism who actually proclaimed itself a techno-utopianism that assumes acceleration to be an emancipatory power in itself (Avanessian and Hester 2015, 12).

Even though these proposals center around the acceleration of technical production to achieve destruction of everything, even gender, this recourse seems more akin to a political provocation than a strong theoretical proposal, since it's never quite clear what "acceleration" means, to the point of remaining a technophile hope for the future.

In this version of the rapport between feminism and technology the most important criteria are to go beyond the differentiation of nature and culture, even regarding biology and gender, further beyond the obliteration of nature by technology. The final expression that claims "If nature is unjust, change nature" (Laboria Cuboniks 2017, 161) is an expression seeking for the maximal confrontation.

If Wacjman's technofeminism focused on how gender acts in the sociotechnical process where the materiality of technology propitiates or inhibits the action of subjects entangled in gendered power relations, the expanded technofeminism of xenofeminism seeks to emphasize the agency of subjects not only regardless of their gender, but against any generic hierarchy produced that displaces the exercise of power both in the design and in the circulation, distribution, use and appropriation of technology.

Especially in Latin-American contexts, hackfeminisms have strong mobilizations on the side of access, appropriation and re-writing of technical resources such as algorithms, protocols and servers. Irene Soria is one of the many researchers in Latin America who have been concerned with giving critical visibility to all these strategies that concentrate their efforts on revitalizing the figure of the hacker from the exercise of self-determination of the "raw material" of new technologies: computer programming, to the way in which bodies, territories and subjects are imbricated (Soria 2016, 16). Special attention is deserved by the multiplication of local servers, the amplification of digital communities which main concerns are collective learning, self-defense and digital autonomy. The Red de Telefonía Celular Comunitaria (Cellphone Communitary Network) from Oaxaca, Mexico is the paradigmatic example of how indigenous and community efforts can be put together to bring to the communities themselves services that are monopolized by private enterprises and where the role of the state continues to be another mechanism for justifying expropriation.

Be it democratizing the access to the internet, foster the reproduction of devices that emancipate women from domestic labor or even the old dream, now a nightmare, of assisted conception, many of the proposals layed out are founded on the instrumentalist approach that conceives technology as the industrial production of discrete objects that serve as the emancipation of a particular political subject: women. Many of these criticisms start from a very clear critique of the complete political identity to which they intend to subsume the conditions of technical production so that, finally, the technical still seems the unthinkable outside the margins of the anticipated political decision.

Prior to this mapping of relations between feminisms and feminizations as appropriations of technology that seek to rewrite it – from the more specific production as the code, to the more abstract but structural condition as the institutions of knowledge –, some questions arise: is it enough to change the condition of "enslavement" of technology to that of "emancipation" to favor other technical dynamics? Is the feminist characterization enough for another type of technical production? These questions point to a transformation in the way of approaching the relations between technology and gender, women and feminism frameworks, where the question of the political power of technology takes a 180-degree turn towards the question of technological power itself: a question that pays special attention to the modes of development of the technical, that allows technology to become an ontological category rather than remaining a general concept that encompasses various instruments.

Technicity and Technology: A New Invention

In what follows I would like to bring back the reconceptualization of technology developed by Gilbert Simondon in order to think alternatives to our relation to technical objects. What is of interest to us regarding this conception is that it is entangled to the process of individuation and individualization, e. g., the modal condition through which the real becomes real (Simondon 2014, 20–25). This is not the old problem of the being and how being splits. I assume that all beings have a load of being that doesn't exhaust its possibilities, e. g., an excess from where new potencies emanate. Individuation is precisely the process where what is "becomes" in its modality. When Simondon asks about the particular ways in which the technical realizes itself, the answer is a process of technicity that, in general, is a process of concretization of technical objects (Simondon 2007, 90). The question of technicity is the answer to the question of the technical as such. Where Heidegger (2007) thought that the essence of techné wasn't technical, e. g., where the essence of modern techné had to be sought in the way techné was a modal condition of being in its unfolding to the human, Simondon turns the screw. The essence of techné is properly technical: it resides in the way of proceeding of the unfolding of the technical-real, e. g., technical objects.

What looks like an engineerism that goes through the processes of production of tools, machines and assemblages is actually a philosophical reconceptualization of the problem of the technical. We then start to talk about technical objects not as particular objects (that include even institutions and organizations), but in the sense of a complex network of operatory and functional relations that produce individuals and assemblages. The technical object, a set of schemas of function and structure, is not the result of a design choice; it is a process that is constantly changing, a process of concretization where the human participates only as a crystalized gesture (Simondon 2007). To discover such a process as the proper realm of the unfolding of the technical is technology itself. Technology such understood goes from the particulars built in the industrial revolution until today towards a process of philosophical thinking that encounters the technical in itself (Simondon 2017, 237).

This theoretical approach does not feed from the accelerationist utopia that finds its root in technocratic aspiration, and neither does the image of the cyborg, with its contemporary iteration found in the transhumanist paraphernalia: problematic approaches, for they forget about the technical production in an operative sense and end up making up a robotic ideal with the biases of a humanism that disowns itself. The potency of the technical does not come from the emancipatory mode in which technical objects can be used. I'd say, with Stiegler (2020), that all technique is a *pharmakon* that can be both venom and antidote; yet its potency is not in either side, but in the concretizing act revealed by the technical process as its operation: invention.

In the same way, when talking about bodies, as in women's bodies or feminized bodies, it's not about biology, but about operatory structures that organize and reorganize, that form meanings and produce sense. When speaking about technical potency of the bodies I don't mean to diverge on the waters of the human's prosthetic condition, whose technical inflection centers around an extended biology. With this idea we look to displace the problem of the subject's determination with a stable, clear and distinct identity, for example, woman. Contrary to this resolve, grounded in an abstract political subject or a particular individual in the fashion of neoliberal marketing, technical inventiveness is the germ that triggers collective individualization.

For Simondon, the concept of invention refers to "the emergence of the extrinsic compatibility between medium and organism, and the intrinsic compatibility between the subsets of the act" (Simondon 2013, 158, Translation EB). This means invention can be understood as a produced object that mediates relations but also, and more importantly, as an act that allows the creation and modification of them. The inventive act is a catalytic activity of movement that produces not only objects but new ways of inhabiting life. The relevancy of every inventive act is the effect it produces, not only in regard to its results or object but in the operation itself on which it relies, on which it is founded and from which it derives its structures. "The Invention is induced by a necessity of internal compatibility effectuated and expressed in the organized system that includes as subset of the living being through which it advents" (Simondon 2013, 210, Translation EB). Every inventive operation, in its technical sense, is a modification or creation of a structure. While it refers to heterogeneous mediations, it also has a functional place among different orders and as such allows the subject's action to take place. We insist that such invention does not only refer to the practical use which serves to solve a problem, but the act that expresses and leads to life (Simondon 2017, 303–318) – the construction of a relational realm. In this sense, more than a spontaneous activity, it's about a creative dynamism that emerges in the directed interaction of bodies to the resolution of a conflict or tension: what I've referred to as "operation".

This concept of invention is not the same as innovation, nor does it stand in relation to productive intentionality but with psico-social individuation, or with the transinidividual, to call it as Simondon does: the complex and systemic unit that exceeds the individual and at the same time interiorizes it: the collective formation (Simondon 2014, 360). If innovation finds itself on the side of production, as an intentional idealization that has its end in the object market, the conceptual force of invention, understood as a re-structuring operation that solves a conflict, lies in its technical and political thrust. The operation enhances new models of relational conformation both inside technical production itself as well as in the political organization with others, understood not as separate realms but in their real and practical intertwining. It isn't an amalgamation of cybernetic dreams between the biological and the technical or artificial, but an operatory analogy that inspires us to think other ways of acting together.

To Keep Thinking

Thus, a technological attitude centered around inventive activity implies the acknowledgment of operative potentialities that can promote other symbolic and bodily exchanges, e. g., a production in terms of individuation instead of creation. It's all about a new ontology in a sense that is not centered around the differences among beings, but an ontology of becoming that materializes along an ontogenetic process where the technological potential remains as an operatory unfolding. Such generated action is not lead by an effervescence lacking control of any virtuality, but it tends to functional registers and possible restructurings. Technical invention is a political ontology and insofar an activity that expresses life, produces sense. What we want to keep focusing on with this approach is the possibility of the invention of a technological potency of politics. That we can recall technology in its own terms with a dialogue from the feminist perspectives in its dimensional diversity. This requires not just one type of techno or cyber feminism but an ontology that keeps in mind that there are, as well as the human individuals, technical individuals and others that enable different alliances.

References

Avanessian, A. and Hester, H. (Eds.) (2015). *Dea ex machina.* Berlin: Merve.
Firestone, S. (2003). *Dialectics of Sex.* New York: Farrar, Straus and Giroux.
Franklin, S. (2010). "Revisiting Reprotech: Shulamith Firestone and the Question of Technology". In Merck, M. and Sandford, S. (Eds.), *The Further Adventures of the Dialectic of Sex.* London: Palgrave Macmillan, 29–60.
Haraway, D. (1988). "Situated Knowledge. The Science Question in Feminism and the Privilege of Partial Perspective". *Feminist Studies* 14(3), 575–599.
Haraway, D. (2003). *The Companion Species Manifesto: Dogs, People, and Significant Otherness.* Chicago: Prickly Paradigm Press.
Haraway, D. (2004). "A Manifesto for Cyborgs: Science, Technology and Socialist Feminism in the 1980s". In Haraway, D., *The Haraway Reader.* New York: Routledge, 7–46.
Heidegger, M. (2007). "La pregunta por la técnica in Soler". In Soler, F. and Acevedo, J. (Eds.), *Martin Heidegger. Filosofía, ciencia y técnica.* Santiago de Chile: Editorial Universitaria.
Laboria Cuboniks (2017). "Xenofeminism: A Politics for Alienation". In Gunkel, H., Hameed, A. and O'Sullivan, S. (Eds.), *Futures and Fictions.* London: Repeater, 152–161.
Lewis, S. (2019). *Full Surrogacy Now. Feminism against Family.* London: Verso.
Medina, E. (2014). *Cybernetic Revolutionaries: Technology and Politics in Allende's Chile.* Cambridge, MA: MIT Press.
Paasonen, S. (2010). "From Cybernation to Feminization: Firestone and Cyberfeminism". In Merck, M. and Sandford, S. (Eds.), *The Further Adventures of the Dialectic of Sex.* London: Palgrave Macmillan, 61–83.
Parisi, L. (2017). "Automate Sex: Xenofeminism, Hyperstition and Alienation". In Gunkel, H., Hameed, A. and O'Sullivan, S. (Eds.), *Futures and Fictions.* London: Repeater, 152–161.
Plant, S. (2020). "On the Matrix: Cyberfeminis Simulations". In Thomas, T. and Wishermann, U. (Eds.), *Feminist Theory and Critical Media Culture Analysis. Starting Points and Perspectives.* Bielefeld: Trascript, 325–336.
Simondon, G. (2007). *El modo de existencia de los objetos técnicos.* Buenos Aires: Cactus.
Simondon, G. (2013). *Imaginación e invención.* Buenos Aires: Cactus.

Simondon, G. (2014). *La individuación a la luz de las nociones de forma e información.* Buenos Aires: Cactus.
Simondon, G. (2017). *Sobre la técnica.* Buenos Aires: Cactus.
Soria, I. (Ed.) (2016). *Ética Hacker, seguridad y vigilancia.* Mexico: Universidad del Claustro de Sor Juana.
Stiegler, B. (2020). "Elements for a General Organology". DOI: 10.3366/drt.2020.0220.
Torrano, A. and Fischetti, N. (2020). "Feminist Philosophy of Technics and Technology. Notes for an Activist Latin American Academy". DOI: 10.26694/pensando.v11i23.11058.
Vergés Borsch, N. (2013). "Teorías feministas de la tecnología: evolución y principales debates". Digital Repository University of Barcelona URL: http://diposit.ub.edu/dspace/handle/2445/45624 (last accessed 03 January 2023).
Wacjman, J. (2006). *Technofeminism.* Cambridge: Polity Press.
Wacjman, J. (2009). "Feminist Theories of Technology". DOI: 10.1093/cje/ben057.
Wolfe, C. (2010). *What Is Posthumanism?* Minneapolis: University of Minnesota Press.

Ruth Edith Hagengruber

The Third Knowledge Dimension: From a Binary System to a Three-limbed Epistemology

Abstract: The thesis of this paper is that a new kind of epistemology evolves from the use of artificial intelligence. The path it takes changes our understanding of the world, of human values and also of science and will be irreversible. The question that arises is whether this form of intelligence also influences our knowledge structure. By this I mean the area that we outline philosophically as the epistemological area. So the question is, under these circumstances, is the way we gain knowledge today still comparable to the definitions that philosophy has provided us with for centuries? The answer is: No! The paper sketches in broad outlines what the cornerstones of change will be and what consequences this will have for our way of understanding.

Introduction

Artificial intelligence is everywhere. Many things in our daily life, most of what we know and what we do is either accompanied or supported or provided by it. It has become a part of our daily life, in the house, in the working place, in leisure time, not to speak of scientific insight, economic trade and development and last but not least for medical need and support. Many areas would not exist as they do today without it. Trade and transport, supply and maintenance, technology and effortless living, administration, institutions, depend on it to a high degree. Behind most processes are real processes. We have analyzed, transported, managed, even without this artificial intelligence support. How does it change these processes, how does it change our perception of life?

The question that arises is whether this form of intelligence also influences our knowledge structure. By this I mean the area that we outline philosophically as the epistemological area. Is the way we gain knowledge today still comparable to the definitions that philosophy has provided us with for centuries? The answer given in this paper is: No! The reason given for this is that, firstly, the binary organization of knowledge as it is built up from Aristotelian ontology has proved to be deficient in many regards, though it is established as the most powerful knowledge organization we use, also in the machines we are talking about here. Secondly, there have always been alternatives to epistemological framing, other than the Aristotelian kind of building knowledge ontologies. The Platonic-maieutic technique for generating knowledge is one; further attempts were made in Renaissance philosophy. These different kinds and alternatives are briefly addressed here, in order to demonstrate the need for a present-day recapitulation of our categorical approach to the ordering of knowledge in the world.

These alternative concepts of knowledge today give clues as to how we can design a world of knowledge that organizes the construction of knowledge in a far more dynamic way. What is presented here as the third dimension of knowledge, means nothing other than the need to catch up with the knowledge production of artificial intelligence in our epistemic coordinate system.

Aristotle and the End of Anthropocentric Epistemology?

So far, our culture praised itself and did not have any doubts that anthropocentric dominance is the determining force of our reality, its description, its definition, its development. Such a perspective has been justified mostly with a reference to the Bible and religion that made man think to be a partly nature partly godly entity, part of nature, part of heaven, who determines "to on", that, what is; as Aristotle describes this in his first chapter of his *Politics*.

This perspective finds its exemplarily illustration in Aristotle's ontology. It corresponds well to a hierarchical anthropocentric edifice of thought, not to say it has created the kind of hierarchy. From there it impacted the structure of our knowledge world and still does. Exemplified in its concept of knowledge as the dominion of the man of reason, also drafted in the Aristotelian Book One of his *Politics*. The rational man is the thinker and ruler; slaves, women and children are subject to him. He rules the house, its inhabitants and orders the polis in foresight. To his rational order corresponds the order of knowledge that captures the essence of things in what it is according to this knowledge system. What ever is, is described as the defined container of knowledge, a part of the ordered variety of objects in the world in their linguistic description. The variety of possible connections between them is forced into an order that we can manage logically. It determines the telos and function of the things in the world and how we organize it.

The Aristotelian structure of knowledge ordering impacted the Western tradition, it formed our knowledge system and as well and in consequence also our social system. Both were squeezed into an ontology of hierarchies of knowledge and dominion, subjected to the white man's power of what he defined to be "reason". There was a man, a wife and a slave, a house and a community and all this formed the bricks of the "boxes" that gained their essential meaning by being "part of" a function-driven hierarchy. This system of boxes was applied to communities, countries, and science. For centuries, it formed the basic of the European ontology and knowledge system.

As powerful as this ontology proved to be, it had its limits. There is no ontological skeleton that could deliver the backbones of reality. There is no access to an independent metaphysical framing, though up to today the aim of an "objective" framing through ontologies remains an ideal.[1]

There is an underlying metaphysical strive to grasp the Archimedean point beyond the world to allow its determination and mastery of the multiplicity of objects. Since Aristotle, this has been the white man's perspective. Its claims have long been critically reflected by feminist work, but its validity in the scientific realm seems to remain unchallenged.

The Limits of Our Knowledge World

Luciano Floridi reflects on the Aristotelian knowledge structure as a Lego-like system of which it would be a mistake if its application were continued as one that moves within the frames of a fixed structure. Built up like a building-block system, of which we have excellent command (Floridi 2020, 311). Floridi's critique of the Aristotelian primordial philosophy of things is extended to the Newtonian conception of space, as it expresses the sectoral one-dimensionality in which our thinking is trained today, as he holds (Floridi 2020, 313).

Even space and time in this tradition, and this history are according to Floridi rigid frames of reference; "containers" that tend towards an ideal final stability. Floridi even analogizes the lack of dynamism of this structure with the fascist tendencies to define a habitat: "Imagine a big box, a room, in which the person-building blocks interact in a linear and irreversible way along the arrow of time." He employs an analogy to the fascist concept of the "spazio vitale" and the National Socialist concept of "Lebensraum", both as ideological derailments of this primor-

---

[1] "To be widely accepted an ontology must be neutral as between different data communities, and there is, as experience has shown, a formidable trade-off between this constraint of neutrality and the requirement that an ontology be maximally wide-ranging and expressively powerful – that it should contain canonical definitions for the largest possible number of terms. One solution to this trade-off problem is a top-level ontology, which would confine itself to the specification of such highly general (domain-independent) categories as: time, space, inherence, instantiation, identity, measure, quantity, functional dependence, process, event, attribute, boundary, and so on" (Smith 2003, 159).

dial Newtonian philosophy of physical space as a geographical territory where the physical time is a calendar (Floridi 2020, 313). "In other words, the Aristotelian-Newtonian Ur-philo-sophy is natural, intuitive, familiar, does not easily show its limits, and has worked in the past. The alternative is untested, counter-intuitive, unfamiliar, it is not how we conceptualize the world and our societies in it" (Floridi 2020, 314). Floridi's radical reduction is underpinned with his reference to a quote from Margret Thatcher. She denies, he says that there is a phenomenon like "society", beyond the "bricks" of individuals, families, and so forth. These supposedly definite building blocks of knowledge organization, is however, according to Floridi arbitrary. He asks, where does something like a "family" end? Are the lines as clear as those Aristotelian-trained action makers in our society think it to be? Society is not a Lego system and Newtonian physics comes to its end when it should make us understand subatomic realms. We are struggling to find a new scientific system and we need new categories to grasp the new order of our world. Floridi assumes to find it with Ernst Cassirer (1923). He suggests to replace the concept of *substance* with that of *function*, as Cassirer did, with a function in the mathematical sense, as an unambiguous relation defined to describe a change and thus, not to grasp an entity, but a relation by which all things are connected with one another.[2] Thus, Floridi holds, changes the implicit operating model, which is no longer that of the Aristotelian-Newtonian mechanism, rather rigid and restrictive, but that of the force field or relational network, much more flexible, inclusive, and unbounded.

> Social relations tend to be intertwined and continuous, with varying degrees of intensity, from weak to strong. In our example, we may be better off by speaking of Italian citizens who have relations with French citizens and vice versa in a variety of ways, i. e. relations that are more or less intensive, superficial, fruit-ful, frequent etc. As a consequence, in a "relation-oriented" and not "thing-or-iented" policy, it is no longer the quantifiable amount of "performance" of things that is the main parameter of evaluation, but the degree of solidity and resilience of the relations that constitute things and bind them together, citizens included. (Floridi 2020, 316)

---

[2] Floridi explains the relation thus: "Here, 'relation' is to be understood in the logico-mathematical sense, as anything that qualifies every thing – human, natural, artificial – individually (e. g. Alice is unmarried, which is a unary relation) or not individually (e. g. Alice and Bob are married, which is a binary relation; or Carol is sitting between Alice and Bob, which is a ternary relation; and so forth for any n-ary relation)" (Floridi 2020, 315 note 6).

Emerging Knowledge – Different Approaches in History

For a long time, philosophy has worked with the Aristotelian ontological scheme and Floridi is not the first to point out these shortcomings of the Aristotelian conception of knowledge. It is criticized from an intercultural and feminist perspective, it is also criticized for its rigid character. Renaissance philosophers criticized the Aristotelian ontology and successfully changed the path of science in the period. It was one of the most eloquent and also effective forms of critique regarding to its outcome. The critique of Aristotle's rigid knowledge structure gave rise to the new worldview of modernity. This critique broadened the horizon considerably and moved the man and the earth out of the centre. The Platonic concept of *emerging* knowledge has, of course, always been an alternative to Aristotle rigid epistemology. Aristotle's concept precisely rebut this fluid knowledge conception. Moreover, Plato pretends a self-productive conception of knowledge. He describes a self-generating access to knowledge for all, men, women, slaves, children. In the *Symposium*, Diotima teaches Socrates and criticizes his rigid and object fixed knowledge access. This dialogue can well be referred to in order to understand why this kind of "Lego-like" structures knowledge shall be rebuked, as it does not give space to knowledge growth. What the Diotima figure is telling the young Socrates is that there are no things, but everything we refer to is a relation for which we go. This difference in understanding the object as something of becoming and being in relation to whatever is given with it changes the access to knowledge and he condition of its availability, which is always and only partly and singular in regard to something or someone.

Knowledge thus appears only as an emerging process of knowledge gain. There is always something that must be overcome; it only serves as a basic for further striving to relate the difference by letting something new out of this process. Entities emerge to overcome difference. This kind of dialectic relational thought inspired many Renaissance thinkers, males and females. It is still a widely unknown tradition of women's contribution to the metaphysics of love in the period.

The Aristotelian relation of understanding presents an observer and the observed. In the Renaissance period it had been criticized as not sufficient to explain the things in the world. To some extent, philosophers in the Renaissance have been interested in inventing knowledge and providing alternative techniques to collect knowledge, instead of relying on the "given". The knowledge of the universe was created, for example in Giulio Camillo's memory theater or in the combinatorial "wheels" of Giordano Bruno, who sought to make new connections and knowledge about the world accessible from supposedly non-arbitrary essences and categories

(Hagengruber 2007). Another influential thinker of the period, the long-time prisoner Tommaso Campanella invented with his Utopia *Civitas Solis* another theater of memory that simultaneously demonstrated how to organize the *scientia scientiarum*, where all kinds of knowledge are brought together and new knowledge emerged. The highlight of the machines he presents is that they do not consume any energy. He thus already thinks the innovative in the metaphysical context of a materialistic conservatio. He gives some examples of rain and water and wind machines. The highlight of the machines he presents is that they do not consume any energy. He thus already thinks the innovative in the metaphysical context of a materialistic conservatio. Campanella's "machines" were based on a third element that he had described in his book, titled "Il senso delle Cose e della Magia", later developed further in his metaphysics and historically successfully visualized his idea in his utopia. Following the metaphysical and materialistic claim that things are related to each other, but as a whole sustain itself, the crucial idea is to gain the knowledge of how to realize this "conservation" by combining the right matter for the best effect. There is no nothing; everything is something. Nothing should be lost, everything should be put in the place where it is of greatest use, using its specific relation. This philosophy aims at gaining the utmost relational knowledge of all particularities in their relation, presupposing that there is a kind of stable essence, matter, that forms the variety and that inspires the innovation of relation. An infinite knowledge growth about how to use the relevant matter makes life ever more pleasant. People become two-hundred years old and live healthy and happy, according to their knowledge about these relations. The Utopians do not absorb energy nor do they exploit nature as everything is what it is in its relatedness. People act without consuming energies and return everything they have consumed to the earth which is growing again out from the wast thus preserving the world and all in it. Things, humans, all living and matter is cared for not to be harmed as everything is important in relation to something. Necessary extraction is repaid. A great cycle where knowledge is defined to identify the most specific and fruitful connection for a specific goal, keeps the search running. Exchange of elements is part of this process, as being different secures conservation and the exchange of the different is the process that keeps it going.

Of course, this is a utopia and neither Campanella, nor we today, had the capacities to organize such an immense use of knowledge in such an optimized way. But the ideal was created and presented in that novel. At least, Campanella suffered for its inventive ideas for twenty-eight years in prison.

Remarkable is how he describes a different kind of knowledge process than was presented within the Aristotelian model and it seems that this Renaissance model is closer to how we understand a machine driven epistemology today. Campanella's claim, that everything and everyone measures its world from its own measure is crucial. This specific being guides the exchange of experience and knowledge. Its specifity and sensus is unknown, but to be experienced. It is not rigidly closed or firmly framed, though framed by material condition the entity as an object of knowledge emerges from that process. Campanella calls it "sensus" which leads us to understand the basic relation in the world, the specifity of its connectedness and the riddle of its conservation. Sensus is that which is common to all things, because they thereby enter into a relationship with one another. Campanella's utopia can also be used as an ontological figure for the changes in epistemology brought about by the new technology.

The Third Knowledge Dimension: From a Binary System to a Three-limbed Epistemology

The turn from a part-whole driven ontology to a perspective of things as objects which are no longer solely objects of information but emerging knowledge entities is also taking place in current technology. The critique of the binary epistemology can be met by relating to the tradition of "emerging knowledge" systems to extend the binary scheme of a determining, but narrow framing definition of the binary knowledge system.

There is no Archimedean point of view for humans. Knowledge exists only in being part of a big "infosphere", Floridi claims (Floridi 2014, 24). The new knowledge presented and becoming possible through AI expresses itself in its relationality of dependencies. These cover our expectations to a huge extent. But they also multiply our mistakes. AI today is a data fed system that mirrors knowledge conditions, prejudices and in general limited knowledge, it is evidently not open to experience. It still acts within the brickstone-like system of knowledge, framed, rigid and often also wrong and unreliable.

A first step towards a new epistemology, to overcome the binary system as determining and not sufficient, could however be thought of by the support of AI. While the human is the cause of AI's capacities and deficiency, namely forming and shaping an insufficiently and limited picture of the world, the machine driven knowledge could be used to enhance our understanding and to support the growth of knowledge if it was freed from a certain framing. The human being is not the exclusive determinant of knowledge. Every cat, every tree, every living being is a such and our ontology must be understood that way. Everything is nested in its world according to its abilities and survival relations. Most of these conditions of its nestedness are still completely unknown to us. To reflect about this fact is not new; new is however that we might overcome the limitedness thanks to AI. Could an independent knowledge production represent a generation of knowledge?

Machine knowledge transcends us in many ways. What is meant herewith is not that these machines were completely autonomous or producing a different "kind". Of knowledge. On the contrary, these machines depend to a large extent on an Aristotelian ontology. The point to be made is that the knowledge production of these machines surpasses the capacity of human knowledge production. The tasks that will evolve from this fact will lead into a different system of knowledge production, knowledge distribution and knowledge analysis. The epistemic system we are used to, is changing, foremostly because the hereby created knowledge community is no longer limited to humans. Machines analyze and synthesize knowledge. It is not possible to determine the difference between its own analytic combinatoric and its synthetic processes. Layer over layer prevent us to understand as quickly as the machine is able to proceed what the determining categories are. From now on we share our world of (sense-making) entities with our AI machines. It is through this fact that we learn, the binary model of cognition is replaced.

This change in the crucial determinants of the world of knowledge will also have decisive consequences for our social world. And here I am not talking about the changes in the social world, in the sense of a spread between rich and poor, between those who are able to deal with these machines and those who aren't, either not yet or not any more. The point here is rather to understand how the world of the social changes from this altered perspective of knowledge. For by implication, the social processes that are co-determined by this kind of knowledge, that are analysed by it, will be considerably more fluid than is the case today. Thus, one can say, this epistemological liquefaction of the social will prove to be the counterpart to the dreaded hardening and spreading in the ontological realm of the social.

This kind of machine "knowledge" will become a third element in our world explanation system. Just as constant as we and the (natural) world, it will shape our world of knowledge. The knowledge machine is a "child" grown out of our constructive mind and has now part in the formation of our understanding and interpretation of the world. It delivers support, deviance and all that any knowledge actor has ever been delivering. With a decisive difference, or even not: It is widely independent from us. The knowledge content and interpretation serves as a third source of making understandable, of presented connections, relations, sometimes nonsense, sometimes opposed, more often accepted as a plausible argument. It does not always go unchallenged, but it is still a source of knowledge to which we respond. This third element changes our knowledge relation which until then had only existed in two components of which we thought one to be "free", at least partly and another one to be "determined" by natural law. Knowledge machines break this binary scheme. They emerge as a third element that is as productive of knowledge as we are. That provides new insights, just as nature does. Together and separately, we are creating a new dimension of knowledge. What will count as knowledge is confirmed by reciprocal processes between the three elements of which each is able to accept and to reject. The acceptance of machine-produced knowledge depends on the cultural network of knowledge confirmation. It will compete with our understanding of creativity (Hagengruber 2017). According to René Descartes (1596–1650) animals and machines are equal in their inability to think, for him "automated" modes of knowledge were active in both. Turing objected to that view, claiming there is not a difference between machine and human knowledge (Turing 1950, 454). But it is not Turing's intention to prove an act of "thought" when he speaks about the "thinking capacities" of machines. He rebuts Lovelace's argument that machines never will compete with human's creativity and affirms that also the teacher is ignorant of what is going on inside of the learning machine, speaking of students. He was right when he said that "most of the programs which we can put into the machine result in its doing something we cannot make sense of".

Knowledge production of artificial intelligence must be seen as an independent factor of our epistemic world and cannot be reduced to the first two elements, neither to the human understanding nor to the knowledge provider as which we understand nature. It constitutes a *third dimension* of knowledge. Artificial intelligence generates its own dimension of contexts and categorial orders. The dominance of the human subject as the sole producer of knowledge will vanish; while those who will continue to use the AI for their own purpose and aims, subjecting the machine to their will will not find a way out of a limited (Aristotelian) knowledge restriction.[3]

Those who will accept the productivity and analytic creativity of this third knowledge dimension will get a chance to multiply their knowledge of the world and its processes. An epistemology that presents itself three-limbed will lead us into a different world views and open up to new experience. It will anchor us differently in nature and society than before. Algorithmic methods, new ways of knowledge aggregation and changed compositions of knowledge clusters structure knowledge of the world in new ways.

---

[3] See in addition my paper "Die 'dritte Wissensdimension. Eine Epistemologie für eine neue Wissenswelt" (2022). See also "The Third Knowledge Dimension. How AI Changes Epistemology" (Digital Talk at *Ethics and Digitalization* (Hagengruber 2021b).

Feminists have often claimed that binary ontologies determine and narrow our understand of gender and its representation. This new ontology presents itself as an ontology that is not designed from a selective human or male perspective, as it was the Aristotelian one that defined the male and the female for the use of fertility. This was one aspect of life that determined our culture for a long period of time. The task is now to shaping our understanding of the world on the basis of a growing dimension of knowledge which is organized as a triangular epistemology that nests us differently in nature and society.

The turn from a primary hierarchy and function-driven ontology into a primarily knowledge-driven ontology comes along with an ontology that sets out new relations as it follows new goals striving to nest everything and everyone to a place of its utmost flourishing existence. There is no place for humanity's supremacy over nature and the cosmos, and certainly not one for a hierarchy of genders and races.

References

Campanella, T. (1637). "Instauratio in prologum instauratarum scientiarum". In: *Philosophia realis.* Paris, 1–33.

Cassirer, E. (1923). *Substance and Function, and Einstein's Theory of Relativity.* Chicago: Open Court Publishing.

Floridi, L. (2014). "The Fourth Revolution in Our Self-Understanding". In Hagengruber, R. and Riss, U. (Eds.), *Philosophy, Computing and Information Science.* London: Pickering and Chatoo, 19–29.

Floridi, L. (2020). "The Green and the Blue. A New Political Ontology of a Mature Information Society". *Philosophisches Jahrbuch* 2, 307–338.

Hagengruber, R. E. (1994). *Tommaso Campanella. Eine Philosophie der Ähnlichkeit.* Sankt Augustin: Academia.

Hagengruber, R. E. (2015). "Tommaso Campanella. Soziale Organisation und enzyklopädisches Interesse". In Höffe, O. (Ed.), *Politische Utopien der Neuzeit.* Berlin and Boston: De Gruyter, 139–171.

Hagengruber, R. E. (2017). "Creative Algorithms and the Construction of Meaning". In Wernecke, J., Pietsch, W. and Ott, M. (Eds.), *Berechenbarkeit der Welt?* Wiesbaden: Springer, 331–341.

Hagengruber, R. E. (2022). "Die 'dritte Wissensdimension'. Eine Epistemologie für eine neue Wissenswelt". In: Banse, G. and Fuchs-Kittowski, K. (Eds.), *Cyberscience – Wissenschaftsforschung und Informatik. Digitale Medien und die Zukunft der Kultur wissenschaftlicher Tätigkeit.* Berlin: Trafo, 253–258.

Smith, B. (2003). "Ontology". In Floridi, L. (Ed.), *Blackwell Guide to the Philosophy of Computing and Information.* Oxford: Blackwell, 155–167.

Turing, A. M. (1950). "Computing Machinery and Intelligence". *Mind* 49, 433–460.

Sabine Thürmel
Social Machines in a Data-driven World

Abstract: In the last decades, social machines have evolved from supporting the collaborative and creative endeavors of humans to being proactive experts themselves. In many cases they are no longer mere tools but interaction partners. Algorithmic innovations in Big Data-based analytics and machine learning result in less influence for the human collaborators and more power for these machines. Examples from medicine and pharmacy demonstrate that Big Data analytics promises to provide not just insights but foresight: predictive analytics is used for optimizing the discovery path in drug discovery and decision processes in medical environments. The anticipatory governance in medical early warning systems and preventive healthcare systems allows medical decision processes to be supported or even automated. Thus, it may be exemplified that so-called social machines have evolved from technology-enabled social systems towards expert systems relying on the latest developments in the computational sciences.

Introduction and Overview

Currently we find a wide variety of social machines on the web supporting the original version of Tim Berners-Lee's definition of social machines, being "processes in which the people do the creative work and the machine does the administration" (Berners-Lee and Fischetti 1999, 172–175). Today these "technology-enabled social systems" (Shadbolt et al. 2019) consist of public service social machines, knowledge sharing social machines, and citizen science social machines among others. Social media are both widely used and widely criticized for the impact on social interactions and opinion forming. Current platforms show the huge impact technology has on the interaction between humans.

Social machines perceived as "digitally mediated human networks – governed by AI and machine learning" (MIT Laboratory for Social Machines 2019) are also on the rise. They "are shaping more and more of what we perceive, remember, plan, and do" (MIT Laboratory for Social Machines 2019). This definition rightly stresses that human networks are not only given a "platform to build social networks or social relations among people" (Smart and Shadbolt 2014, 8) but are more and more governed by AI and machine learning.

Digitally mediated human networks have been discussed by scholars in media studies since their beginning. The evolution of social machines has been studied less intensely, especially when one focuses on the objectives of current social machines. Following Smart and Shadbolt current social machines may be understood as "systems in which human and machine components make complementary contributions with respect to the performance of some larger joint process" (Smart and Shadbolt 2014, 3) profiting from the extraordinary progress AI has made in the last years. In contrast to the last decades where AI promised at lot but showed meager results the advent of deep learning techniques reversed this trend. Even popular journals like the *Economist* inform the general public of the "return of the machinery question", that is of the impact of AI as a technique which "enables machines to perform tasks that could previously be done only by humans" (Economist 2016, 1). Already in June 2016 the *Economist* dedicated the afore-mentioned special report on AI to deep learning which can be applied to many different domains. Examples include language translation, facial recognition and others where until now mostly humans excelled. So how will an AI-enabled future change social machines? Will the "machinery" of social machines become (semi-)autonomous and will the human control of social machines be challenged by this development.

In this paper the ongoing evolution of social machines – and the changing role of humans in the collaborative process is presented by focusing on a specific topic, namely the development of clinical support systems. Two stages in this process are highlighted: an early vision of the automation of medical decision processes and the current reliance on Big Data analytics.

Social Machines and the Art of Healing

More than 50 years ago, in November 1966, an article was published in the *Bayerisches Ärzeblatt* (Bavarian Medical Journal): "automation – a medical provocation? replacement of the physician by technology". The author, Bruno Friton, being both a physician and an engineer, was convinced that "the medicine of tomorrow will be dominated by electronic data processing equipment. [...] Therefore humanitarian and professional ethos should be the guiding principle. This is the only way to free both physician and patient from the phobia of automation". He concluded his manifesto with following words: "we physicians neither adore the technology nor do we perceive it as a curse but we approve of it. Additional rationalization and further automation, namely an increase in creativity – these are the tasks for the future" (Friton 1966, Translation ST,888).

Bruno Friton was convinced, like many of his peers, that the automation and streamlining of the medical workflow, similar to the automation in manufacturing being on the rise at that time, was feasible in the near future. This would allow the physician to become more efficient and would free him from repetitive, cumbersome tasks. It took perhaps longer than he anticipated but clinical decision support systems are well established.

The most common clinical support systems involve medication dosing and order support as well as alerts and reminders where information relevant to the medical task at hand is displayed in pop-up-style windows. Workflow support provided by clinical guidelines are prevalent, too. However, other than Friton expected, the deployment of these tools does not necessarily lead to an "increase in creativity". On the contrary, the autonomy of physicians is more and more curtailed since the clinical support systems have evolved from descriptive, "user-initiated" tools like reference tables to clinical guidelines up to prescriptive, "system-initiated" clinical protocols as well as documentation templates and alerts and reminders that call for the user to take a specified action (Sholler et al. 2016, 176). These "point-of-care electronic prompts" (Schwann et al. 2011, 869) are intended to constrain and direct their users. Rationales have to be provided if one wants to deviate from the directive given by the clinical support system. Thus, 50 years after Friton's enthusiastic embrace of automation in medicine, not only Dan Sholler et al. (2016) wonder what the future of the art of healing will be in times when clinical health systems guide the medical personnel and medical decision processes get more and more automated.

Big Data Analytics in Medicine and Pharmacy

Human intelligence is enhanced by the technical components which serve as tools for the human's use. The deployment of Big Data technologies forms an integral part of the latest generation of such social machines. Data-intensive science has started to influence both medical knowledge and medical practice. In 2017 nearly 10,000 scientists competed in the Data Science Bowl to develop machine learning algorithms that can more accurately detect cancerous lesions in CT scans (Olavsrud 2017). Computational pathology based on computer vision and machine learning already offers Big Data-based approaches being as good as humans in analyzing biopsies (Ehteshami et al. 2017). One has to keep in mind that human labelers produce annotations to train and to evaluate computational algorithms, thus humans continue to play an important part in the detection of malignant cells. At Cornell University among others, Big Data analytics is used for cancer genomics and is applied for drug discovery, thus supporting the precision medicine paradigm which is intended to lead to cancer prevention, diagnostics, treatment, and cure (Elemento Lab 2023). Moreover, Big Data-based predictive algorithms allow the focus to be shifted from reactive measures to proactive prevention. They are experimentally used in early warning systems providing a continuous assessment of the "not yet". They may be employed to monitor neural anomalies in intensive care, e. g. in order to detect and predict epileptic seizures. In addition, drug discovery supported by deep learning demonstrates how data-intensive science changes and accelerates explorative research processes by applying novel heuristics. In the "data-driven world" medical diagnostics and treatment as well as drug discovery will increasingly profit from Big Data analytics. One might even say that well-established forms of "knowing that" and "knowing how" will be disrupted by the current wave of AI technologies. Authors like Kenneth Cukier wholeheartedly embrace this development: "anything that requires highly specialized training, judgement and decision-making under conditions of uncertainty will the done better by an algorithm than a human" (2017).

As the examples given above show "actionable data", the output of the predictive algorithms, intend to provide a link between "knowing that" and "knowing how". In drug discovery systems they lead the way to further optimizing the discovery path given ("knowing that"), the explorative experimentation until that moment and the options presented at that moment ("knowing how"). In preventive health care systems, the "actionable data" are aimed at nudging or even pushing the patients towards a healthier life style.

The goal is "to know ahead and to act before". In case of path optimization unproductive explorations can be avoided if the actionable data are conclusive and provide an anticipatory guidance. The researchers are steered towards more fruitful next steps based on the insights gained in computational sciences which are the epistemic authority for this kind of endeavor. In the case of preventive health systems, the actionable data may result in micro-directives guiding both machines and humans. The epistemic authority of these anticipatory governance practices is based on the insights of the computational and behavioral sciences. However, it speaks no longer with a human voice but an artificial one. Thus, we find a novel coupling of anticipatory governance and epistemic authority provided via computational and behavioral sciences.

In these "learning healthcare systems" knowledge is generated by the AI tools. Operational and tactical decisions are mostly system-initiated. However, such systems are autonomous only in so far as they are capable of operative and strategic control. The normative control remains in the hands of the human operators (Gransche et al. 2014).

Due to the promises of "the age of analytics", "data and analytics can enable faster and more evidence based decision making" (McKinsey Institute 2016), medical practice will continue to evolve. Moreover, these techniques have begun to influence the agenda of promoting preventive health care and personalized medicine on the basis of behavioral, genetic and molecular data.

It has to be noted that Big Data approaches form a unique algorithmic culture: they focus on patterns and correlations instead of causal relationships. Since they are based on the stark opposite of easily comprehensible and transparent procedures, trust in the results of these processes often may not be reinforced by expert views: Even if the underlying (mathematical) principles of these models are understood they lack an explicit declarative knowledge representation. Therefore, it is difficult, to say the least, to generate the underlying explanatory structures. Thus, the epistemic authority of these methods is not easily challenged or validated. Currently, researchers work on a first step towards reviewing these procedures: they work on systems enabling to make decisions transparent, understandable and explainable (see e. g. Holzinger et al. 2017 for an overview of the field for the medical domain).

Considerable similarities exist between data-intensive science and the engineering sciences as Wolfgang Pietsch points out (2016): both predominantly stay on the phenomenological level. They are strongly inductive relying on exploratory experimentation or related methods. Often, explanations are not available beyond establishing the causal relevance of certain conditions. The reliance on phenomena may explain the success of data-driven approaches in medicine and pharmaceutics. The proximity to engineering sciences may change the *ars medicina*, the art of healing, in fundamental ways: what is the adequate division of labor between the human practitioner and the medical diagnostics and treatment tools? On one end of the spectrum, where pattern recognition is the main task, highly specialized training and Big Data sets are available, fully automated decision making will prevail in the future – as predicted Kenneth Cukier for computational pathology.

However, Big Data algorithms are not suited to problems where no (or no sufficient) data exist. As Agrawal, Gans and Goldfar note: "machines are bad at prediction for rare events" (2018, 102). In contrast, humans may make use of analogies or rely on their experience gained in similar situations. Therefore, Agrawal, Gans and Goldfar anticipate "a rise in *human prediction by exception* whereby machines generate most predictions because they are predicted on routine, regular data, but when rare events occur the machine recognizes that it is not able to produce a prediction with confidence, and so calls for human assistance. The human provides prediction by exception" (2018, 68). Yet, the "prediction machines are better than humans at factoring in complex interactions among different indicators, especially in settings with rich data" (2018, 69). Therefore, a suitable division of labor is called for. Concluding, it must be noted, that both humans and machines cannot predict truly new events from past data. Thus, shaping the future by predictive analysis has clear limits.

In economic parlance, one might even say that well-established forms of holding on to a commonly shared perspective on reality will be disrupted by the current wave of AI technologies. One example is the use of computational techniques in Computational Psychiatry. This field aims to classify psychiatric phenomena no longer according to the established manual of diagnosis (ICD-10-GM; DIMDI n. d.) but in novel, more fluid models of reduced cognitive, affective and social functions (Hoff 2019, 18) where "computational techniques facilitate the measurement of intrapsychic processes that are not otherwise directly observable" (Huys 2017). Thus, Computational Psychiatry intends to provide transformative decision support systems discarding the established modes of characterizing mental disorders and replacing the social memory of medical specialists – at least in part – with new data and new correlations.

Conclusion

Social machines have evolved from technology-enabled social systems towards expert systems relying on the latest developments in the computational sciences. In the "data-driven world" medical diagnostics and treatment as well as drug discovery are increasingly profiting from Big Data analytics. In diagnostics and pharmaceutical research these practices embody the insights of computational science – and in health care the findings of behavioral science – in order to nudge the patients to the desired behavior. Big Data-based predictive algorithms allow the focus to be shifted from reactive measures to proactive prevention. They are experimentally used in early warning systems providing a continuous assessment of the "not yet". In addition, scientific discovery supported by deep learning demonstrates how data-intensive science changes and accelerates explorative research processes by applying novel heuristics.

This development has not only broadened the scope of the so-called social machines but starts to change how we perceive computer systems. They are no longer passive tools but have begun to be an active or even proactive part in research and development processes which in the natural sciences and engineering are always collaborative endeavors.

References

Agrawal, A., Gans, J. and Goldfarb, A. (2018). *Prediction Machines: The Simple Economics of Artificial Intelligence.* Cambridge, MA: Harvard Business Review Press.

Berners-Lee, T. and Fischetti, M. (1999). *Weaving the Web: The Original Design and Ultimate Destiny of the World Wide Web by Its Inventor.* London: Orion Business.

Cukier, K. (2017). "The Data-driven World". In Franklin, D. (Ed.), *Megatech: Technology in 2050.* London: The Economist Books.

DIMDI (n. d.). ICD-10-GM. URL: https://www.dimdi.de/dynamic/de/klassifikationen/icd/icd-10-gm/ (last accessed 18 November 2022).

Economist (2016) "The Return of the Machinery Question". Special Report on AI, June 2016, 1–15.

Ehteshami, B. et al. (2017). "Diagnostic Assessment of Deep Learning Algorithms for Detection of Lymph Node Metastases in Women with Breast Cancer". *JAMA* 318(22), 2199–2210. DOI: 10.1001/jama.2017.14585.

Elemento Lab (2018). "Cancer Genomics". Weil Cornell Medicine Elemento Lab URL: https://elementolab.weill.cornell.edu/research/cancer-genomics (last accessed 19 January 2023).

Friton, B. (1966). "Automation – eine medizinische Provokation? Ablösung des Arztes durch die Technik?" *Bayerisches Ärzteblatt* 21(11), 88–896.

Gransche, B., Shala, E., Hubig, Ch., Alpsancar, S. and Harrach, S. (2014). Wandel von Autonomie und Kontrolle durch neue Mensch-Technik Interaktionen. Grundsatzfragen autonomieorientierter Mensch-Technik-Verhältnisse. Stuttgart: Frauenhofer.

Hoff, P. (2019). "Psychiatrische Diagnostik: Big Data und die therapeutische Beziehung". *NZZ*, 28 August.

Huys, P. (2017). "Computational Psychiatry". DOI: 10.1024/1661–4747/a000297.

Holzinger, A., Biemann, Ch., Pattichis, C. and Kell, D. (2017). "What Do We Need to Build Explainable {AI} Systems for the Medical Domain?" arXiv:1712.09923.

McKinsey Global Institute (2016). *The Age of Analytics: Competing in a Data-driven World.* Full Report. URL: https://www.mckinsey.com/~/media/mckinsey/industries/public%20and%20social%20sector/our%20insights/the%20age%20of%20analytics%20competing%20in%20a%20data%20driven%20world/mgi-the-age-of-analytics-full-report.pdf (last accessed 03 January 2023).

MIT Laboratory for Social Machines (2019). *Understanding and Empowering Human Networks.* URL: http://socialmachines.media.mit.edu/ (last accessed 5 September 2019).

Olavsrud, T. (2017). "Big Data Scientists Compete to Create Cancer Detection Algorithms". *CIO Journal*, May 4, 2017. Online Article. URL: https://www.cio.com/article/234978/data-scientists-compete-to-create-cancer-detection-algorithms.html (last accessed 03 January 2023).

Pietsch, W. (2016). "Engineering Complex Phenomena Using Big Data. Some Methodological Reflections". Presentation at the Symposium *Ethics of Big Data: The Engineering of the "Not Yet"*. IACAP.

Schwann, N., Bretz, K., Eid, S., Burger, T., Frey, D., Ackler, F., Evans, P., ... and McLoughlin Jr., T. (2011). "Point-of-Care Eletronic Prompts: An Effective Means of Increasing Compliance, Demonstrating Quality, and Improving Outcome". *Anesthesia and Analgesia* 113(4), 869–876.

Shadbolt, N., Kieron O'Hara, K., De Roure, D. and Hall, W. (2019). *The Theory and Practice of Social Machines. Lecture Notes in Social Networks.* Cham: Springer.

Sholler, D., Bailey, D. E. and Rennecker, J. (2016). "Big Data in Medicine: Potential, Reality, and Implications". In Sugimoto, C. R., Ekbia, H. R. and Mattioli, M. (Eds.), *Big Data Is Not a Monolith.* Cambridge, MA: MIT Press, 173–186.

Smart, P. and Shadbolt, N. (2014). "Social Machines". In Khosrow-Pour, M. (Ed.), *Encyclopedia of Information Science and Technology.* Hershey, PA: IGI Global.

Laura Roberts
Smart Feminist Cities: The Case of Barcelona en Comú

Abstract: Barcelona en Comú, the feminist political platform currently running the city of Barcelona, is cultivating a Smart Feminist City aiming to put technology at the service of the people rather than, for example, selling citizen data to corporations. This paper extends Elizabeth Grosz's theorisation of the Bodies-Cities interface to a Bodies-Cities-Technologies interface to think through the implications of the ways in which a feminist city such as Barcelona is reversing the neoliberal Smart City paradigm through its harnessing of technology to use for the common good and to challenge social discrimination. In doing so, this paper prompts us to think through the implications of these changes on the production of subjectivities through the Bodies-Cities-Technologies interface.

Using a feminist philosophical framework this paper considers the case of Barcelona en Comú, the explicitly feminist political platform currently running Barcelona, to illustrate how thinking through the lens of feminist philosophy enables us to appreciate how Barcelona en Comú is reimagining *Smart Cities* as ethical, feminist and anti-racist cities that harness and develop technology for the common good of all citizens rather than for profit of private capital and the elites. This work takes seriously our relations with technology and in framing these using feminist philosophy and political activism, imagines these as a force for social change. In doing so, I hope to gesture toward a feminist philosophy of technology that theorizes the ways in which particular practices of feminist cities like Barcelona open spaces for the figuration of explicitly feminist political subjectivities. Engaging with these ideas, using a feminist philosophical framework helps us to think deeper about the types of subjectivities cities are nurturing, urging us to consider the ethical and political projects relating to the entanglements of human being and technology without erasing our lived differences of gender. Ultimately, this paper hopes to contribute to emerging conversations offering critical feminist and anti-capitalist perspectives on technology, with a focus on feminist cities, in order to articulate and imagine new ways of being in the world that recognize the entanglement of human and non-human, as well as the algorithms of oppression (Noble 2018) in which we are all now embedded.

Bodies-Cities and Feminist Philosophy

In "Bodies-Cities", a chapter from *Space, Time, and Perversion: Essays on the Politics of Bodies* (1995), Australian philosopher Elizabeth Grosz is interested in how to think the relations between bodies and cities. Grosz argues that "the city is one of the crucial factors in the social production of (sexed) corporeality" noting that "the built environment provides the context and coordinates for contemporary forms of body" (Grosz 1995, 104). Grosz's work points out that it is the city which organizes and "automatically links otherwise unrelated bodies: it is the condition and milieu in which corporeality is socially, sexually, and discursively produced" (Grosz 1995, 104). Given this notion that the city is the frame and context in which bodies are sexually produced and gendered I agree with Grosz when she suggests that "the relations between bodies and cities are more complex than may have been realized" (Grosz 1995, 104). And, when thinking through the idea of a feminist city as we will in this paper, these relations become even more interesting.

Grosz ultimately argues that we can understand the relations between bodies and cities as constitutive and mutually defining but she first takes us through two traditional models that articulate the interrelation of bodies and cities (Grosz 1995, 104). First, there is a view undergirded by Western traditions of humanism, that "the city is a reflection, projection, or product of bodies" (Grosz 1995, 105). The second model, elaborated by liberal political philosophers like Hobbes, Locke and Rosseau, "suggests a parallelism or isomorphism between the body and the city, or the body and the state" (Grosz 1995, 105). Grosz points out that while the body is seen as parallel, the body is "rarely attributed a sex" (Grosz 1995, 106). Critically assessing these two models which, it is important to stress, still underlie conceptions of civic and public architecture as well as town planning Grosz notes that there is a slippage from conceptions of the state to city (Grosz 1995, 106–107).[1] And, as the work of Barcelona en Comú demonstrates, sometimes the interests of states and cities are in conflict and what is "good for the nation or state is not necessarily good for the city" (Grosz 1995, 107). Grosz thus offers a third model of how to think the relations between bodies and cities that combines elements of each of these models (Grosz 1995, 108). On her model Grosz suggests that the lived (and thus sexed and gendered and raced) body is active in production of the city, however the two are not causally linked rather they are "mutually defining" (Grosz 1995, 108). Grosz ultimately argues that while "there may be an isomorphism between

---

[1] She writes that "there is a slippage from conceptions of the state, which as a legal entity, raises political questions of sovereignty, to conceptions of the city, a cultural entity whose crucial political questions revolve around commerce" (Grosz 1995, 106–107).

the body and the city" it is not a mirror and rather "there is a two-way linkage that could be defined as an interface" (Grosz 1995, 108). Ultimately Grosz argues that cities and bodies define and establish each other through this model of an interface (Grosz 1995, 108). The implication of this model means that cities, like bodies, can be conceived of as gendered and raced and classed. And, consequently, we can begin to understand how cities can privilege certain genders, races, classes, and able-bodied citizens.

Importantly, for Grosz, while the city is not the most significant ingredient in the social construction of bodies it is nevertheless an important element because "the form, structure, and norms of the city seep into and affect all the other elements that go into the constitution of corporeality" (Grosz 1995, 108). Grosz's articulation of the Bodies-Cities interface thus offers a framework from which to think through the effects of the often patriarchal and racist social norms underlying contemporary neoliberal *Smart Cities*. It also offers, however, the possibilities of challenging these norms. Thinking through the interface, Grosz notes, "in turn, the body (as cultural product) transforms, reinscribes the urban landscape according to its changing (demographic) needs" (Grosz 1995, 109). The city, then, can be imagined as a "hinge between the population and the individual, the body, its distribution, habits, alignments, pleasures, norms, and ideals are the ostensive object of governmental regulation" (Grosz 1995, 109). The city, for Grosz, can be understood as "both a mode for the regulation and administration of subjects but also an urban space in turn reinscribed by the particularities of its occupation and use" (Grosz 1995, 109).

Grosz works through a number of implications from this schematic survey but the one I am interested in here is the point she makes about social rules and the production and circulation of power. Grosz writes:

> The city's form and structure provides the context in which social rules and expectations are internalized or habituated in order to ensure social conformity or, failing this, position social marginality at a safe distance (ghettoization). This means that the city must be seen as the most immediate locus for the production and circulation of power. (Grosz 1995, 109)

Grosz's point is clear: we must understand the interface of the city as locus "for the production and circulation of power" (Grosz 1995, 109). This interface of Bodies-Cities becomes a particularly interesting model to think through the ways in which a feminist city has strategic opportunities to challenge the power of patriarchal elites and ultimately channel and circulate the power back to and through the diverse citizens of the city. Grosz concludes this short chapter with a particularly prescient remark noting (remembering this paper was published in 1995) that if indeed the city is "an active force in constituting bodies, and always leaves its traces on the subject's corporeality" the dramatic "transformation of the city as a result of the information revolution" will have direct "effects on the inscription of bodies" (Grosz 1995, 110). But she writes, "only time will tell" (Grosz 1995, 110). In the 25 years since this chapter has been published the information and technological revolution has truly taken hold and it seems crucial, perhaps even more urgent than ever, to critically think through the ways in which multiple technologies we engage with daily mediate our lives, are entangled in the production of our subjectivities, our politics, and, of course, our experiences of so-called *Smart Cities*.

Thinking more recently about technology and cities, architect Alejandro Zaero-Polo raises similar concerns as those that Grosz gestured toward in 1995 in his article "The Posthuman City: Imminent Urban Commons" (Zaero-Polo 2017) in *Architectural Design*. He is critical of urban planning which remains within the humanist framework and argues this is no longer effective at addressing "the urgent questions cities are facing today" (Zaero-Polo 2017). He argues that cities have become "a crucial intersection between technology and politics where the equations between wealth, labour, resources and energy have to be reset to address the current shortcomings of neo-liberal economies" (Zaero-Polo 2017, 29). He further argues that cities must become "devices for the common good" and that "imminent urban technologies need to locate resources and technologies at their core" (Zaero-Polo 2017, 29). He refers to these as "imminent urban commons" and argues that these commons "need to become instructions of devolution and ecological awareness, constructed transversally across technologies and resources" (Zaero-Polo 2017, 29).

Bringing a feminist lens to Zaero-Polo's thinking on cities and technology it is important to recognize that many contemporary feminist and anti-racist scholars point out that technology is not neutral, and that it is, as Safiya Noble argues in her work in *Algorithms of Oppression*, socially constructed (Noble 2018; Bishop et al. 2020). Contemporary conversations in feminist technoscience, feminist media studies and critical algorithmic studies point out that the technology we engage with daily is undergirded by sexist and racist epistemologies and ontologies. Indeed, there is still much work to be done that brings together feminist and anti-racist critiques of technology with critiques of *Smart Cities*. Using a philosophical lens enables this exploration to go deeper and offers the opportunity to think critically about the interface of Bodies-Cities and technologies that Grosz articulates. This paper thus asks the reader to consider how bodies (in all their lived differences), cities and technologies are constitutive and mutually defining (Grosz 1995, 104). Ultimately, we will build on Grosz's ideas here to think through the interface of bodies-cites-technologies in feminist *Smart Cities*.

This paper thus poses the following questions: If the *Smart City* along with its increased technological surveillance and harvesting of data for profit is the most immediate locus for the production and circulation of power, how does a feminist city challenge this model? What can we learn from a city that is challenging the norms and forms of the status quo (the neoliberal patriarchal elites)? Do feminist cities produce feminist subjectivities? How is the feminist city contributing to/producing social imaginaries in which our subjectivities are made and remade?

Barcelona: A Smart Feminist City

While I cannot answer all these questions here this paper hopes to open space for these future conversations to take place. But first, what is a feminist city? The website for the Barcelona city council explains:

> We're a feminist city, applying the gender perspective in all municipal policies and taking a collective stand against gender violence. We're a city which takes into account and combats the everyday difficulties faced by women in terms of care, job insecurity and labour discrimination, safety at home and in the streets. We're a feminist city, which protects and stands up for sexual and gender diversity, which has created a pioneering LGBTI centre and which fights LGBTI-phobia. We're a city based on feminism, reinventing ourselves every day to achieve a space which is free and safe for everybody. (Info Barcelona n. d.)

Barcelona en Comú is the political platform currently running the city of Barcelona and this platform is part of what has become known as the International New Municipalist movement. International New Municipalism emerged out of the wake of the global uprisings of 2010–11 concerned with creating "new ways of doing electoral politics" and challenging the current capitalist political and economic models (Shea Baird 2016). In 2015 many of these citizen platforms across Spain "swept to victory … on a wave of public indignation at cuts and corruption" (Shea Baird and Miralles 2021). These citizen platforms, often made up of activists, were intent on occupying the corrupt political institutions in order to create change.

Most basically in International New Municipalism there is a practical and pragmatic commitment to grassroots radical democracy and the needs of the local communities and neighborhoods. Common life and community are refigured in International New Municipalism. As it is international, it is also about connecting local communities and activists on a global scale. Kate Shea Baird writes:

> … municipalism constructs alternative forms of collective identity and citizenship based on residence and participation. Municipalism is pragmatic and goal-based: in a neoliberal system that tells us 'there is no alternative', municipalism proves that things can be done differently through small, but concrete, victories, like remuncipalizing basic services or providing local ID schemes for undocumented immigrants. Municipalism allows us to reclaim individual

and collective autonomy; in response to citizen demands for real democracy, municipalism opens up forms of participation that go beyond voting once every few years. (Shea Baird 2017)

Along with these demands for real democracy and the multi-pronged challenges the platforms throw at neoliberal political institutions and systems, the International New Municipalist movement views feminism as key. Barcelona en Comú are committed to what they refer to as the feminization of politics. Kate Shea Baird and Laura Roth explain:

> ... the feminisation of politics, beyond its concern for increasing the presence of women in decision-making spaces and implementing public policies to promote gender equality, is about changing the way politics is done [...] It aims to shatter masculine patterns that reward behaviours such as competition, urgency, hierarchy and homogeneity, which are less common in – or appealing to – women. Instead, a feminized politics seeks to emphasize the importance of the small, the relational, the everyday, challenging the artificial division between the personal and political. This is how we change the underlying dynamics of the system and construct emancipatory alternatives. (Shea Baird and Roth 2017)

This changing of the way politics is done, from a feminist perspective, plays a central role in Barcelona becoming a feminist city. This feminizing of politics also plays out in concrete ways in the landscape of the city. In 2015, after the election of Mayor Ada Colau and Barcelona en Comú to government, the city council began implementing strategic feminist initiatives, policies and protocols in the governing of the city. Barcelona en Comú have a city councilor dedicated to feminist and LGBTI issues. They have a Strategic Plan for Gender Justice and a Strategic Plan Against Sexism in the City (2017–2021). There are many initiatives and campaigns including the protocol against sexual assault and harassment in night clubs, improved public lighting in most neighborhoods, free municipal childcare and all urban planning takes a gender perspective. The new Gender Justice Plan (2021–2025) aims to consolidate municipal policies of recent years and eradicate inequalities between men and women "promoting a fairer and more equal city for all inhabitants" (BEC Gender Justice Plan 2021–2025). The new plan takes into account the impact of the Covid-19 crisis on equality between men and women and is based around four areas: 1) Institutional change; 2) Economy for life and organization of time: "to achieve a fairer and more sustainable economy which guarantees equality in life conditions between men and women, we must recognize the fundamental role of all work necessary for subsistence, reproduction and people's wellbeing, as well as joint responsibility in assuming care work". This point includes the fight against the digital gender divide and women's access to ICT industries; 3) City of rights; 4) Close and sustainable neighborhoods (BEC Gender Justice Plan 2021–2025).

What I am particularly interested in here is the critical and feminist view Barcelona en Comú has on so-called *Smart Cities*. Barcelona offers an excellent example of how a feminist city can challenge the neoliberal *Smart City* narrative through its attention to the ways in which technology can be used for the common good and how it may help to challenge many forms of social discrimination. Barcelona en Comú proposes ethical and innovative uses of technology to recognize the inequalities in lived differences between men and women and illustrates how technology can be put to use in creating a city which eradicates these inequalities in various ways. Understanding the relations between Bodies-Cities-Technologies as an interface we can now appreciate how gendered, raced, classed and differently abled bodies in this feminist city are producing and being produced by the city in new ways. Critiquing the neoliberal *Smart City* from this philosophical perspective and thinking about the ways in which the Barcelona city council are using technology highlights, I think, the urgency and value of theorizing this work. I argue it opens the way toward a feminist philosophy of technology.

Framing these developments is the Barcelona Digital City Plan (2015–2019) which includes the important subtitle "Putting technology at the service of the people". Francesca Bria, the former Digital Innovation Commissioner in the Barcelona City Council who put the Barcelona Digital City Plan into motion explains how the plan aimed to rethink the *Smart City* aiming to transcend its technological objectives to better respond to the needs of the citizens (Bria 2017). Bria notes that cities cannot "solve all our digital problems: many of them need urgent attention at the national and global level. But cities can run smart, data-intensive, algorithmic public transportation, housing, health and education – all based on a logic of *solidarity, social cooperation and collective rights*" (Bria 2018).

An important aspect of the Digital Plan views technology and Big Data as a common good of the city (Bria 2018).[2] Bria explains Barcelona en Comú are "reversing the smart city paradigm" and instead of "extracting all the data we can before thinking about how to use it, we started aligning the tech agenda with the agenda of the city … We want to move from a model of surveillance capitalism, where data is opaque and not transparent, to a model where citizens themselves can own the data" (Bria 2018).[3] In making city data openly accessible, rather than

---

[2] "We are introducing clauses into contracts, like data sovereignty and public ownership of data", says Bria. "For example, now we have a big contract with Vodafone, and every month Vodafone has to give machine readable data to city hall. Before, that didn't happen. They just took all the data and used it for their own benefit" (2018).

[3] "I think in the technological world it's very important to put forward a narrative that's different to the surveillance capitalism from Silicon Valley, and the dystopian Chinese model, with its Social

selling it off to corporations, the city helps, as Bria notes, over "13,000 local tech companies to build future data-driven services through a blockchain-based platform that we are developing in the *DECODE* project" (Bria 2017). An explicitly feminist example of this is an app the Barcelona city council has recently launched. It allows people to report sexual harassment which the city council can then evaluate to determine "hot spots" in the city and act accordingly.

The city has also made headway into digital participatory democracy which aims to harness technology to increase participation in the democratic and policy-making process. To do so they are using their own digital platform, Decidim Barcelona (in English "We Decide"). In doing so, the *Smart City* really is being developed from the ground up (Bria 2017). As Bria notes:

> Now the public can participate directly in government as they would on social media, by suggesting ideas, debating them, and voting with their thumbs. Decidim taps into the potential of social networks: the information spreading on Twitter, or the relationships on Facebook. All of these apply to politics and Decidim seeks to channel them, while guaranteeing personal privacy and public transparency in a way these platforms don't. (Bria 2018)

Considering these examples that are happening in a feminist city alongside certain feminist philosophical perspectives thus enables us to appreciate how the feminist politics of Barcelona en Comú and their progressive new municipalist governance allows us to hope and imagine the future and relations with others in community differently. Moreover, these are just some of the examples of the ways in which the feminist city council of Barcelona are challenging the neoliberal *Smart City* narrative and creating cultural transformations in everyday lives through institutional politics and policies related to technology. They are creating a fearless feminist city founded upon the ideas of the common good and rethinking social relations through education campaigns and protocols and technology to challenge the neoliberal ideas that there is "no alternative", offering instead radical emancipatory imaginaries and hope for the future.

Reading these initiatives and, in particular, the core aspects of the Digital Plan I return to consider Grosz's work. Building on Grosz's work I suggest we can think of Bodies-Cities-Technologies as forming relational interface. An interface in which Bodies-Cities-Technologies define and establish each other (Grosz 1995, 108). They are constitutive and mutually defining. The implication of this, is that cities, like bodies, and technologies can be conceived of as gendered and raced and classed. Consequently, we can begin to have a more intimate view on how *Smart Cities*

Credit System that uses citizen data to give them a rating that then gives them access to certain services", says Bria. "We want to lead Europe to put forward an alternative model" (2018).

can privilege certain groups of citizens but, on the other hand, rethinking the *Smart City* from a feminist perspective we can begin to imagine how feminist *Smart Cities* can work for the common good. Moreover, if we agree with Grosz's analysis of the importance of the city in the formation of subjectivity and the power the city holds in production of social norms, it seems Barcelona en Comú's Feminist City and Digital Plan is a crucial and central way in which we can challenge the insidiously neoliberal systems that cause harm to us all, but particularly women and gender non-conforming folks and all those that do not fit the mold of the patriarch. Much more theorizing and work is required here to think through the ways in which technology works in the subjectification of Bodies-Cities but given what I have outlined here, I am hopeful that a feminist *Smart City* is on the way to nurturing and producing feminist political subjectivities. To echo Grosz in 1995, however, "only time will tell".

References

Basu, M. (2017). Interview with Francesca Bria. 15 December 2017. *GovInsider.* URL: https://govinsider.asia/security/francesca-chief-technology-digital-innovation-officer-barcelona-city-council/ (last accessed 18 November 2022).

Bishop, S., Bradbury-Rance, C., Conor, B., Feldman, Z. and Saunders, R. (2020). Introduction to the Special Issue "Algorithms for Her? Feminist Claims to Technical Language". *Feminist Media Studies* 20(5), 730–732.

Bria, F. (2015). *Barcelona Digital City Plan.* Ajuntament de Barcelona. URL: https://ajuntament.barcelona.cat/digital/en (last accessed 18 November 2022).

Bria, F. (2018). "Our Data is Valuable. Here's How We Can Take That Value Back". *The Guardian*, 5 April 2018. URL: https://www.theguardian.com/commentisfree/2018/apr/05/data-valuable-citizens-silicon-valley-barcelona (last accessed 18 November 2022).

Department for Feminisms and LGTBI (2016). *Plan for Gender Justice 2016–2020.* Ajuntament de Barcelona. URL: https://ajuntament.barcelona.cat/dones/sites/default/files/documentacio/plan-for-gender-justice-2016-2020_ang.pdf (last accessed 18 November 2022).

Department for Feminisms and LGTBI (2017). *Plan estratégico contra el sexismo en la ciudad 2017–2022.* Ajuntament de Barcelona. URL: https://ajuntament.barcelona.cat/dones/sites/default/files/documentacio/estrategia_contra_el_sexisme_2017_es.pdf (last accessed 3 January 2023).

Department for Feminisms and LGTBI (2021). *Plan for Gender Justice 2021–2025.* Ajuntament de Barcelona. URL: https://ajuntament.barcelona.cat/dones/sites/default/files/documentacio/estrategia_contra_el_sexisme_2017_es.pdf (last accessed 18 November 2022).

Grosz, E. (1995). *Space, Time and Perversion: Essays on the Politics of Bodies.* London: Routledge.

Info Barcelona (n. d.) "Barcelona, Feminist City". URL: https://www.barcelona.cat/infobarcelona/en/actions-and-services/barcelona-feminist-city_773983.html (last accessed 13 December 2022).

Noble, S. U. (2018). *Algorithms of Oppression: How Search Engines Reinforce Racism.* New York: New York University Press.

Shea Baird, K. (2016). "How to Build a Movement-party: Lessons from Rosario's Future City". *OpenDemoncracy*, 15 November. URL: https://beta.opendemocracy.net/en/democraciaabierta/

how-to-build-movement-party-lessons-from-rosario-s-future-city/ (last accessed 18 November 2022).

Shea Baird, K. (2017). "A New International Municipalist Movement Is on the Rise – From Small Victories to Global Alternatives". *OpenDemocracy*, 7 June. URL: https://www.opendemocracy.net/en/can-europe-make-it/new-international-municipalist-movement-is-on-rise-from-small-vic/ (last accessed 18 November 2022).

Shea Baird, K. and Roth, L. (2017). "Municipalism and the Feminization of Politics". *ROAR Magazine*, June (6). URL: https://roarmag.org/magazine/municipalism-feminization-urban-politics/ (last accessed 13 January 2023).

Shea Baird, K. and Miralles, J. (2021). "What Happened to the Municipalists in Spain?" *ROAR Magazine*, 1 June 2021. URL: https://roarmag.org/essays/fearless-cities-municipalism-spain/ (last accessed 13 January 2023).

Zaero-Polo, A. (2017). "The Posthuman City: Imminent Urban Commons". *Architectural Design* 87(1), 26–35.

Tatiana Kolomeitceva
User Experience as Enlightenment: User Experience for Women Philosophers' Presentation

Abstract: The notion of user experience concerns a huge variety of different aspects of the interaction between the end-user and the company. The article focuses on user experience in the digital world (websites and apps). The theory of UX based on Dawkins' notion of memes is shown in its biological, historical and philosophical perspective. The article aims at giving an epistemological critique of UX theory and to discuss its practice with the help of the concepts of Enlightenment by Kant and Ankersmit, as well as "Being-ready-to-hand" by Heidegger. The concept of Enlightenment allows thinking of UX as the field which deals with not only cognitive but also anthropological and socio-historical ideas. Practical suggestions on better presentation of women philosophers in the digital world are given according to the conclusions of the theoretical part of the article. The digital world has to provide the opportunity for women to be thinkers and creators.

Introduction

During the last ten years media anthropology has been examining the bias of the digital world (De Seta 2020). Gender aspects in training the machines in AI research have also been analyzed (Pagliacco 2020). The digital specialists are still not being enough trained to avoid gender prejudices. Such prejudices often translate into biased interface (Barth 2012). The field of user experience testing has also been criticized for unfair recruitment (Teixeira 2018).

The field of user experience theory is not very young, it's almost ten years old. It spreads all over the world and tends to be a global phenomenon. There are user experience writing and design textbooks that postulate a unified approach to writing texts and designing for websites and apps. We have come to a situation where we have a unified approach of the interaction between the digital and humans and this approach is spreading global. The article analyzes one of the most powerful

Acknowledgments: I want to thank Veronika Detel for the warm discussion of the concept of my conference paper. I would also like to express my great appreciation to Dr. Waltraud Ernst and Luciana Santos for the methodical material I used in working on the text.

parts of this approach: the base of user experience theory is Dawkins' theory of memes (Evans 2017).

Writing and action are the key categories of user experience theory (writing makes the end-user act in a certain way). On the one hand, the field of user experience presents itself as practical and takes science as its starting point. On the other hand, user experience writing theory concerns texts. It can be expected that this field contains methodological problems and that an epistemological critique of it would be perspective.

The article suggests a philosophical critique of user experience in the digital world and then makes some practical notes on how the ideas of such a critique may be able to improve the opportunities of women philosophers' presentations. Firstly, it develops some thoughts on the epistemological critique of user experience theory. Secondly, it suggests the philosophical critique of user experience practice. The third part of the article is dedicated to practical suggestions a better presentation of women philosophersin the digital world.

Method

First of all, Dawkins' theory of memes is considered in the light of the critique given by Toledo (2009). Toledo questions the scientific validity of Dawkins' views: empirical evidence is replaced by the compilation of plausible stories about evolution. This provides an opportunity to use Ankersmit's analysis of a historical phenomenon, language and reality (Ankersmit 1994).

The article also uses Ankersmit's concept of Enlightenment to show that virtual reality and social reality today seem to be in two different eras. Kant's epistemological critique therefore becomes relevant: people in virtual reality must ask themselves again the well-known four questions ("What can I know?", "What must I do?", "What may I hope?", "What is man?"). The article refers to two works by Kant: *Beantwortung der Frage: Was ist Aufklärung?* (Kant 1784) and *KantsLogik* (Kant 1800).

The practical suggestions are formulated using a variety of theoretical and practical views in order to broaden the range of topics that need to be discussed when talking about user experience. The article uses Heidegger's notion of "Being-ready-to-hand" which allows thinking of websites and apps as tools (Heidegger 1927). But as Alison Stone has shown, Heidegger's methodology has a major disadvantage in that it emphasizes the loneliness of man, whereas he is fundamentally not alone (Stone 2019). So the article highlights the importance of changing the work of user experience specialists to become an "'intra-active' network of 'becoming with'": this notion was developed by Waltraud Ernst while researching the process of communication of people using tools (Ernst 2017).

The Epistemological Critique of User Experience Theory

According to user experience theory the information in the digital world must be packed well in order to go through "the psychological bottleneck" of attention (Evans 2017). The memes that fit the human nature will survive, others will die. Unfortunately, Dawkins' meme theory is highly criticized within the biology community: it does not meet the criterion of scientific validity. As Gustavo Leal Toledo points out, Dawkins engages in an interesting process of creating stories of evolution instead of writing scientific history.[1]

Of course today we have many good examples of books where biological or paleontological facts become the basis for thinking about society. For instance, new information on upright walking of our ancestors from millions of years ago helps to develop the idea that from the very beginning it was a life of mutual assistance and empathy rather than competition (Desilva 2021).[2] Unfortunately, a meme is not a gene, much less a fragment of a human ancestor's bone. Meme theory imitates science, as Toledo shows.

Our century continues to be fascinated by stories of evolution and it shows an interest in humanity's past and a belief in science. Strikingly, Dawkins' lack of evidence for a scientific meme theory as pointed out by Toledo echoes Ankersmit's separation of language, fact and historical narrative (Ankersmit 1994).[3] But in

---

[1] Toledo uses a wordplay involving "história" and "estória": "Uma boa narrativa memética necessita ter, como pano de fundo, uma análise empírica mais detalhada, bem como análises psicológicas explicando o motivo de certos memes terem mais sucesso do que outros. Não basta construir uma história interessante, pois uma história assim é apenas uma estória" (Toledo 2009, 149). The English language fully follows this wordplay: "A good memetic narrative needs to have, as a backdrop, more detailed empirical analysis, as well as psychological analysis explaining why certain memes are more successful than others. It is not enough to construct an interesting history, because such a history is just a story" (Translation TK).
[2] In fact, Jeremy Desilva questions patriarchy: "Are we innately violent and restrain our aggressive tendencies through rules and group norms, or are we peaceful by nature and become aggressive in oppressive societies that celebrate violence and the patriarchy" (Desilva 2021, 258).
[3] Ankersmit points out that "a universally agreed-upon proposal has hardened into a historical phenomenon which is part of the past itself" (Ankersmit 1994, 91). This is probably what happened with meme theory. It has gained so much flesh that it has become the basis for textbooks on user experiencewriting.

the case of memes there is the whole biological discussion which suggests that we do not deal with facts here.[4]

Ankersmit suggests that historical narratives can also contain philosophical concepts, as is characteristic of history when we think of Hegel or Marx, for example. Citing Ruse, Toledo directly points out that modern evolutionary narratives do not contain scientific knowledge but rather a metaphysical concept.[5]

When discussing historical narratives, Ankersmit separates two eras: the Enlightenment and Romanticism (Ankersmit 1994). In the Enlightenment, the historian believes that there is no gap between socio-historical reality and himself. Romanticism adds to the separation between man and history. The Enlightenment believes that the acquisition of knowledge can improve the world. Romanticism already sees the past as a mystery and the process of comprehension takes on its own dark tones.

The interaction between humans and gadgets today is based on a simple empirical basis, on experience. There seems to be no gap between the reality of the experience of using websites and apps. Perhaps using Ankersmit's approach we should say that for modern people there is no gap between the socio-historical reality of virtuality and themselves. And two conclusions may follow. First, we need a critique of virtual reality "from within" this Enlightenment situation. Second, we need the distance of Romanticism, since, according to Ankersmit, it is this distance that, together with loneliness, provides a reflection of the self. And we need the

---

4 Toledo's way of thinking about Dawkins' theory as just a "story" is what Ankersmit writes about the importance of the criteria "from the outside": "narrative unity and coherence always come "from the outside", as it were: they do not have their source so much in narrative itself – at least not exclusively so – as in what happens in the controversy concerning several narratives on the same topic" (Ankersmit 1994, 94).

5 Toledo writes: "Nas palavras de Ruse: Eles [Gould e outros] argumentam que para todos os casos os entusiastas da evolução conseguem arranjar uma história 'mais ou menos' adaptacionista. Em conseqüência, acabamos por ter diante de nós um quadro pseudo-científico, panglossiano e metafísico do mundo, no qual tudo acontece da melhor maneira possível, do ponto de vista da adaptação, por força da seleção natural (Ruse 1995, 43) Esta estratégia foi chamada de Panglossiana, uma referência ao personagem que Voltaire criou para parodiar a idéia do melhor dos mundos possíveis de Leibniz" (Toledo 2009, 123).("In Ruse's words: They [Gould and others] argue that for all cases evolution enthusiasts can come up with a 'more or less' adaptationist story. As a result, we end up with a pseudoscientific, Panglossian, metaphysical picture of the world, in which everything happens in the best possible way, from the point of view of adaptation, by force of natural selection (Ruse 1995, 43) This strategy was called Panglossian, a reference to the character that Voltaire created to parody Leibniz's idea of the best of all possible worlds" Translation TK). Remarkably, Toledo follows this up with a critique of Dennett's meme theory as well, which means that it would be impossible to pull Dawkins out and just frame Dennett in it. This branch of evolutionary theory is in great doubt.

reflection of the individual as a user of sites and applications. Otherwise, together with the meme theory, we will get thousands of pseudoscientific explanations as to why memes about women in the history of science and philosophy have not reached our time.

So at the end of this epistemological part of the critique we can follow the first path described above and perform some kind of Cartesian or Kantian algorithm of philosophical critique of particular websites and apps and the user experience theory on the whole. The practice of doubting one's experience and believing that things can be explained are the key points of the project of Enlightenment. As Kant said: "Sapere audi! Be brave to use your own mind!" (Kant 1784) We need to question user experience theory that pretends to provide the knowledge in the field of psychology and neuroscience in order to rule human attention. All the memes of awebsite or an app must go "through the psychological bottle-neck" (Evans 2017). Kant would say in this situation that people are like cattle who don't move without their nannies and they forget their freedom and they will be very careful and even suspicious if they are given their freedom.

Enlightenment is the independence of thought, the independence of choice. Kant also speaks about laziness as one of the main reason preventing people from thinking freely (Kant 1784). The algorithms of user experience theory develop such a laziness in humans. So, both Dawkins and Kant speculate onthe experience of the borders of human mind.

Four questions from Kant's *Logic* (Kant 1800) apply to user experience theory:
1) "What can I know?" The base of user experience theory is psychology and neuroscience appealing to Dawkins' theory of memes. On one hand, this can lead to a new stage of critique of psychology in a Husserlian way. On the other hand, user experience usage of the meme concept resembles the logic of expelling women from the history of philosophy: "A meme that never enters a brain ... it doesn't exist" (Evans 2017). So if people don't know about women philosophers, their writing doesn't exist. By the way, we can criticize Kant for the similar passage that I have mentioned. He does not speak about bottlenecks but about the sieve, like screen or flour-sifter. The best writings of the past went through this flour-sifter, we have only the best in present. That passage can be found in Kant's *Logic*, Kant's history of philosophy also does not speak about women philosophers.
2) The second question is "What must I do?" In the digital world according to user experience theory we must suggest content or design in any writing in order to catch attention.
3) The third question is "What may I hope?" User experience theory proposes its own pragmatic teleology with setting the main marketing goal and cut-

ting any practice that would not be appropriate for the "psychological bottleneck".

4) The fourth question is "What is man?" Here we have a certain concept of human nature: in the digital world "the memes that are optimized for receptivity will go on to dominate, while those that are misaligned with human nature will be selected against and ... ultimately go extinct, suffering the silent, ignored death of most digital inventions" (Evans 2017). Can we say that we don't know much about women philosophers' writings because they don't fit the human nature? This resembles how it used to be in the medical sciences before the 19th century: no experiments on rats, no chemistry, but a huge belief in human nature. You don't survive ... well your case is against human nature. Here we also may notice the metaphorical way of thinking using the notion of "human nature".

And of course there must be more metaphors. The human being is suggested to be a user, both of buttons and words (Metts Welfie 2020). Evans believes that people are "cognitive misers ... meaning that we will allocate the least possible processing power to determine your value to us" (Evans 2017).

A Critique of User Experience Practice

User experience aims at gadgets to become the main tools of humans. We can use Heidegger's concept of "Being-ready-to-hand" here (Heidegger 1927). If a tool is "Being-ready-to-hand" for Heidegger we can speculate of humans using it in a way that goes beyond its being just a tool. For instance, the ax gives us the information of our hand. We can hold the ax. This example is given by Heidegger. If there are buttons on gadgets, our hand can press them. Websites and apps can tell a lot about people if they are "Being-ready-to-hand". User experience specialists do their best to design and write the websites and apps in order to fit the psychological peculiarities of a person. User experience aims to make websites and apps "Being-ready-to-hand" in this way.

When we look at a website we can find banners that say "Subscribe" or "Buy now". This gives us the knowledge that the human hand can press these banners and the human mind can leave such sayings without asking: "Do I have the capacity to do anything else?".

All these sayings are in the imperative, which implies that we are dealing with instructions that are to be followed. No discussion. It is perfectly easy to repeat and remember those instructions. And people become the creatures pressing the banners on websites where they don't have room to question the whole process.

But what if, instead of these sayings like "Share" or "Subscribe", we rather had "Share your opinion with us?": not an imperative but a question?

Women need a space where they can be not only passive consumers but thinkers. It's hard to be a thinker on websites with banners and sayings in the imperative. The imperative creates hierarchy. Hierarchy leads to women's being expelled from the discourse. Websites and apps with banners that have questions on them would be "Being-ready-to-hand" as well. But such websites and apps, as "Being-ready-to-hand", would tell us that there is room for discussion, for using our mind and that all persons are subjects, including women.

Women need room for being treated like subjects, like thinkers in the digital world, not just consumers, but subjects who can express their opinion freely.

To conclude my critique of user experience practice, I would like to mention that all sayings in the imperative (even "Share your opinion") are inefficient if we want some room to answer questions. Banners with the words "What do you think of" would be more appropriate.

Practical Suggestions on Women Philosophers' Presentation in the Digital World

Practical suggestions for the promotion of women philosophers in the digital world will follow the logic of the theoretical part of the article.

Firstly, we may exploit our contemporaries' fascination with stories about evolution. Intellectual detective stories about searching for the missing branch of evolution could find their echo in the search for the truly missing link: the ideas of women scientists and philosophers who influenced men, famous in science and philosophy. Even three or five examples would suffice; it would be like finding the missing part in a dinosaur skeleton that has been on display in a museum for a hundred years. For publicity purposes, one could even put forward a provocative slogan or question containing the message that men' scientific writings descended from women's ideas. The concept of exadaptation can also be used here. An example of exadaptation is the fact, roughly speaking, that animal ear bones used to be part of the jaw in reptiles. And if women's ideas are used and developed by men – this could be called exaptation for promotional purposes.

The second suggestion is inspired by Dawkins' idea of a virtual museum of all possible animals. For biologists, this means bringing together in one space all the possible lineages of development of living organisms, including those that have not come to fruition in the course of evolution. The suggestion is to create a virtual museum of all philosophers, but concentrating not on inventing new possible philosophies, but rather on bringing together all the historical male and female figures in philosophy, including mothers, grandmothers, sisters, nannies, governesses, and anyone else who influenced the upbringing of the philosopher, not to mention influenced his ideas. In this way we would show that male philosophers were never alone from the very beginning (and this would illustrate Alison Stone's ideas (Alison Stone 2019)). The history of 19th-century Russian Empire has a beautiful example: the artist Arkhip Kuindzhi's wife Vera Shapovalova translated articles by the chemist Mendeleev from Russian into French. Perhaps it would be more promising to create a virtual museum that includes artists and scientists as well. For imperial Russia this would have been justified, since educated people at a certain historical period usually belonged to a more or less homogeneous stratum of society.

The third suggestion comes from a desire for user experience theory to have a scientific basis. Waltraud Ernst proposes a materialistic, human-machine interaction-based study of how those who directly use machines in their work can be improved (Ernst 2017). Writers and designers in the field of user experience can benefit from such an experience because it involves the active participation of workers in production changes, their reflection on both their work and themselves, and ultimately it leads to the creation of conditions for emancipation (becoming "'intra-active' network of 'becoming with'").

The fourth suggestion moves on with a critique of the theory from within the Enlightenment situation, as well as a call to create a virtual space where women can express themselves not as consumers but as thinkers: we need to rethink the process of moderating of websites. Now moderators are not so well-paid and well-trained. If we want the digital world to have room for discussion we should improve the moderation of it. At this point the idea of Enlightenment could be useful too. Kant speculates about how to manage the freedom of speech and justice and peace in a society (Kant 1784). So I would say that in our case the answer is good moderation and obeying the rules of moderation by all users.

The fifth suggestion follows the discussion of "Being-ready-to-hand". We could provide the texts of women philosophers and about women philosophers with audio versions. Headphones are another very popular gadgets that also can be named "Being-ready-to-hand", or "Being-ready-to-ear". And with audio versions texts of women philosophers could become resources of education for people leading active ways of life, for instance, going infor sports. In audio versions such texts could be posted on websites that contain books, music, audiobooks, podcasts, bookshops, etc., even in ITunes.

Results

User experience as a standardized and global branch of knowledge carries a controversial meme narrative containing metaphysics. This controversial theory opens the door to any discriminatory stories about why something or someone is unworthy of audience attention. At the same time, the experience of web and gadget users gives the illusory impression that there is no gap between the person and their user experience. The concept of Enlightenment can be a starting point for a critique of this situation from within. The concept of "Being-ready-to-hand" allows us to analyze the virtual world as well as gadgets as tools. At the heart of any proposal to promote women philosophers in the digital world must be the understanding that human beings are not existentially alone in their user experience. Rather, they can carry a liberating potential if the situation of solitude is avoided and conditions for reflection and discussion are created.

Our aim should be to rethink user experience theory and to create a new type of the digital where women are not only users but authors and creators.

References

Ankersmit, F. R. (1994). *History and Tropology: The Rise and Fall of Metaphor.* Berkeley: University of California Press.

Barth, D. (2012). "Designing the Gender-neutral User Experience". URL: https://web.wpi.edu/Pubs/E-project/Available/E-project-042612-150925/unrestricted/Designing_the_Gender-Neutral_User_Experience.pdf (last accessed 3 January 2023).

De Seta, G. (2020). "Three Lies of Digital Ethnography". *Journal of Digital Social Research* 2(1), 77–97.

DeSilva, J. (2021). *First Steps. How Upright Walking Made Us Human.* New York: Harper Collins.

Ernst, W. (2017). "Emancipatory Interferences with Machines?" *International Journal of Gender, Science and Technology* 9(2), 178–196.

Evans, D. C. (2017). *Bottlenecks: Aligning UX Design with User Psychology.* New York: Apress.

Heidegger, M. (1927). *Sein und Zeit.* Tübingen: Max Niemeyer.

Kant, I. (1784). "Beantwortung der Frage: Was ist Aufklärung?" *Berlinische Monatsschrift*, December, 481–494.

Kant, I. (1800). *Immanuel Kants Logik.* Königsberg: Friedrich Nicolovius.

Metts, M. and Welfie, A. (2020). *Writing Is Designing. Words and the User Experience.* New York: Rosenfeld.

Pagliacco, S. (2020). "Understanding Gender and Racial Bias in AI". URL: https://www.uxmatters.com/mt/archives/2020/11/understanding-gender-and-racial-bias-in-ai.php?fbclid=IwAR3dzTXvSo7a8850oQtlGN1TmvY-vYty8CUeYJxu-vxNP04VTw4yGAyAo (last accessed 17 November 2022).

Stone, A. (2019). *Being Born. Birth and Philosophy.* Oxford: Oxford University Press.

Teixeira, F. (2018). "Why Are You Still Recruiting User Test Participants by Gender?" URL: https://uxdesign.cc/why-are-you-still-recruiting-user-test-participants-by-gender-ed21ec6cff61?fbclid=IwAR28_WQqQFXUJ0gdmT9IT_PKp4F16JbPL6NywDnqSTIcGB1YUakVENfWQ_U&gi=7199-b0a72a0a (last accessed 17 November 2022).

Toledo, G. L. (2009). *Controvérsias meméticas: a ciência dos memes e o darwinismo universal em Dawkins, Dennett e Blackmore.* Rio de Janeiro: Pontifícia Universidade Católica do Rio de Janeiro.

Talya Ucaryilmaz Deibel and Eric Deibel

Artificial Intelligence in Ancient Rome: Classical Roman Philosophy on Legal Subjectivity

Abstract: Conceiving of technology in its relation to modern society in terms of power imbalances dates back to antiquity. Particularly the understanding that there are 'instruments' of 'instruments' has its roots in the Aristotelian conception of slavery as a morally unacceptable institution both historically and today. In antiquity, slaves were seen as tools in symbioses: The prosthetic extensions of others, simultaneously persons and things. When we conceive of digital technology as a communicative artefact that is an extension of technological reason we face the same dilemma today. This paper seeks to draw historical connections between cybernetics and slavery around the general question: will AI technology result in a new type of slavery? As such this requires us to rethink the intricate concepts of humanness, subjectivity and sovereignty in Roman philosophy in order to apply them to the contempaorary ethical questions on artificial agents and digitization of technology.

Introduction

The anthropomorphization of machines and the mechanization of humans blur the lines between 'humans' and 'things', opening a plethora of metaphysical and ontological discussions. The involvement of artificial agents in the 'political ecology' requires us to rethink the concept of legal subjectivity. The mastery and control relationship in cybernetics has always been central. Such sovereignity relationship referred as *domenica potestas* in Roman philosophy, was the key concept around which the Roman society organized its labor relations. Roman law, reflecting the tension between natural law traditions and pragmatism, demonstrated the traditional dualism of *persona* and *res* in legal subjectivity.

In ancient Rome, slaves were not considered as 'persons'. However, acknowledging the 'humanness' of slaves, Roman philosophy considered slavery being against the laws of nature and recognized the derivative legal subjectivity of the slaves. Such derivative subjectivity could be traced back to the Aristotelian idea that the slaves were inanimate tools, the prosthetic extensions of the owners or the 'instruments' of the 'instruments'. As such, AI, being the extension of technological reason, faces the same dilemma today. Artificial agents that are almost 'humans' with their epistemological decision making mechanisms, are owned by human masters as communicative artefacts. Being such 'actants' makes them capable of legal subjectivity.

As the historical connections between cybernetics and slavery resulted in the juxtaposition of the Roman slaves and artificial agents, this paper concerns itself with the dualist approach of Roman philosophy on legal subjectivity: being a person and a thing at the same time. Roman legal philosophy is not only the history of ideas, but also the future of legal relationships. Being the ultimate sci-fi of its era, the works of Roman jurists started to be considered as a model for the practical problems arising from AI technology.[1]

Roman Philosophy on the Dual Characteristics of Slaves

There is a common and reasonable misunderstanding that slaves were not considered human in ancient Rome (Chopra and White 2011). In the classical era, legal subjectivity was not determined based on humanness. It was formed based on different social and political status given to the human beings concerned. These forms of status were *status libertatis* (the liberty status), *status civitatis* (the status of citizenship) and *status familiae* (the family status). As such, only free citizens of Rome who were not under the sovereignty of another family member could be considered as a legal subject, a person who can have rights or obligations. These forms of status did not have the same gravity when determining one's personhood. The *status libertatis* was considered as the most important element when defining legal subjectivity. As such, if one lost his or her freedom he or she faced *capitis demunitio maxima*, the maximum loss of personhood (Buckland 1950; Watsons 1987; Borkowski and Du Plessis 2020). The relationship between master and slave revolved around *domenica potestas*, which was the reason why slaves were subjected to the dominion of another; or better put: to the law of another. It referred to the patronage relation between the master and the slave, a type of sovereignty performed over a human being.

Nevertheless, the sources on classical Roman philosophy, notably the works of Cicero and the Stoicist school, demonstrate that even though slaves were not con-

---

[1] The legal implications and the liability of AI with contractual and delictual nature are discussed in depth in another paper. As part of the general project, this paper contains the philosophical considerations and challenges that are necessary for the legal architecture of the AI technology. For more information about the practical implications, see Ucaryilmaz Deibel 2021.

sidered as persons in the legal and institutional sense, they were acknowledged as human beings. This was a dictate of natural law. In other words, the philosophical works reflected the obvious tension between how the status of slavery prevented legal personhood, making slaves the object of the legal system, and how at the same time their natural status of humanness could never be denied. Such concrete effect of the classical natural law tradition survived via Justinian's compilation of Roman law in the post-classical era, the *Corpus Iuris Civilis*.

This text did not only constitute a civil law codification of the Byzantine era but also a text book of law and legal philosophy, which demonstrated the different views of the classical legal philosophers. The first book of the compilation contained an explanation, stating "all legal rules are related either to persons or to property or actions" (*omne ius quo utimur vel ad personas pertinet vel ad res vel ad* actione) (Ins. 1.2.12, Goudy 1910) In this sense, the status of the slaves was expected to be addressed in the law related to property, as the slaves were thought nothing but a mere thing. As such, the classical jurists Ulpianus and Paulus presented us with a naturalistic understanding of personhood: *Servus nullum caput habet*, the slave has no personality. The word 'caput' which means head in Latin reflected the precarious nature of their existence: The slaves could never be subjects (Gaius, Ins. 1.86).

Classical Roman texts also addressed slavery as an institution within the book on persons, acknowledging they are as human as any free person can be. The slaves were not only *res*. They had full responsibility from their criminal actions, delicts, and the decisions they made. The sentence in Latin was not constructed with the word *aut* (or), but instead, the word *vel* (rather, or...) was used. This is generally accepted as a conscious linguistic decision as *vel* as a disjunctive conjunction indicates a contrast depending on a subjective choice whereas *aut* refers to an objective situation. In other words, *aut* indicates excluding the other possibility, whereas *vel* underlines interchangeability (Buckland 2010). To support this view, Theophilus clarified this statement in the 6th century as he acknowledged that the division between human beings and things was not definite (Theophilus, *Paraphrasis Institutionum* Ad. In.1.3.pr.). There was no black and white. Orlando Patterson sees this dualism of being a person and thing at the same time as a practical achievement that leaves no place for vagueness (Patterson 1982).

What Patterson emphasizes is that Romans developed numerous remedies to overcome this duality. They positioned their legal system as opposed to their natural law tradition to address the challenges based on simply policies. This story reminds us today of the status of AI as it establishes a basis from where to look at a future interchangeable interrelationship between *persona* and *res*. AI as a human and a thing and as person and property. In the contemporary world, the machines are acting like humans, realized as a dynamic and interchangeable relationship between master and machine wherein we are convinced the machines are like us. Not quite, of course, with this symbiosis of man and machine, a legal relationship is gradually materializing that inescapably returns us to the Roman roots of law – to when this relationship was not about machines and their masters, but about masters and slaves. Then, just as today, we are not just speaking philosophically, as with Hegelian dialectics, but literally about the return to the origin of contemporary law, which lies in how Roman society organized its trade and business around its laws of slavery (Wiener 1989).

Modern history of cybernetics – ergo robotics –, returns to us something that was always already central to history, and hereby legal philosophy and subjectivity is forced to face its roots. How is it that with the spread of AI throughout our lives come conceptualizations and practical implementations that have their origin 2000 years ago? It is redundant to state that such a focus on the Roman view on legal subjectivity from the lens of slavery and its relation to AI should not in any case be formulated or interpreted as a defense of slavery as an institution that lacks morality, both historically and today. This applies to how slavery exists in today's world for many millions of living people, to the law as well as to how we imagine the possibilities for AI gaining self-awareness (Pagallo 2011).

Roman legal philosophy owes tremendously to Greek thinkers, as Romans were never as philosophically minded as their Greek contemporaries. As such the Roman approach to slavery is distinctively similar to the works of Aristotle. In *Politica*, Aristotle discussed the slavery as either artificial or natural (Aristotle, *Politica* 1.1255a.). Natural slaves were the ones that were born slaves, they had the aptitude for physical labor. They did not share the cultural similarities with the Greek and they were obedient. On the other hand, some slaves were unnaturally under *domenica potestas*. They were war captures, or criminals condemned to slavery – *servi poenae* – and later demonstrated a fear of rebellion as a result of 'unnatural' slavery and of a clash of consciousness between masters and slaves (Smith 1983). Coming from Greek philosophy via Stoicism, Romans acknowledged slavery as *contra naturam*. As opposed to the Aristotelian view, they did not differentiate between types of slavery, rather they condemned all sorts of slavery relations as being against nature (Gaius., Ins. 1.52, Ins. 1.3.2–3, D.1.5.4.1 Florus 9 inst.).[2]

In ancient Greece and Rome, slaves were not seen different from masters. They were merely considered as his extremities. Aristotle uses the word 'organon' as he refers to the position of the slaves. They were the animate tools, the instruments that the master utilizes. In other words, their existence was derivative to the

---

2 The expression reads as follows: *"Servitus est constitutio iuris gentium, qua quis dominio alieno contra naturam subicitur."*

existence of the master (Aristotle, *Politica* 1255b). The Romans adopted this view of Aristotle as 'slaves as masters' and designed their juridical system based on the secondary and derivative legal subjectivity of the slaves. This system is proposed to be adopted when it comes to the legal acts of AI in our contemporary world.

AI: More Human than Human

Artificial intelligence (AI) is often used as an umbrella term and as such, has connotations that are reductive in regard of what counts as intelligence and by extension, 'being human'. In this regard its challenge to the notion of humanness centers on 'intelligence' as the ability to think and to create. When AI has the ability to display a certain behavior that might have been epistemologically categorized as intelligent, we are describing it as more or less similar to the agency of a human beings (McCarthy 1990). Such an approach is obviously fallacious in the sense that it is overly simplistic in how it seeks to define and standardizing the notion of intelligence.

Treating intelligence as an engineering benchmark, however, reflects the *modus operandi* of machines to execute cognitive and analytical human-like functions. Accordingly, scientists distinguish between different scales and capabilities of AI. Sometimes this is presented with computers as the principle instrument whereby cognitive processes are investigated and imitated, but increasingly no such tools are mentioned but rather AI is imagined in terms of complex and distributed self-learning processes that lack clear supervision. Identifying output streams, aka machine learning is an essential part of such a *modus*. The idea is to let systems evolve and learn on their own, meaning that they will evolve in an exponential manner in terms of capability (LaGrandeur 2013).

Such a process therefore relies on its own previous knowledge and experiences, once again humanizing machines so that we can imagine them to be thinking and acting rationally. In this sense machine learning shows such anthropomorphism in how it imagines the famous Turing test and similar imitation games can be passed. If a machine has natural language processing, knowledge representation, automated reasoning and machine learning skills, it is considered as an agent thinking like a human being. A similar approach is seen in 'deep learning', which refers to the building and usage of neural networks as decision making nodes, mimicking human neurology (Kelleher 2018; Peters and Besley 2019).

In other words, we cannot understand what is going on in that machine-like brain as it increasingly is presented to us like a black box with nontransparent and incalculable internal dynamics (Teubner 2006). Therefore, artificial intelligence as a discipline is based on the premise that every aspect of learning can be simulated by a machine. Simulation is the key concept here: Cameras as eyes, microphones as ears, speakers as mouth, sensors as skin and nose, which creates the humanness of the machine.

The questions can also be reversed as humans can also be considered machines. Our neurological activities include mechanical steps, making us organic, natural machines. Human beings are composed of information, where life is coded in their DNA. Information theory also suggests that feelings and intelligence is nothing but impulses. In other words, humans are conceptualized as feedback loops, as information that is generated within the constant interplay between biology and informatics. In this sense, AI refers to the artificial brain and robotics refers to the artificial biology.

There are many expectations about the end-result of this interaction between human and machine. Some visionaries are predicting that humans in the conventional sense will be extinct by the time of fully sentient AI. Whether or not that means we are enslaved by the AI is open for debate as one could argue that human intelligence would be persuaded to become part of 'artificial general intelligence'. Such speculation, however, is not crucial to the argument proposed here. Such visions (like general AI) might turn out to be exaggerating the expectations about AI, deep learning, machine learning etc. in how it invariably relies on anthropomorphization of human-machine relations. Whether or not this might be a form of (science) fiction, such expectations have real consequences: The anthropomorphism of the machines comes with the mechanization of human beings.

Roman philosophy helps us to draw the analogy between slaves and AI with its legal and pragmatic understanding of the possible dual state of agents: One can simultaneously be a *persona* and a *res*. Slavery reflected a *sui generis* status as a compromise between the unique characteristics of humanness and property in the "liberal economy of Rome". Roman philosophy provides us with the first examples of hybrids visible in the inter-changeable relationships of the master and the slave. Today, we are witnessing these hybrid structures as the association of human and non-human actors where personality serves as the element that allows for their structural coupling (Teubner 2006; Luhmann 2012).

It is instructive here to consider for a second the term cybernetics as a predecessor of AI and the information age (Kline 2015). The term cybernetic, as the predecessor of AI, first used by Norbert Wiener, comes from Greek *kubernetes*, steersman, referring to devices that could self-steer. The connection between slavery and cybernetics was therefore revolving around *domenica potestas*. What classical Roman philosophy shows us is that humanness was never an inherent property when determining legal subjectivity. While a sentient, human mimicking robot is *a fortiori* easy to analogize to a natural person, this is not necessary. There is no need to naturalize humanness or assume a human spirit as the foundation of legal personality, as is the case with the Hegelian understanding of legal personality. No analogy between natural persons is required when we refer to how corporations, foundations and associations have legal personality which had already started to be established in Roman law.

In other words, personifying non-humans is a social reality today. Recently the Whanganui River in New Zealand was accepted as having legal subjectivity (Stone 1972; O'Donnell and Talbot-Jones 2018). This may well be a legal necessity for the future AI. Law attributes legal personality to flows of communications to stabilize social expectations (Teubner 2006). Teubner proposes the non-human objects to be personified as the Latourian concept of *actants:* Communicative structures to which "the apparatus of science has given a voice". (Teubner 2006, p.510). Today, new hybrids and *actants* are entering the commercial scene and transforming the political ecology, challenging yesterday's anthropocentric view and transforming it to the ecocentric view of legal relationships (Latour 1996; Teubner 2006).

Going Back to the Classical Debate

Legal subjectivity and the social challenges arising from AI are widely discussed in today's legal scholarship. The relationship between philosophy, law, technology and society might never have been this concrete. Yet, classical philosophy on the blurred lines between persons and things shows us that the challenges are not new. It is within that context that Roman law remedies are again relevant for today's predicament as they open up a perspective to break through the juxtaposition of the machine and the human that is making it difficult to manage the plethora of practical issues that come with the development of AI. This similarity is even visible in official documents, such as those by the EU expert group on the liability of AI which referred to Roman remedies as a possible solution to govern AI.[3]

However, such a practical perspective comes at a price, opening up the relation between master (*dominus*) and slave (*servus*) that clashes with our modern understanding of what is to be a fully emancipated liberal agent (Kant 1998). Sensible as this perspective is when trying to understand the relation between legal and technical subjectivity in practical terms, the problem begins when pushing this argument on to the question of the unity and the continuity of human nature. Such an argument might give the impression that the declassification and disqualification of human exceptionalism is a given, considering that it is based on an 'inaccurate' split of law/ethics and technology. After all, if humans with their laws

---

[3] European Union Expert Group on Liability and New Technologies (2019).

and ethics were never isolated from technology, is the human as a bearer of right an illusion that modern science strips from us? Perhaps we never had the dignity, autonomy and reason we pride ourselves for to begin with? (Žižek 2004; Tamminen and Deibel, 2019)

In other words, we should be aware that such versions usually come with a concept of the liberal agent that is presented in a distinctly non-Roman conception of free will, dignity and autonomy that belongs to the history of liberal democracy's commitment to the freedom and equality of individual citizens. This is not how the Romans understood the individual, which matters when we enter the murky terrain of AI-consciousness and self-awareness and by extension begin chipping away at historically static or universal understandings of what is unique about 'the human' and whether or how we should be committed to moral autonomy of human individuals as the highest human good in liberal societies as organized around the rule of law.

Such a more fundamental philosophical debate about what it is to be human has different sides in its relation to technology. For example, there is a strong current in STS scholarship that finds these problems relevant to law through its critique of how law is usually understood as following technological developments. The idea that technological developments and societies are separate and independent is still around (Wyatt 2008). Instead, other STS scholars like Jasanoff argue that legal philosophy and technology mutually shape each other and this process does not revolve around two separable, independent worlds. Both the material and the social construction of technology and law need to be acknowledged (Jasenoff 2004).

This also applies to Roman philosophy and its relation to technology which presents us with a legal example of how the introduction of a novel technology did not simply change the legal rules of its time. Rather, it helped to shape the legal paradigm continuously. This included the practice and management of slavery as a Roman institution, which in this version of events turns into an illustration of how technology and law were the socio-technical infrastructures of its day and how both were always embedded in social contexts. Not only does it involve human actors deciding to use technology morally or not, legal ethics depend on relationships between human and technologies, existing in hybrid networks (Jones 2018).

Roman law of slavery was revolutionary in including 'hybrids' or 'actants' in commercial life (Latour 1996; Teubner 2006). Such perspective might inevitably result in the assignment of a *sui generis* legal subjectivity to AI (Solum 1992). What is important in such a future scenario would be considering this solution from the perspective of the classical Roman philosophy which requires not to be trapped in the early-modern conception of humanness. Legal subjectivity is not a uniform concept. Rather, it refers to a bundle of fundamental capacities such as having rights, obligations, responsibility, accountability and so on. In this sense, in the future if AI will ever be granted some of these capabilities, its legal subjectivity will be based on the fiction that they have human-like characteristics. In other words, they would be *persona ficta*.[4]

Conclusion

The inevitable cyborgization of humans would definitely be a change for tomorrow's post-humanist world, if not danger (Fuller and Lipinska 2014). This novelty brings classical questions about humanness into the spotlight again. What was human yesterday and what will it be tomorrow? In the near future it is predicted that some AI will be treated as business partners or family members instead of simple tools. Just like the slaves being integral to business-life in ancient Rome, the AI will *de facto* be capable of making decisions which will affect the subjectivity of others. Facing the new technological paradigm with the current development of AI, we can also decide to go back 2000 years to look for answers. We are invariably going to be confronted with similar questions as the ones that the Romans had. This is urgent, considering that we are dealing with a variety of debates over how to deal with the technology-driven dualism in the legal world.

In ancient Rome, slavery was never a definite status. The master could emancipate the slave any time. The emancipation (*manumissio*) resulted with a change of *cives* on the side of the slave who became a *libertinus* (the freedman). This ended the *domenica potestas*, that is the power of sovereignty of the master on the slave. Yet it created a new patronate relationship with the former master who became a *patronus* and the former slave, *libertinus*. Ultimately our analysis brings us closer to the Aristotelian idea of "slaves as masters, not others". This shows two sides, changing *cives* and, in time, re-inventing the patronage relationship.

In this sense there is no contradiction with modern ideas but a continuity from antiquity to the legal theories of agency from Aristotle to Hegel's dialectic of lordship and bondage (Hegel 1977). Hegel, as a reader of ancient Rome, juxtaposed Roman philosophy to the political developments of his time. The narrative about the power relations between two people changing positions over time, ending bondage, reflects the concept of *manumissio* in Rome. Hegel's struggle of bondsman and the lordship is focused on consciousness before the social roles were

---

[4] The theory of *persona ficta* was developed in Canon law, mostly attributed to post-glossator jurist Bartholus. The legal subjectivity of all non-humans such as companies, guilds, associations etc. is based on this theory.

changed. This idea is also applicable to our questions: Can the sophisticated AI be a quasi-*libertinus* after being granted a *sui generis* legal subjectivity? Is the AI more likely become enslaved by humans or will the consciousness of robots enslave humans?

The word *persona* in Latin comes from the ancient Greek word *prosperon*, often referred to the outward appearance of the man (van den Hoven van Genderen 2018): just like today's AI technology is an extension of the human intellect and intentions. Today the position of AI is frequently formulated as a false dilemma that would have us choose between robots as objects or robots as sentient entities. This logically implies that we are dealing with subjects, ones that eventually might legitimately ask to be fully emancipated entities on the premise that they have degrees of autonomy, dignity and a functioning consciously. Even if we are modest about the notion of self-aware AIs, the opposite also applies. Nonetheless, this type of 'return of slavery' should not be understood as a toleration of any type of slavery whether it is race-/class-oriented or simply referring to our merger with machines. Quite the opposite, we should remain critical and be aware of its past as it exits in Roman legal philosophy.

References

Aristotle. *Aristotelis Politica* (translated and edited by Sir W.D. Ross, 1957). Oxford: Clarendon Press.
Borkowski, A. and Du Plessis, P. (2020). *A Textbook on Roman Law*. Oxford and New York: Oxford University Press.
Buckland, W. W. (1950). *A Textbook of Roman Law from Augustus to Justinian*. Cambridge: Cambridge University Press.
Buckland, W. W. (2010). *The Roman Law of Slavery*. Cambridge: Cambridge University Press.
Chopra, S. and White, L.(2011). *A Legal Theory for Autonomous Agents*. Ann Arbor: University of Michigan Press.
European Union Expert Group on Liability and New Technologies – New Technologies Formation (2019). "Liability for Artificial Intelligence and Other Emerging Technologies" URL: https://op.europa.eu/de/publication-detail/-/publication/1c5e30be-1197-11ea-8c1f-01aa75ed71a1 (last accessed 1 November 2021).
Fuller, S. and Lipinska, V. (2014). *The Proactionary Imperative: A Foundation for Transhumanism*. London: Palgrave Macmillan.
Gaius. *Institutiones.*, Vol.1–2, (translated and edited by Francis de Zulueta, 1946). Oxford: Clarendon Press.
Goudy, H. (1910). *Trichotomy in Roman Law*. Oxford: Oxford Clarendon Press.
Hegel, G. W. F. (1977). *Phenomenology of Spirit*. Trans. by A. V. Miller. Oxford and New York: Oxford University Press.
Jasanoff, S. (2004). "Ordering Knowledge, Ordering Society". In Jasanoff, S. (Ed.), *States of Knowledge: Co-production of Science and the Social Order*. London: Routledge, 13–45.
John McCarthy, J. (1990). *Formalizing Common Sense*. Ed. by V. Lifschitz. Norwood: Ablex.

Jones, M. L. (2018). "Does Technology Drive the Law? The Dilemma of Technological Exceptionalism in Cyber Law". *Journal of Law, Technology and Policy* 2, 249–284.

Kant, I (1998). *Critique of Pure Reason*. Ed. by P. Guyer and A. W. Wood. Cambridge: Cambridge University Press.

Kelleher, J. D. (2018). *Deep Learning*. Cambridge, MA: MIT Press.

Kevin LaGrandeur, K. (2013). *Androids and Intelligent Networks in Early Modern Literature and Culture*. London and New York: Routledge.

Kline, R. (2015). *The Cybernetics Moment or Why We Call Our Age the Information Age*. Baltimore: John Hopkins University Press.

Latour, B (1996). "On Actor-network Theory: A Few Clarifications". *Soziale Welt* 47(4), 369–381.

Luhmann, N. (2012). *Theory of Society*, vol. 1. Trans. by R. Barett. Palo Alto, CA: Stanford University Press.

O'Donnell, E. L. and Talbot-Jones, J. (2018). "Creating Legal Rights for Rivers: Lessons from Australia, New Zealand, and India". *Ecology and Society* 23(1), 7–14.

Pagallo, U (2011). "Killers, Fridges and Slaves: A Legal Journey on Robotics". *AI & Society* 26(4), 347–354.

Patterson, O (1982). *Slavery and Social Death: A Comparative Study*. Cambridge, MA: Harvard University Press.

Peters, M. and Besley, T. (2019). "Critical Philosophy of the Post-Digital". *Postdigital Science and Education* 1(1), 29–42.

Smith, N.(1983). "Aristotle's Theory of Natural Slavery". *Phoenix* 37(2), 109–122.

Solum, L. (1992). "Legal Personality of Artificial Agents". *North Carolina Law Review* 70(4), 1231–1288.

Stone, C. (1972). "Should Trees Have Standing?" *Southern California Law Review* 45, 450–501.

Tamminen, S. and Deibel, E. (2019). *Recoding Life: Information and Biopolitical*. London and New York: Routledge.

Teubner, G. (2006). "Rights of Non-Humans? Electronic Agents and Animals as New Actors in Politics and Law". *Journal of Law and Society* 33(4), 497–521.

Ucaryilmaz Deibel, T. (2021). "Back to (for) the Future: AI and The Dualism of Persona and Res in Roman Law". *European Journal of Law and Technology* 12(2), 1–27.

Van den Hoven van Genderen, R. (2018). "Legal Personhood, Robotics". In Corrales, M. et al. (Eds.), *AI and the Future of Law*. London: Springer, 257–290.

Watson, A. (1987). *Roman Slave Law*. Baltimore: John Hopkins University Press.

Watson, A. (1985) *The Digest of Iustinian*. Vol.1–4. Philadelphia: University of Pennsylvania Press.

Wiener, N. (1989). *The Human Use of Human Beings, Cybernetics and Society*. London: Free Associations Books.

Wyatt, S. (2008). "Technological Determinism is Dead. Long Live Technological Determinism". In Hackett, E. J. et al. (Eds.), *Handbook of STS Studies*. Cambridge, MA: MIT Press, 165–180.

Žižek, S. (2004). *Organs without Bodies: On Deleuze and Consequences*. London and New York: Routledge 2004.

Part III: **History (Non-Western and Western)**

Priyanka Jha
Pursuits of Global Gendered Intellectual History: Stories from India

Abstract: The key argument that this paper poses is the need for intellectual history to be gendered as well as inclusive in its orientation, bringing voices from the post-colonial and non-Western worlds. Building from the narratives and experiences of India, and the multiple feminist interventions and contributions in sites of knowledge and thinking, this paper argues for the urgency of making global gendered intellectual history of ideas inclusive and diverse. It emphasizes the urgency of a shift towards it invoking the deep diversities in the world of women thinking, drawing from multiple experiences resulting from distinct contexts, locations and temporalities. This paper also makes a case for identifying the common and similar ideas that women thinkers share, but at the same time, the necessity for a context-specific focus on positionalities that are crucial in shaping those ideas.

The Indian Experience

The Context

India's interaction with Modernity was mediated by Colonialism and like many post colonial socities, witnessed colonial modernity, which shaped certain trajectories in these societies. As a result, colonies and their future normativities even at the moment of their independence were enmeshed in borrowed ideas to some extent. Like other specters, this was reflected in the pedagogical moorings of the universities and syllabus of the of the schools and universities in these newly independent nations. With the shift from the colonized past to the uncolonized and free present, in the wake of selfhood and autonomy in political, economic and social processes, there was still an absence of freedom and autonomy in the thinking and systems of knowledge, as the many educational institutions as well as processes reeled under the burden of the colonial imprint. Knowledge was one of the sites that failed in decolonizing itself and was under the remnants of colonialism.[1] In

---

[1] The argument for the decolonizing of mind and knowledge has been an important one in post-colonial societies, posed in the African and Asian thinking. Nandy (1983) is a crucial work on this thesis.

the independent times, from 1950s onwards, what one witnessed, that the curricula and syllabus of the schools and universities in India and other African and South Asian nations drew from the Western and European frameworks. Much of the research and teaching resources were derived from colonial frameworks.

Over time and with a growing demand for indigenizing the pedagogies, the educational system evolved. Some form of autonomy was reflected in the shape of teaching one's history, philosophy and thinking. Humanities and Social Sciences as two fields attempted to decolonize themselves from the epistemic control, as one witnessed the entry of Indian thinkers and political philosophers in the curriculum. The native thinkers were being taught along with the Western thinkers like Plato, Aristotle, Social Contractarians and others. However, despite indigenizing the intellectual history, there was a serious lapse on part of the scholars and academicians in gendering the discourse. This was evident as a failure in terms of bringing indigenous women thinkers and their work to attention. Women thinkers were missing from the pedagogy as well as the syllabus. It can't be a matter of coincidence that the thinkers and philosophers with positions on key concepts were all men, whether transatlantic or native. It would be difficult to imagine that women did not have an active contribution in the domains of the social, political, economic and cultural concerns in India and other societies.

From the post-colonial perspective, there were two big problems that the global intellectual history or Indian socio-political thought[2] suffered from: firstly, either women thinkers were excluded entirely or even if there was some success in bringing certain women thinkers to attention, they were not native and indigenous but from the West and Europe. The second concern was the challenge of finding women thinkers from one's own context as well. The important issue here is the absence of indigenous women thinkers in the discourse and the necessity of invoking them in an equal manner.

Recalling from my first interaction as undergraduate student majoring in Political Science, in India many of the women thinkers that were taught or engaged in various courses of thought and theory were drawn from the West.[3] This was a crucial moment for me as a student of ideas and theory as I was privileged enough to be introduced to the ideas of important women thinkers in a context in which women thinkers were missed completely.[4] My inception to political theory and

---

2 In India, Intellectual History is taught as Indian Political Thought, Sociological Thought and also as Socio-Political Thought in many universities.
3 West here represents Europe and the transatlantic world.
4 It is important to highlight here that teaching women thinkers are not usually the norm in Indian universities, however, certain places consciously teach women thinkers. The very reason that some of us were introduced to the writings, works and contributions of women thinkers was be-

thought was gendered. I was taught key political ideas and concepts from the writings and works of thinkers like Mary Wollstonecraft, Rosa Luxembourg, Simone de Beauvoir, Hannah Arendt and many other great women, who shaped my consciousness and understanding of the human condition. But at the same time it was also difficult and problematic to not find enough Indian or South Asian women thinkers as part of the course. This was a problem, as I knew extremely well that many women thinkers from the subcontinent who had positions over key sociological, economic, cultural and political debates were missing. The important issue that needs attention here is that even in the narration of exemplary women, often these are drawn from the Western world, which is extremely important in circumstances of patriarchal listings without women, but then it is devoid of the native and indigenous women thinking.

In the present time, when there are growing pressures on intellectual history, to be global in its orientation. It needs to be gendered at the same time, bringing in experiences and voices from the non West. This paper argues that the pursuit of the global gendered intellectual history of ideas has to be non-Eurocentric in approach and invoke the diversities of women thinking from across the world. It needs to bring in voices, experiences and subjectivities of women from the non-Western world and draw from post-colonial subjectivities.

Tracing the Indian Intellectual History: History Troubles, Feminist Revisions

It is a common saying that history is written by the victors, which takes us closer to the fact that this kind of history is always a partial rendition of the moments and events. This sort of history is limited and distant from providing us with a multiplicity of facets that might give us the true picture. The narration then is from one's location and standpoint, in this case this is a male position of what we know as history. It has been written and narrated by men for the 'others'.[5] In India, like in other societies, our history was never narrated by one of us, women, but for the longest time it has been narrated by men.

---

cause of the conscious efforts of the 'feminist teachers' we had in our colleges and universities. I was also lucky to be introduced to Indian women thinkers at this stage but this cannot be generalized as the norm usually is the absence of native Indian women thinking across Indian universities.

5 'The other' is seen as those who were marginalized, women, subalterns, Dalit, tribal and others at the fringes.

The rationality behind this, as it was men who secured for themselves the sole position of writing, narrating, recording and later putting out the results for 'the others to read'. Right from the times of antiquity to modern times, knowledge has been presented as a male domain. In India, this was justified from the ancient societies on with text with Texts like the Dharmashastras including Manusmriti, that kept women outside the fold of knowledge, denied them access to it. This male custodianship was problematic but was never questioned, it was routinized and legitimized by various sources. Religion is a primary source that was used to justify keeping women out of these domains.[6] Most of the Indian religions like Hinduism, Islam, Buddhism, Sikhism were prescriptive concerning the women's role and position in society and were responsible for limiting women's access to knowledge. The key role that women were prescribed was the dutiful mother, wife and daughter, denying them any autonomous selfhood. This was a global phenomenon: testimonies can be found for the sexual division of labor legitimized by religion all over the world.

The sexual division of labor found its justfication and legitimacy in a variety of sources found support in the writings of male thinkers, interestingly even in liberal celebrated male thinkers, heralded as the cornerstone of intellectual thinking. It is in their works and writings that we find the hardening of the gender roles. The construction of women as being emotional and non-rational was another brilliant way of keeping women outside the fold of knowledge, either in creation or dissemination. So this situation worked in ways and manners that made the existing privileged position of men better. As a result, what was written as well as recorded suffered from the male gaze and bias.[7] It was largely male historians who wrote histories and it was from their histories, that the list of thinkers deemed as foundational for intellectual history was excavated. For many years, it was the result of these histories that led to the shaping of constructions around women. This was also central to the definition of the contours of the society, which also led to the

---

[6] There are historical records drawn from across cultures that testify to the fact that men systematically kept the others outside the fold of knowledge. One of the big justifications for legitimizing limited knowledge was down from the cannons of religions. Religion was a used as a tool for the status quo which was a clear demarcation in the form of gender roles. In India, Hinduism and texts like Manusmriti were deployed from the ancient times to keep women and the other marginalized outside the fold of knowledge. It instructed the readers that women, animals and the lower castes were not evolved enough to receive any kind of education or knowledge.

Two important texts that engage with this issue are Uma Chakravarti's *Gendering Caste: Through a Feminist Lens* (2018) and Sharmila Rege's *Against the Madness of Manu: B R Ambedkar's Writings on Caste* (2013).

[7] Feminist historians like Gerda Lerner, Mary Beard, Joan Scott and Uma Chakravarti have articulated their views on the relationship between patriarchy and history.

greatest misogynist public-private divide. As a common global phenomenon, the core and peripheries were constructed as it was men in the center/core of the discourse, the ones who ruled and stayed in the center/core of undertakings of knowledge and relegated the women to the peripheries. Society was thus constructed that women had no contribution in the larger male public domain. Men took on themselves of not just shaping the outlines of the public but also had a say on the undertakings of the private.

Power translated not only in terms of control over the institutions, systems, processes but most importantly knowledge. It was men who were in charge of what was considered important for recording, documenting and disseminating. Like any domain of knowledge, history and intellectual history of ideas succumbed to this power dynamics. Men were in control of history whereas women were being pushed outside. The process of male historical narration was the mainstream which invisibilized women and their contributions outside the records. This led to one of the longest processes of marginalization that many societies have encouraged without alterations.

However, despite many barriers, women struggled to make space for themselves and much later in modern times, made many attempts towards transforming the given of the male articulations. It is important to make it clear that right from the times of antiquity to the present, women were also creating, recording and disseminating knowledge equally through their indigenous ways. The trouble was not the absence or dearth of resources, materials and contributions, but the ignorance of it. The great annals of written history and the hegemonic male history failed in mentioning the ideas, teachings and knowledge that women produced. In the case of colonial societies, this emerged as a bigger problem as the history was written by two kinds of men, the native and the foreigners, the colonized and the colonizers. Many of the histories on the Indian Subcontinent, present South Asia, were undertaken by British historians like James Mill, Mountstuart Elphinstone, Vincent Smith, William H. Hunter and W. H. Moreland who narrated the history with imperial sympathies and failed to mention the contribution of the many women who in an equal manner had a role to play. This was emulated by the native Indian historians as well who suffered from the male bias themselves. These nationalist historians like Jadunath Sarkar, R. C. Dutt, Tara Chand and others, who made huge contributions towards giving these societies their narrative, have failed to do justice to the issue of gender in these narratives.

I remember very well, as a student of history, the school textbooks failed seriously in this domain. Even if there were certain references towards the inclusion of women regarding the nationalist struggle for independence, this was never narrated in the manner of women as autonomous beings but they were referred to as dependants, to be channelized by great leaders who all happened to be men.[8] There was another aspect to this kind of narrativization, that even if very few women were discussed and invoked as the iconic women leaders, they were few.[9] Even to this day, how history is taught in Indian schools has very little reference to women who participated in the nationalist struggle for independence. The trouble with this kind of narrative stems from the fact, that women are portrayed as bearing no autonomous agency and they were led by male leaders. It is not possible that women did not have an active role. Women were active agents of transformation and change; borrowing from Meera Kosambi's work, they were crossing multiple thresholds. They were leading their struggle and were creating their paths for themselves and many others.

Cracks in the Narration: Feminist Inroads and Laying the Groundwork for a Gendered Intellectual History of Ideas in India

Some of the writings and works that have now been resurfacing across societies concerning women's contribution have been possible due to the untiring efforts of feminist historians. Gerda Lerner, Mary Beard, Joan Scott for the West and for India by Tanika Sarkar, Uma Chakravarti, Mrinalni Sinha, Kumkum Sangari, Sudesh Vaid and others gave to the people gendered history.

One of the biggest contributions of feminist historians was the transformation and alteration in the discourse and narrative of events. It showed to the masses the missing and invisible women. It was in these histories, that one found the active contributions and participation of the many women in important historical events and moments. The works produced by these historians deconstructed the perspective of women as passive recipients, invoking them as agents of transformations. Before these seminal interventions, mainstream history portrayed women as passive, being dependent on male leaders for change.

---

8 An instance of this could be that women's entry into the nationalist movement in India was portrayed as Gandhi's contribution. In some of the key historical writings and later carried forward in the school textbooks the view is expressed that it was Mahatma Gandhi who led to the entry of women in the movement as he invented methods that led to a large number of women entering. This fact has been critiqued by many feminist historians who argue that women were very much part of the struggle way before Gandhi entered into the picture. There are many narratives that tell us about women who were active in the social reform and other moments of agitation that preceded Gandhi's arrival in India after his time in South Africa.
9 It will be an interesting perspective to study the choices of invoking certain women over others.

The gendered history of social reforms in Modern India was instrumental in invoking articulations of women bearing agency in their uplifting. The narratives of autonomous negotiations led by women in resolution of tropes of injustices were central. From the writings of women thinkers, many myths were shattered, one being the nature and role of great reformers. It was found out that many of the so-called liberal male leaders themselves worked with a patriarchal orientation, to the extent that they were obstructive to the works of many women social reformers.

The existing historical discourse on social reforms in colonial India in the late 19th century before the feminist historical interventions constructed the colonial masters and liberal native men as the harbingers of change: in ways and means invisibilizing the contribution of many women thinkers who were fighting against multiple patriarchies, the indigenous as well as the foreign, the native and the masters. The resolution of social evils like child marriage, conditions of widowhood, women education and many other issues were credited to the liberal reformist men. However, towards the 1980s, with the emergence of social histories, this narrative on social reforms suffered massive critiques with the works of feminist historians like Meera Kosambi, Uma Chakravarti, Tanika Sarkar, Rosalin O Hanolin and Geraldine Forbes who successfully brought to the public significant works of women thinkers who played a catalyst role in social reforms. It was from social histories that the readers were introduced to women thinkers like Pandita Ramabai, Savitiribai Phule, Ramabai Ranade, Kanshibai Kanitkar, Anandibai Joshee and many others for the first time.

The work and contribution of women thinkers were retrieved from a multiplicity of sources like autobiographies, speeches, letters, works, biographies and literary contributions. These sources not only informed the audience about the nature of work that women waged for their emancipation but also the kind of struggles they risked. From being ostracized to public ridicule or humiliation, the struggles were umpteen. When Savitribai Phule along with Fatima Sheikh started the first school for widows and women from the depressed classes, they were ostracized and ridiculed, to the extent that they were physically stopped on their way on umpteen occasions. But they remained undeterred. Feminist social histories also provided the audience with many organizations, established and run by women themselves, reflecting on the leadership that women had.

Education as a field of historical investigation helped in bringing out the role of women a catalyst of change. Geraldine Forbes's *Women in Colonial India* and *Women in Modern India* were instrumental in bringing to our attention that Indian women who not only were self-trained themselves but also set up institutions for women's education. These texts were central in introducing exemplary women like Rassundari Devi, Dr Hemabati Sen, Begum Rokeya and others from the colonized world who were instrumental in opening the field for young girls and women during the times when education was always a privilege of men and in ways was constructed as an all-male terrain. Many of these women were, in the truest sense, the real pioneers of women education in India. It was not the Macaulays of British India that led to women's education being considered as something constructed. Prior to Forbes's kind of contribution, the education of women and the other marginalized was narrated as emerging in the benevolence of men – whether foreign or native.

Along with feminist historians, literary critics as well produced voluminous scholarship on voluminious contributions, works produced by women in India. The multiplicity of texts in the forms of novels, poems, plays and other creative engagements gave insights into the lives of women, lifeworlds and their engagements with patriarchy. The role of feminist literary criticism provided avenues in the form of understanding the misogyny and sexism that plagued some of the classics. These were crucial in not only inverting the canon but also provided the multiple sites in which women were creating their imaginaries. It was in these works that one could locate the alternative imaginations that women were writing about. These writings helped in developing new strategies to open up canonical texts for feminist readings.

Feminist critics turning to women authors presented many different imaginations that authors wanted to convey. In this trajectory, one of the central works, Sussie Tharu and K. Lalita's *Women Writing in India: 600 B. C. to the Present* was significant in bringing the diversity of literary women's voices across the regions of India from ancient to contemporary times. This work was phenomenal, as an intervention when there were claims of an absence of women from literary fields. It made available those women literary icons in a context where only male authors were considered as writers. What was rather fascinating was the fact that it reinvented myths and epics which portrayed women in domestic patriarchal roles. There were new roles that women were creating for themselves, many times in a sexualized manner. Women sociologists and the establishment of many centers for women studies equally played a pivotal role in bringing gender into the discourse.

Women's movements across the globe are of significance here, because they connects us to the common struggles that women wage across the different parts of the world. However, the need to recognize the role that context plays in the shaping of the demands requires attention. Despite the commonality of goals that women aspire for, the articulation and aspirations are enmeshed in local patriarchies. These movements provided us with distinct frameowrks for undertaking Global Intellectual History. One has to recognize that many of the gains that women in contemporary times enjoy are the results of long drawn-struggles led by extraordinary women. In India, many of the women studies departments that were set up in India since the 1980s were the result of the women's movement in India. Led by feminist thinkers Veena Majumdar, Lotika Sarkar, Devaki Jain and others, the pressures mounted by the women's movement led to the emergence of many women studies center in India. The Centre for Women's Development Studies (CWDS), founded in 1980, was one of the first to be established in Delhi. In India, the movement, activism and academics go hand in hand, shaping the demand for gendering sites of education. It is this triad that played a significant role in shaping the discourse on gender.

Diversity and Subjectivity Reflected in Women's Movements

The women's movement in India also informs us about the nature of distinct concerns. It also informs about the differential nature of struggles waged by women in the non-West. The position of women in Western societies was different from women in this part, as the struggles aimed at basic human rights. The struggle in the West for the attainment of basic rights was overcome many years. At the time, when women's movements had succeeded in making suffrage rights a reality in the West in the late 18th century, women in this part of the colonized world were demanding basic rights in the form of education, health, maternity-related matters, marriage and measures against child marriage. One cannot deny that women across the world waged significant movements, but the nature of concerns varied and so did the strategies. This is also true for contemporary times when we compare the situation in the transatlantic and post-colonial worlds. One also has to understand that in the colonized societies, the women struggles were twin-fold in nature as they waged struggles against two kinds of patriarchies in their fight for basic rights, the colonial oppressors and the native men. This theme also guides the Global South Feminism, which stems from this vantage point, that societies and nature of oppression – and thus, the struggles –vary. Therefore, the gendered intellectual history of ideas needs to be framed with this unique positionality, as there is no meta-narrative of this understanding.

One of the most important reflections drawn from the Indian experience of gendering knowledge is that women writings and experiences cannot be essentialized. Women have waged struggles in different parts of the world and they continue to do so, and there is so much commonality to these struggles, however, the nature of concerns is deeply rooted in one's positionality. It becomes central for those engaging with these ideas and concerns to also give adequate attention to diversities. There are differences in the way women have envisioned emancipation, as the context and location play a crucial role in those envisions. Therefore one of the most important tasks of the gendered intellectual history of ideas is to invoke these diversities, and in its pursuit of becoming global, it will have to include the women thinkers from the non-West, from post-colonial societies. These women thinkers who could not be successful in gaining attention or fame, like others, need to be equally engaged. Their contributions and works would add perspectives making the discourse richer and diverse.

Failure of Intellectual History to Take the Gains of the Feminist Scholarship

The contributions of each of these gendered sites, whether in the form of history, sociology, or literary studies, are of huge significance for gendered intellectual history. The groundwork has been prepared for the intellectual historians to work with. In the present form, intellectual history, either in India or globally, has failed being gendered in its orientation, despite this groundwork. One can say, as a result, that intellectual history has been myopic and limited. In India, despite the voluminous feminist contributions, intellectual history fails to grasp the gains from the feminist readings of history, sociology, literary works and social movements. What one witness is a certain continuity of the kind of fixity that exists in forms of engagement largely and sometimes solely with male thinkers and their ideas. In many ways, it is the male thinkers who are included and the female thinkers are excluded. And even if certain women thinkers are invoked, these are the mainstream celebratory names which existed even before the feminist interventions. But the important concern here is that despite the feminist contributions in the form of giving to the nation and the audience the missing, invisibilized and marginalized thinkers, intellectual history continues to be of a status quo kind in its orientation.

It is crucial for Intellectual history of Ideas to be gendered in its orientation, incorporating and adding the many gains of feminist interventions. The lost, missing and invisibilized voices are accessible. The corpus of women writings and engagements is available to us now creating the base of knowledge which we did not have and this is the very foundation on which the superstructure of intellectual history needs to be established. With this as the background, let us now explore the arguments that support the shifts towards global gendered intellectual history and the possible ways and means of doing that.

Global Gendered Intellectual History

Before we locate the arguments for the necessity of shift towards global gendered intellectual history, it is crucial to understand how this paper understands gendered intellectual history (GIH). It is a field of knowledge that is primarily based on the works and contributions of women thinkers from across the world. Invoking the multiple diversities and subjectivities that shape ideas and thinking, this way of doing ideas in history is based on positionality, context specificness and temporality.

The Need for Global Gendered Intellectual History

Gendered intellectual history as a field of knowledge is not simply an epistemic issue, but an act of politics, subversive politics. It will contributing towrads alternative reading and invocation of normative values and concerns like liberty, eqaulity, dignity, justice and many others. As a result, instead of these ideas emerging in strands and tropes of emancipation and autonomy for women, it succumbs to the frameworks of domesticity encouraged through prescriptions and expectations for women.

Gendered intellectual history of ideas bears within itself the capacity of transformation as it provides us with the exemplars and philosphers that women rarely encounter. What women usually are socialized into are the narratives of the heroes, kings, saints and wise men. As a result, the narration of the big attainments of human civilization is then reflected as the deeds of these men. These narrations, missing the queens, heroines, revolutionary women, don't bear any autonomous ideas for girls and women, as they are restricted to the conventional roles as good mothers, daughters, wives. They fail to provide a reference for the non-conventional. Women who would question, challenge or critique the social norms are referred to as deviant and revolutionary woman. They should be part of the conversations, deliberations, narratives and discourse. The change and shift towards gendered intellectual history would aid in deconstructing the roles and norms for women. It will provide articulations on distinct roles and imaginations for womanhood and girlhood.

It would present women as active agents in making history and societal change. Women who were creating, acting, transforming in their national histories. This would aid in waning the perceptions built around women as passive recipients and make them visible as active agents instead. Involved in politics and reforms, this would give them role models. As testified from the history of the social reform movement in India, many women who worked towards the emancipation of women were not simply at the receiving end, as narrated by the various schools of history, either nationalist, Cambridge or Marxian school. Gendered intellectual history of ideas bears the responsibility of invoking and mainstreaming these agents of transformation. Otherwise many of the exemplary women thinkers would be buried in anonymity.

The need to popularize the active agent imagination of women is a crucial task because of the nature of consequences it bears on the lives of women. The selective memory on part of men and male historians has been responsible for adding passivity in the lives of women. This also rendered women's work and their contributions non-significant and made activities of men important and meaningful. This history of selective memory and great forgetting had consequences for women, as in the absence of their history, women were presented as being inconsequential in the shaping of historical events.

Gerda Lerner writes: "'The great forgetting', selective memory has a special significance for women. Women are half of humankind, they have always carried out half of the world's work and duties and have been active agents in history. Yet in the recorded history they have only appeared only as 'marginal' contributors to human development" (Lerner 1997, 52).

Not only women thought and contributed to the entire process of thinking. Invoking the contributions through the means of gendered intellectual history will have ramifications on patriarchy, deconstructing the historical conditioning. Feminist historians like Mary Beard, Gerda Lerner, Uma Chakravarti and Tanika Sarkar have written on patriarchy and its role in shaping history. This mode of doing history of ideas leads to the twin process of alteration of historical conditioning and creation of consciousness at the same time. How history has been narrativized tends to uphold sexual division of labor relegating women within the confines of the homes. This particularly also informs about the shaping of the perception of one's own being and selfhood, of looking at oneself through the eyes of the other. This is degenerative as it embarks on solidification of the inferiority thesis, routinized and socialized through patriarchy.

Lerner writes: "Men similarly miseducated through a distorted image of the past, have been reinforced in their culturally created sense of superiority and the conviction that a sex based division of labour justifies male dominance" (Lerner 1997, 120–121).

The ideas of passivity and inferiority which get entrenched through the many ways in which history is recorded and disseminated further through other social processes. The reinforcement of historical psyhological complex impacts the future for the girls and women, who find themselves situated in frameworks reinforced by the one-sided history which is lopsided, failing to bring on fore the multiplicity of roles that women played. There are no heroines, no queens in the stories that have been given to us. There are no images and pictures on the walls in which the young girls grow up. There are very fewer role models for the new generation. Young girls and women need their exemplars and role models. GIH would provide exemplars and role models. Therefore the act of GIH is not just political but social as well.

Need for Diversities and Subjectivities in Gendered Intellectual Histories

Gendered intellectual history of ideas will also have to be inclusive in its orientation, as it will need to bring to the fore diversities of experiences. There is a need to underscore that subjectivities, positionalities are of importance here. Despite the commonality of certain experiences that women have, there is also the need to understand that the engagements with these experiences are different for women. Location and positionalities shape one's subjectivities, and the need to also bring in diversities of voices and subjectivities in the study. What men would consider as normal and conventional would be oppressive and exploitative for women, and it works in the same way for women. One's understanding is shaped by one's location in the society and by the situatedness in power relations. Some women are more empowered than the women, sheerly because of their location in political, economic and social strata. India like many other societies has a vast array of diversities in the form of cultural and social identities emanating from the tropes of religion caste, ethnicities and even linguistics. For instance, Caste plays a very important role in India, as it is a form of social stratification and it formalizes into class. Indian women are divided on caste and class lines and one's location in the caste order defines the nature of opportunities available. The possibilities are not similar for upper caste and lower caste women and their lifeworld would be shaped by positionality in the society. To understand the ideas and politics of the marginalized women it becomes important to invoke experiential epistemology. This mode emphasizes the experiences of oneself emanating from one's location, in this case, Caste. As a result, two experiences cannot be the same. Therefore it would be faulty to juxtapose the diversities of experiences that women share as one.[10] Tribal women in India would have distinct experi-

---

[10] Dalit feminism becomes a major strand of thinking in feminist politics. Works of thinkers like Gopal Guru, Sharmila Rege, Ruth Manorama and Kalpana Kannabiran have been instrumental in bringing the lines of distinction to attention. Gopal Guru's "Dalit Women Talk Differently" (1995) and Rege's *Dalit Feminist Standpoint* (1998) can be referred to here.

ences from the ones faced by Dalit women or upper caste women. It is a crucial aspect that this project has to consider. It becomes crucial to invoke subjectivities to be inclusive and not essentialize women's experiences from across the world as being one and the same.

Tasks Ahead: Possibilities and Ways

Global gendered Intellectaul hsitory requires urgency and cannot be ignored. The following section reflects on the possible modalities of undertaking the task in certain ways and manners. These suggestions despite being centric to India have global orientation as well.

Redrafting the Curriculum

The first important aspect of making intellectual history of ideas more gender-sensitive is bringing more works of women thinkers in the curriculum in schools and universities. There is enough evidence that can be drawn globally that women thinkers are conspicuous by their absence. Courses on political theory, thought and political philosophies in various disciplines in India have been failing to be gendered. Especially courses on Indian political thought and sociological thinkers fail to give adequate attention to women thinkers. Taking a look at some of the course designs of the big Indian universities, one finds a paucity of women thinkers, whereby even to this day the majority of thinkers are men. Even if there are some women thinkers to be taught, there are limited, mostly the more celebrated and famous ones are taught.

These courses demand rigorous revaluation as it leads to essentialization, as some few women thinkers can't be representative of the diversities of ideas, thoughts and experiences. The issue of syllabus revisions is an important point of consideration. Despite the annual or bi-annual revisions in the syllabus, the chances of incorporating women thinkers are still on the weaker side. There has been a growing demand for making the syllabus gendered, but there is still a long way to go. This also makes us think about the pedagogical aspects of social sciences and humanities. The teaching in itself will have to be gendered, which doesn't mean teaching a separate module on gender. The orientation with which courses are taught shall have to be gendered, with the narration of events or the explanation of social, political and economic processes in a gendered way. There is no add and stir phenomenon but it will have gender as a key category in dissemination.

Also in societies where there is a huge interface of the political establishment in the domain of education the difficulties are bigger as the administrators in the form of bureaucrats, mostly men, are involved in making policies of education. Most of them are distant from the gendered perspective, mirroring the larger societal ways of thinking, and don't feel the need to incorporate the aspect of gender or pedagogy. They think like policy practitioners, specialists and bureaucrats and are not teachers. It might not even be a crucial aspect for them. So for them missing the gendered aspect might not be a matter of consideration. But for the academicians and teachers, it is. Therefore, the need to reexamine, revise, reform the syllabus and pedagogies from a gendered lens becomes a key concern. There is also the need to have more research funding for gender and women studies as many of the centers grapple with the concern of paucity of funds.

Creation of Archives and Making Women's Writings Available

There is the need to create new archives. With the contribution of feminist historians, literary critics and sociologists, a large number of feminist works have surfaced and a certain archive has been created. It is crucial to extend the existing archives to incorporate the missing women voices and at the same time to create new archives. Archives are very important as memories, histories and acts are stored here. The memories and histories of women's struggles managed to create a space for themselves in the larger imagination of the nation, but there are many more processes and events that require the urgency of the feminist lens. Not only should more research on women thinkers be encouraged but this should be done with rigor – as it will open more sites and terrains which will contribute to the larger archives in making. These archives will open new ideas, new perspectives and standpoints which might be an alternative to the normative ones.

This also shows the need for making the archives and works of women thinkers available and accessible for all. In the present time, when the world is moving digitally beyond boundaries and borders, it is a wonderful opportunity to familiarize with the diversity of women's writings and ideas all over the world. This will have to be supported in the framework of 'open access'. One witnesses the rise of many feminist digital platforms adding to the discourse; there is the need to see more of them.

The Need for Translation

Most of the writings written by women were in their native tongue. India is a linguistically diverse nation and the 8th Schedule of the Constitution of India recognizes 22 languages and many dialects. One needs to understand that English became the medium of instruction only with British colonialism, and it is a legacy that was taken on after the Independence. In contemporary times, Hindi and English are used as language for official communication in India, but each state also has a mother tongue. Many of the women writers used their mother tongue to communicate their ideas and as result, a large number of works were produced in Bengali, Marathi, Gujarati, Punjabi, Sindhi, Konkani, Maithali – the list is endless. One of the most important tasks that lie ahead is to draw to attention many of these unseen works. They need to be invoked in popular spaces, which requires extensive translations. One of the reasons that many of these works have been missing is because of not being translated. Intellectual history of ideas shall have to invoke the translated works. This is an important consideration because, in the non-transatlantic worlds, many thinkers use their language instead of English as the medium of communication.

Invoking Women Thinkers in the National Imagination

One of the primary reasons for the absence of women thinkers from the public imagination can be attributed to the failure of the government's actions. The failure has been on part of everyone involved in the knowlege production and dissemination, as they have failed to include women thinkers and writers in an egalitarian manner, as they have done with the male thinking. Many of the South Asian nations since attaining independence have been actively involved in commemorating the great leaders who played an important role in the nation's independence. They are hailed as role models, and one finds them in the form of statues or images in the public spaces or on the walls of public institutions like schools, universities and government offices. The public world is filled with the busts of these exemplary men. This makes sense as the nation wants to keep them alive in the public memory, but when this phenomenon is looked through the lens of gender, it raises many objections. Women thinkers are not invoked along with these men with these men. One hardly finds the images of the extraordinary women who played an equal role in the attainment of independence and in the shaping of the national consciousness. One rarely finds these women in the galleries and walls, neither their statues, along with the men. In India, Gandhi's statues are the most common ones, as he is also invoked as the father of the nation. But the women who stood with Gandhi are missing. One rarely finds the statues of women leaders like Kamla Devi Chattopadhyay, Sarojini Naidu, Annie Beasant who played an equally important role as any other male leader. Symbols are central to nationalist imaginations, as they have meanings. But if the symbols of the nation are limited and only of a certain kind, the kind of impact this has is of a certain kind. If these women leaders and thinkers are invoked at the same level and specter as the male thinkers and leaders, there is the possibility of this translating in other realms as well, most importantly in the realm of knowledge and the possibility of them finding a place in the syllabus and pedagogies of the nations' education.

Women-centered Intellectual History of Ideas

As Gerda Lerner suggested, in the pursuit of finding the missing and absent women's history, there is a need for the shift towards 'women-centered history'. This makes a compelling argument for the women-centered intellectual history of ideas. The task is not simple but can be undertaken. One possible way of doing this could be rigorous engagements with the key ideas of normativity, through the works and writings of women thinkers. For example, the ideas of freedom or equality can be mapped through the works of women thinkers and the possibilities of finding an alternative understanding, as a result of differential experiences and subjectivities of women. For instance, if we engage with the writings of thinkers like Tarabai Shinde on the idea of equality in India, her essay (Shinde 1991) brings to the readers very interesting insights on the meaning of equality in comparison to male thinkers like Jaya Prakash Narayan. Equality as an idea would have a completely different understanding.

A woman-centered intellectual history of ideas can be undertaken by bringing women thinkers to positionality on these ideas. This can be done by putting a spotlight on women thinkers, for example in the Indian Scenario, by invoking thinkers like Pandita Ramabai on religion, Tarabai Shinde on equality, Savitribai Phule on caste and oppression, Anadibai Joshee on body and subjectivity, Begum Rokeya on education, Kamla Devi Chattopdhayaya on rights and freedom, Godavari Parulekar on labor. This list can be continued endlessly as there has been so much written by these thinkers on the key thematic concerns. There are also the possibilities of offering separate papers and courses on gendered intellectual history in the departments, whereby the key ideas and themes may be engaged solely with the works of women thinkers. Another interesting way is to teach an equal number of women thinkers along with the male thinkers. Saying this, one should realize that it should not be the sole responsibility of departments of gender studies or women studies centers to be teaching gender or gendered intellectual history of ideas, but it should be the conscious decision of departments in general to teach in a gendered manner.

Conclusion

In the background of the larger argument regarding the shift towards gender intellectual history stands the fact that it also needs to be global at the same time. It needs to draw from the diverse corpus of women writings and engagements. In its pursuit to be global, it needs to draw from the non-Western societies which are post-colonial, where colonialism shaped and impacted the thinking of women in ways and manners that were distinct from other parts of the world.

The key aspect of this global gendered intellectual history is to be context-specific and temporal. Contexts are very central not just in understanding the life world of thinkers. We will not fully understand the nature of their works and the lines of distinctions without understanding the context. This way of doing history of ideas cannot solely be an actress-oriented approach, but rather it has to be a comprehensive approach. This kind of intellectual history has to be deeply entrenched in the diversity of experiences. It will help us move beyond the given frames and would also give us a sense of the frames and references different from our own. A global gendered intellectual history would also help in mapping and drawing connections across societies. It is not just an act of being there or having lists of women being taught, but it is a statement of presence. We were there and we made history.

The domain of intellectual history of ideas becomes more important for certain societies that still do not treat women equally, where there are still struggles for human rights, where women are still far away from being part of the discourse, despite shaping them. When women have shaped their destinies and paved the way for many others, it becomes all the more reason for them to have a body of knowledge in the form of a global intellectual history of ideas as a frame of reference. The task is not just limited to providing them with a corpus of writings and engagements, but it also includes the possibilities of inspiring them to shape their own lives and trajectories.

References

Chakravarti, U. (2013). *Rewriting History: The Times and Lives of Pandita Ramabai*. New Delhi: Zubaan.
Chakravarti, U. (2018). *Gendering Caste: Through a Feminist Len*s. Revised Edition. New Delhi: Sage and Stree.
Dubois, E. C. and Vinay, L. (2017). *A Passionate Life: Writings by and on Kamladevi Chattopadhyay*. New Delhi: Zubaan.
Forbes, G. (1996). *Women in Modern India*. Cambridge: Cambridge University Press.
Forbes, G. (2005). *Women in Colonial India: Essays on Politics, Medicines and Historiography*. New Delhi: Chronicle Books.
Guru, G. (1995). "Dalit Women Talk Differently". *Economic and Political Weekly*, 14–21 October, 2548–2549.
Kamladevi, C. (2014). *Inner Recesses Outer Spaces: Memoirs*. New Delhi: IIC and Niyogi.
Kosambi, M. (2007). *Crossing Multiple Thresholds: Feminist Essays in Social History*. New Delhi: Permanent Black.
Kumar, R. (1993). *The History of Doing: An Illustrated Account of Movements for Women's Rights and Feminism in India, 1800–1900*. New Delhi: Kali for Women.
Lerner, G. (1997). *Why History Matters: Life and Thought*. Oxford: Oxford University Press.
Majumdar, V. (1995). *Emergence of Women's Question and Role of Women Studies*. New Delhi: CWDS.
Mani, B. and Sardar, P. (2008). *A Forgotten Liberator: The Life and Struggle of Savitri Bai Phule*. Delhi: Manohar.
Mehta, V. R. (1992). *Foundations of Indian Political Thought*. New Delhi: Manohar.
Nandy, A. (1983). *The Intimate Enemy: Loss and Recovery of Self under Colonialism*. Delhi: Oxford University Press.
O'Hanlon, R. (1994). *A Comparison between Women and Men: Tarabai Shinde and the Critique of Gender Relations in Colonial India*. Madras: Oxford University Press.
Pantham, T. and Deutsch, K. L. (Eds.) (1986). *Political Thought in Modern India*. New Delhi: Sage.
Rege, S. (2013). *Against the Madness of Manu: B. R Ambedkar's Writings on Brahmanical Patriarchy*. New Delhi: Navayana.
Rege, S. (1998). "Dalit Women Talk Differently: A Critique of Difference and Towards a Dalit Feminist Standpoint". *Economic and Political Weekly* 33(44), WS39–WS46.
Rege, S. (1998). "Dalit Feminist Standpoint", *Seminar* 471, 47–52.
Sangari, K. and Vaid, S. (1990). *Recasting Women: Essays in Indian Colonial History*. New Brunswick, NJ: Rutgers University Press.
Sarkar, T. (2001). *Hindu Wife, Hindu Nation: Community, Religion and Cultural Nationalism*. New Delhi: Permanent Black.
Sarkar, S. and Sarkar, T. (2008). *Women and Social Reform in Modern India*. Bloomington: Indiana University Press.
Shinde, T. (1991). Stri Purush Tulana (A Comparison of Men and Women). In: Tharu, S. and Lalita, K. (Eds.), *Women Writing in India 600 BC to the Present*. Delhi: Oxford University Press, 223–235.
Tharu, S. and Lalita, K. (Eds.) (1993). *Women Writing in India: 600 B.C to the Present*. New York: Feminist Press.
Young, I. M. (1990). *Justice and the Politics of Difference*. Princeton: Princeton University Press.

Toyomi Iwawaki-Riebel
Yosano Akiko's Philosophy and Poetry – Modernization of Japan and Women's Liberation

Abstract: The purpose of the examination of women's liberation theory in the thoughts of Yosano Akiko (1878–1942) is to reconstruct the processes of modernization and internationalization in Japan in the Meiji era (1868–1912). Akiko argued about the issue of women's liberation, refuting "the protection of mothers by the nation", and expanded the cultural criticisms and poetics on political, educational, and social issues. Touring through Europe and studying modern Western philosophy (1912) also opened the horizon of poetry and philosophy. Akiko spoke of ways to improve her position, including the need for women's higher education and financial independence. Despite the problems of feudal and ultra-nationalist propaganda of women's education as "good wives and wise mothers" in the Post-Meiji era, Akiko defined the free and cultural way of women toward the future. This paper reviews Akiko's fundamental considerations on the "Theory of remodelling of women" not only in pre-modern Japanese contexts, but also in modern and intercultural contexts.

Introduction

Yosano Akiko has been a subject of modern Japanese women's history. She lived in the turbulent period from the modernization of the Meiji era (1868–1912) throughout the Taishō democracy (1912–1926) until World War II during the Shōwa era (1926–1989). By rethinking the transition of Yosano Akiko's ideas, we can now refine her criticism in the 21st century, as it is more widely globalized in human life such as politics, economy, numerous wars, and epidemics. How can we develop Akiko's ideas that reach across time and borders?

Yosano Akiko was born in 1878 (Meiji 11) at the dawn of modern Japan which was characterized by free civil rights and globalization. She was familiar with classical literature such as *The Tale of Genji* by Murasaki Shikibu and participated in the literary activities of *waka* poetry early on. She ran away from her feudal home in 1901 (Meiji 34) and married the poet Yosano Tekkan. In the same year she gained her fame with the publication of *Midaregami* (Tangled Hair) and became the representative of the magazine *Myōjō* (Venus), which led the movement of Meiji Romantic poetry. The anti-war poem for her younger brother who went to the

Russo-Japanese War (1904–1905), *O My Brother, You Must Not Die*, and her publication of the *New Translation of Genji Monogatari* are also famous. Nevertheless, from the end of the Meiji era, Akiko worked on social criticism such as issues of women's rights, education, and suffrage. She has founded the *Bunka Gakuin* in the latter half of the Taishō era and has been promoting girls' education based on the spirit of liberalism.

As an important background of Japanese society and literature, let us consider the transition from romanticism to naturalism after the Russo-Japanese War (1904–1905). Akiko also made political and social critiques by "the true pursuit of humanity" from "the literature of non-political, non-social individualistic expressions" of her inner world. She helped the establishment of modern individuals and the realization of "democratic nationalism".[1] It was a transitional period from an era of universal ideals for human beings and a world without any doubt about the policy of modernization, to a nationalistic era in which that universality is lost. Akiko died in 1942 (Shōwa 17) without seeing the end of World War II, leaving behind the problems of women which had not been resolved during the war.

Akiko's Starting Point

"yawahada no	"soft skin
atsuki chishio ni	warm with heated blood
furemo mide	not touching it
sabishikarazu ya	on the path of virtue
nichi wo toku kimi"	aren't you lonely?"

(Yosano 2010 [1901], 9; Reichhold and Kobayashi 2014, 39)

This *waka* has been read worldwide. Janine Beichman passionately translates this *waka* poem as follows:

"This hot tide of blood
Beneath soft skin and you don't
Even brush it with a fingertip
Aren't you lonely then
You who preach the Way?" (Beichman 2002, 105)

Akiko revolutionizingly wrote *waka* poems about the body and sensuality of women, which leads back to the Heian era (794–1185) literature, while overturning

---

[1] See *"minshushugiteki nashonarizumu"* (Odagiri 1961, 137 and 241).

the established ethical view of women from the perspective of free love in early poetry anthologies such as *Midaregami* (Tangled Hair). It is indeed her motivation to raise awareness of the independence of women who have "given birth". The turning points that determined Akiko's poetry and thoughts were her first encounter with Western thoughts based on her experience of traveling to Europe (1912 Meiji 45) and also her *bosei hogo ronsō* (dispute over motherhood-protection) with Hiratsuka Raichō (1918–1919). Akiko emphasized the importance of rational thinking and education for women in the relationship between herself, the nation and the world through her departure from the traditional *ie* (house) system and her cross-cultural experiences.

Akiko's "World Citizen" and Her Journey to Europe

1909 Yosano Akiko criticized the trend of values of men and women after the Russo-Japanese War: "(Men and women) live in cooperation with each other and take charge of work that suits them. I would like to make sure that neither men nor women have the eccentric thoughts of being filthy because they give birth to children and being precious because they go to war" (Yosano 1987 [1909] a, 35).

At that time, the problem of women's education in Japan was to teach ethics that should be "*ryōsai kenbo* (good wife, wise motherhood)" and "*shudō saishō* (husband leads, wife harmonizes)" (Yosano 1909b, 45). These were a gender ideological pair with the national slogans "*fukoku kyōhei* (Enrich the Country, Strengthen the Armed Forces)" and "*shokusan kōgyō* (encouragement of new industry)". The cultural concept of a complete "human" was not formed by scholarship and wisdom there.

In *Women and Thoughts*, published in 1911, the year before traveling to Europe, Akiko said that Japanese people especially women, lacked rational thinking. Akiko herself had no university education. She was proposing that there is an urgent need to make "a woman who considers, a woman who thinks, a woman of brains, a woman who works concurrently, a woman of hands". She also thought that "a new qualification to remodel herself and be a solution to women's problems" is an urgent task. Her ideas of peace and coexistence enumerate the ancient and modern philosophical values that she has maintained throughout her life:

> "Who am I?" "I am a human. Even though there is a gender distinction between men and women, their value as a human is equal." "I can see all things with human beings as the basis, and I can see myself as one of all things or living things." "I am one of the world's citizen and one of the Japanese." "I don't know what purpose I was born in. Like I don't know the

purpose of the universe." "I have a desire to live." "I have a desire to go as completely abundantly as possible." "Human cannot live alone. They need a communal life." "Men and women are the starting point of communal living. A couple is established here. Next, parents, children, and society." "If there is a society, naturally an organization of the ruled person will be created to facilitate the communal life of the society. Also, due to the individual genius and education, which is the basis of the society, there will be differences in wisdom, feelings, and will. It creates a distinction between occupations." "People, both as individuals and as members of society, must enjoy all kinds of happiness. The best of happiness is to demonstrate individuality and do our best, and to understand and appreciate each other's individuality" (Yosano 1987 [1911] a, 59).

Here we can also see the phenomenological effect of G. W. Hegel (1770–1831) on Akiko. Hegel discusses "the pure concept of approval" in Chapter IV, the beginning of Section A of "Self-consciousness" in *The Phenomenology of Spirit*, and the "recognition of others" is also meaningful for Akiko's social thought of self-establishment. Hegel's argument is thus expressed: "Self-consciousness can only be satisfied in a different self-consciousness (through absolute negation)". In the movement of this process "I and the other acknowledge each other as mutually appreciative" (Hegel 1991 [1807], 144). Akiko had a more or less Hegelian basis, which was already known in Japan at that time.

From the end of the Meiji era, Marxism became rather popular, and its influence in Akiko's works is also visible. Akiko cites Leo Tolstoy (1828–1910):[2] "Improving oneself is the best act of life" (Yosano 1987 [1911] a, 61). She maintained this in connection with the Shintō tradition, "we Japanese women should hurry to make ourselves wise, sensitive, and indulgent 'one person'", and concludes with: "Women in the country who worship *Amaterasu Ōmikami* want to get rid of all the menial old customs and take pride in setting the model of civilized women" (Yosano 1987 [1911] a, 61). In 1911, Hiratsuka, Raichō (1886–1971), who was a later opponent, published *Seitō* (Bluestocking) with the opening remark that "In the beginning, woman was truly the sun." (Hiratsuka 2011 [1911], 1148). There, Akiko wrote the poem *The Day When the Mountains Move*, followed by "Write only in the first person. / I am a woman. / Write only in the first person. / I am. I am. (Yosano 2019 [1911], 1). It expresses the declaration of recovery of the self-consciousness (*jiko kaifuku sengen*) of modern Japanese women.[3]

---

[2] In Japan, Tolstoy has been widely influenced on writers, religious figures, and socialists. Since he was first translated in 1886 (Meiji 19), Mori Ōgai and Kōda Rohan have also translated short stories. See Sekai Bungaku Daijiten Henshū Iinkai 1997, 244–245. *Ivan the Fool* was first translated into Japanese in 1902, and there are some parts that seem to have influenced Akiko.
[3] *"Josei no jiko kaifuku sengen"*. See Kano 2002, 38.

Akiko already had a dialectical vision to build a life in which individuals, Japan as a nation, and citizens of the world were united. Modern women were able to gain awareness of women's liberty rights and make good use of their freedom of thought to come into contact with the wisdom of the world in order to become civilized women. It is said that not only the *Kyōiku chokugo* (Imperial Rescript on Education) that insisted on moral education such as "loyalty and filial piety" should be understood, but also the "fundamental spirit" of the *Dainipponkoku kenpō* (Dai-nippon Empire Constitution) of the liberty rights of the nation that became modern Japan.[4] This spirit is exactly Japanese "democratic nationalism".[5] However, Akiko's belief was that the happiness of women who have a diligent and intelligent profession and are economically independent is transformed into the happiness of women and humankind.

Akiko struggled with her husband's unemployment and with having many children, but as a working woman, she supported her family by writing. Akiko financed her husband and poet, Yosano Tekkan, to travel to France in 1911 (Meiji 44), and she later went to European countries such as France for four months. In *Pari yori* (From Paris) (1914), co-authored with Tekkan, "From Paris' Travel Window", Akiko said from a comparative perspective: "European women are active, oriental women are stationary", observing: "Japanese women have a request principle in their hearts, and they are willing to live, and they lack the motivation to enrich and enjoy their lives" (Yosano, H. and Yosano, A. 1914, 232).

She also admired the composition of society from the lives of Westerners by looking at the modern ego and the traffic rules of courage and harmony:

> I had to be surprised to see Londoner and Parisian horses and crowds march lightly without any quarrels or clashes on the busy streets of Piccadilly and Grand Bruval. And I learned that those who walk freely devise their own wise rules and walk. (Yosano 1987 [1915], 95)

Akiko, who was writing poetry for her inner world, realized that after returning from Europe, her interest shifted to "ideal problems and concrete problems (war and politics) that led to real life rather than art". In a form rooted in life consciousness, she began to philosophically reconstruct what the nation, the society, the individual were for her. According to "First Impressions in Paris" published in the Paris literary magazine *Les Annales*, 29 Sept. 1912: "Since the beginning of the 21st century happiness is given to this civilization. Educate men and women on an equal footing. At the same time, stand on an equal footing in society and act. Thus, it is my desire to obtain social rights on an equal footing". "Men and

---

4 *"Joshi no dokuritsu jiei"*. See Yosano 1987 [1911] b, 64.
5 See footnote 1 (Odagiri 1961, 137 and 241).

women want to do their best for each other, have equal obligations, and enjoy life with equal happiness" (Yosano, H. and Yosano, A. 1914, 233). Akiko states that as the development of society progresses, class conflicts and gender conflicts will disappear. She respects family but declares that a cooperative society in which the free development of each individual person is possible is the condition for the free development of all people. This happiness can be based on a mutual recognition of freedom.

The universal suffrage could try to make Japanese politics – rich in love and reason – a true democracy. Akiko said: "A solid and positive cultural dweller has the right to freedom and independence so that human beings are not overwhelmed by any power other than their own" (Yosano 1987 [1919] a, 253). In the sense of orthodox free thought and democracy, Akiko insisted on "freedom of education, freedom of thought, freedom of speech, freedom of profession". She also emphasized: "In order to contribute to all systems of life (individual life, family life, national life and world life), individuals have the right to the opportunity to develop this ability, that is, the right to equality" (Yosano 1987 [1919] a, 255).

The following can be considered as counterevidence of Akiko's ideal "life of united three sides". The cause of misfortune in life is that the three sides of the individual, the nation, and the world are inconsistent, clashing, and bursting. The interests of a nation do not become the happiness of individuals or the human beings of the world if they are invading each other, for example, in a war (Yosano 1987 [1916], 136). While observing World War I, Akiko linked art and science through the global cooperation of love and economy and became a driving force for the common well-being of human life. This leads to the pacifism of building life, national life, and world life. She consistently maintains the whole human philosophy that is achieved after all individuals, not just women, are freed from alienation.

What Can Be Seen from the Motherhood-protection-debate

Prior to the dispute over maternity protection with Raichō Hiratsuka and women in 1918–1919, Akiko argued, "Eliminate the emphasis on maternity", in light of her own idea of holistic human beings. The Swedish thinker Ellen Key (1849–1926) and Tolstoy are the subject of her criticism: "According to Tolstoy, a woman must devote herself to the mission that is inevitably placed on herself, the natural mission of giving birth to as many children as possible for work and raising and educating them. And according to Ellen Key the central element of a woman's life is to be a mother" (Yosano 1987 [1918] a, 178). Tolstoy's "natural mission" and Key's "natural restriction of individual rights" make infinite human activities other than motherhood secondary activities. However, in reality, human beings must change their own lifestyles according to their personal sexuality and circumstances. Akiko referred to the equality of "humanity" against external discrimination, which is broadly divided into gender differences. Not only motherhood, but also labor, artistry, national character, world, etc., the center of life is constantly changing, so even for Ellen Key, the absolute motherhood principle is an unrealistic old concept, and there are an infinite number of "dignified lives that demonstrate human duties" other than the life of parents.

However, Ellen Key's idealistic considerations would not necessarily have agreed with Akiko:

> Working women not only need the will to improve their own lives, but above all a more active feeling for the organization of the whole. Their personal demands for education, tranquility, beauty, love, motherhood must be brought into connection with those of everyone so that you also begin to demand for others what they want for themselves. (Key 1905, 216)

Key lays the values on the individual, if it serves for the whole, that is, for "humanity". Unlike Akiko, this does not show a development of consciousness from the individual to the nation and to the "world citizen".

The motherhood debate in Japan began when Hiratsuka Raichō criticized Akiko's position that always advocated an "ideal for girls' lives to be mentally and economically independent" and her insistence on "protection of the mother's body by state". Akiko continued, "we already consider it a *slave morality* for women to live off on men through reproductive service. We must also refuse to eat at the nation for the same reason" (Yosano 1987 [1918] b, 200).

> It has become normal for both boys and girls to sustain material life by engaging in some kind of physical and mental labor, if we make our labor system in general the most suitable for us, in other words, "it is expected that this can be easily achieved in a happy era when the majority of workers can safely marry and deliver, as long as humans create a system that fairs the distribution of wealth." (Yosano 1987 [1918] b, 204)

Continuing the criticism of Hiratsuka Raichō, Akiko said that we can only push forward the "national remodeling" from the foundation by "individual remodeling" without expecting much from the "nation". The translations of Nietzsche's *Sklavenmoral* and *Herrenmoral* (Slave Moral and Lord Moral)[6] were well-known, judging from other poems and critiques, at least Nietzsche and *Weiblein*,[7]

---

6 See Nietzsche 1988 [1886], 280 (*Jenseits von Gut und Böse*, § 260). Nietzsche gives two types of

> *Woman*
> *"Don't forget the whip"*
> *Zarathustra said.*
> *"Women even are cows and sheep."*
> *In addition, I will say,*
> *"Leave them in the field."* (Yosano 1929)

She tried to achieve a female remodeling with a self-consciousness freed from *herd slave morality*. From there, instead of being enslaved to capitalism, it envisions a class struggle based on culturalism in which laborers are completely freed from the rule of capitalists and create individuals from the rigors of real freedom and equality.

When it comes to *slave morality*, alternatively, Hegel's idea of *Herr* and *Knecht* (lord and servant) and Marx's materialistic concepts such as *bourgeois* and *proletariat* can be considered, but rather than aiming for a revolution, the ideal of "fair distribution of wealth" is talked about, as a form of moderate socialism. It could be refined as sustainable "ethical capitalism" which includes a criticism of Marx etc.

Akiko also wrote for "better order": "Capitalism must be ruled out as long as it jeopardizes free and independent survival of 'the only natural right of each person'", as Kant calls it.[8] For the "proletariat", human beings must consciously strive to create a new social order purposefully (Yosano 1987 [1918] b, 226). In the modern welfare state, there is an aspect in which Akiko's ideals are fused with Hiratsuka Raichō who insists on national assistance.

Conclusion with Epidemic

Finally, Akiko talked about "basic consideration of women's remodeling" based on "culturalism", "gender equality", "humanity's classless collective responsibility", and "pan-laborism". She quotes *Die ethischen Grundfragen* (1899) by Theodor Lipps (1851–1914) also, and she states, "Because the Diet requires that interests

---

moralities: Lord moral and slave moral. The type of slave moral is: If the raped, depressed, suffering, unfree, self-uncertain and tired moralize, "the appreciation will express a pessimistic suspicion of the whole situation of man, perhaps a condemnation of its man as a whole location. [...] The slave's view is unfavorable to the virtues of the mighty: he has skepticism and mistrust. [...] The slave moral is essentially utility moral".

7 See Nietzsche 1988 [1883], 86 (*Also sprach Zarathustra*). Zarathustra speaks on the old and young females: "Do you go to women? Don't forget the whip!"

8 See Kant 1983 [1783], 53 (*Was ist Aufklärung?*). Kant calls: "Have the courage to use your own understanding! is therefore the motto of the Enlightenment".

in all directions be represented, women must also be represented there" (Yosano 1987 [1919] b, 269).

1918–1919 is a year of turbulence both internationally and domestically with the end of World War I, the surge in prices, the rice riots, the Siberian intervention, and the outbreak of the Spanish flu much like the recent corona pandemic. This epidemic killed about 450,000 people in Japan and 20 to 45 million people worldwide. Akiko Yosano also wrote about this "flu". In her article "From the Bed of the Cold", which was published in *Yokohama Bōeki Shinpō* (Yokohama Trading Newspaper) on 10 November 1918, she criticized the government severely. In 2021, when the infection of Covid-19 has not converged at all, Akiko's aspect as a thinker is drawing attention. Akiko had criticized the same slow epidemic prevention measures and unfair infection treatments as the current government did in a 100-year-old critique. Her work, which combines her literary expressiveness and logical thinking, is now being reviewed in Japanese newspapers *Asahi Shinbun* and *Nikkei Shinbun* etc. and is widely studied (Sazanami 2020; Shiota 2020).

> The dramatic harm of infectious diseases immediately deprives the majority of humans of their health and workforce. Why didn't the government order the temporary closure of many crowded places such as kimono fabrics shops, schools, entertainments, large factories, and large exhibitions in order to prevent this danger as soon as possible? [...] Due to the lack of unity and thoroughness in social facilities, the people cannot avoid the evils that should be avoided. [...] At the same time, while being a person living together in a group, he could not take the most effective first-ranked antipyretic just because he was a poor person. Feeling imperiled is certainly unreasonable, even in light of today's new ethical consciousness. (Yosano 2002, 172)

"Equality did not begin with Rousseau", Akiko transculturally cited the ancient Chinese philosopher Confucius (551–479 BCE), "I'm not worried about poverty, I'm worried about being unequalized", and Liezi (ca. 400 BCE), "Being equal is the essence of the world".

Akiko does not break the stance of equal rights from the perspective of various systems of life, even during a pandemic. She was under the oppression of class and gender struggles. The awareness of peace in gender cooperation begins with the difference between men and women, and develops a world philosophy that extends beyond the differences between men and women to the point where individuals realize equal rights as world citizens.

References

Beichman, J. (2002). *Embracing the Firebird. Yosano Akiko and the Birth of the Female Voice in Modern Japanese Poetry*. Honolulu: University of Hawai'i Press.

Hegel, G. W. F. (1991 [1807]). *Phänomenologie des Geistes*. In: *G. W. F. Hegel: Werke in 20 Bänden*, vol. 3. Ed. by E. Moldenhauer and K. M. Michel. Frankfurt/M.: Suhrkamp.

Hiratsuka, R. (2011 [1911]). Two Manifestos. The Foundation of Seitō, the Blustocking Society. In: *Japanese Philosophy. A Soucebook*. Ed. By J. W. Heisig, T. P. Kasulis and J. C. Maraldo. Honolulu: University of Hawai'I Press, 1148–1150.

Kano, M. (2002). *Nihon no kindai shisōshi*. Tokyo: Iwanami Shoten.

Kano, M. and Kōuchi, N. (Eds.) (1987 [1985]). *Yosano Akiko Hyōronshū*. Tokyo: Iwanami Shoten.

Kant, I. (1983 [1783]). "Beantwortung der Frage: Was ist Aufklärung?" In: *Immanuel Kant: Werke in sechs Bänden*. Vol. 6: *Schriften zur Anthologie, Geschichtsphilosophie, Politik und Pädagogik*. Ed. by W. Weischedel. Darmstadt: Wissenschaftliche Buchgesellschaft, 53–61.

Key, E. (1905). *Über die liebe und Ehe*. Berlin: S. Fischer.

Lipps, T. (2015 [1899]). *Rinrigaku no konpon mondai*. Trans. by Abe, jirō. Tokyo: NDL shozōkosho POD.

Nietzsche, F. (1988 [1883]). "Also sprach Zarathustra I". In: *Friedrich Nietzsche: Sämtliche Werke. Kritische Studienausgabe*, vol. 4. Ed. by G. Colli and M. Montinari. Munich: Deutscher Taschenbuch Verlag/Berlin and New York: Walter de Gruyter, 9–102.

Nietzsche, F. (1988 [1886]). "Jenseits von Gut und Böse. Vorspiel einer Philosophie der Zukunft". In: *Friedrich Nietzsche: Sämtliche Werke. Kritische Studienausgabe*, vol. 5. Munich: Deutscher Taschenbuch Verlag/Berlin and New York: Walter de Gruyter, 11–243.

Odagiri, H. (1961). *Nihon gendaishi taikei. Bungakushi*. Tōyōkeizai Shinpōsha.

Reichhold, J. and Kobayashi, M. (Trans.) (2014). *Yosano Akiko. A Girl with Tangled Hair*. Gualala.: AHA Books.

Sazanami, Y. (2020). "Gote ni mawatta kuni no kansen taisaku ni katsu. Yosano akiko jidai sakidori". *Asahi Shimbun*, 6 September 2020. URL: https://www.asahi.com/articles/ASN943S6WN8QUCVL003.html (last accessed 20 October 2021).

Sekai Bungaku Daijiten Henshū Iinkai (1997). *Shūeisha sekai bungaku daijiten* 3. Tokyo: Shūeisha, 244–245.

Shiota, H. (2020). "Shisōka Yosano Akiko ni hikari. Supeinkaze taisaku wo hihan". *Nikkei Shinbun*, 6 August 2020. URL: https://www.nikkei.com/article/DGXMZO62318870V00C20A8AA1P00/ (last accessed 20 October 2021).

Yosano, A. (2010 [1901]). "Midaregami". In Yosano, A. (Ed.), *Yosano Akiko Kashū. Yosano Akiko jisen*. Tokyo: Iwanami Shoten, 9–10.

Yosano, A. (1987 [1909] a). "Ubuya monogatari". In Kano, M. and Kōuchi, N. (Eds.), *Yosano Akiko Hyōronshū*. Tokyo: Iwanami Shoten, 32–41.

Yosano, A. (1987 [1909] b). "Rikon ni tsuite". In Kano, M. and Kōuchi, N. (Eds.), *Yosano Akiko Hyōronshū*. Tokyo: Iwanami Shoten, 42–52.

Yosano, A. (1987 [1911] a). "Fujin to shisō". In Kano, M. and Kōuchi, N. (Eds.), *Yosano Akiko Hyōronshū*. Tokyo: Iwanami Shoten, 54–61.

Yosano, A. (1987 [1911] b). "Joshi no dokuritsu jiei". In Kano, M. and Kōuchi, N. (Eds.), *Yosano Akiko Hyōronshū*. Tokyo: Iwanami Shoten, 62–69.

Yosano, A. (2019 [1911] c). "Sozorogoto". In Hiratsuka, R. Und Itō, N. (Eds.), *Seitō* 1. volume n° 1. Tokyo: Seitō-sha. URL: https://www.aozora.gr.jp/cards/000885/files/59150_68035.html (last accessed 20 January 2023).

Yosano, A. (1987 [1915]). "Kyōshin tōgo shō". In Kano, M. and Kōuchi, N. (Eds.), *Yosano Akiko Hyōronshū*. Tokyo: Iwanami Shoten, 91–109.

Yosano, A. (1987 [1916]). "Bosei henchō wo haisu". In Kano, M. and Kōuchi, N. (Eds.), *Yosano Akiko Hyōronshū*. Tokyo: Iwanami Shoten, 136–147.

Yosano, A. (1987 [1918] a). "Sanmen ittai no seikatsu e". In Kano, M. and Kōuchi, N. (Eds.), *Yosano Akiko Hyōronshū*. Tokyo: Iwanami Shoten, 178–191.

Yosano, A. (1987 [1918] b). "Hiratsuka san to watashi no ronsō". In Kano, M. and Kōuchi, N. (Eds.), *Yosano Akiko Hyōronshū*. Tokyo: Iwanami Shoten, 200–210.

Yosano, A. (1987 [1918] c). "Hiratsuka, Yamakawa, Yamada sanjoshi ni kotau". In Kano, M. and Kōuchi, N. (Eds.), *Yosano Akiko Hyōronshū*. Tokyo: Iwanami Shoten, 219–236.

Yosano, A. (1987 [1919] a). "Fujin mo sanseiken wo yōkyū su". In Kano, M. and Kōuchi, N. (Eds.), *Yosano Akiko Hyōronshū*. Tokyo: Iwanami Shoten, 253–261.

Yosano, A. (1987 [1919] b). "Fujin kaizō no kisoteki kōsatsu". In Kano, M. and Kōuchi, N. (Eds.), *Yosano Akiko Hyōronshū*. Tokyo: Iwanami Shoten, 262–276.

Yosano, A. (1929). *Akiko Shihen Zenshū*. Tokyo: Jitsugyō no Nihonsha. URL: https://www.aozora.gr.jp/cards/000885/files/2557_15784.html (last accessed 20 October 2021).

Yosano, A. (2010 [1943]). *Yosano Akiko Kashū. Yosano Akiko jisen.* Tokyo: Iwanami Shoten.

Yosano, A. (2002). *Yosano Akiko hyōron chosakushū.* Vol. 18. Tokyo: Ryūkei Shosha.

Yosano, H. and Yosano, A. (1914). *Pari yori.* Tokyo: Kanao Buneidō. URL: https://dl.ndl.go.jp/info:ndljp/pid/951380 (last accessed 20 October 2021).

Timothy DeGriselles
A Philosophical Defense of Self-Defense: Examining Sor Juana Inés de la Cruz' *Reply to Sor Filotea*

Abstract: Sor Juana Inés de la Cruz wrote the *Reply to Sor Filotea* to defend herself from accusations from powerful church leaders at her time. Sor Juana compares her struggles to others such as Jesus Christ and Socrates. This essay examines the similarities between the persecution and the defense of Sor Juana to that of Socrates' self-defense found in Plato's *Apology*. Both thinkers were accused of not following the commands of their deities and of studying things of the world. Sor Juana uses similar arguments in *The Reply* that shows that her studies and beliefs in no way hinder Sor Juana's relationship with God but proves that her studies and writings improve her relationship. In the end, Socrates and Sor Juana are persecuted in similar ways and defend themselves by proving their superior, divinely inspired minds to that of their accusers. One major difference is that in the *Apology*, Socrates accepts death while at the end of *The Reply* Sor Juana seemingly capitulates to continue her philosophical journey.

Introduction

In 1691, Sor Juana Inés de la Cruz wrote a philosophical self-defense in a letter replying to a set of admonitions that a powerful bishop of the Catholic church had leveled against her. In this letter, Sor Juana compares her intellectual and spiritual persecution to the persecution of Jesus Christ and Socrates. Sor Juana explains that Jesus Christ was hated for his miracles, but it was "Christ's sacred head and divine mind [that] were reservoirs of his wisdom". Sor Juana claims this to be why Christ's accusers placed the crown of thorns on his head. Because "in this world, it is not enough for the wise mind to be ridiculed, [the Divine mind] also must be injured and mistreated"[1] (De la Cruz 2009, 66). The unjust persecution and killing of Christ were due to his divine mind. Similarly, Sor Juana claims that the law used in ancient Athens to persecute and ultimately kill Socrates was based on the fear that the leaders around him had towards his superiority.

---

1 *La sagrada cabeza de Cristo y aquel divino cerebro eran depósito de la sabiduría; y cerebro sabio en el mundo no basta que esté escarnecido, ha de estar también lastimado y maltratado.*

In this essay, I will focus on her relationship to Socrates, showing how Sor Juana uses the similarities between their cases to stage her own self-defense.

Sor Juana broke boundaries in the society of 17th-century New Spain by educating herself, using classic and scholastic texts from her grandfather's extensive library. Using this self-education as a foundation, Sor Juana wrote in varied genres and fought for her freedom to study as a woman. A prolific thinker, she wrote dramas, responses to theological debates, poetry, and hymns for the Catholic church. Sor Juana's entire life was dedicated to the project of wanting to remove herself of ignorance.[2] During her life, Sor Juana's works were published, performed, and applauded throughout the Spanish-speaking world (Warnke 1987, 11). Sor Juana wrote *The Reply* to prove that her education, writing, and studies should be within her right as a woman and nun.

Until recently, *The Reply* was thought to be the first and only instance of self-defense that we had by Sor Juana against a leader persecuting and censuring her. In 1980, a letter was found written denouncing her confessor Father Antonio Nuñez de Miranda which she had written in the year 1681/82.[3] Much like *The Reply*, the earlier letter of 1681/82 is a response to criticism of Sor Juana's use of verse, her studying sciences, and ultimately the state of her soul in the eyes of God.

The letter of 1681/82 gives insight into the difficulties that Sor Juana must have been facing long before 1690 due to her studious nature. With only the single data point of *The Reply*, it could appear as a single event of friction between Sor Juana and some members of the hierarchy of the church. However, as Octavio Paz observes in his book *Sor Juana, or Traps of the Faith:*

> There is correspondence between the documents because, even though separated by ten years, they mark two stages of the same conflict... [The letter of 1681/82] confirms that Sor Juana's difficulties with various dignitaries of the Church predated the affair of [*The Reply* in 1691] and must have begun around 1680. (Paz 1988, 492)

The conflict that Sor Juana responds to in *The Reply* is a continuation of her earlier self-defense.

While not all who are persecuted for their ideas are able or willing to defend themselves, the action of self-defense is philosophical. Philosophers like Sor Juana

---

2 The biographical part of my work has been taken from Sor Juana's *La respuesta a Sor Filotea* (De la Cruz 1997) and three main secondary sources: Octavio Paz's *Sor Juana, or The Traps of Faith* translated by Margaret Sayers Peden (1988), Electa Arenal and Amanda Powell's introduction to *The Answer/La Respuesta: Sor Juana Inés de la Cruz*, 2nd ed. (2009), and Frank J. Warnke's book *Three Women Poets: Renaissance and Baroque* (1987).

3 For clarities sake, I will refer to this as the letter of 1681/82, following Arenal's labeling.

and Socrates use their self-defense as a form of intellectual autobiography. Examining these self-defenses can serve as a window into what is most important to these thinkers. In the case of Sor Juana and Socrates, we can see how they articulate a vision of pursuing divinely inspired wisdom against the limited conceptions of the leaders of their respective communities.

In the letter of 1681/82, Sor Juana renounces Nuñez de Miranda as her confessor, and confronts him about the claims he has made against her. The letter shows insight into the frustration Sor Juana must have felt with a man who she was supposed to trust completely as her confessor. Paz remarks that this earlier document was "written with undisguised impatience and anger in reaction to the defamatory gossip of Father Nuñez de Miranda" (1988, 492). Paz also remarks that this is clearly a private letter, intimate in its wording, and meant for her confessor alone. Where the letter of 1681/82 was meant to be private, *The Reply* is meant as a public self-defense.

In *The Reply*, Sor Juana's defense is threefold: first, she shows that studying the secular sciences is well within her rights as a nun and women based on her capabilities. Next Sor Juana asserts that the use of verse is allowed within the church and that therefore she should not be prohibited to write poetry. Finally, she claims that all of her inclinations to study and write go back to the fact that she has been given the desire to write and study by God himself, so her salvation is not in question. These arguments in her defense in *The Reply* are written to skirt any scrutiny by the Inquisition to allow the letter to be published. While the 70-year-old Socrates ultimately accepts his death at the end of his self-defense, believing himself to be at the end of his life anyway, Sor Juana capitulates to the Inquisition, and acts humble. I assert that her humility shows that she sees her intellectual journey in New Spain as ongoing, while Socrates had accepted his arrival at his destination.

Sor Juana's self-defense is philosophical in the same way that Socrates defends himself in Plato's *Apology*. Due to the public nature, Socrates is able to answer questions surrounding his purpose in Athens as the gadfly, how his wisdom is greater for not-knowing, and what his relation to the gods of Athens is. Both were accused by their communities – the Church and Athens respectively – of going against their god or gods and studying improper things. Both dealt with similar persecutions and in turn defended themselves by showing that the laws and rules used to judge them were flawed. They did not fall outside of the social structure but surpassed it due to their personal relationship with the divine.

The Reply as Self-Defense

The Reply is a direct response to an open letter from Bishop Fernández de Santa Cruz. The letter, written under the pseudonym Sor Filotea, was itself a response to a letter in which Sor Juana attacked a Jesuit orator from Portugal. In the bishop's letter, "Sor Filotea" praised Sor Juana for many of her talents, even naming Sor Juana's critique *La Carta atenagórica,* a letter worthy of Athena.[4] However, much of *La Carta* chastised Sor Juana for studying non-sacred texts and for writing in verse. "Sor Filotea" claimed to worry for the state of the soul of Sor Juana. While in the letter "Sor Filotea" seems to genuinely care for Sor Juana, and while the bishop was supposedly her friend, we can only speculate on the intent of this chastisement, whether it was meant as correction or was a provocation. In any case Sor Juana took it as a harsh provocation and defended herself in a strong way.

Because Sor Juana was a nun, "Sor Filotea" had rebuked Sor Juana for writing on secular topics and not focusing solely on sacred matters. In response, Sor Juana states her decision of what to study it is not a sign of favor for one area over another. Professing humility, Sor Juana claims that her attention to secular texts was due to her lack of skill, intelligence, and practice. She writes:

> And speaking more specifically, I confess to you that ... for to not have written much on sacred topics has not been dislike, nor the fault from lack of application, rather it has been extra fear and reverence necessary for those Sacred Texts, for I know of myself that my intelligence is lacking, as well as being unworthy, to handle them. (De la Cruz 2009, 44)[5]

Here, Sor Juana asserts that if the highest of the sciences is theology, using the analogy of regality, then her studying sciences and humanities is not an affront to the "Queen". In fact, this is the only path to reach the peak of true understanding. By arguing that her studies prepare her to reach a level of knowledge that will make her able to understand theology, Sor Juana takes the venom from her critics. Instead of Sor Juana needing to devote her time to sacred matters, Sor Juana claims that her studies of the world only improve herself and let her study theology more wholly.

---

4 Will be referred to as *La Carta*, following Arenal and Powell, Paz, etc.
5 *Y hablando con más especialidad os confieso, con la ingenuidad que ante vos es debida y con la verdad y claridad que en mí siempre es natural costumbre, que el no haber escrito mucho de asuntos sagrado no ha sido desafición, ni de aplicación la falta, sino sobra de temor y reverencia debida a aquellas Sagradas Letras, para cuya inteligencia yo me conozco tan incapaz y para cuyo manejo soy tan indigna.*

Sor Juana shows the connections between the supposedly baser sciences and specific moments in theology, arguing that these initial studies improve her understanding of theology. Sor Juana continues the argument by asking how she could understand how the Holy Scriptures were written without first understanding the field of logic? If she does not understand musical theory, how could she know whether a miracle occurred when David healed with his song or whether the healing was just a natural facet of music? How could Sor Juana be able to understand the Books of Laws if she had no concept of the branches of law (De la Cruz 2009, 52–56)? She makes connections to different fields of study, such as astronomy, geometry, architecture, and rhetoric. Sor Juana does so to show that the study of any of these subjects was not useless. If every field is seen as enhancing the understanding of God, it would be preposterous to not study such things.

To be clear, Sor Juana's argument is not the only reason to study other subjects is from a desire to better know God. She is not naïve. She knows there are plenty of those who study the earth and such who do not have faith like her. The difference between Sor Juana and these others lies in her own connection to the divine. She asserts that prayer offers a bridge, between secular knowledge and sacred knowledge. Sor Juana emphasizes:

> And after knowing all [of these sciences], one must ask for another help than what was said, and that is a purity of heart and continuous prayer, in order to receive from God that cleansing of the spirit and illumination of the mind that is necessary for understanding such sacred things. And if [the purity of heart and prayer] things are missing, then these other sciences serve no purpose. (De la Cruz 2009, 54–56)[6]

Sor Juana makes explicit that these sciences that she studies are not enough for her. Despite the criticism and harassment that she receives, Sor Juana's faith is a central part of her studies. Without her faith, the knowledge would make her divine right to study obsolete. The qualification that faith is essential to her reasons for study, coupled with her conception of the sciences as interconnected provides a clearer picture of her motivations. This clearer picture refutes the idea that Sor Juana's studies show a lack of care of God and the sacred.

Sor Juana's defense of her studies culminates in a metaphysical point. Sor Juana reminds those who have made it their mission to persecute her for the studies that she has done, that in addition to the connections she has already made, there is a single point that guarantees the value of her studying secular fields of

---

6 *Y después de saberlas todas, pide otra circunstancia más que todo lo dicho, que es una continua oración y pureza de vida, para impetrar de Dios aquella purgación de ánimo e iluminación de mente que es menester para la inteligencia de cosas tan altas; y si esto falta, nada sirve de lo demás.*

knowledge. Sor Juana explains: "All things come from God, who is the center and at the same time the circumference, where all created lines begin and where they all end" (De la Cruz 2009, 56).[7] No matter what persecutions are heaped against Sor Juana by leaders of the church, they cannot dispute this point. The fields that they dismiss and judge her for all must derive from theology, the one that they hold in the highest esteem. So, anyone who demands that Sor Juana study theology and the sacred should also acknowledge that her secular studies come from that same God. In this way, Sor Juana roots her self-defense in the shared theological and metaphysical commitments of her critics. To prevent Sor Juana from studying the things that she wants to study is to deny those fields' connections to God and theology.

Sor Juana's defense of her choice to write poetry is multifaceted, focused on both her own relationship with poetry and the inherent merit of poetry in relation to God. She writes:

> If I now turn my eyes unto the ability to write in verse which has been much harassed, seeing that it has been condemned and incriminated to such an extent, I have searched diligently in which way it can have caused harm and I have not yet found any. (De la Cruz 2009, 94)[8]

This strategy again proceeds from a position of modesty. Acknowledging that her poetry and verse have been criticized for a long time, Sor Juana professes that and even so, after all this time, she has not been able to find any harm that verse can cause on its own. To cement this point, Sor Juana uses the authority of the church and a 16th-century theologian named Casidoro de Reina. With the quotation speaking in praise of verse, Sor Juana extrapolates the use of verse by the church itself. She explains:

> And as Casidoro says, "All poetic speech had its origin in the Holy Scriptures." However, our Catholic Church not only does not scorn verse, rather it uses verse in its hymns and recites those by San Ambrosio, Santo Tomás, de San Isidoro and others. (De la Cruz 2009, 94)[9]

---

7 *Todas las cosas salen de Dios, que es el centro a un tiempo y la circunferencia de donde salen y donde paran todas las líneas criadas.*

8 *Pues si vuelvo los ojos a la tan perseguida habilidad de hacer versos, viéndola condenar a tantos tanto y acriminar, he buscado muy de propósito cual sea el daño que puedan tener y no lo he hallado.*

9 *Y así dice Casiodoro:* Omnis poetica locutio a Divinis scripturis sumpsit exordium. *Pues nuestra iglesia católica no solo no los desdeña, más los usa en sus himnos y recita los de San Ambrosio, Santo Tomás, de San Isidoro y otros.* Latin translation found in De la Cruz 2009.

Sor Juana uses these authorities to show that verse is revered and sacred. The origin of verse, according to Casidoro, is in the sacred texts that Sor Juana is supposedly ignoring by writing in verse. While "Sor Filotea" claims that Sor Juana's habit of writing in verse is not seemly for a nun, the fact that different leaders are recited in verse, and the church itself uses verse in its sacred text, shows the error in the fictional nun's accusations.

Sor Juana asserts that since the church uses verse, she has the right to as well. The assertion of this right leads her to a general defense of poetry. Sor Juana posits:

> The art is not to blame for its misuse, but that of the bad actor who turns it to vice, and making it into the snares of the devil, which happens in all of the humanities and sciences. (De la Cruz 2009, 94)[10]

This point is twofold: first, art is not to blame for any misuse, but it is the practitioner of the art who is at fault; and second, this misuse happens in all the fields of study and sciences – whose queen is theology. Therefore, if any art could be vilified for the practitioners of a few, then the same vilification would need to be done to all sciences. But Sor Juana knows that Bishop Fernández would never make the claim that a whole science (theology, for example) is worthless because some people misuse it for personal gains. By the same token, no one can attack poetry in and of itself without also criticizing hymns and church approved poetry. Since Bishop Fernández would not do that, he cannot criticize poetry as such.

Having shown that poetry is not inherently evil, Sor Juana claims there must be another basis for the attacks by Nuñez de Miranda and Bishop Fernández. Sor Juana concludes that the difference must be that she is a woman. Sor Juana examines how else poetry could be evil and writes:

> Well, if the evil is found due to the use of a woman, we can already see how many have done so in a laudable fashion. So, in which way is it in my case? I certainly confess of my baseness and vileness, but I figure that not even one indecent couplet that comes from me has been seen. (De la Cruz 2009, 96)[11]

Here, Sor Juana asserts that if the criticism comes from her gender, then it is still misplaced. There have been other women that were lauded in the church that wrote in verse, yet Sor Juana is still targeted. And even if Sor Juana accepts, through

---
10 *El mal uso no es culpa del arte, si no del mal profesor que los vicia, haciendo de ellos lazos del demonio; y esto en todas las facultades y ciencias sucede.*
11 *Pues si está el mal en que los use una mujer, ya se ve cuántos los han usado loablemente; pues ¿en qué está serlo yo? Confieso desde luego mi ruindad y vileza; pero no juzgo que se habrá visto una copla mía indecente.*

either real or feigned humility, her "baseness and vileness" she is unwilling to accept that any of her own verses have harmed anyone, because she has never written any poetry that was indecent to begin with – or, at least, that anyone has ever seen. With this, Sor Juana proves that the criticisms against writing in verse and studying secular sciences are illogical, and she moves on to the criticisms regarding the sanctity of her soul. It is here that Sor Juana will defend her right as a woman to an intellectual life.

Sor Juana acknowledges that this argument is a difficult criticism to dismantle; yet she needs to engage with it. But rather than engaging head on, Sor Juana instead asks whether her persecutors even have the right to make this criticism at all. Towards the beginning of *The Reply*, Sor Juana speaks of the fear that her soul might be in jeopardy, and writes:

> And thus, when I consider this on my own, I often say: Blessed art thou, Lord, for not only did you not want my judgement in the hands of any other creature, nor even in my hands did you place it, rather that you kept in thine hands, and freed me of myself and the judgement that I would place upon myself—which, driven by my own understanding, it could not have been anything less than condemnation—and thou reservist to thy mercy, because thou lovest me more than I can love myself. (De la Cruz 2009, 40)[12]

Here, Sor Juana disarms the denunciation in a brilliant move. It does not matter what the church leaders – as mere creatures – say about Sor Juana's soul, because that judgment is in God's hands alone. Those who claim to judge the sanctity of her soul are in no position to do so, because not even she herself can make the condemnation that these critics make. Their claims have no effect on her because only God can condemn. This disarms the entire critique from the beginning.

After removing the power of judgment from the hands of these critics, Sor Juana continues to show that even if they could judge her, there is no merit to the claims. Sor Juana begins to show that even if her studies were problematic, the origin of her desires to study would still justify them. Sor Juana claims that "the desire to write has never been from myself, but an outside force; that I can say this truthfully: Thou hast compelled me" (De la Cruz 2009, 46).[13] It is her creator who compelled her to write. This desire to study and write cannot be a flaw, be-

---

[12] *Y así, cuando esto considero acá a mis solas, suelo decir: Bendito seáis vos, Señor, que no sólo no quisisteis en manos de otra criatura el juzgarme, y que ni aun en la mía lo pusisteis, sino que lo reservasteis a la vuestra, y me libristeis a mí de mí y de la sentencia que yo misma me daría—que, forzada de mi propio conocimiento, no pudiera ser menos que la condenación—, y vos la reservasteis a vuestra misericordia, porque me amáis más de lo que yo me puedo amar*

[13] *El escribir nunca ha sido dictamen propio, sino fuerza ajena; que les pudiera decir con verdad: Vos me coegistis.*

cause it is a strong impulsion that was placed in her by a perfect being. Sor Juana emphasizes the divine origin of these desires by the capitalization of *Vos*,[14] which was used throughout this text when speaking of or to God, to show His superiority. If her desire to write is an innate part of her soul, how could it possibly be reason to condemn her?

Sor Juana then entertains the possibility that writing is a vice. But even in this case, there would still be another layer of the criticism that was problematic. Sor Juana writes "Blessed be God who wished that it was unto letters I was inclined and not towards some other vice, which would have been nearly insurmountable to me" (De la Cruz 2009, 60).[15] If her writing is truly her only vice, then she is blessed, because there are so many more that would be much worse for her soul. This minimizes the weight of any future criticism, while simultaneously demonstrating her writing is insufficient grounds for her damnation.

No other mortal is privileged enough to assign her blame and stop her from studying. On this basis, Sor Juana asks "Sor Filotea" to clarify in what way Sor Juana has been wrong. Sor Juana writes:

> If the crime is within the *Carta atenagórica*, was there anything more than just my simple opinion which was granted to me as permission by our Sacred Mother Church? And if She, with her holy authority, does not prohibit me to do so, why is it that any others can prohibit me? (De la Cruz 2009, 90)[16]

Here, Sor Juana sticks the nail in the coffin. Up to this point, Sor Juana has shown that she has done nothing wrong in her work. The Church herself,[17] through her scriptures, has never prohibited any of her studies or writings. So, if the Church herself has never condemned her studies as wrong, then it is impossible for Bishop Fernández, or any other accuser, to have the right to attack her and stop her from her work.

Sor Juana defends herself in a straightforward manner, using examples from theologians of the past and from the scriptures themselves to show that the prohibitions against studying and writing in verse are unwarranted and that Sor Juana followed the dictates of the Church better than her own leaders. Step by

---

[14] An older form of "tú" which is still used in some parts of Latin America.
[15] *Bendito sea Dios que quiso fuese hacia las letras y no hacia otro vicio, que fuera en mí casi insuperable.*
[16] *Si el crimen está en la Carta Atenagórica ¿fue aquélla más que referir sencillamente mi sentir con todas las venias que debo a nuestra Santa Madre Iglesia? Pues si ella, con su santísima autoridad, no me lo prohíbe, ¿Por qué me lo han de prohibir otros?*
[17] Sor Juana refers to the church in the quote as a "her", as a turn of phrase. In Latin and Spanish, "church" is feminine. See notes on paragraph (40), De la Curz 2009, 139.

step, Sor Juana concedes a little, just to show that her writing and her studies do not put her soul in danger, and that the accusers only attack her because of who and what she is, and in doing so proves that the critics have no authority to condemn her. In this way, Sor Juana defends her right as a woman of faith to pursue divinely inspired wisdom on her own, through secular sciences and poetry.

Socrates and the Self-defense of the *Apology*

During her own defense, Sor Juana refers to Socrates in a roundabout way. She speaks of the law that was used against Socrates, that was intended to banish him from Athens, but ultimately was used to put him to death. Sor Juana writes that the "politically barbarous law from Athens ... still stands". Although the law was ostensibly in place to protect Athens from those who would have harmed it, it had a more sinister motive, and that was "to hate those that outshine others" (De la Cruz 2009, 62).[18] By examining Socrates' self-defense, Sor Juana shows that Socrates' conception of wisdom (knowing that one knows nothing) invalidates the attack on his character and shows that the leaders of Athens did not understand the law that they used to condemn Socrates.

In the *Apology*,[19] Socrates defends himself against persecutors who have been after him for years. Just as Sor Juana was accused of studying secular matters and not following her religious obligations, Socrates was accused of studying the earth and sky, and therefore not following the deities of Athens (Plato 2002, 19b). And like Sor Juana, Socrates uses philosophical autobiography to show that his investigations were for the sake of divinely inspired wisdom. He tells a story of a friend who went to the oracle at Delphi and asked who the wisest person of all of Athens was, to which the god of that place replied that none was wiser than Socrates (2002, 21a). Socrates then describes the journey he took to understand how he could be the wisest person in Athens.

While the god claimed that no one was wiser than Socrates, Socrates needed to have proof of this, because so many people seemed wise in Athens. To Socrates, the

---

18 *Aquella ley políticamente bárbara de Atenas, por la cual salía desterrado de su republica el que señalaba emprendas y virtudes porque no tiranizase con ellas la libertad publica, todavía dura, todavía se observa en nuestros tiempos, aunque no hay ya aquel motivo de los atenienses; pero hay otro, no menos eficaz, aunque no tan bien fundado, pues parece máxima del impío Maquiavelo: que es aborrecer al que se señala porque desluce a otros. Así sucede y así sucedió siempre.* I put the entire quote, which I used above in English, but only selections.
19 In Greek, *apologia* means defense. As Grube notes, "there is nothing apologetic about this speech". See Grube in Plato 2002, 21, footnote 1.

claim was strange. He says "[w]hatever does the god mean? What is this riddle? I am very conscious that I am not wise at all; what then does he mean by saying that I am the wisest" (2002, 21b)? For Socrates, the search for wisdom is the search to understand the god at Delphi.

To better answer his question, Socrates questions leading Athenian men that seem to have knowledge, looking for evidence of someone wiser than him. But in these exchanges, Socrates learned that the other person had no knowledge, even if they claimed to. Socrates observes:

> I am wiser than this man; It is likely that neither of us knows anything worthwhile, but he thinks he knows something when he does not, whereas when I do not know, neither do I think I know; so, I am likely to be wiser than he to this small extent, that I do not think I know what I do not know. (Plato 2002, 21d)

This is a situation in which Socrates at least is wiser because unlike the others, at least Socrates is aware of his lack of knowledge. This shows that divinely inspired wisdom consists in the knowledge of one's own ignorance. Therefore, his search for knowledge and studying the things of the earth and sky was not contrary to the gods, as Socrates' accusers claimed, but was a way in which Socrates was honoring the god at Delphi in trying to understand the prophecy.

By defending himself, Socrates shows that wisdom was the most important reason for his search, and that he did not go counter to the gods but rather that his actions were those of a virtuous follower of his divine calling. Even though the accusers at his trial were ultimately successful in their prosecution, his defense of his life lends credence to Sor Juana's assertion that the reason for the prosecution of Socrates was due to resentment of the way in which his understanding outshone others. And this is the same reason that Sor Juana gives for why the accusers of her own time attack her. It is not for the same reasons that the accusers claim – that these two thinkers spent too much time studying the world and not enough time in the devotion to their respective deities – but rather for the reason that these two philosophers, as Sor Juana asserts, outshine their society's leaders in their understanding and virtue providing examples of a pursuit of divinely inspired wisdom outside traditional institutional structures. This was why they both had to be removed.

Conclusion

At the end of both of their defenses, both Sor Juana and Socrates show that their ideas and questions are worthy pursuits. While both agreed that the accusations of heresy were groundless, both Sor Juana and Socrates had to decide in what way they were going to continue their respective philosophical journeys. At the end of the *Apology*, Meletus proposed that Socrates be given the death penalty. In the Athenian system, the accused had the opportunity to raise a counteroffer, and the jurors would choose which option is better. While Socrates was expected to choose exile – which the jurors would have accepted (Plato 2002, 37c) – Socrates presents the penalty of being treated greater than even an Olympian athlete and being given free food for the rest of his life. Because this penalty was preposterous, Socrates was accepting death as the penalty of the false accusation. His philosophical journey had reached its end.

Sor Juana could have reached the same destination, because at that time, the Inquisition was in full force. Throughout *The Reply*, Sor Juana references the Inquisition, and knows what will happen if she is officially denounced and persecuted by this Holy Office.[20] But, Sor Juana is careful throughout *The Reply* to show that her opinion is not heretical, and in the end, capitulates to "Sor Filotea" by showing the bishop humility.

In the second to last paragraph, Sor Juana cleverly points out that she knows "Sor Filotea" is not a nun, and referring to Bishop Fernández by his pseudonym within the entire letter was a way to avert the Inquisitions wrath. Sor Juana writes:

> If the style of my letter, my venerable Lady, has not been as you deserve, I ask thee forgiveness for the comfortable familiarity or less authoritative way in treating you as a nun of the veil, my sister, I have forgotten the distance between your very illustrious personage and myself, which would not have occurred if I had seen you unveiled. (De la Cruz 2009, 40)[21]

"Sor Filotea" was supposedly a nun from a different cloister, and was a literal distance between herself and Sor Juana, and did not know Sor Juana personally. Therefore, Sor Juana would, if "Sor Filotea" were real, need to apologize for being so familiar and comfortable in her self-defense. Sor Juana claims that she was so personal because they are both nuns and would never have written this way if "Sor Filotea" were unveiled, and no longer a sister of the cloth.

However, there is also a double meaning with distance and unveiled. Sor Juana knew "Sor Filotea" was the Bishop Fernández, so there was a figurative distance

---

[20] Sor Juana refers to this in four places directly throughout this letter. Twice in paragraph 5, once in paragraph 26 and again in paragraph 40.

[21] *Si el estilo, venerable Señora mía, de esta carta, no hubiere sido como a vos es debido, os pido perdón de la casera familiaridad o menos autoridad de que tratándoos como una religiosa de velo, hermana mía, se me ha olvidado la distancia de vuestra ilustrísima persona, que ha veros yo sin velo, no sucediera así.*

between the station of the two, and by treating the bishop as a nun, Sor Juana was able to speak much more openly than otherwise would have been possible. Thus, this letter would never have occurred if "Sor Filotea" were to be unveiled as Bishop Fernández.

By responding in a seemingly humble way, Sor Juana avoided the anger of the Inquisition. She was able to defend herself from her accusers in a public manner and work philosophically through these questions of her worthiness of her soul, her right to study what she wished, and be able to write poetry. Sor Juana engaged in an inherently philosophical endeavor much like Socrates did millennia before her, by showing the righteousness of her soul. Her divinely inspired mind was capable of study, and so she should be free to study in the way best suited to accomplish her desire in order to better her connection with her divinity. Socrates chose to end his philosophical journey. However, at the point of *The Reply*, Sor Juana was not willing to end her philosophical enquiries quite yet. After *The Reply*, Sor Juana continued writing and was able to publish another volume of her work less than a year later.

References

De la Cruz, J. I. (1997 [1691]). "Respuesta de la poetisa a la muy ilustre Sor Filotea de la Cruz". *Poems, Protests, and a Dream*. London: Penguin Books, 1–74.

De la Cruz, J. I. (2009). *The Answer/La Respuesta*, ed. and trans. by Arenal, E. and Powell, A. 2nd ed. New York: Feminist Press.

Paz, O. (1988). *Sor Juana, or The Traps of Faith*. Trans. by Margaret Sayers Peden. Cambridge, MA: Harvard University Press.

Plato (2002). "The Apology". In Plato, *Five Dialogues*. Trans. by G. M. A. Grube. Indianapolis, IN: Hackett.

Warnke, F. J. (1987). *Three Women Poets: Renaissance and Baroque, Louise Labé, Gaspara Stampa, and Sor Juana Inés de la Cruz*. Lewisburg, PA: Bucknell University Press.

Demin XU

Le rôle des œuvres de Rousseau dans les mouvements féministes en Chine moderne

Abstract: The feminist movement in modern China was originally – between the end of the 19th century and the very beginning of the 20th century – mainly led by intellectual men who called for gender equality and women's empowerment. Among them were Liang Qichao (1873–1929), Ma Junwu (1881–1940) and Jin Tianhe (1873–1947), promoters of Rousseau's thought, and intellectuals of the May Fourth Movement of 1919 such as Chen Duxiu (1879–1942), Hu Shi (1891–1962) and Lu Xun (1881–1936). «Man was born free», Rousseau, since his introduction in China, sowed the seeds of the revolution of mores in Chinese society, and opened the discussion on the «New woman» in the late Qing dynasty (1644–1911) and the early Republic of China (1912–1949).

Résumé: Le mouvement féministe en Chine qui remonte à la fin du XIXe siècle était principalement animé par les hommes intellectuels qui en appelaient à l'égalité des sexes et à l'émancipation des femmes. Parmi eux se trouvaient Liang Qichao (1873–1929), Ma Junwu (1881–1940) et Jin Tianhe (1873–1947), promoteurs de la pensée de Rousseau dont Huang Zunxian (1848–1905) fut probablement le premier lecteur, et les protagonistes du Mouvement du 4 mai 1919 tels que Chen Duxiu (1879–1942), Hu Shi (1891–1962) et Lu Xun (1881–1936). Influencés par Rousseau, Liang, Ma et Jin conçoivent la nécessité aux femmes de recevoir une éducation et de détenir un emploi. «L'homme est né libre», Rousseau, dès son introduction en Chine, a semé les graines de la révolution des mœurs dans la société chinoise, et a ouvert la discussion sur la «Nouvelle femme» à la fin de la dynastie Qing (1644–1911) et au début de la République de Chine (1912–1949).

Note on the author: Demin XU est Docteur en philosophie, chercheuse post-doctorante au LLCP – Université Paris VIII. Ses domaines de recherche couvrent la démocratie moderne, la liberté individuelle et la liberté politique, la politique et la société chinoises.

Introduction

Depuis leur adoption en Chine, Rousseau et sa théorie du contrat social sont un symbole révolutionnaire des mouvements sociaux y compris le mouvement féministe à l'orée du XXème siècle, à tel point qu'on le rapproche parfois de Confucius, même si son influence reste encore confinée dans le cercle des intellectuels. Sa thèse selon laquelle «L'homme est né libre» a introduit la discussion sur la «Nouvelle femme»[1] à la fin de la dynastie Qing (1644–1911) et au début de la République de Chine (1912–1949).[2] C'est notamment après le Mouvement du 4 mai 1919 que les femmes chinoises commencent à rechercher activement l'égalité des droits dans tous les aspects, à savoir, politiques, économiques, culturels et sociaux.

Le premier mouvement féministe moderne en Chine était principalement animé par des hommes intellectuels qui en appelaient à l'égalité des sexes et à l'émancipation des femmes. Cette particularité chinoise ne se retrouve pas dans d'autres pays. Parmi eux se trouvent Liang Qichao 梁启超 (1873–1929),[3] Ma Junwu 马君武 (1881–1940)[4] et Jin Tianhe金天翮 (1873–1947),[5] promoteurs de la pensée de Rousseau, et les intellectuels du Mouvement du 4 mai 1919, à l'instar de Chen Duxiu 陈独秀 (1879–1942),[6] Hu Shi胡适 (1891–1962)[7] et Lu Xun 鲁迅 (1881–1936).[8]

Une révolution sous le signe du *Contrat social*

Si on parle des circonstances de l'établissement du mouvement féministe en Chine moderne, Rousseau en est un passage incontournable. Il est connu depuis 1878

---

[1] Idéal féminin de l'époque, à comparer aux « Femmes d'autrefois » (*jiu nüxing* 旧女性).
[2] On parle ici du régime politique instauré en Chine de 1912 à 1949, après la chute de la dynastie Qing, dynastie impériale régnante depuis 1644.
[3] Journaliste, philosophe et réformiste, l'un des dirigeants de la Réforme des Cents Jours de 1898.
[4] Fondateur de l'Université de Guangxi, puis président de plusieurs autres universités. La première traduction en chinois du *Manifeste du parti communiste* est faite par lui aussi, elle paraît dans le *Min Bao* à l'été 1906.
[5] Dans les années 1930, avec Zhang Taiyan 章太炎, Qian Jibo 钱基博 et Tang Wenzhi 唐文治, il est connu comme l'un des quatre maîtres d'études chinoises. Jin Tianhe a consacré la seconde moitié de sa vie à la science de l'éducation.
[6] Figure de proue du Mouvement de la Nouvelle Culture (1915–1923), intellectuel radical bien connu et doyen de la faculté des sciences humaines de l'Université de Beijing de janvier 1917 à avril 1919.
[7] Philosophe et figure du Mouvement de la Nouvelle Culture, il a été professeur de littérature anglo-américaine à l'Université de Beijing, puis président de la même Université. Par la suite, il deviendra ambassadeur de la République de Chine aux États-Unis et président de l'Académie Sinica.
[8] Nom de plume de Zhou Shuren 周树人, écrivain et l'un des fondateurs de la littérature chinoise contemporaine.

grâce à Guo Songtao 郭嵩焘 (1818–1891),[9] premier diplomate permanent sous l'ère Qing dans les pays occidentaux, qui, à l'occasion d'une visite officielle en Grande-Bretagne, puis en France, le mentionne dans le *Lundun yu Bali riji* 伦敦与巴黎日记 (Journal de Londres à Paris) : « Rousseau et Voltaire s'attaquent aux pouvoirs du clergé, la classe privilégiée »,[10] ce qui va par la suite chambouler ses perceptions. Bien que Guo ne trouve aucune relation directe entre Rousseau et la Révolution française, il n'en néglige pas pour autant sa contribution à l'instauration de la démocratie en France. Notons qu'il voyage au moment du centenaire de la mort de ces deux grands hommes. Ainsi, arrivait Rousseau dans l'histoire chinoise. Guo envoie son journal à la Chancellerie une fois terminé et stéréotypé sous le titre de *Notes de Mission diplomatique à l'Ouest*, provoquant un tollé général à la Cour. Sa planche d'imprimerie sera ensuite détruite par un décret impérial, il ne pourra être réimprimé et diffusé que tardivement, au tournant des années 1980.

En 1882, Nakae Chomin 中江兆民 (1847–1901, son prénom Chomin est issu du *Livre des Odes*),[11] penseur politique japonais, traduit *Du Contrat social* en chinois dans son pays. Sa publication aura une grande influence auprès de la jeunesse japonaise engagée dans le Mouvement pour la liberté et les droits du peuple. Le traducteur et penseur gagne la réputation d'être le « Rousseau du Japon ». Il est important de noter que sous l'ère Meïji (1868–1912), l'enseignement de la langue chinoise est encouragé pour des raisons d'expansion en direction du continent. Aussi, s'ouvre de nombreuses institutions dans lesquelles s'effectuera le passage du nankinois (南京官话)[12] au pékinois (北京官话), langue officielle du pays convoité à cette époque. Nakae Chomin apprend le chinois dès son enfance, surtout au travers du *Tchouang-tseu* 庄子, œuvre taoïste du IIIe siècle av J.-C. et des *Mémoires Historiques* (*Shiji* 史记) rédigées en 109–191 av J.-C. par Sima Qian.[13] Huang Zun-

---

9 L'un des fondateurs de l'armée du Hunan, haut fonctionnaire de la dynastie Qing, ministre plénipotentiaire en Grande Bretagne à partir de 1875, et aussi en France en 1878. Il démissionne l'année suivante.
10 Guo Sontao, *Lundun yu Bali riji*, Yuelu shushe, Changsha 1984, 562
11 Théoricien et activiste des mouvements de droits civils, homme politique, philosophe matérialiste à l'ère Meiji du Japon, il a fait ses études à Paris et à Lyon.
12 Langues officielles des dynasties précédentes sont toutes à la base du mandarin de Nankin. Depuis le milieu de la dynastie Qing, le pékinois devient sa langue standard.
13 Néanmoins, en tant que théoricien des droits civiques, ses motivations s'expliquent par son discours : « Nous devrions nous éveiller à ce qui est le devoir naturel du Japon, pour envisager notre propre destin dans les cent ans à venir [...] peu importe la force de notre pays, la faiblesse de notre voisin, si nous lui envoyons des troupes sans aucune raison, quels en seront alors les résultats ? Après tout, la superficialité ne peut vaincre la justice ». (Dernière œuvre de Chomin, *Un an et demi, suivi un an et demi*, Éditions de Presse de Commerce, 1997, Beijing, p. 17) La décadence institutionnelle de son pays confirmera pleinement sa prédiction.

xian 黄遵宪 (1848–1905), érudit fonctionnaire et écrivain, fut probablement le premier lecteur de cette traduction. Dans une lettre à Liang Qichao, il fait part de ses réflexions et incite à sa diffusion en Chine. La 1ère partie de l'ouvrage est publiée en 1898 par la Maison d'Éditions Tongwen de Shanghai (上海同文书局). La même année, a lieu la Réforme des Cent jours (*Bairi weixin*, 百日维新),[14] initiée par le jeune empereur Guangxu 光绪 (règne 1875–1908) et ses conseillers réformistes : entre autres, Kang Youwei 康有为 (1858–1927)[15] et Liang Qichao. La Réforme propose l'abandon de la monarchie absolue au profit d'une monarchie constitutionnelle, dans le but de moderniser et de rendre puissant le pays. Mais finalement, ce sont l'impératrice douairière Cixi 慈禧 (1835–1908) et les conservateurs qui gagnent la lutte au sein du Palais : l'empereur Guangxu sera confinée à l'intérieur de la Cité Interdite jusqu'à son décès en 1908 ; « six martyrs favorables à la Réforme »[16] seront exécutés par décapitation ; Kang Youwei et Liang Qichao, deux promoteurs (un troisième, Tan Sitong refusera de partir et sera parmi les six) s'enfuirent au Japon où ils fondèrent la Société de protection de l'empereur (*Baohuang hui* 保皇会). Hu Shi dira lors des événements du 4 mai, « il y a 20 ans, Kang Youwei était trop avancé pour son époque ; 20 ans plus tard, au contraire, il est trop conservateur ».[17]

Une édition intégrale de l'ouvrage *Du Contrat social*, traduite par un étudiant chinois au Japon, Yang Tingdong 杨廷栋 (1879–1950),[18] est publiée à Shanghai en 1902, ce qui permettra une plus grande diffusion de la doctrine rousseauiste. Entre 1901 et 1902, Liang Qichao publie deux articles, « Lusuo Xue'an » 卢梭学案 (L'école de Rousseau) et « *Minyue Lun* juzi Lusuo zhi xueshuo » 民约论巨子卢梭之学说 (La pensée du grand Rousseau du *Contrat social*), où il présente la biographie de Rousseau, les principes de sa doctrine, les relations entre la volonté générale et la souveraineté, celles entre la souveraineté et le droit, celles entre le droit et le gouvernement. Ces articles offrent une introduction précieuse à Rousseau avec une vue assez large, bien que parfois erronée. Son maître, Kang Youwei, lui fait

---

14 Mouvement réformiste, du 11 juin au 21 septembre 1898, dure en réalité 104 jours. *Wuxu* est le nom de l'année dans le cycle sexagésimal.
15 Lettré et théoricien politique, l'un des dirigeants de la Réforme des Cents Jours de 1898.
16 Ils sont aussi appelés « six gentilshommes » (*Wuxu liu junzi* 戊戌六君子) : Tan Sitong 谭嗣同, Lin Xu 林旭, Yang Rui 杨锐, Yang Shenxiu 杨深秀, Liu Guangdi 刘光第 et Kang Guangren 康广仁.
17 Hu Shi, *Hu Shi xuanji* 胡适选集 (Textes choisis de Hu Shi), Ershiyi shiji chubanshe, Beijing, 2013, p. 74.
18 En mars 1898, Yang Tingdong arrive à Tokyo, il est parmi les premiers étudiants chinois financés par l'État. D'après le *Guide de la constitution de l'école Nichika*, il est entré en janvier de la 32e année de l'ère Meiji (1899). Pour les traductions chinoises du *Contrat social*, voir Wang Xiaoling, *Jean-Jacques Rousseau en Chine (de 1871 à nos jours)*, Musée Jean-Jacques Rousseau, Montmorency, 2010.

quelques remarques, ce qui l'amène à mieux réfléchir sur les idées de Rousseau, aussi conclut-il : « il est vrai que la doctrine de Rousseau est quelque peu radicale, néanmoins elle est un bon remède pour la Chine ».[19]

Certes, les traductions de cette période ne sont pas totalement fidèles au texte original. Yang Tingdong introduit même une nouvelle traduction du nom de Rousseau : *Lu Suo* 路索, signifiant « explorer le chemin », il le considère comme l'homme sage qui incarne la voie pour sauver le pays. En fin de compte, ces erreurs ont peu d'importance dans cette période historiquement exceptionnelle, car l'ouvrage permet aux intellectuels chinois d'entrer directement en contact avec la pensée occidentale moderne et de dénoncer la tyrannie impériale.

Zou Rong 邹容 (1885–1905), nationaliste et révolutionnaire à la fin de la dynastie Qing, mènera une lecture approfondie du texte durant ses études au Dobunshoin de Tokyo (同文书院). De retour en Chine, il publiera en 1903 un pamphlet, *L'Armée Révolutionnaire* (*Gemingjun* 革命军), considéré comme une première « Déclaration des droits de l'homme en Chine », lu par Hu Shi et Chiang Kai-shek 蒋介石 (1887–1975)[20] dans leur jeunesse. Son appel à la souveraineté du peuple chinois inclut la création d'un parlement, l'accès à l'égalité des droits pour les femmes, l'obtention de la liberté d'expression et de presse, en somme, tout ce qui inspirera Sun Yat-sen 孙中山 (1866–1925)[21] pour la Révolution républicaine de 1911 (*Xinhai Geming* 辛亥革命).[22]

Rousseau devient une référence de la révolution dans la société chinoise. De nombreux admirateurs prennent des noms de plume dans des journaux progressistes : *Lusuo zhi tu* 卢梭之徒 (disciple de Rousseau), *Lusuo hun* 卢梭魂 (âme de Rousseau), *Pingdeng ge zhuren* 平等阁主人 (maître du studio de l'égalité), *Jingping* 竞平 (lutte pour l'égalité,), *Ziyou* 自由 (liberté), *Renquan* 人权 (droits de l'homme), *Minyou* 民友 (ami du peuple), *Zhige* 志革 (idéal de la révolution). Le

---

19 Liang Qichao, *Yinbingshi heji* (Œuvres de Liang Qichao), tome 4, Zhonghua shuju, Beijing, 1989, p. 97
20 Homme politique et militaire, dirigeant du parti nationaliste depuis 1925 et président de la République de Chine de 1948 à 1975. Dans les années 1930, il a lancé le mouvement de la nouvelle vie dans le but de promouvoir la réforme culturelle et la moralité sociale néo-confucéenne et finalement d'unir la Chine sous une idéologie centralisée suite à l'émergence entre autres du communisme.
21 Leader de la Révolution républicaine de 1911 et homme d'État chinois, il est considéré comme « le père de la Chine moderne ».
22 Elle renverse la dynastie Qing après 268 ans de règne (1644–1911). Le système impérial gouvernant la Chine depuis deux millénaires disparaît.

premier numéro de *Min Bao* 民报,[23] publication officielle de La Ligue Unie (aussi connue sous le nom de *Tongmenhui* 同盟会, Alliance révolutionnaire), contient dans ses pages un portrait de Rousseau, le nommant «Premier homme des droits civiques du monde». Liu Yazi 柳亚子 (1887-1958), déjà rebaptisé *Renquan* (Droits de l'homme), souhaite être «Yalu» 亚庐 (le Rousseau de l'Asie). Après sa lecture, Von Maolong 冯懋龙 (1882-1958), né dans une famille cantonaise à Yokohama), plus tard rebaptisé Von Ziyou 冯自由 (liberté), suivra la révolution républicaine et Sun Yat-sen toute sa vie.

Toutefois, devant l'urgence des besoins de la nation, sa survie, les droits des individus se voient relégués au second plan. Et l'œuvre de Rousseau cède très vite la place aux préoccupations des démocrates révolutionnaires. Liang Qichao se tourne également vers le «nationalisme», préconisant le «despotisme éclairé». Étant le premier critique de la théorie du droit divin, Yan Fu 严复 (1854-1921), après la première guerre sino-japonaise (1894), affirme clairement que «la liberté du peuple est un droit inaliénable». Cependant, en février 1914, il publie un «*Minyue* pingyi» 民约评议 (Commentaire du *Contrat social*) dans le journal *Yongyan* 庸言 (Propos ordinaires),[24] où il l'attaque en l'accusant d'être à l'origine des «inondations et [du règne] des bêtes sauvages et féroces».[25] Cela s'explique pour trois raisons : tout d'abord, il le rejette du point de vue de ce qu'il imagine comme origine de la société ; puis, il montre son opposition au «culte de la liberté» ; enfin, il ne veut plus refuser «la monarchie absolue».[26]

Pour réactiver l'attention à Rousseau, tout en corrigeant les erreurs de Chomin et celles de la version qualifiée de «fraude absurde illisible» de Yang Tingdong, Ma Junwu en propose en 1916 une traduction plus proche de l'originale, avec la certification de sa traduction anglaise par H. J. Tozer. Il mettra 80 jours pour en arriver à bout, et la publiera aux Éditions Zhonghua shju 中华书局 sous le titre de *Zuben Lusao* Minyue Lun 足本卢骚民约论 (L'édition intégrale du *Contrat Social*), en 1918. De plus, il confirme que «la doctrine de Rousseau, violemment attaquée dans les temps modernes, affirme le principe de la souveraineté du peuple, à tel point que le livre deviendra la force motrice de la Révolution française. Jamais dépassé depuis deux cents ans, il est l'un des grands classiques du monde».[27]

---

23 Fondé en 1905 à Tokyo. Dans sa profession de foi, Sun Yat-sen, dirigeant de la Ligue, y annonce pour la première fois les Trois Principes du Peuple : nationalisme, démocratie et bien-être du peuple.

24 Fondé par Liang Qichao en 1912 à Tianjin, c'était une plateforme permettant la propagation du concept de constitution.

25 *Hongshui mengshou* 洪水猛兽, expression empruntée à Mencius.

26 Yan Fu, *Yan Fu ji* 严复集 (Œuvres de Yan Fu), Zhonghua shuju, Beijing, 1986, pp. 333–340.

27 Ma Junwu écrit dans l'introduction de sa traduction.

Bien que les révolutionnaires reconnaissent ses idées, très peu comprennent véritablement sa pensée. En particulier, la notion de contrat social ne trouve tout simplement pas d'équivalent dans leurs discours. Cependant, beaucoup y trouveront une pensée de la « révolution » de par cette « vague » rousseauiste.

Une émancipation prônée par des intellectuels masculins

Rappelons que depuis deux mille ans la Chine est une société confucéenne et hiérarchisée, ainsi l'ordre des genres se justifie par la supériorité masculine et l'infériorité féminine. Dans ce contexte patriarcal et arbitraire, l'autonomie des femmes n'a jamais été prise en considération, ni dans la vie familiale, ni dans la société. Les « droits des femmes » sont restés pendant longtemps inconnus au niveau langagier.

Comme nous l'avons mentionné plus haut, le mouvement féministe en Chine moderne a d'abord été initié par des hommes intellectuels, tels que Liang Qichao, Ma Junwu et Jin Tianhe, ce qui diffère des autres pays. Cela permet de poser les questions suivantes : pourquoi les hommes promeuvent-ils les droits des femmes ? Et quel est leur point de départ ? Influencés par la théorie des droits de l'homme rousseauistes, ils reconnaissent que les femmes ne sont pas intrinsèquement faibles et qu'il faut leur donner l'opportunité de recevoir une éducation et de détenir un emploi afin qu'elles puissent exercer les mêmes droits que les hommes.

Néanmoins, les mouvements féministes en Chine moderne sont étroitement liés au développement national. La lutte pour les intérêts des femmes, en tant que groupe social indépendant, n'est jamais devenue un mouvement dominant, bien qu'il y ait toujours eu des femmes féministes qui réclament et défendent activement leurs droits, et montrent alors une attitude différente de celles des leurs compères masculins. On peut voir plus en détail le rôle joué par chacun de ces penseurs.

Liang Qichao

La défense prise par Liang des intérêts des femmes est très influente. Ses opinions s'expliquent par le principe de l'universalité des droits de l'homme, tels que les droits humains naturels, la liberté, l'égalité... Quant à la réalisation du droit des femmes, il préconise la protection de leur santé, le soutient de leur éducation, la défense des mouvements féministes et enfin leur émancipation.

De prime abord, il estime que les aptitudes des femmes ne sont pas intrinsèquement moindres, mais qu'elles peuvent être mieux développées.[28] Son affirmation renverse l'opinion dominante de l'époque à propos de la « faiblesse naturelle » des femmes, et incite ces dernières à changer leurs conditions de vie et leur état d'esprit grâce à l'éducation. Il a donc conseillé aux femmes de dire « Non » au bandage des pieds[29] et de créer des écoles de filles. Pour Liang, le degré de la puissance d'un pays dépend en grande partie de l'accès des femmes aux domaines de l'esprit, tant culturels que professionnels.[30] « Si on veut rendre notre pays puissant, il faudra miser sur l'éducation des femmes ».[31]

De 1902 à 1906, Liang Qichao avance ses idées dans une série d'articles publiés dans le journal *Xinmin Congbao* 新民丛报 (Le Nouveau Peuple). À propos du retard économique de la Chine, il affirme que le pouvoir national dépend du nombre de producteurs et de consommateurs : si les producteurs sont nombreux mais les consommateurs sont peu nombreux, cela peut rendre le pays prospère et le peuple fort ; à contrario, si les consommateurs sont plus nombreux que les producteurs, alors il sera difficile d'échapper à la pauvreté et à la faiblesse. Dans ce sens, il ne faut que les femmes jouent seulement le rôle de consommateur, mais aussi celui de producteur. Son opinion trouve un écho dans le mouvement de défense des professions féminines de 1915 à 1923. L'indépendance économique était en effet primordiale dans l'émancipation des femmes.

D'après Sudo Mizuyo, chercheuse à l'Université Hitotsubashi, le terme de *nüquan* 女权 (féminisme en chinois), serait probablement introduit en Chine par l'intermédiaire du Japon. Bien que Liang Qichao emploie rarement ce mot dans ses œuvres, les questions qu'il soulève sur le bandage des pieds et l'éducation des femmes provoquera ensuite un épanouissement des mouvements féministes dans le pays. Cette première génération a non seulement favorisé le développement de l'éducation féminine, mais a également rendu populaire l'idée de l'indépendance et de l'émancipation féminines.

Le 6 novembre 1922, Liang Qichao publie un texte intitulé « Renquan yu nüquan » 人权与女权 (Droits de l'homme et droits des femmes). Aujourd'hui on le

---

28 Liang Qichao, *Yinbingshi heji*, tome 1, Zhonghua shuju, Beijing, 1989, p. 121
29 La coutume des pieds bandés est une pratique chinoise allant du Xe au début du XXe siècle, sur les filles et les jeunes femmes issues des classes sociales favorisées, puis plus largement imposée dans la société chinoise.
30 Sudo Mizuyo, *Zhongguo nüquan gainian de bianqian* 中国 "女权" 概念的变迁 (Changements du concept de « féminisme » en Chine), trad. Yao Yi, Zhongguo shehui kexue wenxian chubanshe, Beijing, 2010, pp. 33–35.
31 Liang Qichao, « Lun nüxue » 论女学 (Sur l'étude des femmes), in *Yinbingshi heji*, tome 1, *op. cit.*, pp. 37–44

considère comme un chef-d'œuvre d'introduction à la sociologie ayant servi à éclairer la pensée du peuple. Il dénonce la mise à l'écart des femmes en matière des droits de l'homme, comme si ce n'était pas «leur affaire». Pour lui, le mouvement des droits humains revêt trois significations : le droit à l'égalité dans l'éducation ; le droit à l'égalité dans le travail et le droit à l'égalité en politique.[32] Aussi approuve-t-il les mouvements des droits des femmes pour leur accès à l'éducation, au travail et à la vie politique.

Ma Junwu

Le terme *nüquan* (féminisme) commence à être répandu dans les milieux intellectuels chinois entre 1902 et 1903. Ma Junwu et Jin Tianhe ont apporté leurs contributions. Ma Junwu, traducteur de Rousseau et également de Spencer (1820–1903), publie en 1902 «Les droits des femmes chez Spencer et l'évolution sociale chez Darwin», texte dans lequel il présente les pensées féministes de Spencer. Ma est en phase avec Liang Qichao sur deux points principaux : «les aptitudes des femmes ne sont pas intrinsèquement moindres» ; «la puissance d'un pays dépend de l'accès des femmes aux choses de l'esprit, tant culturelles que professionnelles». Mais subsistent des différences entre eux. Pour Ma, les femmes se positionnent comme sujet de droit, aussi est-il favorable à l'égalité conjugale et à la participation des femmes en politique. Le but ultime de la pensée féministe de Liang est la prospérité et la puissance de la nation chinoise, tandis que pour Ma, les femmes doivent avoir les mêmes droits publics que les hommes, cela suppose une révolution sociale.

En 1903, Ma Junwu publie dans *Le Nouveau Peuple* une introduction à la théorie féministe de John Stuart Mill (1806–1873) : *The Subjection of Women* (*De l'assujettissement des femmes*).[33] Il ne l'a pas entièrement traduit, au contraire, son texte est très bref, mêlé de ses propres réflexions. Il souhaite principalement utiliser les deux auteurs (Spencer et Mill) pour préconiser «l'égalité entre les hommes et les femmes» et «la révolution féministe». Liang et Ma ont profondément influencé les discours féministes de la fin de la dynastie Qing et du début de la République de Chine. Ils ont également façonné l'imagination populaire quant au féminisme européen de l'époque. Les traductions de Ma Junwu ont séduit son contemporain Jin Tianhe.

---

32 «Renquan yu nüquan», texte repris dans le *Yinbingshi heji, op. cit.*, pp. 81–85.
33 Essai de John Stuart Mill publié en 1869. L'auteur y défend des idées en faveur de l'égalité entre les sexes et du droit de vote des femmes.

En 1906, Ma publie un article intitulé «Dimin shuo» 帝民说 (Du Peuple-Empereur) dans le deuxième numéro du *Min Bao* pour présenter le principal concept de Rousseau : la souveraineté du peuple. Il transforme la sentence «le peuple est le souverain» en «le peuple est l'empereur», ceci afin de faciliter la compréhension et la réception avant la chute de l'empire.

Jin Tianhe

Jin Tianhe est connu comme le «père des Lumières féministes dans la Chine moderne» et comparé à un «Rousseau pour les cercles féminins» par Lin Zongsu 林宗素 (1878–1944), sa préfacière. Un point intéressant à souligner est que grâce à lui et Liu Yazi, Zou Rong a pu publier *L'armée révolutionnaire* en mai 1903. Trois mois plus tard, Jin fait paraître le *Nüjie zhong* 女界钟 (Cloche du monde des femmes). Si le premier fait fureur dans le pays et cela jusqu'à la veille de la Révolution républicaine, le second est non-seulement considéré comme «la première monographie sur la théorie féministe dans la Chine moderne», mais aussi comme la première œuvre dédiée aux recherches sur la problématique féminine. L'auteur affirme que «les femmes sont la mère de la nation» et proclame pour la première fois dans l'histoire chinoise : «Vive les droits des femmes», ce qui deviendra le cri unanime pour nombre de mouvements féministes ultérieurs.

Par ailleurs, il souligne : «Le progrès ou la régression du monde sont aussi de la responsabilité des femmes». Sous l'influence de penseurs occidentaux, tels que Stuart et Spencer, Jin Tianhe s'intéresse aux droits des femmes en matière d'éducation, de mariage, d'économie et de politique. En même temps, il les classe en droits publics et privés : le droit d'entrer à l'école, le droit de se faire des amis, le droit de faire des affaires, le droit de posséder des biens, le droit de migrer et l'exercice de leur liberté dans le mariage.[34]

Avant lui, Kang Youwei et Liang Qichao avaient déjà appelé à l'émancipation des femmes, mais ils se concentraient sur l'abolition du bandage des pieds et l'éducation des femmes, car pour ces derniers le bandage des pieds est une honte de la nation et la puissance du pays ne peut se passer de l'éducation des femmes. Autrement dit, libérer les femmes fait partie des moyens de réformer le pays. Le *Nüjie zhong* a clairement mis en avant le concept du droit des femmes (*nüquan*) : «Les droits des femmes et les droits civils sont directement liés, et ne sont pas deux problèmes distincts ... La révolution politique est la lute pour la liberté de tous les citoyens ; la révolution familiale est la lute pour la liberté individuelle des citoyens.

---

[34] Jin Tianhe, *Nüjie zhong*, Shanghai guji chubanshe, Shanghai, 2003, pp. 60–63.

L'objectif des deux est le même ».³⁵ Sur cette base, Jin préconise l'égalité entre les hommes et les femmes, la liberté du mariage, la participation des femmes à la politique :

> Les femmes, c'est la mère de la nation. Si nous voulons rénover la Chine, nous devrions avoir des Nouvelles femmes ; Si nous voulons une Chine puissante, nous devrions renforcer les femmes ; Si nous voulons une Chine civilisée, nous devrions d'abord cultiver les femmes ; Si nous voulons sauver la Chine, nous devrions d'abord sauver les femmes. Il n'y a aucun doute.
>
> Les femmes, c'est la mère d'une civilisation.³⁶

La défense des droits des femmes par les hommes intellectuels est également liée aux changements du statut international de la Chine. Au début du *Nüjie zhong*, Jin Tianhe imagine qu'il se promenait dans les rues de Paris, et pas dans les rues de Pékin, ce qui démontre sa perspective internationale. Les buts de promotion par ces hommes de la « Nouvelle Femme » correspondent à l'image féminine, telle qu'elle est perçue en Ocident. He Zhen 何震 (1884–1920), féministe chinoise du début du XXᵉ siècle et l'une des premières lectrices de Jin Tianhe, écrit : les hommes chinois imitaient les décisions des hommes européens, américains et japonais, c'était tout simplement du point de vue de la différence des civilisations ; c'était une affaire purement égoïste. Pour elle, la lutte féministe ne doit pas être subordonnée à la lutte nationaliste, ethnocentrique ou à la modernisation capitaliste.

Liberté individuelle et auto-émancipation des femmes

À la fin de la dynastie Qing et au début de la République de Chine, diverses discussions sur la « Nouvelle Femme » se sont engagées. Celles-ci portaient sur l'image idéale de la femme et se déroulaient en trois étapes. Tout d'abord, le bandage des petits pieds devenait signe de « déclin » et de « barbarie ». Ensuite, un programme était dressé pour une adaptation intellectuelle et physique des femmes aux conditions de travail en vigueur dans le pays. Enfin, l'entrée des femmes elles-mêmes dans les revendications féministes d'abord prônées par les hommes voit se

---

35 Ding Zuyin 丁祖荫, « Nüzi jiating geming shuo » 女子家庭革命说 (De la révolution familiale des Femmes), *Nüzi shijie* 女子世界 (Le Monde des Femmes), 1904(4), p. 2.
36 Jin Tianhe, Éditorial, *Nüzi shijie* 女子世界 (Le Monde des Femmes), 17 janvier 1904.

développer un discours d'indépendance et de conscience de soi en vue de forger des droits selon leurs espérances.

La réception du *Contrat social* de Rousseau a non seulement suscité l'éveil de la majorité des intellectuels masculins, mais également alerté beaucoup d'intellectuelles féminines et même des femmes du peuple. Les femmes opprimées depuis toujours s'aperçoivent qu'elles ont aussi des personnalités complexes et complètes, tout comme les hommes. Cette prise de conscience les incite à poursuivre vivement leurs droits à la politique, à l'économie, à la culture et à la vie sociale.

Qiu Jin

Qiu Jin 秋瑾 (1875–1907), fille d'une famille de lettrés et fonctionnaires distingués de la dynastie Qing, mère de deux enfants, a été la première femme à rejoindre le mouvement de l'émancipation des femmes dans l'histoire chinoise moderne.[37] En mai 1904, après avoir rompu avec son mari, Wang Tingjun 王廷钧 (1879–1909), fils d'un riche marchand de la province du Hunan, elle vent tous ses bijoux, embarque en direction du Japon pour étudier. De ce fait, Qiu Jin est aussi appelée la «Nora chinoise», d'après le personnage emblématique de la pièce d'Henrik Ibsen (1828–1906), *Une maison de poupée* (1879). Lors de son séjour au Japon, elle rejoint la Sanhe hui 三合会 (Triade chinoise), association organisée par Von Ziyou, lecteur du *Contrat social*.[38] L'association visait à «Renverser la dynastie Qing et à Régénérer la Chine», elle est nommée conseillère (*baishan* 白扇). Ses activités révolutionnaires au Japon se répandent rapidement dans le Hunan, ce qui incitera une vingtaine de jeunes femmes à la rejoindre en novembre 1904.

L'émergence de femmes qui étudient à l'étranger est extraordinaire. Cela signifie que les femmes chinoises opprimées et maltraitées pendant de nombreux siècles ont commencé à se libérer du règne des familles traditionnelles, à savoir, ne plus être liées au patriarche, au père, au frère, au mari ou tout autre membre masculin de la famille, ce qui provoquera de grands changements dans le statut familial des femmes.

---

37 Bien qu'il y ait Kang Tongbi 康同璧, fille de Kang Youwei, Li Huixian 李惠仙, l'épouse de Liang Qichao, qui revendiquaient aussi l'égalité entre les hommes et les femmes, on les considère encore comme des femmes «passives», selon la distinction établie par Emmanuel-Joseph Sieyès (1748–1836), car ce sont leur père et époux qui les promeuvent.

38 Von a également reçu l'ordre de Sun Yat-sen de contacter les révolutionnaires chinois au Japon. En 1904, il participe à la création de la Ligue chinoise avec ce dernier.

Bien que Kang Youwei, Liang Qichao et d'autres soient très critiques envers l'éthique traditionnelle et notamment l'inégalité des sexes, on ne peut pas dire d'eux que ce sont des féministes au sens strict, alors que Qiu Jin, par son souhait d'indépendance, peut être considérée comme pionnière dans l'émancipation de la femme chinoise. À cet effet, son engagement est tout un symbole, elle a acquis la stature d'une révolutionnaire sur la scène historique du pays. D'ailleurs, elle associe toujours la révolution féministe à une révolution plus totale qui embraserait tout le pays. Pour elle, les deux sont intimement liées et atteindront le même but : si les femmes sont libérées et peuvent participer aux diverses activités sociales, alors la patrie sera sauvée. Aussi, estime-t-elle que l'émancipation des femmes est un préalable à la prospérité du pays. Là on voit que son féminisme rejoint celui des hommes intellectuels, à savoir qu'il est d'abord envisagé sous l'angle de la puissance du pays, et non pas centré sur l'émancipation des femmes en tant que telle. Ainsi, propose-t-elle que les femmes quittent leur famille et viennent participer à la vie sociale.

La pensée féministe de Qiu Jin émane aussi de sa lecture de Rousseau, de Montesquieu et d'autres penseurs occidentaux. Son opposition aux pieds bandés s'articule autour de la physiologie et de l'humanisme. « Si nous voulons nous émanciper, il faut commencer par libérer nos pieds ».[39] Sa vive défense de l'égalité entre les hommes et les femmes puisse sa source dans la doctrine des « droits naturels ». Elle dit : « La révolution débute dans la famille, c'est pour cette raison qu'on réclame des droits pour les femmes ».[40] Son appel à la création d'écoles de filles provient des idées féministes occidentales. « Les femmes devront avoir de la culture, rechercher l'autonomie et ne plus dépendre des hommes ».[41] Elle recommande aux femmes sa pratique de l'auto-émancipation : être « indépendantes – travailleuses – engagées » («自立-学艺-合群»). Première héroïne et martyre à la Révolution républicaine de Chine, Qiu Jin lègue un héritage inégal dans le féminisme chinois, notamment dans la participation politique et l'engagement militaire des femmes.

Zhongguo nübao 中国女报 (Femmes Chinoise), périodique créé par Qiu Jin en 1906, est l'une des premières publications féminines en Chine. Son éditorial du 14 janvier 1907 écrit par elle-même est un manifeste politique pour l'émancipation des femmes chinoises. Elle a ainsi publié « Un avertissement à nos sœurs » (« Jinggao jiemeimen » 敬告姐妹们), « Chanson des droits des femmes » (« Nüquan

---

39 Guo Changhai 郭长海, *Qiu Jin quanji jianzhu* 秋瑾全集笺注 (Œuvres de Qiu Jin, édition critique), Jilin wenyi chubanshe, Changchun, 2003, p. 362.
40 *Ibid.*, pp. 377–399.
41 *Ibid.*

ge» 女权歌) et d'autres critiques et œuvres littéraires pour encourager ses compatriotes féminines.

La liberté individuelle est brandie pour la première fois

Malgré tout, la transformation de la société ne se construit pas en un jour, comme Hu Shi, philosophe et figure du Mouvement de la Nouvelle Culture (1915–1923), l'affirme : « Ce n'est pas comme un beau matin où le monde se serait soudainement amélioré ; l'individu ne doit pas se satisfaire de l'air du temps pour bien commencer ».[42] Ne restant qu'au niveau de « l'esprit d'une politique constitutionnelle », la Révolution républicaine de 1911 restera superficielle. Pour atteindre une véritable efficacité, il faut attendre jusqu'au 15 septembre 1915, jour de la création de *La Jeunesse* (*Xin Qingnian* 新青年)[43] à Shanghai, inaugurant par là le Mouvement de la Nouvelle Culture dans le pays. Dans le premier numéro, son fondateur Chen Duxiu publie un article intitulé *La France et la civilisation moderne*,[44] où il appelle vigoureusement à importer « les doctrines de l'indépendance, de l'égalité et des droits de l'homme » et dans un même mouvement à déraciner « les fondements de l'éthique et de la politique de notre pays »,[45] c'est-à-dire, le confucianisme. Plus tard, il démontre la corrélation entre vie moderne et indépendance individuelle : « Il n'est pas nécessaire que le fils se conforme à son père, que la femme se conforme à son mari » ; « La veuve qui se remarie ne sera jamais méprisée » ; « Dans la société moderne, c'est une pratique courante que les hommes et les femmes communiquent entre eux » ; « Les femmes occidentales mènent une vie indépendante, exercent toutes sortes de professions, avocats, médecins, vendeuses ou ouvrières ».[46] Les exemples qu'il cite ici sont loin de la réalité chinoise de l'époque.

---

42 Hu Shi écrit dans son journal du 30 avril 1921.
43 Revue mensuelle, fondée par Chen Duxiu le 15 septembre 1915 à Shanghai. Elle joue un rôle majeur dans l'introduction des idées occidentales tant libérales que marxistes au début du XXe siècle avant de devenir une revue du Parti communiste chinois.
44 *Fanlanxi he jinshi wenming* 法兰西和近世文明, publié dans *La Jeunesse*, vol. 1, n°. 1, 15 janvier 1915, repris dans *Duxiu wencun* 独秀文存 (Œuvres de Chen Duxiu), tome I, Waiwen chubanshe, Beijing, 2013, p. 11.
45 *Duxiu wencun*, tome I, Waiwen chubanshe, Beijing, 2013, p. 103.
46 *Kongzi zhi Dao yu Xiandai Shenghuo* 孔子之道与现代生活, publié dans *La Jeunesse*, vol. 2, n°. 4, 1er décembre 1916, repris dans *Duxiu wencun*, tome I, Waiwen chubanshe, Beijing, 2013, p. 118.

Pour Hu Shi, la jeunesse chinoise devrait s'*émanciper* par elle-même, afin de mieux participer à la société, il fait de « l'ibsénisme » : « Soyez vous-mêmes la colonne de l'État, pour servir la société ; être soi-même, c'est le plus bénéfique pour un individu ».[47] En juin 1918, la revue *La Jeunesse* publie un numéro spécial sur Ibsen, Hu Shi y traduit *Une maison de poupée* en coopération avec son élève, Luo Jialun 罗家伦 (1897–1969). En même temps, il publie un article, « L'ibsénisme » (« Yibusheng zhuyi » 易卜生主义), connu pour être sa proclamation de la « libération de l'individu » qui aura une énorme influence sur la jeunesse de l'époque.

Les auteurs de la revue montrent une grande ouverture au libéralisme occidental et sont particulièrement intéressés par la démocratie, la science, la liberté individuelle, et l'émancipation des femmes et de la jeunesse. Ils attaquent violemment les idées, les valeurs et les institutions traditionnelles, notamment le confucianisme. Pendant cette période, la jeunesse chinoise vit un bouleversement total. Elle lutte pour abattre le système de la famille, les vieilles religions, la morale et les coutumes anciennes, tels que les principes éthiques de la piété filiale (*xiao* 孝) et de la fidélité de l'épouse (*jie* 节), elle lutte aussi pour briser toutes les institutions traditionnelles. Fu Sinian 傅斯年 (1896–1950) déclare que le système corrompu de la famille est « la source de tous les maux ».[48] Lu Xun stigmatise la fidélité de l'épouse comme morale inhumaine, et critique la piété filiale qu'il juge antiévolutionniste.[49] Dans *Le Journal d'un fou* (*Kuangren riji* 狂人日记, 1918),[50] il dénonce la persécution de la culture traditionnelle sur les individus, qu'il identifie au cannibalisme (*chi ren* 吃人).

C'est la première fois que les traditions sont critiquées dans des termes radicaux. C'est aussi la première fois que le confucianisme, au moins dans son interprétation classique et orthodoxe, subit une attaque aussi frontale. Ce n'est pas une réforme en demi-teinte ou une rénovation partielle qui est préconisée, mais un vaste détrônement des fondements mêmes de la tradition en vue d'un nouvel idéal. Dans ses discours et romans, Lu Xun estime que l'émancipation des femmes devrait aboutir à l'autonomie de la pensée féminine et à l'indépendance économique. Pour lui, ce n'est qu'une fois ces deux aspects remplis que le chemin de l'émancipation des femmes pourra s'élargir et s'approfondir.

---

47 *Yibusheng zhuyi*, publié dans *La Jeunesse*, vol. 4, n°. 6, 15 juin 1918, republié dans *Hu Shi Wencun* 胡适文存 (Œuvres de Hu Shi), tome I–4, Waiwen chubanshe, Beijing, 2013, pp. 13–38.
48 Fu Sinian, « Wan'e zhi yuan » 万恶之源 (La source de tous maux), in *Xinchao* 新潮 (Renaissance), vol.1, n°. 1, janvier 1919.
49 Lu Xun, « Wo zhi jie lie guan » 我之节烈观 (Mon avis sur la chasteté), in *La Jeunesse*, vol. 5, n°. 2, août 1918.
50 Première œuvre de la littérature chinoise moderne écrite en vernaculaire, c'est aussi l'œuvre maitresse de Lu Xun.

Mouvement du 4 mai 1919, Mouvement féministe et le marxisme

Le Mouvement du 4 mai 1919 va engendrer non seulement une descente dans la rue des étudiants, mais encore un rapprochement de ceux-ci avec les travailleurs de toutes catégories. Cette manifestation est due à l'acceptation par le gouvernement, contre son peuple, des termes du Traité de Versailles concernant la Chine. Précédemment, il n'y avait pas de mixité en Chine. Dans cette atmosphère d'égalité, de liberté, de démocratie et d'anti-impérialisme, la participation féminine à travers tout le pays est particulièrement importante. Un grand nombre de femmes et d'étudiantes commencent à résister aux valeurs traditionnelles, des jeunes filles coupent leurs cheveux, réclament l'émancipation. Dès lors, la scolarité mixte fait son apparition en Chine.

À cette occasion, émerge l'Union des étudiants de Beijing, fondement de l'unification des étudiants de toutes les écoles secondaires et établissements universitaires de la ville, filles comprises. Ainsi, les étudiantes ont pu rayonner dans ce foisonnement étudiant et travailler avec leur *alter ego* masculin. Enfin, vient le triomphe du mouvement, sous les pressions, le gouvernement est obligé de refuser de signer le Traité. Guidés par des jeunes intellectuels progressistes, les étudiants et les étudiantes ont également dénoncé le poids des traditions, le pouvoir des mandarins, ainsi que l'oppression des femmes.

Par conséquent, le Mouvement du 4 mai permet à la société chinoise de progressivement prendre conscience des problèmes des femmes : la liberté de mariage, l'émancipation des femmes, les écoles mixtes, etc. Tout cela s'exprimera constamment dans un nombre inestimable d'œuvres littéraires. Aujourd'hui, si on concluait, l'un des meilleurs fruits que le Mouvement a porté, serait qu'il engendra une suite de mouvements féministes enregistrés dans l'histoire de la pensée chinoise.

Si le mouvement féministe préconisé par les hommes intellectuels a dans un certain sens tendance à rendre célèbre le credo suivant : «perfection de sa personne, régulation de ses affaires familiales, mise en bon ordre d'une principauté et apport de la paix dans le monde» (*Xiushen, Qijia, Zhiguo, Pingtianxia* 修身、齐家、治国、平天下)[51] auprès des cercles féminins, il en ira de même ultérieurement avec les communistes qui appliqueront leurs principes communistes à ce mouvement. La raison en est que les féministes (féminins comme masculins) ont

---

[51] L'idée confucianiste, provient d'un grand classique, *Les Rites*, Chapitre *La Grande Étude*, c'est aussi un credo des confucéens depuis deux millénaires.

décelé une forte contradiction entre l'idée des droits de l'homme et ceux des femmes, et le système étatique et le régime politique. De sorte qu'ils réorientent leur lutte dans une visée marxiste, adoptant le concept de dictature du prolétariat.

Conclusion

En Occident, on associe souvent la lutte pour les droits des femmes à Olympe de Gouges (1749–1793)[52] qui adressa à la reine Marie-Antoinette en septembre 1791 cette affirmation : « La Femme naît libre et demeure égale à l'homme en droits. Les distinctions sociales ne peuvent être fondées que sur l'utilité commune ».[53] Cette « Déclaration des droits de la femme et de la citoyenne » résonne encore dans le monde de nos jours.

Les premiers penseurs et les pionnières féministes de la Chine moderne ont apporté une contribution indélébile au mouvement de libération des femmes, bien qu'ils soient limités par le contexte socio-politique de leur époque, comme le fait de subordonner la libération des femmes à la prospérité de la patrie. Liang Qichao, Jin Tianhe et Qiu Jin incluent leurs réflexions sur les conditions des femmes et leur amélioration pour la société chinoise dans une perspective politique qui consiste essentiellement en renforcement de l'État-nation chinois, alors que Ma Junwu et He Zhen mettent l'accent sur le destin et les intérêts individuels des femmes. C'est pour cette raison que les premiers sont considérés comme défenseurs d'un « féminisme patriarcal ».

Les idées de Rousseau, connues et divulguées en Chine depuis 1898 grâce à nos penseurs étudiés, suscitent immédiatement une sympathie chez les jeunes intellectuels. Ils convoquent le vocabulaire traditionnel chinois pour rendre les concepts rousseauistes de liberté, d'égalité et de droits. Rousseau et sa pensée deviennent une source primordiale dans la Révolution de 1911 qui a mis un terme à l'Empire. Dans une certaine mesure, Rousseau aurait pris la place de Confucius, dont les valeurs ont été mises en cause lors du mouvement de la nouvelle culture au début du XXe siècle. Les traces de sa pensée continuent à marquer les revendications des féministes en Chine.

---

52 Écrivaine polygraphe, guillotinée le 3 novembre 1793 à Paris, elle est aussi pionnière du mouvement féministe lors de la Révolution française.
53 Le premier article de la *Déclaration des droits de la femme et de la citoyenne* (septembre 1791)

Bibliographie

Butler, J. (2002). *Marché au sexe*, avec Gayle S. Rubin. Paris: EPEL.
Butler, J. (2004). *Le Pouvoir des mots*, trad. Charlotte Nordmann avec la collaboration de Jérôme Vidal. Paris: Éditions Amsterdam.
Butler, J. (2005). *Trouble dans le genre*, trad. Cynthia Kraus. Paris: La Découverte.
Butler, J. (2010). *Sois mon corps*, avec Catherine Malabou. Paris: Bayard.
Butler, J. (2021). *Le Vivable et l'Invivable*, avec Frédéric Worms. Paris: PUF.
Chen Duxiu 陈独秀 (2013). *Duxiu Wencun* 独秀文存 (Œuvres de Chen Duxiu), tome 1. Beijing: Waiwen chubanshe.
De Beauvoir, S. (1986). *Le deuxième sexe*, tome 1-2, Folio essais. Paris: Gallimard.
Durkheim, É. (1966). *Montesquieu et Rousseau. Précurseurs de la sociologie.* Paris: Librairie Marcel Rivière et Cie.
Ferry, L. (2013). *Rousseau et Tocqueville. L'invention de la démocratie moderne.* Collection Sagesses d'hier ez d'aujourd'hui Vol. 10 Paris: Le Figaro Éditions.
Guo Songtao 郭嵩焘(1984). *Lundun yu Bali riji* 伦敦与巴黎日记 (Journal de Londres à Paris). Changsha: Yuelu shushe.
Guo Yanli 郭延礼(1987). *Qiu Jin yanjiu ziliao* 秋瑾研究资料 (Documents de recherches sur Qiu Jin). Jinan: Shangdong jiaoyu chubanshe.
Guo Yanli 郭延礼 (éd.) (1987). *Qiu Jin wenxue lungao* 秋瑾文学论稿 (Essais littéraire de Qiu Jin). Xi'an: Shaanxi renmin chubanshe.
Guo Changhai 郭长海(2003). *Qiu Jin quanji jianzhu* 秋瑾全集笺注 (Œuvres de Qiu Jin, édition critique). Changchun: Jilin wenyi chubanshe.
Hu Shi 胡适(2013a). *Hu Shi xuanji* 胡适选集 (Textes choisis de Hu Shi). Beijing: Ershiyi shiji chubanshe.
Hu Shi 胡适(2013b). *Hu Shi wencun* 胡适文存 (Œuvres de Hu Shi), tome 1-4. Beijing: Waiwen chubanshe.
Jin, T. (2003). *Nüjie zhong* 女界钟 (Horloge du monde féminin). Shanghai: Guji chubanshe.
Kristeva, J. (2001). *Des Chinoises*. Paris: Éditions Pauvert.
Liang Qichao 梁启超 (1989). *Yinbingshi heji* 饮冰室合集 (Œuvres de Liang Qichao), tome 1-45. Beijing: Zhonghua shuju.
Lu Yanzhen 卢燕贞(1990). *Zhongguo jindai nüzi jiaoyu shi* 中国近代女子教育史 (Histoire de l'éducation féminine dans la Chine moderne). Taipai: Wenzhe chubanshe.
Mill, J. S. (2016). *L'asservissement des femmes*, trad. Marie-Françoise Cachin. Paris: Payot.
Montesquieu, M. de (1979). *De l'esprit des lois*, tome 1-2. Paris: Garnier-Flammarion.
Rosanvallon, P. (1998). *Le peuple introuvable.* Paris: Gallimard.
Rousseau, J.-J. (1992a). *Discours sur l'origine et les fondements de l'inégalité parmi les hommes. Discours sur les sciences et les arts.* Paris: Garnier-Flammarion.
Rousseau, J.-J. (1992b). *Du Contrat Social.* Paris: Garnier-Flammarion.
Rousseau, J.-J. (2011). *Du Contrat Social.* Paris: Éditions Flammarion.
Schwarcz, V. (1986). *The Chinese Enlightenment.* Berkeley, CA: University of California Press.
Sudo, M. (2010). *Zhongguo nüquan gainian de bianqian* 中国"女权"概念的变迁 (Changements du concept de « féminisme » en Chine), trad. Yao Yi. Beijing: Zhong sheke wenxian chubanshe.
Wang, X. (2010). *Jean-Jacques Rousseau en Chine (de 1871 à nos jours).* Montmorency: Musée Jean-Jacques Rousseau.
Yan Fu (1986). 严复, *Yan Fu ji* 严复集 (Œuvres de Yan Fu). Beijing: Zhonghua shuju.

Pedro Falcão Pricladnitzky
Mind of Nature: Cavendish's Argument for Panpsychism

Abstract: In this text, I intend to present one of Cavendish's arguments for the thesis that nature, or all individuals that make up nature, have mental properties. Cavendish offered many arguments to show that matter has the capacity to think, but her central argument for the position is drawn from an observation that, for her, is evident and unquestionable: bodies, or the parts of matter that make up nature, behave in an orderly and variable way and this is only possible if they have sensitivity and rationality. Cavendish's position is not just that matter has the capacity to think or that the view that some material beings can think. Her view that intends to explain the phenomena that occurs in nature rests on a stronger thesis: all matter, by its very nature, thinks.

Cavendish asserts that intelligence, cognition and thinking are characteristics present in all aspects of nature. The materialism espoused by Margaret Cavendish thus puts experience and consciousness in rather peculiar terms. Furthermore, the organization and order patently demonstrated by bodies that exist in nature is explained by this characteristic as being inherent in matter.

In the *Observations Upon Experimental Philosophy*, Cavendish states:

> Nay, were it possible that there could be a single part, that is, a part separated from all the rest; yet being a part of nature, it must consist of the same substance as nature herself; but nature is an infinite composition of rational, sensitive and inanimate matter: which although they do constitute but one body. (OEP, 127)[1]

Cavendish tried to characterize and explain nature as a whole in terms of matter. However, unlike many 17th-century philosophers, she did not hold that mind represented a peculiar and separate aspect of physical reality and that consciousness

---

1 Cf. "... you ask whether Nature hath Infinite souls? I answer: That Infinite Nature is but one Infinite body, divided into Infinite parts, which we call Creatures; and therefore it may as well be said, That Nature is composed of Infinite Creatures or Parts, as she is divided into Infinite Creatures or Parts; for Nature being Material, is dividable, and composable. The same may be said of Nature's Soul, which is the Rational part of the onely infinite Matter, as also of Nature's Life, which is the sensitive part of the onely Infinite self-moving Matter..., for Infinite Material Nature hath an Infinite Material Soul, Life, and Body" (PL, 433).

https://doi.org/10.1515/9783111051802-022

should be explained in terms of a singular ontological category. Her materialism reached out to perceptions, thoughts and emotions. In this sense, there is no major metaphysical distinction between human beings and the rest of nature. Inasmuch as human beings are indisputably thinking beings and are composed of the same constituent elements of nature, the difficulty is not so much in explaining how rational we are, but in explaining how the rest of nature is not.

This version of materialism is a constant in her work:

> Nature is purely corporeal or material, and there is nothing that belongs to, or is a part of nature, which is not corporeal; so that natural and material, or corporeal, are one and the same; and therefore spiritualbeings, non-beings, mixt-beings, and whatsoever distinctions the learned do make, are no ways belonging to nature. Neither is there any such thing as an incorporeal motion; for all actions of nature are corporeal, being natural; and there can no abstraction be made of motion or figure, from matter or body, but they are inseparably one thing. [Wherefore no spiritual being, can have local motion]. (OEP, 137)[2]

None of the actions and operations of bodies are to be explained in terms of an immaterial faculty or agent, be it a mind or a substantial form. Bodies themselves have the necessary and sufficient requirements to accomplish all the things we can see them doing. For Cavendish, there is no part of nature that is not filled with matter; there are no voids or empty spaces.[3] Every body is infinitely divisible:

> Although I am of opinion, that nature is a self-moving, and consequently a self-living and self-knowing infinite body, divisible into infinite parts; yet I do not mean, that these parts are atoms; for there can be no atom, that is, an indivisible body in nature; because whatsoever has body, or is material, has quantity; and what has quantity, is divisible. But some may say, If a part be finite, it cannot be divisible into infinite. (OEP, 125)[4]

And all bodies that are part of nature, at all levels of division, are sensitive and rational, possessing consciousness and thinking:

---

[2] See also: "Nature is material, or corporeal and so are all her creatures, and whatsoever is not material is no part of nature, neither doth it belong to any ways to nature" (PL, 320–321). Cf. GNP, I, 1–2.

[3] Cf. PL, 451–452: "Truly, Madam, an incorporeal dimension or extension, seems, in my opinion, a mere contradiction; for I cannot conceive how nothing can have a dimension or extension, having nothing to be extended or measured".

[4] "Neither am I able to conceive the truth of his assertion, that all lines are derived from points, and all numbers from unity, and all figures from a circle: for, there can be no such thing as a single point, a single unity, a single circle in nature, by reason nature is infinitely divisible and compoundable; neither can they be principles, because they are all but effects" (OEP, 259).

> When I say, that "none of nature's parts can be called inanimate, or soulless" I do not mean the constitutive parts of nature, which are, as it were, the ingredients whereof nature consists, and is made up; whereof there is an inanimate part or degree of matter, as well as animate; but I mean the parts or effects of this composed body of nature, of which I say, that none can be called inanimate; for, though some philosophers think that nothing is animate, or has life in nature, but animals and vegetables; yet it is probable, that since nature consists of a commixture of animate and inanimate matter, and is self-moving, there can be no part or particle of this composed body of nature, were it an atom, that may be called inanimate, by reason there is none that has not its share of animate, as well as inanimate matter, and the commixture of these degrees being so close, it is impossible one should be without the other. (OEP, 16)[5]

One of Cavendish's motivations for this perspective on the nature of matter is that the widespread order in nature that we are able to patently perceive is explainable by the rationality of the constituent elements of the physical world. Material beings, therefore, are not inferior or less perfect beings. To maintain that minds are corporeal aspects that constitute all beings is also not to diminish the complexity present in thought.

> But some imagine the rational motions to be so gross as the Trotting of a Horse, and that all the motions of Animate matter are as rude and course as renting or tearing asunder, or that all impressions must needs make dents or creases. But as Nature hath degrees of corporeal matter, so she hath also degrees of corporeal motions, Matter and Motion being but one substance; and it is absurd to judge of the interior motions of self-moving matter, by artificial or exterior gross motions, as that all motions must be like the tearing of a sheet of Paper, or that the printing and patterning of several figures of rational and sensitive matter must be like the printing of Books… and so the curious actions of the purest rational matter are neither rude nor rough; but although this matter is so subtil and pure, as not subject to exterior human senses and organs, yet certainly it is dividable, not onely in several Creatures, but in the several parts of one and the same Creature, as well as the sensitive, which is the Life of Nature, as the other is the Soul; not the Divine, but natural Soul; neither is this Soul Immaterial, but Corporeal; not composed of raggs and shreds, but it is the purest, simplest and matter in Nature. (PL, 180)

Every material and bodily activity for Cavendish is a complex and sophisticated event of nature. Philosophical perspectives that identify the more subtle and abstract actions that take place in the natural world with an immaterial agent or faculty are mistaken because they have not been able to understand the true essence of the body.[6]

Holding that all motion is evidence of life and that all things in nature are composed of matter and motion, Cavendish assumes that life pervades the entire

---

[5] Other relevant text is found in OEP, 156.
[6] David Cunning in his book *Cavendish* (2016) presents an interesting development, cf. 185–196.

natural world, including what we would call inanimate objects. For her, such objects would be alive insofar as they have motion. While the motion they exhibit is not as complex as the motion expressed by humans and other animals, this does not imply rejecting that they have some level of motion and therefore some form of life. By proposing an intrinsic link between movement and cognitive abilities, Cavendish will defend that cognition is present in an unrestricted way in nature.[7] Thus, life and cognition are, for Cavendish, natural properties and are present in every aspect of the natural world, albeit in a range of complexity.[8]

In this text, I intend to present one of Cavendish's main reasonings for the thesis that nature, or all individuals that make up nature, have mental properties, that is, consciousness, perception and cognitive capacity. In this way, I will analyze a fundamental argument for what has come to be known as Cavendish's panpsychism.[9] Cavendish offered many arguments to show that matter has the capacity to think, but her central argument for the position is drawn from an observation that, for her, is evident and unquestionable: bodies, or the parts of matter that make up nature, behave in an orderly and variable way and this is only possible if they have sensitivity and rationality. That is, the natural world, to express its most easily identified characteristics, demands awareness and thought.[10] Cavendish's position is not just that matter has the capacity to think or that the view that some material being, by the very nature of matter, thinks is compatible with its nature. Her view that intends to explain the phenomena of nature rests on a stronger thesis: all matter, by its very nature, thinks.

At first, I intend to clarify the concepts of thought and consciousness in Cavendish's philosophy of nature. After that, I will present a proposal for reconstructing the structure of the argument that Cavendish exposes for the position that the variable organization exhibited by nature demands thought. This perspective of Cavendish is directly linked to the thesis of complete blending that will be discussed at the end of this text.

Cavendish constantly introduces mental life jargon into her work, but she does not seem to introduce this expressly in her views on the nature of thought and consciousness. However, in two passages from *Observations Upon Experimental Philosophy* and in one of the *Grounds of Natural Philosophy*, we see an effort to define what thought would be as well as the notions that would be associated with it.

---

7 The perspective that the totality of matter has mental characteristics is also discussed in the following texts: Detlefsen 2007, Duncan 2014, and Cunning 2016.
8 Eugene Marshall in his introduction to the *Observations Upon Experimental Philosophy* discuss this aspect (Marshall 2016).
9 See O'Neill 2001, XXV, and Detlefsen 2018, 147–148.
10 Cunning 2016, 93–94; cf. p. 77.

At first, we have a definition of thought in terms of representation and intentionality:

> For instance, when I see an object, I have also a thought of that object; and that thought is a copy of the object, made of the rational part of matter, but not the sensitive pattern; so that there is a great difference betwixt the rational perception and the sensitive. For a second instance, the sensitive perception of light in the eye, is one thing; the rational perception or thought of light, is another; which I mention, to express in some manner the nature of perception rational; though at the same time I understand, there are infinite perceptions rational, as well as infinite perceptions sensitive: wherefore I cannot say, that all rational perceptions are like to human thoughts, otherwise, than in respect of purity; for we may perceive in ourselves a greater purity and subtlety of the rational, than of the sensitive. (OEP, 179–180)

Cavendish, in the opening of the quote, is explicit: Seeing an object is thinking about that object. Thinking necessarily involves content. Cavendish assumes that any thought must have an object, that is, that the correct description of the thought process is relational. It involves a subject that thinks and something that is thought of. What is the content of such an act? Cavendish answers: a copy of the object. So here, she is developing a representationalist perspective of thinking. The act of thinking is identified with seeing and also with the content of such an act. When we think of an object, such as the sun, we have the act and a representational content. The intentionality of thinking can also be related to the awareness that is gained through perception.

Identifying thinking and seeing, Cavendish allows the interpretation that to think is the same as to perceive. But here, she makes an important distinction. There is rational perception and sensitive perception. Thought is related with the kind of perception that is produced by the rational aspect of matter and the sensitive perception does not immediately generate thought. It is not quit clear what Cavendish means by such a distinction but she says that the rational perception involves a more pure and subtle kind of perceiving. We might say, through her example, that sensing the light is different from thinking the light because sensing involves the affection aspect of perception. Sensitive perception is the direct and immediate interaction of a body with another that is perceiving. And the rational perception is the representational awareness of such interaction. This interpretation, however, might turn out problematic considering Cavendish's perspective on causal efficacy.

This causal aspect that is relevant to her theory of thought is considered some pages further:

> Besides, it is to be observed, that in the mentioned book, I compare thoughts, which are the actions of the rational figurative motions, to the sensitive touch; so that, touch is like a thought in sense, and thought like a touch in reason: But there is great difference in their purity; for,

though the actions of touch and thought are much after the same manner, yet the different degrees of sense and reason, or of animate, sensitive and rational matter, cause great difference between them; and as all sensitive perception is a kind of touch, so all rational perception is a kind of thoughtfulness: But mistake me not, when I say, thought is like touch; for I do not mean, that the rational perception is caused by the conjunction or joining of one part to another, or that it is an exterior touch, an interior knowledge; for all self-knowledge is a kind of thoughtfulness, and that thought is a rational touch, as touch is a sensitive thought; for the exterior perceptions of reason resemble the interior actions or knowledge of sense. (OEP, 182)

In this quotation, Cavendish offers yet another definition of thought as the action of rational figurative movements. Unlike the previous passage where the focus was to define thought through the content that necessarily constitutes every act of thought, here Cavendish is exposing the process that can engender thought. What generates thought seems to be analogous to the process that occurs when we have the sensation of touch: "touch is like a thought in sense, and thought like a touch in reason". To say that a touch or an affection is like a thought in the senses is to say that being affected by a body can generate the figurative movements that form sensations. Analogously, to say that thinking is like exerting a touch on reason seems to mean that thinking involves the figurative movements of the rational aspect of matter. The process that generates sensation is similar to the process that generates thought; both are produced by figurative movements of matter. The difference is that thought is linked to figurative movements of rational animate matter and sensations are linked to figurative movements of sensitive animate matter. Again, here Cavendish presents a difference in the level of purity and subtlety present in thoughts, purer and subtler, with respect to sensations, grosser and more rudimentary movements. The introduction of the notion 'touching', in turn, seems to reinforce the interpretation presented above that the foundation of the difference between thinking and feeling, that is, between rational perceptions and sensitive perceptions, for Cavendish lies in the fact that sensation involves the affection of a body and thought is the result of a reflexive process that is indirectly linked to an affection without directly depending on it.

The causal model of perception reappears in the *Grounds of Natural Philosophy*, where Cavendish also draws an approximation between perceiving and knowing:

Chapter IX: Of Perception in General: *Perception* is a sort of Knowledg that hath reference to Objects; that is, Some Parts to know other Parts: But yet Objects are not the cause of Perception; for the cause of Perception is Self-motion. But some would say, *If there were no Object, there could be no Perception.* I answer: It is true; for, that cannot be perceived, that is not: but yet, corporeal motions cannot be without Parts, and so not without Perception. But, put an impossible case, as, That there could be a single Corporeal Motion, and no more in Nature; that Corporeal Motion may make several Changes, somewhat like *Conceptions*, although not *Perceptions:* but, Nature being Corporeal, is composed of Parts, and therefore there cannot be a want of Objects. But there are Infinite several manners and ways of Perception; which proves, That the Objects are not the Cause: for, every several kind and sort of Creatures, have several kinds and sorts of Perception, according to the nature and property of such a kind or sort of Composition, as makes such a kind or sort of Creature; as I shall treat of, more fully, in the following Parts of this Book. (GNP, 8)

Here we see the specific reference to the concept of self-motion as ultimately responsible for the formation of perceptions and thoughts. That is, for Cavendish what, in fact, produces a perception or a thought is not an object that is perceived or the eventual affection that this object can provoke in some subject of perception, but the very motions of that body that perceives it. The bodies that are around it and would be considered its objects of perception would be occasional causes of perception, but they would not engender, at least not in the form of an efficient cause, is its thought or its perception.[11] The act of thinking in this way for Cavendish involves a complex web of motions between parts of matter. She recognizes that thought is intentional, there is no objectless thought. However, in the causal aspect, the object only suggests its perception to the body that perceives it. It is by an individual decision of a part of matter to form the perception that it has of an object. So to say that A perceives B, following Cavendish's model, means that A through its own self-motion generates its perception of B and that B can provoke an affect in A that would suggest, but not directly cause, the formation of such a perception.[12]

With the understanding we gained from the interpretation of these passages, we can more clearly propose what would be panpsychism for Cavendish. In the *Observations Upon Experimental Philosophy*, Cavendish says:

[...] animate matter is the life and soul of nature, and consequently of man, and all other creatures; for we cannot in reason conceive that man should be the only creature that partakes of this soul of nature, and that all the rest of nature's parts, or most of them, should be soulless or (which is all one) irrational, although they are commonly called, nay, believed to be such. Truly, if all other creatures cannot be denied to be material, they can neither be accounted irrational, insensible, or inanimate, by reason there is no part, nay, not the smallest particle in nature, our reason is able to conceive, which is not composed of animate matter, as well as of inanimate; of life and soul, as well as of body; and therefore no particular creature can claim a prerogative in this case before another; for there is a thorough mixture of animate and inanimate matter in nature, and all her parts. (OEP, 221)

---

11 Cf. Detlefsen 2006 and Eileen O'Neill and her discussion of causation in her 'Introduction' to *Observations Upon Experimental Philosophy* (O'Neill 2001).
12 Cf. Boyle 2015.

Animated matter is the characteristic responsible for motion and, in this sense, for any and all changes in nature. The sense in which the aspect of matter is responsible for every action is being animated has at least two aspects: 1) as it is the promoter of all motion in nature and 2) to be able to move it is necessary for it to have self-awareness and cognition of its surroundings. Cavendish, in the *Observations*'s passage, identifies the rational soul with the soul of nature. There is no distinction from an ontological perspective in the rationality of a human being and the rationality of nature; both would have the same soul configuration. Every expression of thought and consciousness is an aspect of animate matter. The metaphysics that Cavendish suggests to us is a description of reality that is both materialistic and cognitive:

> But some may object, that if there be sense and reason in every part of nature, it must be in all parts alike; and then a stone, or any other the like creature, may have reason, or a rational soul, as well as man. To which I answer: I do not deny that a stone has reason, or doth partake of the rational soul of nature, as well as man doth, because it is part of the same matter man consists of; but yet it has not animal or human sense and reason, because it is not of animal kind; but being a mineral, it has mineral sense and reason; for it is to be observed, that as animate self-moving matter moves not one and the same way in all creatures, so there can neither be the same way of knowledge and understanding, which is sense and reason, in all creatures alike; but nature being various, not only in her parts, but in her actions, it causes a variety also amongst her creatures; and hence come so many kinds, sorts and particulars of natural creatures, quite different from each other; though not in the general and universal principle of nature, which is self-moving matter, (for in this they agree all) yet in their particular interior natures, figures and proprieties. (OEP, 221)

We have an important distinction in Cavendish's panpsychism. Even though every part of matter has thought, that is, is animated, the different configurations of matter have a specific type of thought, which is constituted through its own nature. The animate aspect of matter is omnipresent in nature, but it is not qualitatively evenly distributed among the parts of nature. Human beings and rocks, insofar as they are material and move, must have animate matter. However, Cavendish asserts in the above passage, they do not share the same rationality. The thinking of humans and other animals seems to be more complex and sophisticated than the thinking of minerals, vegetables and even artifacts.[13] However, when Cavendish asserts that the rationality of human beings is not the same rationality as that of minerals, it is not clear whether they have different *types* of rationality or would possess rationality in different *degrees*. As we saw in the previous definitions, rationality implies the representation of principles that generate motion,

---

13 Cf. Cunning 2016, 104–105.

that is, the ordering and regulation of matter in nature. Thus, it is not clear whether Cavendish admits that there is a variation in the attribution in the *degree* of complexity of these principles between parts of matter in which a rock would have the same rationality as a human being, only to a less sophisticated degree, or if they would possess a different *kind* of rationality. In that case, we should investigate whether there is an ambiguity in the use of reason in Cavendish.[14]

> Thus, although there be sense and reason, which is not only motion, but a regular and well-ordered self-motion, apparent in the wonderful and various productions, generations, transformations, dissolutions, compositions, and other actions of nature, in all nature's parts and particles; yet by reason of the variety of this self-motion, whose ways and modes do differ according to the nature of each particular figure, no figure or creature can have the same sense and reason, that is, the same natural motions which another has; and therefore no stone can be said to feel pain as an animal doth, or be called blind, because it has no eyes; for this kind of sense, as seeing, hearing, tasting, touching and smelling, is proper only to an animal figure, and not to a stone, which is a mineral; so that those which frame an argument from the want of animal sense and sensitive organs, to the defect of all sense and motion; as for example, that a stone would withdraw itself from the carts going over it, or a piece of iron from the hammering of a smith, conclude, in my opinion, very much against the artificial rules of logic; and although I understand none of them, yet I question not but I shall make a better argument by the rules of natural logic. (OEP, 221–222)

The difference between the expression of rationality and cognition in each part of nature is based on the motions it performs or is able to perform which, in turn, is based on its physical configuration.[15] Due to her criticisms of mechanism and the way in which she defines motion, Cavendish does not reduce this action of nature to spatial displacement.[16] The motions performed by the parts of matter constitute the configurations they adopt or can adopt constituting their identity. This includes not only the disposition and limits that this part occupies, but also how it behaves. Therefore, the types of movements also determine its type of thinking and cognition. For Cavendish, we are able to determine the rationality of something by observing its motions, that is, observing its actions and behavior in nature.

In this context, the concept of 'figure' is fundamental to understanding Cavendish's perspective (OEP, 31). Matter is infinite in virtue of containing an infinite number of parts and parts are finite in virtue of being delimited by certain figures and configurations. As Cavendish points out in the passage, no stone can feel pain like an animal, or be termed blind, for it has no eyes and its sensitivity is not

---

[14] Cf. Boyle 2018, 88.
[15] Cf. Peterman 2019.
[16] Cf. the definition of motion in the *Philosophical and Physical Opinions* (Cavendish 1655, 33).

human-like; does not have the same senses. It has thought, cognition and sensitivity that are typical of the figure of a mineral. The stone moves away from the steps that walk on it as far as its nature and configuration is possible.

Through the concept of figuration Cavendish intends to explain the actions and behaviors of each part of matter and, therefore, it is an essential notion for her perspective on order and variability in nature. She introduces the explanation of the origin of knowledge and perception of each part of matter caused by its self-motion. Cavendish is explicit in the *Observations:*

> But to return to knowledge and perception: I say, they are general and fundamental actions of nature; it being not probable that the infinite parts of nature should move so variously, nay, so orderly and methodically as they do, without knowing what they do, or why, and whether they move; and therefore all particular actions whatsoever in nature, as respiration, digestion, sympathy, antipathy, division, composition, pressure, reaction, etc. are all particular perceptive and knowing actions: for, if a part be divided from other parts, both are sensible of their division: The like may be said of the composition of parts: and as for pressure and reaction, they are as knowing and perceptive as any other particular actions. (OEP, 139–140)

The peculiar actions of parts of matter that are variable due to their different configurations and ordered reflecting their specific knowledge derived from their idiosyncratic constitution in nature. We observe an ordered and varied behavior, this does not seem to be questionable and the explanation of this phenomenon passes necessarily, for Cavendish, by the attribution of mental properties to the parts of nature.

This inference to the best explanation appears in many passages in Cavendish's work. For example, we find it in *Grounds of Natural Philosophy:*

> CHAP. VIII. Of Nature's Knowledg and Perception: IF Nature were not Self-knowing, Self-living, and also Perceptive, she would run into Confusion: for, there could be neither Order, nor Method, in Ignorant motion; neither would there be distinct kinds or sorts of Creatures, nor such exact and methodical Varieties as there are: for, it is impossible to make orderly and methodical Distinctions, or distinct Orders, by Chances: Wherefore, Nature being so exact (as she is) must needs be Self-knowing and Perceptive: And though all her Parts, even the Inanimate Parts, are Self-knowing, and Self-living; yet, onely her Self-moving Parts have an active Life, and a perceptive Knowledg. (GNP, 7)

There is, for Cavendish, deliberation and intentionality in every natural event. Nature manifests itself as a complex network of communication (agreements and disagreements) between its parts. There are many examples that can be pointed out to illustrate her way of seeing the behavior of nature as a sophisticated ecosystem.

The components and elements of an organism indicate this.[17] In the *Observations*, she writes:

> Also in case of Oppression, when one part of the body is oppressed, or in distress, all the other parts endeavour to relieve that distressed or afflicted part. Thus although there is a difference between the particular actions, knowledges and perceptions of every part, which causes an ignorance betwixt them, yet by reason there is knowledg and perception in every part, by which each part doth not onely know it self, and its own actions, but has also a perception of some actions of its neighbouring parts; it causes a general intelligence and information betwixt the particular parts of a composed figure... (OEP, 181)

If one part of an organism imposes itself, for some reason, on another in such a way as to have a negative impact; other parties that are related act in a way to counteract what happened. We could see this, for example, when we have a joint injury in one of our knees and there is a great adaptive behavior in the muscle chain of the thighs and glutes of the injured leg as well as the contralateral leg in order to avoid overloading the injury and thus facilitate the recovery. The eutrophication of bodies of water could be something in the same way of reasoning. Cavendish also makes this clear about the way in which certain medications only manifest an effect on certain organs or parts of the body, even if they have been applied locally or ingested orally:

> [...] none ought to wonder how it is possible, that medicines that must pass through digestions in the body, should, neglecting all other parts, shew themselves friendly onely to the brain or kidnies, or the like parts; for if there be sense and reason in Nature, all things must act wisely and orderly, and not confusedly... (OEP, 78)

We can postulate a possible structuring of an argument that represents Cavendish's perspective for reasoning in defense of panpsychism:
1) Matter as a whole acts in an orderly and variable way.
2) The parts of matter, insofar as they are dependent on the totality of matter, also act in an orderly and variable way.
3) These characteristics demand a cause.
4) Ordering and variation are manifestations of thought, sensitivity and cognition.
5) The best explanation we have to this indisputable behavior is the attribution of mental characteristics to every part of matter.[18]

---

17 Cf. Cunning 2016, 98–100.
18 See also Michaelian 2009 and David Cunning on fallibililism (Cunning 2016, 46).

6) The cause of ordering and variability in nature is the omnipresence of animate matter.

By an inference to the best explanation, Cavendish is led to assert the ubiquity of animate matter. From a metaphysical and ontological perspective, it is necessary, in turn, to introduce the thesis of complete blending in order to explain what the ontological status of matter and its parts is.[19] In the *Observations*, Cavendish says:

> [...] nature is an infinite composition of rational, sensitive and inanimate matter: which although they do constitute but one body, because of their close and inseparable conjunction and commixture; nevertheless, they are several parts, (for one part is not another part) and therefore every part or particle of nature, consisting of the same commixture, cannot be single or indivisible. Thus it remains firm, that selfmotion is the only cause of the various parts and changes of figures; and that when parts move or separate themselves from parts, they move and join to other parts, at the same point of time. (OEP, 127)

Motion presupposes knowledge. Each element or part of nature exhibits behavior that is exemplified by its own motion. Such complexity requires cognition and knowledge. Cavendish through her examination of the nature of matter, concludes that all material beings – all things that exist in nature – have knowledge, sensitivity and rationality. Animate matter can thus account for the conscious mental experience of human beings, as well the other kinds of beings, without the intervention of any special or distinct form of ontological ream. The only kind of substance that exists is the material substance and it has two aspects: animate matter and inanimate matter. Animate matter has two levels of animation: animate sensible matter and animate rational matter. Every aspect and degree of matter is present in every part of nature. There is no arbitrary combination. Rationality, sensation and quantitative matter are principles of determination of nature that are inseparable in reality, albeit conceptually distinct. Animate matter is responsible for every action and motion that occurs in nature and supposes inanimate matter to operate. Inanimate matter is not able to move itself, supporting the operations of sensitive and rational matter. Cavendish is clear about this:

> [...] there is such a commixture of animate and inanimate matter, that no particle in nature can be conceived or imagined, which is not composed of animate matter, as well as of inanimate; and therefore the patient, as well as the agent, having both a commixture of these

---

[19] Karen Detlefsen in her paper "Reason and Freedom: Margaret Cavendish on the Order and Disorder of Nature" (2007) disagrees with this reading. She seeks to present an interpretation in which panpsychism is not necessarily associated with the ordering of nature, but with the freedom and causal effectiveness of the parts of nature.

parts of matter, none can act upon the other, but the patient changes its own parts by its own self-motion, either of its own accord, or by way of imitation; but the inanimate part of matter, considered in itself, or in its own nature, hath no self-motion, nor can it receive any from the animate; but they being both so closely intermixt, that they make but one self-moving body of nature, the animate parts of matter, bear the inanimate with them in all their actions; so that it is impossible for the animate parts to divide, compose, contract, etc. but the inanimate must serve them, or go along with them in all such corporeal figurative actions. (OEP, 158)

We have seen that Cavendish argued that the order and variety which is readily observable in natural phenomena cannot be explained by a mechanistic view of matter as hold by Descartes or Hobbes, as it is in some of her aims in *Philosophical Letters* intended. The type of motion required is more complex and depends on a theory that goes beyond the perspective of transferring a certain amount of motion that is extrinsic to bodies. Motion must be an intrinsic and inseparable characteristic of matter and manifests itself in two aspects: sensitive and rational animated matter. In this controversial context with the mechanistic perspectives of the 17th century, Cavendish's panpsychism emerges. All bodies, including artifacts such as tables and chairs, as well as the constituent parts of organisms such as lungs, kidneys and heart, are cognizant of their movements and are their driving cause. And this metaphysical perspective, according to Cavendish, is the best explanation we can develop to account for natural phenomena.

References

Boyle, D. (2015). "Margaret Cavendish on Perception, Self-Knowledge and Probable Opinion". *Philosophy Compass* 10(7), 438–450.
Boyle, D. (2018). *The Well-Ordered Universe: The Philosophy of Margaret Cavendish.* New York: Oxford University Press.
Cavendish, M. (1655). *Philosophical and Physical Opinions.* London: printed for William Wilson.
Cavendish, M. (1666). *Philosophical Letters.* London.
Cavendish, M. (1668). *Grounds of Natural Philosophy.* Ed. by Colette V. Michael. West Cornwall, CT: Locust Hill Press.
Cavendish, M. (2001). *Observations Upon Experimental Philosophy.* Ed. by Eileen O'Neill. Cambridge: Cambridge University Press.
Cunning, D. (2016). *Cavendish.* London and New York: Routledge.
Detlefsen, K. (2006). "Atomism, Monism, and Causation in the Natural Philosophy of Margaret Cavendish". *Oxford Studies in Early Modern Philosophy* 3, 199–240.
Detlefsen, K. (2007). "Reason and Freedom: Margaret Cavendish on the Order and Disorder of Nature". *Archiv für Geschichte der Philosophie* 89(2), 157–191.
Detlefsen, K. (2018). "Cavendish and Conway on Individual Human Mind". In Copenhaver, R. (Ed.), *Philosophy of Mind in Early Modern and Modern Ages.* London and New York: Routledge, 134–156.

Duncan, S. (2014). "Minds Everywhere: Margaret Cavendish's Antimechanist Materialism" (draft).
Marshall, E. (2016). "Introduction". In: Cavendish, M., *Observations Upon Experimental Philosophy.* Indianapolis, IN: Hackett, VII–XXVII.
Michaelian, K. (2009). "Margaret Cavendish's Epistemology". *British Journal for the History of Philosophy* 17(1), 31–53.
O'Neill, E. (2001). "Introduction". In Cavendish, M., *Observations Upon Experimental Philosophy.* Cambridge: Cambridge University Press, X–XXXVI.
Peterman, A. (2019). "Margaret Cavendish on Motion and Mereology". *Journal of the History of Philosophy* 57(3), 471–499.

Sarah Bonfim
First Principles: The Path to Women's Emancipation in Wollstonecraft's *Rights of Woman*

Abstract: The First Principles function as a strategic resource and an argumentative basis for the emancipation project envisioned by Mary Wollstonecraft. The importance of them lies in understanding more deeply the origins of the arguments Wollstonecraft outlines for the emancipation of women. Using *Vindication of the Rights of Woman* as a standpoint, this article presents the First Principles, the conceptions of reason, virtue and knowledge that work in an interconnected way to demonstrate that women are as much a part of humanity as men. Divided into four sections, I present in this paper each of these conceptions, starting from a general plan, that is, presenting how Wollstonecraft recognizes these conceptions, to a more specific plan for the case of women, their impacts and implications.

Woman's Condition: Subordination and Undeveloped Reason

Mary Wollstonecraft (1759–1797), a philosopher from the 18th century, has made a great contribution to the discussion of women's rights. Wollstonecraft's audacity and courage combined with a revolutionary historical context had, as a result, a work that would become immortal: *Vindication of the Rights of Woman* (1792) [henceforth *Rights of Woman*]. *Rights of Woman* can be read both as a treatise on education and also as a political-philosophical treatise. It is important to say that *Rights of Woman* provides a philosophical basis for Wollstonecraft not only to build her critique of the social model based on private property and oppression of women, but also to pinpoint and recognize who and what is perpetuating the social effects that hold women in the domestic sphere.

It is important to emphasize that *Rights of Woman* is part of a series of texts that were produced during the effervescent period of revolutions. The American Revolution (1776) and the French Revolution (1789) fueled intense debates in English intellectual circles, and the release of *Rights of Woman* marked the questioning of the vacuum of rights that remained for women after the publication of the *Declaration of the Rights of Man and of the Citizen* (1789).

In this paper, my focus is on the women's issue that is at the center of *Rights of Woman*. For this purpose, in the first section, I present what Wollstonecraft calls First Principles. By articulating the conceptions of reason, virtue and knowledge, Wollstonecraft prepares the basis for her argument in favor of women. Later, I present each of the conceptions, starting from a more general plan, specifying its characteristics, and then showing the implications for the case of women. The idea is that, based on the exposition of the First Principles, it is possible to outline Wollstonecraft's contribution to the debate about female emancipation in the history of philosophy.

First Principles: The Path to Emancipation

Reading theorists such as Jean-Jacques Rousseau (1712–1778), Wollstonecraft has found models of femininity that are out of touch with reality. She perceives that such theorists characterize women as unable to think for themselves or even unable to establish some sort of abstract reasoning. With experience and observation of women's circumstances, Wollstonecraft realizes that the problem is not in the female sex itself. Unquestioningly, the situation is a result of a social condition that enforces artificial female manners and also an erroneous conception of femininity that these writers reiterate.

In order to demonstrate that the condition of women is an injustice, Wollstonecraft carries out an investigation into the principles to which she refers as *first*, which guide her arguments throughout *Rights of Woman*. She enunciates the principles in the first chapter as essential in the search for the simplest truths. Wollstonecraft lists them as follows:

> In what does man's pre-eminence over the brute creation consist? The answer is as clear as that a half is less than the whole; in Reason.
>
> What acquirement exalts one being above another? Virtue; we spontaneously reply.
>
> For what purpose were the passions implanted? That man by struggling with them might attain a degree of knowledge denied to the brutes; whispers Experience. (Wollstonecraft 2014, 37)

Establishing these conceptions, Wollstonecraft affirms that knowledge differentiates the type of development that humans have in relation to animals. Similarly, virtue differentiates some men from their peers. Both knowledge and virtue are founded on the faculty of reason, without which it is not possible for virtue and knowledge to be part of human life. From the refinement of knowledge, virtue can be achieved with physical and moral impacts, both from a social and an individual point of view (Wollstonecraft 2014). Although Wollstonecraft uses the term *principles*, in the plural, I will consider them in a singular way. These three conceptions act together in human improvement, which is why it is not possible to see them in a singular plan.

These principles act in such a way as to provide a basis for Wollstonecraft to construct her vindication in a universal and abstract way. Wollstonecraft also implies a Christian metaphysical-theological plan to advocate women's rights. She combines these elements to challenge the established social order, which fails in the parity between the sexes in addition to other injustices, such as social and economic inequality.

What follows is an analysis of reason, virtue and knowledge, highlighting each one from a more general plan down to the particular case of women. My plan is to understand each one of the conceptions and see how they can work in favor of women's emancipation.

Wollstonecraft's Standpoint on Reason, Soul and Improvement

Wollstonecraft states that reason consists of "the simple power of improvement; or, more properly speaking, of discerning truth" (Wollstonecraft 2014, 80). Due to this, Wollstonecraft argues that even though reason is more prominent in some individuals than in others, this faculty is present in the entire human species.

With the power to discern truth, Wollstonecraft refers to the knowledge of worldly facts as they are, without interference from prejudices or opinions. Although Wollstonecraft does not define exactly what she understands as "truth", she states that it is unique for men and women, deductible, and emanates from God (Wollstonecraft 2014, 112). Notwithstanding the fact that speculative truths may prove obscure, moral truths are legitimate, as "they shine clearly, for God is light" (Wollstonecraft 2014, 185). When indicating that the power to discern the truth and to improve oneself is something inherent to human nature, it is important to emphasize that Wollstonecraft understands that regardless of sex, reason is present in equal measure in all human beings, and they must develop their reason to improve themselves (Wollstonecraft 2014, 90).

It is also important to understand that Wollstonecraft bases the conception of reason on two arguments, which work in an interconnected way. First, Wollstonecraft presents the theological argument, which functions to prove that all beings endowed with a soul can be rational. The second is the improvement argument, which states that every being that has an immortal soul is capable of reasoning and has the understanding to improve.

Wollstonecraft's theological argument states that reason has a direct and a close relationship with the metaphysical notion of soul, as it is God who grants the mental strength to seek the development of reason, minting the soul "stamped with the heavenly image". Reason is also, according to Wollstonecraft, "the tie that connects the creature with the Creator" (Wollstonecraft 2014, 80).

Wollstonecraft pinpoints reason in the soul when she states that there is no "trace of the image of God in either sensation or matter" (Wollstonecraft 2014, 90). In assuming such a position, Wollstonecraft excludes the possibility that accidents of the body, such as biological sex, has influence on reason. The theological argument establishes, as shown above, that reason is a potency granted to the human species by God. There are no external limitations. In other words, social or biological components do not define reason and are also a divine gift that exists regardless of social interference.

To this theological argument Wollstonecraft adds the improvement argument. For this purpose, she uses the term *perfectibility*, which assigns a duty to every being that has to perfect their immortal soul through reason. Briefly, all humans need to work for the gradual advancement of the soul. Wollstonecraft considers humans imperfect beings since throughout life, humans develop their reason, reaching more and more towards the possibility of perfect reason. Specifically, Wollstonecraft asserts that reason begins from a common point to reach higher levels of existence, which is why it is in continuous progress.

Wollstonecraft presents an optimistic conception of perfectibility. As she argues, this is what allows human beings to evolve in order to achieve an increasingly better version of themselves. According to Wollstonecraft, perfectibility is what enables people to give up addictions and follow the path of virtue. The relationship that exists between virtue and perfectibility occurs through wisdom, which is the search for improvement and the elevation of the heart.

Concerning women's condition, Wollstonecraft establishes an important dialogue with Jean-Jacques Rousseau's educational theory. After reading *Emile or on Education* (1762), Wollstonecraft agreed with most of its arguments, except for book V, which is the last part of the aforementioned work, in which Rousseau presents Sophia, the spouse of the main character. There are many contradictions in this part; however, I will consider one that is in an initial moment of book V of *Emile*. Rousseau argues that women have the same faculties as men (Rousseau 1979, 357); nevertheless, later in the same book, he argues that women's reason is only practical (Rousseau 1979, 377). According to Rousseau, the characteristic of this kind of reason is that it neither abstracts nor generalizes. By establishing that women's reason is deficient and vacillating, Rousseau sets precedents to justify a social trail that prevents women from fully accessing the faculty of reason.

Wollstonecraft has been opposed to how Rousseau thinks about women's education since the publication of her *Thoughts on the Education* (1788). Always suggesting the opposite of Rousseau, Wollstonecraft defends that women should have an active life, in particular that they must be committed to rational development. For Wollstonecraft, similarly to men, women are endowed with rationality and therefore capable not only of seeing practical scenarios, but also of thinking in an abstract way.

I have argued so far that, for Wollstonecraft, the improvement of reason is what differentiates humankind from animals, allowing both sexes to seek to improve themselves and the species. When affirming that reason is present in the soul and is capable of being perfected, Wollstonecraft lays the foundations of her equality project that seeks to include women in the philosophical aspects of the human species, which until then had been ignored. The questioning position that Wollstonecraft establishes, especially in relation to Rousseau, lays the groundwork for her critique about women's condition. In the next section, I will present how Wollstonecraft's conception of virtue works, and also highlight the obstacles that women have to face to become virtuous.

Virtue, Duty and Affection: A Necessary Relationship

In *Rights of Woman*, virtue is an ability that "exalts one being above another" (Wollstonecraft 2014). Virtue is what distinguishes humans from one another, because some exercise more reason than others. Establishing a connection between reason and virtue, Wollstonecraft understands that there is only one path that guides humanity to the immortality of the soul. This means that every human being who has the faculty of reason must perfect it, and this process should occur in the same way for everyone.

Rational improvement leads to individual improvement, which also expands into the moral and social domains. Indeed, virtue comes to stand beside reason: when someone develops their reason and consequently becomes virtuous, moral progress occurs. From the social point of view, individual virtue allows society to become virtuous, ensuring that the laws and principles that govern it are based solely on reasonable parameters (Wollstonecraft 2014, 37).

Since the development of reason must take place in the same way in all individuals, the conditions of equality between human beings are fundamental. Wollstonecraft refers not only to the sex issue, which separates biological sex, but also to the power and forces that govern society. An example is the monarchy, where riches, heredity, power, and honors are false distinctions among men. According to Wollstonecraft, money and power should not distinguish one man in relation to another. Instead of richness, the benchmark for capacity for virtue must be recognized through the fulfillment of duties and the improvement of reason.

Wollstonecraft argues that duties contribute to the process of human improvement. The enlargement of the faculty of reason is a result of education, which allows acquiring habits of virtue and leads to the practice and fulfillment of duties. In the following, when Wollstonecraft argues about parental duties, I will use as an illustration the relationship between a father and a son, in which duties can be divided into natural and accidental ones.

Wollstonecraft distinguishes natural duty from accidental duty taking a father's intentions as a comparative. On one hand, the natural obligation is when a father has the good intention of training his son by ensuring that the child goes a long way, granting him autonomy. This father tends to strive to form the heart and intends to expand his son's understanding (Wollstonecraft 2014, 184). As a matter of fact, the parent is not only a virtuous being for carrying out this responsible task, but also allows his son to develop virtues. Wollstonecraft assures that natural obligation is a duty that is founded on reason, and the support of this kind of obligation is the moral truth. Unlike speculative truths that God obscures, natural obligations are clear before our eyes. Indeed, Wollstonecraft attributes to individuals the ability to perceive the tasks that will make them more virtuous.

Accidental duty, on the other hand, is based much more on "selfish respect for property" (Wollstonecraft 2014, 187). In other words, the respect that the parent would have for his son is not something genuine. It is a false consideration that is based on vanity and is what promotes hereditary honors, for example. Therefore, it is more in the order of ambition and authority than reason. Accidental duty is degrading, because "The father who is blindly obeyed, is obeyed from sheer weakness, or from motives that degrade the human character" (Wollstonecraft 2014, 187).

Unlike natural duty, accidental duty offers no means of moral improvement. To complete the Wollstonecraftian theoretical framework, it is necessary to note that natural obligation proves to be more relevant than accidental obligation. In addition, it is also necessary to understand that it is from the recurrence of natural obligations that affections arise. Affection refers to "a very faint tie" and is "out of the habitual exercise of a mutual sympathy" (Wollstonecraft 2014, 182). Moreover, affection is also founded on reason and raises in individuals the interests that lead them to fulfill their duties.

Affection acts as an awakening to the need to fulfill duties, which are part of the process of perfecting virtue. These obligations operate in the domestic and public spheres. According to Wollstonecraft, the fulfillment of private duties fosters private virtues. When fulfilling family duties, whether as a parent, child or spouse, people acquire their private virtues while contributing to society, exercising part of their citizenship. The consequence is the improvement of public virtues, the impact of which directly affects morality.

Indeed, it has to be a tautology: to be virtuous is to be free. For the same reason, Wollstonecraft holds that a free being does not submit to any authority other than their own faculty of reason. Therefore, it is necessary that all those who are part of a state be in an equal position in terms of their freedom. In case an individual or a group is subjected to another, the entire society has its freedom and, consequently, its public virtue compromised. Wollstonecraft highlights the importance of this when she argues:

> Moralists have unanimously agreed, that unless virtue be nursed by liberty, it will never attain due strength—and what they say of man I extend to mankind, insisting that in all cases morals must be fixed on immutable principles; and, that the being cannot be termed rational or virtuous, who obeys any authority, but that of reason. (Wollstonecraft 2014, 223–224)

By linking freedom and virtue, Wollstonecraft claims natural rights for women, questioning theorists of the time who deliberately excluded the female sex, reserving these rights only to the male sex. Allowing women to use their own reason and not only respond to external authority, Wollstonecraft opens a new path for her sex to follow.

On the issue of virtues in the case of women, Wollstonecraft takes a position contrary to the theorists of her time. According to such theorists – such as Rousseau –, women were not expected to derive their virtues from reason, but from respect for decorum and external opinion. Wollstonecraft highlights two impediments that theorists sustain to keep women away from becoming virtuous. The first is submission to male authority, which girls are taught to accept from an early age. The second is the continued obstacles that society poses to the development of reason in women. What Wollstonecraft concludes from this is that in learning to repress themselves and not using their own reason, women do not become free and, much less, virtuous. These obstacles not only damage women's lives, but also hinder the progress of humanity as a whole. As I have already argued, for Wollstonecraft, without reason, women cannot contribute positively to society due to the fact that they cannot understand the importance of their duties. Wollstonecraft suggests:

> If indeed this be their destination, arguments may be drawn from reason: and thus augustly supported, the more understanding women acquire, the more they will be attached to their duty—comprehending it—for unless they comprehend it, unless their morals be fixed on the same immutable principle as those of man, no authority can make them discharge it in a virtuous manner. (Wollstonecraft 2014, 23)

In pointing out that women are in a position of slavery, as they are deeply dependent on men, Wollstonecraft also upholds the consequences for the male sex. One of the causes that prevents women from acquiring virtues is linked to a supposedly natural male superiority. The difference that prevails between men and women in the pursuit and promotion of virtue is the result of prejudices, resulting in the relativization of virtues because of sexual labels.

Wollstonecraft inquires: "why should it be increased by prejudices that give a sex to virtue, and confound simple truths with sensual reveries?" (Wollstonecraft 2014, 33). Opposing this observation, Wollstonecraft states that virtue is not relative to sex. In short, Wollstonecraft establishes that virtues are the same for both sexes, and the conduct of men and women must be based on the same principles and must have the same objectives.

According to Wollstonecraft, society expects from women false virtues, such as "patience, docility, good-humor and flexibility". However, they cannot be considered virtues since they are incompatible with the exercise of the intellect. Moreover, they are not true virtues, as they only play the role of restricting female conduct and are not related to reason, being only dictates of sexual behavior, which is why it is problematic to think of virtues that are especially feminine.[1]

Whether married or not, women must have a civil existence. For a woman's private virtue to become a public benefit, she has to have a voice in the state. One of the roles of the legislator is to foster virtue not only in males, but also in females; therefore, Wollstonecraft assigns to the legislator the function of integrating women. The main objective of the one who runs a state is to take advantage of

---

[1] Manners are a way of ordering behavior and have nothing to do with virtues. Virginia Sapiro (2019) highlights this when stating that although social manners are important – as they are intermediaries in the process of socialization and the acquisition of habits – they cannot be considered virtues. Manners are just performances acquired for the purpose of pleasing public opinion. They are not conscious acts, guided towards a moral or virtuous purpose, see Sapiro (2019, 326). For Wollstonecraft, in the case of women, behavior is confused with virtue, which is why it appears that there are sexual virtues. However, Wollstonecraft stresses that the question of conduct must be important not only for women, but also for men. According to Wollstonecraft, women, as well as men, "ought to have the common appetites and passions of their nature, they are only brutal when unchecked by reason: but the obligation to check them is the duty of mankind, not a sexual duty" (see Wollstonecraft 2014, 158).

the individual improvements of absolutely all state components to guarantee the progress of his/her society.

Wollstonecraft argues that "confining girls to their needle" while excluding them from "all political and civil employments" has as a result "narrowing their minds", which prevents them from "fulfilling the peculiar duties that nature has assigned them" (Wollstonecraft 2014, 200). According to Wollstonecraft, for women to know their duties and fulfill them, it is necessary that the field of action allowed for them is greater, so that they can understand how the tasks direct them towards the virtues. Therefore, civic duties do not interfere with their domestic duties, quite the contrary. With the possibility of acting outside the home, as well as with developed reason, women would be fully aware of their duties.

In sum, Wollstonecraft's effort to integrate women into humanity involves giving them not only the right to access and use their own reason, but also to improve themselves, thereby contributing to the progress of humanity. For Wollstonecraft, it is necessary that both sexes act according to the same principles and, most importantly of all: the social compact must be equitable enough to allow them to base their virtues on knowledge.

In the following, I analyze knowledge, the last component of Wollstonecraft's First Principles. The aim is to understand the framework of Wollstonecraft's metaphysical principles: reason, virtue and knowledge and how they contribute to the women's *querelle*.

Knowledge: An Adequate Association of Ideas That Is Free from Prejudice

Wollstonecraft defines knowledge as the "power of generalising ideas, of drawing comprehensive conclusions from individual observations" (Wollstonecraft 2014, 81). The search for knowledge happens according to the need that is imposed on individuals' experiences. When Wollstonecraft holds that necessity is what drives individuals in the search for knowledge, she refers to the renouncement of pleasure as the central motivation of life. Moral and rational progress is what differentiates humans from animals. For Wollstonecraft, unlike animals that use instinct for survival, the passions in human beings are pedagogical in the sense of teaching them what to do or avoid. When discussing the education of young people, the philosopher affirms that it is in the fight against passions that knowledge is acquired.

Passions such as love, ambition, hope and fear work as pathways to learning. For Wollstonecraft, passions are essential in the process of acquiring knowledge, since it is these experiences that will shape the rationality of individuals. According to Wollstonecraft, even the stage of life impacts knowledge and the search for virtue: young people have different experiences than older ones, which makes each one face this process from different angles. She argues:

> Besides, it is not possible to give a young person a just view of life; he must have struggled with his own passions before he can estimate the force of the temptation which betrayed his brother into vice. Those who are entering life, and those who are departing, see the world from such very different points of view, that they can seldom think alike, unless the unfledged reason of the former never attempted a solitary flight. (Wollstonecraft 2014, 139)

That is why, especially in the young, reason deserves special attention. In case knowledge does not derive from the rational faculty, it loses its status and starts to consist only of prejudices. And how do individuals acquire, store and process knowledge? According to Wollstonecraft, this process occurs through the association of ideas.

In a few lines, Wollstonecraft claims that knowledge comes from the outside world, through the association of ideas, which she divides into two types: habitual and instantaneous. Instantaneous association results from a "quick perception of the truth", being so close to intuition that it easily confuses the investigation "and makes us at a loss to determine whether it is reminiscence or ratiocination, lost sight of in its celerity, that opens the dark cloud" (Wollstonecraft 2014, 142). For Wollstonecraft, individuals have some lack of power over this type of association, since when the mind is enlarged, the raw material of this type of association is easily ordered.

Habitual association, according to Wollstonecraft, is about the intellect receiving and storing "the ideas and facts of reality" until there is a relevant event and data to be revealed. The role of this disclosure will be to allow individuals to access the received information "at very different times in life". This information has the ability to come to "mind with illustrative force". This type of association depends more on the "original temperature of mind" than on the will (Wollstonecraft 2014, 142).

When receiving diversity and contrast through education, the understanding becomes malleable and ready to move towards progress. Habitual association "grows with 'our growth'", "has a great effect on the moral character of humanity" and is capable of providing the mind with a transformation that remains throughout life (Wollstonecraft 2014, 143). Despite being more complex than the other types of association, for Wollstonecraft habitual association depends greatly on the instantaneous type. The associations made in the initial period of life, when they are not well managed, can generate nodes that are unlikely to be untied, because, as Wollstonecraft argues: "One idea calls up another, its old associate, and memory, faithful to the first impressions, particularly when the intellectual powers are not employed to cool our sensations, retraces them with mechanical exactness" (Wollstonecraft 2014, 143).

Men and women are affected in what Wollstonecraft calls "habitual slavery to first impressions" (Wollstonecraft 2014, 143). However, especially in the case of women, the effect is deeper. Unlike men, to whom "arid occupations of understanding" mark these impressions, women are more susceptible to becoming slaves to this association of premature ideas. As Wollstonecraft argues, since women do not use their reason properly yet, they can become an easy prey for prejudice. As a result, Wollstonecraft says, women's minds gain a sexual character, as it is the skewed process to which they are subjected that makes them receive information, and they soon transform it into mere impressions and emotions, instead of knowledge.

Although there are theorists who argue that women are naturally emotional and have a deficient reason, for Wollstonecraft this is nothing more than prejudices based on customs and not reason. Knowledge and rationality are women's responsibility as much as they are men's. In making this defense of access to reason and knowledge, Wollstonecraft claims the right of all, with a special focus on women, to become virtuous and attentive to their responsibilities as beings endowed with rights and duties.

Conclusion

Recently, research around the world has been promoting voices that have been neglected in the history of philosophy. Whether due to their geographic location, gender or ethnicity, many thinkers have been left behind. Wollstonecraft was one of those. Although she is not in the hall of "discoveries", there is still much to be studied in Wollstonecraft's works, in particular, her writing as a moral philosopher. In this paper, my objective was to present the First Principles in order to contribute to this consolidation of Wollstonecraft's legacy, both from a political and from a women's defense point of view.

My contribution to the discussion of Wollstonecraft's studies is still under construction and, by now, has raised more questions than answers; however, my intention is to rescue Wollstonecraft's arguments and locate them historically in philosophy. Thus, I intend to contribute to the promotion of a theoretical framework that not only includes women, but is also sensitive to the issues that concern female thinkers. In this sense, understanding the First Principles involves the desire to include them in the aforementioned framework.

Conceptions of reason, virtue and knowledge serve as the philosophical basis for the arguments that Wollstonecraft builds in favor of female emancipation, whether to question the absence of women in public spaces, or to point out in the writings of male writers the injustices that can be found. Although his presence in this paper is small, Rousseau is one of the most frequent interlocutors in Wollstonecraft's works. Wollstonecraft mostly agrees with Rousseau; she is, however, intransigent about how Rousseau treats women and what he attributes to them, such as the "practical reason", which he posits as a female characteristic.

Due to their assumed limited capacity for abstraction, women would not be able to fully develop, and this would affect other fields of life, i. e., consequently, women would not be able to be virtuous or correctly receive and process knowledge. It is precisely at this point that Wollstonecraft concludes that it is not possible for women to be different from men, that is, that they have a reduced capacity only because of their gender.

Alongside other women, such as Christine de Pizan and Catharine Macaulay, Wollstonecraft is a thinker who allows us to rethink the past, rescuing the faded figures in history. Furthermore, the perpetuity of dissatisfaction with the condition of women further highlights the urgency of changing this situation – which, although different from Wollstonecraft's reality, is still not ideal. Finally, Wollstonecraft helps us to define a new kind of future: inclusive, fair and increasingly improved.

References

Bergès, S. (2013). *The Routledge Guidebook to Wollstonecraft's "A Vindication of the Rights of Woman"*. New York: Routledge.
Rousseau, J.-J. (1979). *Emile or On Education*. New York: Basic Books.
Sapiro, V. (2019). "Virtue". In Berges, S., Botting, E. H. and Coffee, A. (Eds.), *The Wollstonecraftian Mind*. New York: Routledge, 323–337.
Wollstonecraft, M. (2004). *Mary*. Ed. by Janet Todd. London: Pickering and Chatto.
Wollstonecraft, M. (2014). *Vindication of the Rights of Woman*. New Heaven and London: Yale University Press.

Annabelle Bonnet

Women's Access to French Philosophy: A Forgotten History (1880–1924)

Abstract: French philosophy from the end of the 19th century and the beginning of the 20th is considered as a masculine domain. This classical narrative expounds that, before that period, women would hardly be present in the history of French philosophy, regarded as no more than exceptions. I will problematize this prejudice through a socio-historical approach to the history of philosophy. On the one hand, I will show that the 1880–1924 period constitutes a blind spot that is necessary to get out of the silence: many women tried to study philosophy. On the other hand, I bring to light the contradiction between the advent of liberal democracy in France and the official prohibition of philosophy for women by the French state. Then, I will argue that the exclusion of women from the right to access philosophical studies must be regarded as an integral part of the contemporary French philosophy.

Introduction: Rethinking the Past – No French Women Philosophers at the End of the 19th Century?

French philosophy from the end of the 19th century and the beginning of the 20th is considered, until now, a masculine domain. According to this interpretation, women would have asserted their place in French philosophy from the second half of the 20th century on, beginning with the works of Simone de Beauvoir and Simone Weil (Châtelet 1972; Revel 1999; Worms 2009). This classical narrative expounds that, before that period, women would hardly be present in the history of French philosophy, regarded as no more than exceptions. The dominant historiography is therefore structured in such a way as to suggest that women generally showed little or no interest in philosophy in the "1900 moment of philosophy" (Worms 2004), a fundamental period of French philosophy, known to have been one of the most intense concerning the advent of democratic principles.

This is one reason why pioneer researchers on the theme of women philosophers in France, as the philosophers Geneviève Fraisse (Fraisse 2020) and Michèle Le Doeuff (Bonnet 2021), often point out that, at the start of their systematical research on the theme in the 1970s, they had no other reference than Simone de

Beauvoir: the history of French women philosophers simply did not exist as a coherent narrative and a legitimate object of study. Since this period, works committed to rethinking this narrative multiplied in France, showing that women had not lost interest in philosophy, but have been excluded for a long time from the French canon of philosophy because of their gender (Collin et al. 2011; Stengers and Despret 2011).

Concerning the middle of the 19th century, researchers have already showed that such an exclusion affected, for example, the philosophical memory of Jenny d'Héricourt who was rediscovered more than one century after her death (Offen 1987). Flora Tristan's writings about the gender bias of the philosophical theories of revolution as well as the figure of Clémence Royer, whose numerous philosophical manuscripts about science have been lost or burned and whose work is therefore partly untraceable (Fraisse 1985), have also been erased from the history of philosophy for long. These three women are most of the time not mentioned in studies on the field of the history of philosophy, despite of their important role in the philosophical field (Bourdieu 1983) of their time.

But how this exclusion happened in France during the referred republican and democratic period remains to be explored. In this article, departing from my doctoral research, I will problematize this prejudice and propose elements to rethink the classical history of philosophy of that moment, focusing on a gender-based point of view.[1] Through a socio-historical approach to the history of philosophy at the end of the 19th and the beginning of the 20th century, some of the ideas that unite this traditional narrative will be questioned. On the one hand, the text points out that the 1880–1924 period constitutes a blind spot that is necessary to get out of the silence. On the other hand, it brings to light the contradiction between the advent of liberal democracy in France and the official prohibition of philosophy for women by the French state, especially in the field of education. The article argues that the exclusion of women from the right to access philosophical studies must be regarded as an integral part of the history of French philosophy, pointing out at the same time that, despite this ban, many women have nevertheless fought for the right to philosophize like men.

---

[1] Bonnet 2022. A partial work has already been published by the Harmattan editions in 2021 (Bonnet 2021).

The Official Prohibition for Women to Philosophize

The end of the 19th century in France marked the advent of liberal democracy. Freedom, equality, autonomy and the right to think for oneself were fundamental liberal principles that structured that new period. Likewise, institutions explicitly addressed, for the first time in France, the issue of free and public basic education for all, even for girls. In this perspective, liberal feminist movements organized themselves in a national scale to claim political, social and intellectual rights for women – most of which would be granted only in 1944 (Mosconi 2017).

In fact, if the Third Republic developed, for the first time in the history of education in France, a public and free education for girls, this access contained a well-defined gender orientation because girls were not considered as future citizens, but as future wives of citizens, deprived of political rights. In this perspective, all knowledge and all teaching programs were "adjusted" to a female public, which shouldn't learn in school the same social roles as the male public. The laws then opposed the family duty of women to their intellectual capacity which, if too developed, would risk destroying the structure of the mononuclear family by diverting them from their *real* role as women (Rogers 2007). Literature, history and science were thereby adapted for a female audience whose goal was to manage their family well, and not to become scientists, historians or writers. The role of literature was to serve as a moral example for future mothers, history classes were to develop love for the French nation, and sciences should be limited to knowledge oriented towards family care, such as hygiene. At the same time, this minimal knowledge was considered useful in face of future husbands, who would not be upset by uneducated wives.

Regarding philosophical knowledge, the situation was rather dramatic. Indeed, it was legally decided that a feminine adaptation of philosophical knowledge would not be possible. In this perspective, promulgated on 21 December 1880, a new law strictly prohibited teaching philosophy to girls and women. Known by the name of its creator, the "Camille Sée law", its general purpose was to define what women could and could not learn from public education institutions. It also marked the official character of the exclusion of women from the philosophical field in France. For the first time in French modern history, women, by law, did not have the right to access philosophical studies. Moreover, philosophy was the only discipline of the humanities and social sciences to which the access was strictly forbidden to women. While historians of philosophy in France have barely remembered the key-date of the sanction of the Camille Sée law, it certainly constitutes a fundamental moment for understanding the history of women philosophers and of French philosophy at the end of the 19th century (Bonnet 2019).

According to reported testimonies, the education commission responsible for monitoring school programs "got scared of allowing young girls to learn philosophy".[2] In fact, the legislative texts affirm that, by reading philosophy, women could distract themselves from their domestic role. Those texts express several times a fear of the presumed use that women could make of the philosophical knowledge. Irony was not absent of the debates concerning the new law: politicians argued, for example, that it should prevent "the happiness, the satisfaction of a poor country doctor who, after a long journey, after having spent his day caring for his patients, will return soaked by the rain to his home and find his wife observing the stars!"[3] The use of their own reason and the learning of concepts would, then, prejudice and disturb the gender balance of the household. In other words, philosophical activity was seen as incompatible with the gendered role of women and, even more, it was potentially destructive of gender social norms and values.

Such a fear might have its roots in certain outcomes of the French Revolution. Since the Revolution and the rise of the Enlightenment period, philosophy had allegedly been invested, in France, with a power of direct action over society, capable more than any other knowledge of influencing social change – and that could include gender issues. Allowing this access could purportedly explode the newly stable society after a century of revolutions. From this point of view, this would disrupt the still fragile social balance of French society. At the same time and for the same reasons, philosophical knowledge was considered as the supreme and most sacred knowledge of human sciences (Fabiani 1988, 2010). In this perspective, women's access to this knowledge would make them fully equal to men and endanger the boundaries between masculine and feminine norms.

Women, at this moment, were not politically equal to men. One of the most influential philosophers of the period, Henri Marion, who was also active at the Ministry of Education, said it clearly in a famous book about women education and its role in French democracy: "Instead of working exactly like us and at the same things, of doubling ourselves in everything, and having the ideal of becoming a Descartes (...)", he wrote, "it is enough that a woman may be seriously interested in supporting the work of men, that she understands them and encourages them" (Marion 1900, 219, Translation AB). To allow women to philosophize seemed impos-

---

[2] Cited in the review Sée 1891, 37, Translation AB.
[3] M. Bourgeois cited in Sée 1888, 204, Translation AB.

sible to him because this option would promote a pernicious competition between men and women.

It is in such an atmosphere that the woman philosopher Clémence Royer was prevented, in 1880, from entering the Sorbonne university to give a course in philosophy of science. Even being a prolific philosopher then, she was prohibited to enter the university building and forced to give lessons in a room of the Town Hall of Paris (Demars 2005). Such a fear of granting philosophy access for women continued decades later in French society, as attested by Simone de Beauvoir's own mother example, who feared that "the study of philosophy mortally corrupts the soul" (Beauvoir 2002, 164) and that her daughter would study philosophy and turn into an unethical and impure woman.

Forty Years of Struggle for Philosophical Equality

The Camille Sée law promoted inequality of access to philosophical knowledge and had serious consequences on French philosophy and the history of French women philosophers. On the one hand, it throwed generations of girls in an education devoid of philosophy and denied them the right to access the art of thinking systematically. On the other hand, they could not, without this education, obtain the bachelor's degree, the baccalaureate, to which philosophy was one of the central tests, and, consequently, they saw their access to the university formally blocked. It should be remembered that at that time, the philosophy program for boys' secondary education accounted for up to 50 percent of compulsory education for future baccalaureate graduates (Poucet 1999). Finally, while the term philosopher was increasingly restricted to an academic space, it was now even more difficult for them to be considered as women philosophers. The Camille Sée law will only be completely abolished in 1924, that is to say more than 40 years after its first application.

It is important to notice that some philosophical knowledge was demanded to enter *every and any* university course, so this interdiction did not impact just women who desired to pursue their studies on this subject, but every woman who aspired to enter university. Without accessible public basic education on this matter, women who wished to study philosophy were forced to go through other means, such as private lessons, family support that allowed them to devote time and money, which was not accessible to all women. A quick overview of the key dates of the feminine conquests in philosophy during this period shows the consequences of such a law, at the same time that their names also constitute signals that women defied the prohibition. The first women bachelors in philosophy appeared just in the 1890s, and it was not until 1905 that Jeanne Baudry became the first female *agrégée*[4] of philosophy, thanks to a derogation request. Since 1825, she was the only women to succeed on this competitive examination until 1920. In 1911, another woman became, for the first time, lecturer of philosophy in a boys' high school, whose name was however forgotten (she is known just as Mme. Rosenberg). In 1913, a woman, Alice Stériad, obtained a doctorate in philosophy, almost a hundred years after the creation of this exam in France. The second woman to obtain a doctorate in philosophy in France (the first French woman, since Stériad was Rumanian), Léontine Zanta, appeared in 1914. It took more than 30 years, under the Camille Sée law, for these women to achieve such successes.

If the official ban on studying philosophy for women does not appear in the classical historiography of this period, the struggles that women and sometimes male philosophers have waged to end these inequalities never are told in the history of philosophy. However, women were not passive face this discrimination. While for men, the philosophical activity was an evidence, women still had to fight for their right to attend philosophy classes. We can cite some of these manifestations. Struggles and attempts to abolish this law had already begun at the end of the 19th century, when the French feminist Mathilde Salomon argued without success, in the Ministry of Education, about the necessity of opening philosophy classes to women. Before the First World War, women philosophers who attended Henri Bergson classes had to stand on the floor, but started to claim chairs to sit and listen to the teacher's lessons. The request was ridiculed by male students, but it was very symbolic: anonym women wanted to have the right to prepare for philosophy exams.

There were strategies to study philosophy in other ways than the official. Some women learned philosophy in feminist associations, or in alternative schools organized by women. Other were accepted by male lecturers and professors in philosophy classes – men who felt the situation was unfair. This is the case of Léontine Zanta, the first French women philosopher to conquer a doctoral degree and who was the first model of success for young women who wanted to study philosophy. She succeeded in her fight because her father was an open-minded college professor and, with his help, she was able to take philosophy courses at the Sorbonne, when she was the only female student of philosophy (Bonnet 2021).

---

[4] Name given to those who pass the competitive exam of the aggregation, an exam for the recruitment of teachers either in secondary education or in higher education.

The 1920s: The Incomplete Conquest of Philosophical Equality

After the First World War, the prohibition set out by the Camille Sée law would appear to be out of tune with time. With men on the front, French society had to be reorganized and women did broadly substitute French male lecturers of philosophy at schools. They accessed the philosophical field that, up to then, was closed, and demonstrated that they were perfectly capable of teaching philosophy. Mentalities on their ability to philosophize had to evolve. In March 1920, they were officially authorized, for the first time, to sit for the *agrégation* exams in philosophy.

However, this authorization was very quickly questioned and cancelled. When men returned from the war, they demanded their places back. After that, the Ministry of Public Instruction intended to divide the teaching competitive exams for philosophy into separate male and female categories. It was then that a vast campaign of denunciation began, notably through the *Société des Agrégées* (Verneuil 2007), to put an end to these inequalities of treatment. For the first time in the history of the French Republic, women organized themselves *collectively* and *officially* to claim their right to philosophize in the same professional conditions as men, a fight that would allow Simone de Beauvoir to obtain, some years later, her full philosophy diploma. These women argued that laws such as the Camille Sée law were archaic, anachronistic and didn't respect the principles of equality. Its members fought for the gender standardization of competitions and philosophical programs. They get their first successes in 1921.

In 1924, under pressure, the Camille Sée law was revoked. Boys and girls had to study the same school programs (philosophy included), women could officially study philosophy at universities and they could take part of the same philosophy exams as men. The situation was better. Even so, the rankings of competitions to be professors of philosophy continued segregated by a gender criterion. There was a ranking for men and a ranking for women. This is why, for example, Simone de Beauvoir and Jean-Paul Sartre did not appear in the same competition rankings, when they passed the competitive exams to be philosophy teachers. Jean-Paul Sartre was the first among men, and Simone de Beauvoir the first among women, and it was considered that she was "second" after Sartre because the ranking of women was always considered lower than the ranking of men. With a unique classification, with a single ranking, maybe Simone de Beauvoir would have been ranked first, as their teachers claimed at that time. "Everyone agreed that SHE was THE philosopher" (Cohen Solal 1999, 116), wrote the philosopher and member of the competition jury Georges Canguilhem about this situation. Through this desire to maintain two rankings, there was still a symbolic issue that refused to affirm gender equality in philosophy.

Conclusion: For Another History of French Philosophy in the 19th and 20th Centuries

The lack of women philosophers in the histories of French philosophy at the turn of the 20th century must be questioned. First, the French philosophy of the period itself invalidated the massive presence of women in its field of research, which is far from being anecdotic. This means that the rejection was thought out and voluntary. Second, it also means that, for more than 40 years, women in France didn't have the right to officially access philosophical studies, even in a democratic framework. Gender-biased considerations prevailed over the democratic question and the gender equality. At the same time, this legal situation pushed women to the fringes of philosophy, while they were deeply interested in the philosophy of their time. Many women philosophers at that period, thanks to other mechanisms, never gave up studying philosophy, but who were not recognized and this marginalization process is still present in our historiography, since they continue to be ignored. Finally, it must be said that women, despite all difficulties and attempts to forbid them, did *never* accept to be expelled from philosophy, and developed individual and collective strategies to surmount those barriers: a chronology of this period and of the women in activity at that moment, made by me in previous researches, ranging from the end of the 19th century to the 1930s, distinguished the presence of 169 women who taught philosophy, 35 who became doctors in philosophy and more than 120 philosophical books written by women. This chapter of our history inside the history of French philosophy is yet to be recovered.

References

Beauvoir, S. (2005). *Memoirs of a Dutiful Daughter.* New York: Harper Prennial Modern Classics.
Bonnet, A. (2019). "Obtenir l'égalité philosophique. L'accès des femmes à la philosophie en France (1868–1918)". *Orbis Linguarum* 53(20), 209–218.
Bonnet, A. (2021). "Entretien avec Michèle Le Doeuff". *Genre & Histoire* 27(1). URL: http://journals.openedition.org/genrehistoire/6393 (last accessed 4 January 2023).
Bonnet, A. (2022). *La barbe ne fait pas le philosophe. Les femmes et la philosophie en France (1880–1949).* Paris: CNRS Éditions.
Bourdieu, P. (1983). "Les sciences sociales et la philosophie". *Actes de la recherche en sciences sociales* 47–48, 45–52.
Châtelet, F. (1973). *Histoire de la philosophie. Idées, Doctrines.* Paris: Hachette.

Cohen Solal, A. (1999). *Sartre (1905–1980).* Paris: Folio.
Collin, F., Pisier, E. and Varikas, E. (2011). *Les femmes de Platon à Derrida. Anthologie critique.* Paris: Dalloz.
Demars, A. (2005). *Clémence Royer l'intrépide: la plus savante des savants: Autobiographie et commentaires par Aline Demars.* Paris: L'Harmattan.
Despret, V. and Strengers, I. (2011). *Les faiseuses d'histoire, que font les femmes à la pensée?* Paris: La Découverte.
Fabiani, J. L. (1988). *Les philosophes de la République.* Paris: Sens Commun.
Fabiani, J. L. (2010). *Qu'est-ce qu'un philosophe français? La vie sociale des concepts (1880–1980).* Paris: Éditions de l'EHESS.
Fraisse, G. (1985). *Clémence Royer. Philosophe et femme de sciences.* Paris: La Découverte.
Fraisse, G. (2020). *Féminisme et philosophie.* Paris: Gallimard.
Fraisse, G. (2021). "Preface". In Bonnet, A. (Ed.), *Léontine Zanta. Histoire oubliée de la première française docteure en philosophie.* Paris: L'Harmattan, 9–12.
Marion, H. (1900). *Psychologie de la femme.* Paris: Armand Colin.
Mosconi, N. (2017). *Genre et éducation des filles. Des clartés de tout.* Paris: L'Harmattan.
Offen, K. (1987). "Qui est Jenny P. d'Héricourt? Une identité retrouvée". *Révolutions et mutations au XIXème siècle* 3, 87–100.
Poucet, B. (1999). *Enseigner la philosophie. Histoire d'une discipline scolaire (1860–1990).* Paris: CNRS Éditions.
Revel, J. F. (2003). *Histoire de la philosophie occidentale.* Paris: Pocket.
Rogers, R. (2007). "L'éducation des filles: un siècle et demi d'historiographie". *Histoire de l'éducation* 115–116, 37–79.
Scott, J. W. (1998). *La citoyenne paradoxale: les féministes françaises et les droits de l'homme.* Paris: Albin Michel.
Sée, C. (1888). "Séance du 19 janvier 1880", *Lycées et collèges de jeunes filles. Documents rapports et discours à la chambre des députés et au Sénat, décrets, arrêtés, circulaires, etc, relatifs à la loi sur l'enseignement secondaire des jeunes filles.* Paris: Léopold Cerf, 173–219.
Sée, C. (1891). "Discours de M. Camille Sée (11 juillet 1880)". *L'Enseignement secondaire des jeunes filles : revue mensuelle*, January 1891. Paris: Léopold Cerf, 34–45.
Verneuil, Y. (2007). "La Société des agrégées, entre féminisme et esprit de catégorie (1920–1948)". *Histoire de l'éducation* 115–116, 195–224.
Worms, F. (Eds.) (2004). *Le moment 1900 en philosophie.* Lille: Presses Universitaires du Septentrion.
Worms, F. (2009). *La philosophie en France au XXème siècle. Moments.* Paris: Folio Essais.

Andrea Pérez-Fernández
Hannah Höch: Notes on Violence and Vulnerability

Abstract: In this text, I reflect on the artistic practice of German artist Hannah Höch (1889–1978), mostly known for her pioneering role in the development of Dadaist inter-war photomontage, and for being the only woman that took part in this movement in Berlin. To do so, I first show the relevance of the Dadaist gaze in her work. Second, I focus on her experience of violence and its relation to the notion of vulnerability. Third, I review Hannah Arendt's idea of contingency as considered by the philosopher Fina Birulés. The purpose of this is to show how Höch's way of describing the common world through the practice of photomontage has a normative character, since pointing out the fragility of the world always acts as a condition for proposing new possible status quos.

"Höch as in *Königin* (queen), not as in *Köchin* (cook)!", claimed an old Hannah Höch (1889–1978) on the correct pronunciation of her name (Höch 2016). In recent times, academic research on this German artist has increased considerably. The editing and publication of her archive after her death, the translation of some of her writings and, above all, the exhibitions that have been held around the world, have revealed her key role in the history of 20th-century art. Born in Gotha into a wealthy family, Höch is mostly known for being one of the pioneering figures of photomontage, but she also excelled in painting, design, or handicrafts. She was also involved in many artistic and intellectual circles, and became friends with figures such as Piet Mondrian, László Moholy-Nagy, Kurt Schwitters or Sophie Taeuber and Jean Arp.[1]

Acknowledgments: This article was made possible by a grant FPU18/03596 and it is framed in the project *Vulnerability in Women's Philosophical Thought: Contributions to the Debate around Present Emergencies* PGC2018-094463-B-100 (MCIU/AEI/FEDER, UE). I would also like to thank David Guerrero and Rocío Thovar for their help.

[1] Hannah Höch's estate is housed in the Berlinische Galerie (Berlin) and partially available in its online collection. There is also a lot of material available in print form AT the Akademie der Künste, and her address book has been published recently (Neckelmann 2018). However, most of it is only in German. For an overview in English, see the catalog of the exhibition *The Photomontages of Hannah Höch* (MOMA, 1996/7), available online at: https://www.moma.org/calendar/exhibitions/241 (last accessed 7 December 2022). *Hannah Höch Picture Book* (Höch 2010) and a printed edition

Having lived through most of the years of what historian Eric Hobsbawm called "the short twentieth century" (Hobsbawm 1994), Höch's artistic career is thus relevant for understanding many of the debates that took place in her time. The rise and fall of the Weimar Republic, the two world wars or Nazi repression delimited the way she approached the world, for which she always felt a great responsibility. The job of a painter was, in her opinion, to be "a filter through which his own time passes" (Höch 2016). She used photographs as poets use words (Höch 1959, 92, Translation APF), and many of her Dada photomontages were an attempt to "capture" such a "turbulent" era. Höch was very clear about what her greatest skill was: "to look, to experience, to classify". But also, she added, she had the will "to bring out again what I have taken in, enriched with what I think and feel about it" (Höch 1976, 24, Translation APF).

In this text, I will reflect on the normative dimension of Höch's way of describing the world through her practice of photomontage. First, as an introduction, I will show that she understands Dadaism not as a specific style, but as a way of seeing the world. Second, I will focus on her experience of violence and its relation to vulnerability, as both notions have been used to describe her work. Having contextualized both categories, I will propose a comprehension of Höch's practice based on contingency, as Hannah Arendt understood it, in order to stress Höch's political dimension.

Introduction: Looking through Dada-glasses

On 9 July 1920, Adolf Behne, co-founder of the German Workers Council for Art (1918–1921), highlighted in the evening edition of the socialist newspaper *Die Freiheit* the "truly brilliant" works (*Klebearbeiten*) of, in this order, Hannah Höch, Raoul Hausmann and George Grosz. In this review of the First International Dada Fair at the Burchardt Gallery, he described the art of this controversial avant-garde group as a direct expression of their time: "It cannot be anything other than what it is today", asserted Behne (1920, Translation APF). Behne referred to photomontages such as *Cut with the Kitchen Knife Dada through the Last Weimar Beer-Belly Cultural Epoch of Germany* (1919–1920), which stood there "as a visual *summa* of Berlin Dada's exuberant condemnation of contemporaneous German society

---

of *Hannah Höch's Life Portrait* (2016) have also been published recently (The Green Box). The bilingual catalog (Spanish-English) of the retrospective curated by Juan Vicente Aliaga at the Reina Sofía (2004) is unfortunately out of print.

and its wholehearted immersion in the revolutionary chaos of post-Wilhelmine Germany" (Boswell 1996, 7).[2]

The technique of collage, that was born then, never ceased to fascinate Höch, even when the movement was already extinct. Although on more than one occasion she claimed to be fed up with being identified only with Dada, she always admitted that such a movement was a way of seeing the world and, therefore, it was not possible for her to completely distance herself from it. The "old Dadaists" could only conceive their existence from then on through those "Dada-glasses" (Höch 1959) with which they interpreted the world. And photomontage was the perfect tool to do this.

As a more concrete example of Höch's practice, we can think about her *Heads of the State* (1918–1920), where Höch parodies Defense Minister Gustav Noske and Reich President Friedrich Ebert "by collaging their paunchy figures atop an iron-on embroidery pattern, associating them not with the traditionally male realm of state formation but with the female domain of leisured relaxation" (Makela 1996a, 28). To do that, she used a well-known photograph of them at a Baltic Sea resort published at the Berlin illustrated Newspaper (*BIZ*), to which she had free access thanks to her work as a designer of embroidered and lace cloths in the handiwork division at the Ullstein Verlag, the largest publishing house in Berlin. She used the same source image in another photomontage named *Dada Panorama*, where she parodied the military alliance of the government by linking Ebert's military dress boots to the phrase "against damp feet", a slogan then used to advertise a popular antiperspirant for feet.

Through their public activities, writings and manifestos, Berlin Dadaists expressed their strong opposition against war, the Weimar government and the conservative bourgeoisie (Elger 2009, 17). In the words of the German writer Richard Huelsenbeck, who inspired Dada in Berlin (Höch 1993), Dada felt itself as the child of a time "which one could insult but not deny" (Huelsenbeck 2015, 38). And although "the political commitment of Berlin Dada was not uniform but bifurcated", the opposition to the Weimar regime – and especially to German chauvinism – meant for these artists a firm support of the socialist revolution, at least during the early Weimar years. However, as the expert on Dada and modernism Richard Sheppard points out, they didn't share a common view on the relation between art and politics:

> The Marxist wing of Berlin Dada thought that the artist could justify his or her existence in a pre-revolutionary situation by creating works that in some way contributed to the revolution. [...] For the Anarchists, however, revolutionary art was revolutionary not by virtue of its ideo-

---

[2] The first comprehensive study of this work was carried out by artist Jula Dech (Dech 1989).

logical purity or politically motivated satirical edge, but by virtue of its "otherness"—its commitment to flux, absurdity, experimentation, and psychic freedom and its inherent opposition to the conventionally ordered world. (Sheppard 2000, 348–349)

According to Sheppard, Höch would have been in the second branch, sharing Raoul Hausmann's "combination of scepticism and Anarchist utopianism" (2000, 333), at least while she was involved with him. It should be noted here that there is no clear overlap between her thinking and that of her peers. A clear example of that is the fact that even if Höch was indeed interested in artistic experimentation beyond politics, her explicit criticism of gender roles is also a sharp internal criticism of the Dada movement itself. At the end of the day, most of their male colleagues "continued for a long while to look upon *us* [their women colleagues] as charming and gifted amateurs, denying *us* implicitly any real professional status" (Höch 1984, 109).

In addition, for Höch, Dada's alliance with communism was much more contingent than programmatic (Höch 1984). And despite her harsh criticism of the monarchy and the *bourgeois* way of life, she never got into politics. At least not besides her participation in the first meetings of the November Group – a heterogeneous group of artists that took its name from the month of the German revolution – and in the exhibition "Women in Need" against the prohibition of abortion in paragraph 218 of the penal code (Pérez-Fernández 2021). In this sense, even though she did not identify herself as a feminist and even though "glorifying the modern woman" was never one of her aims, women's suffering often made her "take a position" (Höch 1976, 27, Translation APF).

With all that, she participated in several Dada activities and took part in its two most important exhibitions – much to the chagrin of her "comrades" George Grosz and John Heartfield – and shared with them their commitment to an ironic and suspicious gaze. While for Dadaists like Hans Richter she was just a "good girl" who "was able to make her small, precise voice heard" and "spoke up for art" when Hausmann proclaimed her doctrine of anti-art (Richter 1997, 132), the Nazis had no doubt that she was a dangerous "cultural Bolshevik", as they labeled her.

Notes on Violence and Vulnerability in Höch's Work

Without doubt, the experience of violence left a huge mark on Höch's production. Insofar as every work is rooted in an economic, social context that shapes and influences it, the force of the inter-war period as a constant echo of war runs through Höch's work. In this respect, art historian Maria Josep Balsach speaks of Höch's 1920s photomontages in terms of a "cartography of violence", as a consequence of the experiences of the First World War. Balsach draws attention to *Cut with the Kitchen Knife* and points out that the figure at the center of it is the face of Käthe Kollwitz, "the painter of the war, the pain, of solidarity and sensibility towards the victims" of violence, especially women (Balsach 2017, 96, Translation APF). In other words, Höch would have chosen the main metaphor of the representation of suffering and war as the articulating element of her personal Dadaist manifesto in images.

The 1920s were also, in Balsach's view, the genesis of later paintings such as *Fear* (1936) or *Dance of Death* (1943), among others. That is, violence would remain at the center of Höch's production as a permanent memory. And she was not the only one. However, the experience of the First World War and its aftermath was something from which many artists like Höch were trying to move away. At the same time, it was nevertheless foundational experience of a new way of understanding art and life, and its relation to politics. The Alsatian sculptor Jean Arp – a close friend of Höch, whom she deeply admired – explained that they "were looking for an elementary art that would, *we* [they] thought, save men from the furious madness of those times" (Arp 2006, 154).

Höch herself said that from that moment on she began to live in a "consciously political way" (Ohff 1968, 11). In her words: "the catastrophe shattered my world. Surveying the consequences for humanity and for myself, I suffered greatly under my world's violent collapse" (Höch 1993, 211). The outbreak of the First World War in 1914 literally interrupted Höch's artistic studies. She had just received a scholarship to attend an exhibition in Cologne and, on her way there, English tourists shout the news from a viewpoint. And talking about the School of Arts and Crafts where she studied and the adjoining facilities, Höch recalled that to access the studios upstairs they had to walk past numerous wounded, as it had served as a military hospital (Ohff 1968, 12). The impact of the repression following the workers' uprisings of 1918 was not less important to her. As the rest of the German left, Höch was shocked by the murder of Rosa Luxemburg and Karl Liebknecht by counterrevolutionary Freikorps irregular troops and under the connivance of Ebert's government. Not to mention the isolation in which she lived for many years since the mid-1930s. As Peter Boswell (1996, 16) details:

> Her dear friend Theo van Doesburg died in 1931. In 1934 a hyperactive thyroid brought her to the brink of death [...]. The following year, Höch and [Til] Brugman parted ways. And with the departure from Germany of Arp, Schwitters, Hausmann (with whom she had resumed contact in 1931) and other friends from the avantgarde, she lived in complete artistic isolation. Just before the outbreak of the war in 1939, she retreated from Berlin to the rural suburb of Heiligensee, a move precipitated by her growing sense of danger.

Until the end of the Second World War in May 1945, Höch lived in almost total solitude, where she spent entire weeks without saying a word. The experience of such events is one of the reasons why Vicente Aliaga, curator of a major Höch retrospective exhibition at the Reina Sofía Museum in Madrid, described her as "an individuality fractured by blows, fragile and strong at the same time, shaped by circumstances and adversity, but with a rare determination to overcome social and political obstacles, as well as an unwavering will to express itself". Accordingly, he highlights the role of "the small, the tiny and the vulnerable" as a "valuable repository of sensations and images" for the artist while referring to her handicraft work. For Aliaga, "Höch's interest in things is usually regarded to be insignificant or 'feminine', that is, handicrafts, fragility and smallness, or evidenced by the numerous *Miniaturen* or minis, the tiny drawings on paper, that she produced at different times throughout her career" (Aliaga 2004, 314).

Given that in the current philosophical context this perspective opens many complex paths, I would like to contribute to contextualize it slightly. If we use "vulnerable" when talking about the materials or the elements that Höch puts into play – e. g., the use of crafts or patterns –, we must consider her writings on embroidery, in which she made an early critique of the hierarchy of artistic materials and genres and ironized about the disdain for crafts traditionally carried out by women. In these articles, published in the prestigious needlework journal *Stickerei- und Spitzen-Rundschau* ("Embroidery and Lace Review", in German), Höch claimed the art of embroidery as another artistic discipline. In 1918 she wrote that embroidery is closely related to painting given that its style changes according to the historical and artistic period. She sentenced: "it is an art and may claim to be treated as such" (Höch 1918, 219, Translation APF). This was also the understanding of some critics of her handicraft work. As Maria Makela explains, Alexander Koch used musical metaphors to review her work, talking about "melodies of lines", "Asian-influenced colour harmonies" or "complex rhythms". Likewise, Adolf Behne emphasized her "thoroughly modern feeling for colour and form" (Makela 1996b, 53). Engaged with the idea of a continuous artistic development of embroidery – a process whose participants were, with no doubt, women who embroider – Höch's vindication didn't consist in idealizing what was "reviled" by the canon but by putting forward her conviction that all gradated classifications were founded on arbitrary principles and should, therefore, be reassessed. In short, she was not trying to stress the wonders of "low art" but trying to destroy the hierarchy between arts and craft genres.

Aliaga also recovers a quotation from Höch, which he links to the symbolic richness of her work and relates to her will to offer different angles and readings of the same phenomenon. When asked about the axes of her work, Höch replied: "Symbols of growth and extinction, love and hate, glorification and rejection, but also the search for beauty; hidden beauty in particular" (Höch 1976, 32, Translation APF). Again, this quote should be understood in a constructive sense. And not as a mere poetic abstraction of her desire to praise the fragile. In this regard, the combination of antithetic principles is probably linked to the idea of balance, which is present in the whole Dadaist movement. As Hanne Bergius states: "always in the tension of a dynamic 'balance of contradictions', the Dadaist opened art on the one hand to chaotic and destructive abysses and invented on the other hand adequate structures". For this Dada expert, "the aesthetic experience of destruction and creation threw light on the productive breaks initiated by Dada: the breaks of multimateriality, polyvalence, multifocality, relativity, fragment, chance, process and the ephemeral" (Bergius 2006, 2). It should be noted, moreover, that this notion of balance between opposites is highly indebted to the philosophy of Salomo Friedlaender (Mynona), with whom Höch was in close contact and whom he quoted in two of her key photomontages (Burmeister 2004). Finally, also in relation with the mentioned quote, it is interesting to emphasize her conception of art as a constant search which, due to its complexity, prevents total control over one's own production, at least in her case. For although she was fully aware that heterogeneity comes at a price, namely the absence of a "personal brand", she confessed (quite proudly) that she was incapable of sticking to a single style (Höch 2001).

A Third Path: Contingency

Having considered the political dimension implicit in the two aspects developed above – that is, the experience of violence as both cause and consequence of a rejection of the existing political order and the vindication of embroidery – I would like to propose a third frame of reading. When reflecting on Höch's thinking and practice of photomontage, I find it more useful to think of violence and fragility as characteristics of the relations that constitute the common world, rather than as attributes of a particular object or individual. In this regard, violence and fragility are related to the extent that the former makes the latter more evident.

Therefore, I would like to focus on a third idea, that of contingency. This is, the idea that something can or cannot be, traditionally opposed in philosophy to necessity (Ferrater 2020). Specifically, I refer to Arendt's comprehension of contingency, which I take from the philosopher Fina Birulés. Arendt understood contingency "as the way of being of politics" and, in doing so, "she tried to restore a positive and specific meaning to politics, focusing not on the question of domination (who should rule whom?) but on freedom and action" (Birulés n. d.).

As Birulés says, "Arendt's point of view is characterized by taking seriously the fact that when we act, we never know the results of our actions; if we knew, we would not be free" (Birulés 2009). And this fact is of great importance in Höch's practice of photomontage. Höch's method was undoubtedly open to spontaneity and chance. The technique of collage meant "to set out on voyages of exploration", and, above all, "to remain receptive to the stimuli of the casual, which, here more than in any other context, are ready to constantly and lavishly regale our imagination" (*Phantasie*), she wrote in 1934 (Höch 1996, 506, Translation APF). Sculptor Siegfried Kühl, a close friend of Höch, explained that they used to brainstorm a title *after* making a composition (Kühl 1991, 11). In a discipline in which the debate about the function of art was the usual frame of discussion, Höch engaged with what she called "free photomontage" as opposed to applied or propagandistic photomontage. In doing this, she embraced the impossibility of knowing the outcome of the process beforehand.

However, as Karoline Hille remarks, "Even if [...] each photomontage is also based on spontaneous ideas or some accidental stimulus, the entire, often protracted development process is calculated and controlled", since this art form not only "required the prior systematic collection", but also was a "medium" to express "her desires, hopes, critiques and fears, and, not least, in which the art of her time, and her time itself" is translated (Hille 2004, 323). But behind this disciplined process lies a clear political commitment:

> I want to erase the fixed boundaries that we humans confidently tend to draw around everything within our reach. I try to convey this, to make it visually perceptible [...]. I want to continue formulating the warning that, in addition to your conceptions and opinions and my own, there are millions and millions of other legitimate viewpoints. [...] I want to help people to experience a much richer world, so that we can engage more benevolently in the world we know. (Höch quoted in Aliaga 2004, 311)

In this sense, the assumption of contingency in Arendt's thought does not mean, as Birulés explains, "a renunciation of thinking or submission to the accidental but, rather, a clear and firm willingness for responsibility toward the world" (Birulés 2009). The philosopher stresses the idea that "we are tied to a world of relationships that we have not chosen and into which we are born unexpectedly, as strangers". And "although it may seem paradoxical, this fragility that Arendt finds in freedom both strengthens and intensifies it", since it links political freedom to the presence of others, that is, to plurality (Birulés 2021).

In doing photomontages, Höch decontextualizes fragments of a common shared reality, cropping them, repositioning them, inverting them... With her method, she shows the arbitrariness of the relations and categories that constitute the world. Precisely, when talking about Dada, Höch said that she and her colleges: "were trying to point out that things could also be done differently and that many of our conventional ways of thinking, dressing or reckoning are no less arbitrary than others which are generally accepted" (Höch 1984, 107). In other words, the fact that relations that constitute the world are not naturally fixed makes it possible to change them. But Höch not only demonstrated that many of the certainties and labels of the time were revisable. By de-naturalizing the present, she also allowed the spectators to imagine other ways of relating to the world.[3] And this brings her practice back to the idea of contingency as an absence of control over one's own actions. That is, Höch invited viewer's participation. As Kay Tabernacle argues, her project consisted in deploying the imagination strategically to transform perception through art and thereby cause social change. And the new image appeared, then, to the viewer "in part as a result of their own experience, memories and internal references, it operates more closely to the realm of the imagination than to its previous context" (Tabernacle 2014, 4). Likewise, Gunda Lynken states that "Höch tried to create novel images which, in her opinion, could only be described as successful when the 'distance' from the basic illustrations was already so radical that it was impossible to recognize the source" (Luyken 2011, Translation APF).

In short, Höch's way of describing the world is not only a consequence of its fragility. For her, this category has a prescriptive character, even as a fact of the world. In this sense, her political responsibility is to point out this fact, and to propose new possible relations that incite the spectator's reflection and imagination.

References

Aliaga, J. V. (2004). "The Total Woman: On the Art of Hannah Höch, Individuality and Gender Issues in Difficult Times". In Aliaga, J. V. (Cord.), *Hannah Höch*. Madrid: Museo Nacional Centro de Arte Reina Sofía/Aldeasa, 311–321.
Balsach, M. J. (2017). "El fotomontatge com a cartografia de la violència, Communication Papers". *Media Literacy & Gender Studies* 6(12), 93–103.
Behne, A. (1920). "Dada". *Die Freizeit* 269(3). URL: https://fes.imageware.de/fes/web/index.html?open=FR03269&page=1 (last accessed 4 January 2023).
Bergius, H. (2006). *"Join Dada!"* [Lecture]. Symposium "Representing Dada", Museum's Titus 1 Theater, New York.
Birulés, F. (n. d.). "Hannah Arendt", *Diccionario Ferrater Mora*. URL: https://www.diccionariodefilosofia.es/es/diccionario/l/4455-arendt-hannah.html (last accessed 28 January 2023).
Birulés, F. (2009). "Contingency, History and Narration in Hannah Arendt". *HannaArendt.net* 1(5). URL: https://www.hannaharendt.net/index.php/han/article/view/149/264 (last accessed 22 November 2022).

---

[3] I have recently further developed the introduction of distance in Hannah Höch's practice of photomontage linking it to Brechtian distancing effect in the light of her photomontage *Mother* and the fight for abortion rights in Germany (Pérez-Fernández 2021).

Birulés, F. (2021). "Vulnerability and amor mundi: Hannah Arendt". In Fuster, L., Laurenzi, E., Birulés, F. and Hoogeveen, T., "Fragments of Vulnerability in Women's Philosophy". *Dictionnaire du genre en traduction/Dictionary of Gender in Translation/Diccionario del género en traducción.* URL: https://worldgender.cnrs.fr/en/entries/fragments-of-vulnerability-in-womens-philosophy/ (last accessed 22 November 2022).

Boswell, P. (1996). "Hannah Höch: Through the Looking Glass". In Höch, H., *The Photomontages of Hannah Höch.* Minneapolis: Walker Art Center, 7–23.

Burmeister, R. (2004). "Balancing the Scales of Difference: Hannah Höch and Salomo Friedlaender/Mynona". In Aliaga, J. V. (Cord.), *Hannah Höch.* Madrid: Museo Nacional Centro de Arte Reina Sofía/Aldeasa, 311–321.

Dech, J. (1989). *Hannah Höch: Schnitt mit dem Küchenmesser.* Frankfurt/M.: Fischer.

Elger, D. (2009). *Dadaismo.* Köln: Taschen.

Ferrater, J. (2020). "Contingencia". *Diccionario Ferrater Mora.* URL: https://www.diccionariodefilosofia.es/es/diccionario/l/856-contingencia.html (last accessed 18 January 2023).

Hille, K. (2004). "'This Never-ending Evolution' Reflected in Her Art – Hannah Höch in the 20th Century". In Aliaga, J. V. (Cord.), *Hannah Höch.* Madrid: Museo Nacional Centro de Arte Reina Sofía/Aldeasa, 322–331.

Hobsbawm, E. (1994). *The Age of Extremes.* London: Abacus.

Höch, H. (1918). "Vom Sticken". *Stickerei- und Spitzen-Rundschau* 18, 219.

Höch, H. (1959). "Brief von Hannah Höch". In Mehring, W. (Ed.), *Berlin – Dada Erinnerungen.* Zurich: Die Arche, 91–92.

Höch, H. (1976). "Suzanne Pagé: Interview avec Hannah Höch". In Dieterich, B. and Krieger, P. (Eds.), *Hannah Höch.* Berlin: Nationalgalerie Berlin, 23–32.

Höch H (1984). "Hannah Höch". In Roditi, E. (Ed.), *More Dialogues on Art.* Santa Barbara: Ross-Erikson, 93–111.

Höch, H. (1993). "A Glance Over My Life". In Lavin, M., *Cut with the Kitchen Knife: The Weimar Photomontages of Hannah Höch.* New Haven: Yale University Press, 211–215.

Höch, H. (1996). "Die ersten Fotomontagen". In Höch, H., *Hannah Höch. Eine Lebenscollage (1921–1945),* vol. 2. Berlin: Hatje, 504–506.

Höch, H. (2001). "Johannes Freisel: 'Das Porträt: Hannah Höch'". See reference in Höch, H., *Hannah Höch. Eine Lebenscollage (1946–1978).* Berlin: Berlinische Galerie, 299.

Höch, H. (2010). *Hannah Höch Picture Book.* Berlin: The Green Box.

Höch, H. (2016). *Life Portrait.* Berlin: The Green Box.

Huelsenbeck, R. (2015). *Almanaque Dadá.* Madrid: Tecnos.

Kühl, S. (1991). "Hannah Höch in Berlin/Interviewed by Mildred Thompson". *Art Papers*, January–February, 10–11.

Makela, M. (1996a). "Heads of State". In Höch, H., *The Photomontages of Hannah Höch.* Minneapolis: Walker Art Center, 28.

Makela, M. (1996b). "By Design: The Early Work of Hannah Höch in Context". In Höch, H., *The Photomontages of Hannah Höch.* Minneapolis: Walker Art Center, 49–79.

Neckelmann, H. (Ed.) (2018). *Hannah Höch: "Mir die Welt geweitet." Das Adressbuch.* Berlin: Transit.

Luyken, G. (2011). "En el reino mágino de la fantasía: El Álbum ilustrado de Hannah Höch". In Höch, H., *Álbum Ilustrado.* Barcelona: Gustavo Gili.

Ohff, H. (1968). *Hannah Höch.* Berlin: Gebr. Mann Verlag.

Pérez-Fernández, A. (2021). "From Compassion to Distance: Hannah Höch's 'Mother'". *European Journal of Women's Studies.* DOI: 10.1177/13505068211028977.

Rendueles, C. et. al. (2006). *Jean Arp. Retrospectiva.* Madrid: Círculo de Bellas Artes.
Richter, H. (1997). *Dada: art and anti-art.* Singapore: Thames & Hudson.
Sheppard, R. (2000). "Dada and Politics". In Sheppard, R., *Modernism-Dada-Postmodernism.* Evanston, IL: Northwestern University Press, 304–350.
Tabernacle, K. (2014). "Distance, Proximity and Hannah Höch's Radical Imagination". *Tropos* 2(1), 2–8.

Part IV: **Gender Issues and Feminist Concepts**

Cristina Sánchez
Feminist Philosophy and Democracy: The Case of Spain

Abstract: What role can feminist philosophy play in the creation and consolidation of democracy? In its enlightened origins, feminist philosophy posed the incompleteness of democracy if women were not included as political subjects. Later, in the 20th century, authors such as Carole Pateman or Anne Phillips questioned the theoretical framework of democracy and citizenship, revealing the sexual contract, the disorder of the private sphere and the importance of a politics of presence. In this paper I present the role that feminist philosophy has played in the consolidation of democracy in Spain. Spanish feminist philosophers in the 1980s highlighted the necessary interdependence between gender equality, modernity, and democracy. To a large extent, the feminism of those years was part of an enlightened feminism of equality that argued for the extension of rights for women. Their inclusion in the political debates of the time managed to influence political institutions and set a solid related conceptual framework that was later going to converge into important legal measures.

Introduction

In 1983, Carole Pateman stated, ironically, that a feminist would not address the relationship between feminism and democracy because for feminists democracy has never existed (Pateman 1983, 204). Indeed, women have not achieved full citizenship in many countries until well into the 20th century, and even today, some rights, such as sexual and reproductive rights, are excluded from citizenship, in an androcentric understanding of the same. However, Pateman adds, feminism has something important to say to theorists of democracy about the foundations of democracy and, as a theory, represents an important challenge and critique to theories of democracy and theories of justice. We can say, in this sense, that contemporary feminist political theory redefines the most important concepts of democracy, or, in other terms, makes us rethink the very grammar of politics itself. In short, according to Anne Phillips, feminist political philosophy challenges democracy to question the core of politics: the who, what and how of democracy and citizenship (Phillips 2013). In the following pages I will briefly analyze the main challenges and proposed changes.

The Who of Citizenship

The critique of liberal democracy and citizenship has been present in feminist theory since its founding moment in the Enlightenment period. Thus, with authors such as Olympe de Gouges and Mary Wollstonecraft, we find the first critical formulations of the Enlightenment in relation to its unfulfilled promises regarding women. "And we are citizens too", demanded the French revolutionary women (Sánchez 2001), a demand that we find in all those historical moments in which democracy is reconsidered or (re-)formulated: from the Enlightenment to the establishment of democracy in Spain in the 80s, and including the current Chile, where women have achieved parity in the new constituent process. Feminist theory – and activism – thus opens up reflections on democracy and citizenship. We could say, in this sense, that there is no democracy without feminism, insofar as showing the paradoxes of citizenship and its exclusions is inherent to feminism since its enlightened origins. This presence of women in such crucial moments for democracy is indicative of something Hannah Arendt pointed out about the voice expressed by popular councils: "We want to participate, we want to discuss, we want to make our voices heard and we want to have a chance to determine the political trajectory of our country" (Arendt 1972, 232). Then, these women's voices evidence the demand for the extension of democracy, the extension of a *demos* that has been exposed as masculine and has yet to incorporate women as political subjects, as full citizens.

Feminist Theory in the 20th century has, to a great extent, questioned and responded to the bases of liberal citizenship, focusing on two fundamental axes of the same construction of the concept of citizenship: firstly, on the notion of *self* implicit in this construction, in what we can call the *ontological critique* (Sánchez 2001), and secondly, on the distinction between the public and the private sphere. Beginning with the classic social contract theories, the *self* is characterized as transcending particularities and differences. In this sense, an examination of classical contractualism reveals an uprooted and disembedded self that, as Hobbes put it, springs from the earth, like mushrooms, and suddenly comes to full maturity, without any kind of mutual commitment (Benhabib 1992, 155). Contemporary versions of the social contract, such as those of Rawls or Habermas (the Rawlsian "veil of ignorance", the Habermasian "ideal speech situations") and other epistemological resources, reveal, once again, the autonomous self *par excellence:* independent, disembodied and without a concrete narrative. The o*ntological critique* shows us the gendered subtext present in the concept of self in modern moral and political theory. The self proposed in these theories is revealed with the attributes of a male who makes a pact between his equals, his peers, and who, as Carole Pateman reminds us, makes a sexual contract – which is forged in the social contract – in order to subdue the "disorder of women", the disorder of selves embedded in nature and in concrete bodies, and to exclude women – negatively essentialized by what they are not – from the public sphere (Pateman 1990). The political pact and the moral intersubjectivity are built on what Benhabib calls a *substitutionalist universalism*, in the sense that the universalism they defend would be the ideal consensus of fictitiously defined selves, identifying the experiences of a specific group of subjects – males – as the paradigmatic case of humans as such (Benhabib 1992). Moreover, such universalism is not only substitutionalist, but also exclusionary, with respect to those other subjects who do not share the characteristics required for their inclusion in the public sphere. The issue, therefore, is not the inclusion of women within the same epistemological framework, but the exclusion of women – coupled with the blindness to emotions, the moral interactions of our daily lives and the exclusions of private matters – show us the shortcomings of that same framework (Benhabib 1992, 13). Subsequently, feminist theory has reformulated this idea of liberal autonomy, underlying the notion of citizenship, proposing a *relational autonomy* (MacKenzie and Stoljar 2000), which denies self-sufficiency and independence as the basis of citizenship. On the contrary, these authors use the term "relational" to indicate that relations of care and interdependence are morally significant, and that our preferences are also shaped by patterns of race, class, gender, and so on. The point is not to give up the idea of autonomy, but it should be a content-neutral value. In fact, in the liberal defense of autonomy, there is an identification of autonomy with values associated with masculinity. Thus, authors such as Marilyn Friedman argue that an agent can choose between different life plans: some conservative and others progressive (Friedman 2002). But the Kantian ideal of autonomy imposes a very specific, androcentric one, and rejects care, relations, interdependence, and emotions.

The What of Democracy and Citizenship

Connected to the above, feminist theory – in relation to democracy – has questioned the division between public and private spheres, which runs through all classical theories of citizenship. From the perspective of political liberalism, the private sphere is the setting for the autonomy of the individual and, consequently, for the non-interference by the state. The neutrality of the state in matters concerning private life and the good life appears as one of the basic foundations of classical liberalism. But we must remember that other paradigms of political theory, such as civic republicanism, also maintain this division between the different spheres. So, we can say that this separation is inherent to the theory of democracy itself. The result is that both the subjects traditionally located in the private sphere – women, children – and the issues assigned to this sphere – "domestic" violence, the reproduction of life, etc. – have remained on the margins of the agendas of democracy. It is precisely feminism that has brought to light issues that concern the good life, such as care and the double working day, for instance. In this sense, the concept of privacy presents a gender subtext. In the words of MacKinnon, state non-interference in the private sphere – one of the basic premises of liberal democracies – in this sense, is largely understood as non-interference in the (mis-) conduct of men: it is not the privacy of women that is protected, but rather the privacy of men (MacKinnon 2014).

Since contemporary feminist theory, however, a differentiation has been made between the *private sphere* and *privacy*. According to Seyla Benhabib, "privacy", "privacy rights" and "private sphere" include three different dimensions: First, "privacy" has been understood in its historical origin as the sphere of moral and religious conscience, impassable to power state, thus highlighting the Church-state separation. Second, and connected to the above, "privacy rights" (classical liberal rights) include economic freedoms, such as the right to property. In this context of historical modernity, "Privacy means non-interference by the State in commercial relations, and in particular, non-intervention in the labor force market" (Benhabib 1992, 91). Finally, "privacy" – and "privacy rights" – mean the sphere of intimacy (the daily necessities of life, sexuality, caring for others …). What would that sphere of non-interference be? It is here where liberal theory, at the origin of the idea of "privacy", has defended that free terrain of state regulation, centered on the autonomy of the individual and linked to freedom of thought at its origin. But in accordance with that private space for the shelter of the self and the flourishing of autonomy, there is an underlying idea of an abstract, disembodied individual, the absolute owner of his actions.

The debate within feminist theory about the value of privacy for women is complex and not without tension. Authors like Martha Nussbaum, for example, ask themselves, *Is Privacy Bad for Women?* and point out how protecting important freedoms under the rubric of "privacy" does not actually present advantages for women (Nussbaum 2000). On the contrary, she argues that what is relevant to justify state intervention is whether there has been a harm – following John Stuart Mill in this point – regardless of whether this harm has taken place in the private or public sphere. However, as other feminist authors add, it is necessary to find a concept of privacy that encompasses women's freedom, equality, bodily integrity, and self-determination. The question, therefore, for some authors (Schneider 1991), would not be to banish the idea of privacy, since this is also important for women, but to develop a more nuanced theory where privacy plays a role that enables the empowerment of women.

The How of Democracy

To explain *the how* of citizenship and democracy, I will focus on the case of women's citizenship in Spain, and the feminist debates around it, in the transition from a dictatorship to a democracy

In Spain, at the end of the 1970s, after the death of the dictator Franco in 1975, there was a process not only of economic and social modernization, but of creation and development of a modernity that had been truncated during the 40 years of the dictatorship. As such, modernity had to establish an ethical, philosophical, and legal framework of universalist principles: freedom, equality, autonomy, within the framework of a new democratic and social state. During Franco's regime, women were legally considered minors, subject to authorization by their husbands to work or to have a bank account. In 1978 the new constitution was approved, very similar to other European constitutions in terms of recognition of rights. What role did feminist philosophy play in this context of the founding of a new democratic regime? I will refer specifically to the academic feminism of the 1980s and early 1990s. This is not to say that there was not also a feminist activism that fought for the right to have rights, in Arendt's words. Since the 1970s we find a great variety of tendencies within Spanish feminism (Folguera 2007). I will focus on academic feminism, and more specifically on that feminism which was linked to philosophical reflection on citizenship and democracy, and was situated, in this sense, within a universalist framework – with all its reformulations – and within a feminism of equality.

The intra-feminist equality-difference debate permeated much of the academic debates not only in Spain, but also in other European countries, such as Italy and France. Although the feminism of difference had important manifestations in Spain, it was the feminism of equality that had the greatest impact on the political philosophy of the time. This can be explained by the need to focus on equality, strengthening and deepening democracy recently achieved in the early 1980s. The feminism of difference, on the other hand, as was happening in Italy at the time, advocated non-involvement in institutions, focusing on personal liberation outside formal politics. What did it mean to opt for a feminism of equality in this context? Far from thinking that it was a matter of accommodation in a pre-established framework, of assimilationism, the Spanish feminist philosophers in this current, proposed the transformation or "re-signification" of the public space, of that still incomplete citizenship, delving into equality as the unfinished task of an unfinished Enlightenment, and even more so in the case of Spain, given its recent history.

To understand the scope of the theoretical interventions of equality feminism at that time, we can use here the notion of *democratic iterations* put forward by Seyla Benhabib, when she explains the reconfigurations of citizenship in today's democracies: With this term, Benhabib refers to the discursive processes in which universal membership rights are renegotiated as "processes of democratic iteration", defined as "complex processes of public argument, deliberation, and learning through which universalist rights claims are contested and contextualized, invoked and revoked, throughout legal and political institutions as well as in the public sphere of liberal democracies" (Benhabib 2004, 179). She takes the term "iteration" from Derrida, who used it in the philosophy of language to indicate that

> in the process of repeating a term or a concept, we never simply reproduce the original first use: each repetition is a form of variation. Each iteration transforms the meaning by adding things that enrich it. Reiteration is the re-appropriation of the "origin"; it is at the same time its dissolution as "the original" and its preservation through its continuous deployment. Each act of iteration involves making sense of an authoritative original in a new and different context. (Benhabib 2004, 180)

Similarly, Spanish feminists for equality took the normative framework of the Enlightenment, re-signifying the very idea of equality and rights, raising new issues on the public-political agenda, such as abortion, and negotiating, in short, not only the *who* and *what* of citizenship, but also the *how* of citizenship, through the inclusion of women in Parliament.

Philosophical Interventions: Celia Amorós, Philosophy and Democracy

In this context of re-signifying the grammar of politics in Spain, I am going to focus on the figure of the philosopher Celia Amorós, one of the most prominent feminist philosophers, and whose philosophical analyses were highly influential in the formulation of a democratic and modern notion of citizenship not only in Spain, but also in Latin America (Femenías 2010). I will highlight here some of her ideas that have been most influential in the development of equality feminism in Spain and in the achievement of relevant laws for women's citizenship. This is not to say that there have not been other women philosophers who have made relevant contributions to this debate, such as Victoria Camps and her proposal for an ethics of care or Fina Birulés, in Barcelona, analyzing the memory of women philosophers in a context of a lack of tradition, of "lack of a legacy", in Hannah Arendt words.[1]

Moving to Celia Amorós work, we have to highlight, firstly, that she proposes a deconstruction of the patriarchal reason that permeates all philosophy, understanding this deconstruction as a political task: "Feminism is political to its very core, it is an 'irrazionalization' of relations of power [...] Feminism is automatically political due to the simple fact that it challenges the definition of politics as laid down by those who divide and define spaces, that is, by those who hold the power" (Amorós 2000, 12, Translation CS). Her book *Toward a Critic of Patriarchal Reason* (Amorós 1985), so important for feminist philosophy in Spain, begins with a re-reading of the history of philosophy, a re-reading of the philosophical canon. But as she says, it is not a question of finding the "misogynist pearls" present in so many philosophers, but rather of analyzing how there has been a patriarchal legitimation of the exclusion of women as political subjects. As another of the important Spanish philosophers of equality of that period points out, Amelia Valcárcel, Amorós' interest was "to seek the mode of construction of universals, and to find the template of patriarchal origin" (Valcárcel 2010, 260, Translation CS). Therefore, while men have been attributed autonomy and individuation, women have been labeled as "the identical", as an undifferentiated group, each woman replaceable by another, because they are identical in their essentialism. Thus, denying them not only autonomy, but the very capacity to be subjects. And without a subject, there is no autonomy. Women, Amorós says, have been "heterodesignated", without being able to "name" themselves, without being able to "self-designate" (Amorós 1987). In this critical exercise, Amorós explores those *veins of Enlightenment* that we can find in authors who demand an "enlightenment of Enlightenment". Unveiling the false universalism of the Enlightenment – the *substitute universalism* in Seyla Benhabib's terms – but without giving up on modernity, the universalist promise of democracy, is the critical task she undertakes.

In the second place, she herself defines her position as a *philosophical feminism*, not a "feminist philosophy", thus emphasizing feminism as theory, as claim and critique, which produces reflexive effects on the philosophical endeavor itself. Feminist theory is, in this sense, conceived as Critical Theory. Taking the original meaning of the word "Theoría" – to make visible" – feminism, for Celia Amorós, "makes visible" socio-political phenomena of inequality that would other-

---

[1] In the Preface of her book *Between Past and Future*, Arendt takes up the words of the French poet René Char: "Our inheritance was left to us by no testament" (Arendt & Kohn 2006, 4). In this sense, Birulés points out in her work the difficulties of feminist philosophers when it comes to establishing genealogies and interpretations in which to recognize this testament (Birules 2003).

wise go unnoticed (Amorós 2005, 427, Translation CS). And in the same way, she "makes us see" the irrationality of the philosophical construction of the contemporary subject, as an abstract, independent, autonomous subject, as a "generalised Other", instead of a "concrete other", using Benhabib's terminology (Benhabib). For Amorós, this task of "making people see" means a task of conceptualizing, and, as she maintains repeatedly throughout her work, "to conceptualise is to politicise" (Amorós 2005, Translation CS).[2] According to this goal, the feminist perspective takes the form of producing epistemological crises of philosophical foundation and, on another level, crises of legitimization of the social and political order. In short, by means of this conceptualization, of "making visible" inequalities and subordinations, feminist theory, as a critical theory of society, leads to a theory of social change.

Thirdly, and linked to the political debate that was very present in Europe in the 1990s, Celia Amorós intervened in the debate on *parity democracy*, to achieve legislative changes in this terrain.[3] Once again, here we find the feminist goal of irrationalizing the male monopoly of power, questioning the main core of democracy, such as the principle of representation. The foundational wound of democracies – the exclusion of certain subjects, betraying universalism – can only be restored through equality and mutual recognition in the social contract. As Anne Phillips points out, the "politics of presence", as opposed to the traditional "politics of ideas", is necessary in deliberative democracy to incorporate the experiences of other subjects and therefore new issues on the public agenda (Phillips 1995). The intense debate in Spain about parity democracy, where academic equality feminism, the presence of a socialist government in power, and the extension of institutionalized feminism in official equality bodies coincided, led to important advances on this issue. Subsequently, in the 2000s, this idea of parity democracy was extended in Spain by means of mandatory regulations to all spheres of power: not only at Parliament, but also to other spheres of decision-making, such as the universities and other public institutions. Again, as we saw at the beginning of these pages, the who, what and how of democracy are very relevant questions for feminism. Celia Amorós, in this sense, points out:

---

[2] This is one of Amorós' most repeated ideas, from which he advocates a nominalist theory of patriarchy.

[3] The debate began in Europe in the early 1990s. In 1992, the first "European Summit of Women in Power" was held in Athens. The *Athens Declaration* was signed by 20 women political leaders, denouncing the "democratic deficit" in all public and political decision-making authorities and bodies at every level – local, regional, national, and European. The Declaration demanded equality of participation by women and men in public and political decision-making. Celia Amorós attended the summit as a speaker.

I believe that feminist discourse today has a very important task: to clarify what democracy is: it must have a whole battery of questions to pass a test of democracy to all types of regimes. Feminism and democracy were born out of the same birth, and now that democracy is in such a difficult situation in some areas because of intransigence and in others because of indifference, the position of women is the ultimate test of democracy. (León Hernández and Amorós 2008, 202, Translation CS)

New Challenges

At the end of the 1990s, and already in the year 2000, Spain passed important laws concerning equality and gender-based violence. 30 years have passed now since those philosophical formulations that I have presented here. In these years, new issues have been incorporated into the feminist debate in Spain, many of them linked to the political performativity of desire, but others also linked to a capitalist horizon of vulnerability and extreme precariousness. There have been ruptures and bitter debates, but over and above these confrontational debates, I would like to highlight a new scenario that directly threatens democracy and women's citizenship: the emergence on the political scene of extreme right-wing parties that have an anti-feminist agenda in their programs. Some of them are already in government in other countries: Hungary, Poland, Brazil... In Spain, the extreme right-wing party Vox is already governing in coalition in regions such as Andalusia and Madrid. They implement, in some places successfully, a real patriarchal counter-reform, carrying out gender violence and denialist political practices, conducting an anti-feminist agenda and hate speech, attacking, in short, the hard-won citizenship.

At the same time, the economic crisis has aggravated the loss of social rights. The situation of women citizens in Southern Europe, traditionally responsible for care work, suffers from the lack of public resources. The introduction of care as a central pillar of citizenship is a demand that is gaining more and more strength. On the other hand, the increase in violence against women during the pandemic lockdown shows the persistence of a patriarchal system that refuses to give up its power. Therefore, social citizenship, care and violence appear as urgent tasks for women's full citizenship. In Nancy Fraser's terms, issues of recognition, redistribution and participation remain the pillars of feminist demands (Fraser 2009). In this sense, we can conclude, in accordance with the link between feminism and democracy that I have been maintaining in these pages, that when women lose, democracy loses.

References

Amorós, C. (1985). *Hacia una Crítica de la razón patriarcal.* Barcelona: Anthropos.
Amorós, C. (1987). "Espacio de los iguales, espacio de las idénticas. Notas sobre poder y principio de individuación". *Arbor* 128, 113–127.
Amorós, C. (Ed.) (2000). *Feminismo y Filosofía.* Madrid: Síntesis.
Amorós, C. (2005). *La gran diferencia y sus pequeñas consecuencias.* Valencia: Cátedra.
Arendt, H. (1972). *Crises of the Republic.* New York: Harcourt Brace.
Arendt, H., and Kohn, J. (2006). *Between past and future.* New York: Penguin.
Benhabib, S. (1992). "Models of Public Space. Hannah Arendt, The Liberal Tradition and Jürgen Habermas". In Calhoun, C. (Ed.), *Habermas and the Public Sphere.* Cambridge, MA: MIT Press.
Benhabib, S. (2004). *The Rights of Others, Aliens, Residents and Citizens.* Cambridge: Cambridge University Press.
Birulés, F. (2003). "La memoria de la muchacha tracia: Mujeres y Filosofía". *Clepsydra: Revista de Estudios de Género y Teoría Feminista* 2, 7–12.
Femenías, M. L. (2010). "Celia Amorós en América Latina: El desafío de su pensamiento". In López Fernández Cao, M. and Posada Kubissa, L. (Eds.), *Pensar con Celia Amorós.* Madrid: Fundamentos, 55–64.
Folguera, P. (Ed.) (2007). *El feminismo en España: Dos siglos de Historia.* Madrid: Fundación Pablo Iglesias.
Fraser, N. (2009). *Scales of Justice: Reimagining Political Space in a Globalizing World.* New York: Cambridge University Press.
Friedman, M. (2002). *Autonomy, Gender, Politics.* New York: Oxford University Press.
León Hernández, L. S. and Amorós, C. (2008). "El feminismo filosófico en España: Entrevista a Celia Amorós". *Isegoría. Revista de Filosofía Moral y Política* 38, 197–203.
Mackenzie, C. and Stoljar, N. (Eds.) (2000). *Relational Autonomy. Feminist Perspectives on Autonomy, Agency, and the Social Self.* New York: Oxford University Press.
MacKinnon, C. (2014). *Feminism Unmodified. Discourses on Life and Law.* Cambridge, MA: Harvard University Press.
Nussbaum, M. (2000). "Is Privacy Bad for Women?" *Boston Review*, 1 April.
Pateman, C. (1983). "Feminism and Democracy". In Duncan, G. (Ed.), *Democratic Theory and Practice.* Cambridge: Cambridge University Press.
Pateman, C. (1990). *The Disorder of Women: Democracy, Feminism and Political Theory.* Stanford: Standford University Press.
Phillips, A. (1995). *The Politics of Presence.* New York: Oxford University Press.
Phillips, A. (2013). *Engendering Democracy.* New York: Polity Press.
Sánchez, C. (2001). "Genealogía de la vindicación". In Beltrán, E. and Maquieira, V. (Eds.), *Femismos. Debates teóricos contemporáneos.* Madrid: Alianza Editorial, 17–73.
Schneider, E. (1991). "The Violence of Privacy". *Conneticut Law Review* 23, 973–999.
Valcárcel, A. (2010). "Celia Amorós, filósofa". In López Fernández Cao, M. and Posada Kubissa, L. (Eds.), *Pensar con Celia Amorós.* Madrid: Fundamentos.

Diana María Acevedo-Zapata and María Lucía Rivera-Sanín

Gender Equality in Colombia's Philosophy Programs: Faculty Participation

Abstract: Professional philosophy has traditionally been a highly masculinized field. Studies have been done in various countries about gender equality in the field, showing that in academic philosophy, as opposed to what happens in other humanities and social sciences, there has been no significant progress toward equality in terms of the participation of women in teaching and research positions. In the Colombian case, there is no information about women's participation in philosophical academia. This study offers a descriptive analysis of women's participation in philosophy programs in Colombia, showing that we are still a long way from gender equality in the field (24.8%). The main objective is to contribute to an understanding of gender inequality in higher education in philosophy in Colombia, in terms of teaching positions occupied by women.

Introduction

Professional philosophy has traditionally been a highly masculinized field. Studies on gender equality in academia in English speaking countries have shown that academic philosophy – contrary to what happens in other fields within the humanities and social sciences – has not significantly advanced towards gender equality in faculty and research positions. In Colombia, although research exists on gender inequality in fields such as sociology and engineering, there have been no studies or publications on women's participation in academic philosophy or on other inequalities. This paper offers a descriptive analysis of female participation in faculties with philosophy programs in higher education in Colombia. The main conclusion is that women are far from having equal participation in faculty and research positions. The goal of the paper is to contribute to the characterization of gender inequality in academic philosophy in Colombia, specifically with regard to female professors and researchers.

Gender Inequality in Higher Education

The *World Atlas for Gender Inequality* published by UNESCO (2012) reports that the number of women in the highest levels of education in every area of knowledge,

i. e., Ph. D. programs and research positions, tend to progressively decrease from the numbers at the undergraduate level. This is a trend in the majority of the 90 countries in the study, except for Latin-American countries, where a larger participation of women in Ph. D. programs can be observed in comparison with other regions of the world.[1] According to UNESCO (2012), the gender gap among students deepens for women in faculty positions and hired researchers in higher education institutions: 71% of male participation against 29% of female participation. In Colombia, the relation fluctuates between 35% and 45% of women in research positions. Although this puts the country above the average of the analyzed countries, women's participation is still far from equal. Specific information on different areas of study and work is needed.

UNESCO's report includes differentiated information regarding life-sciences, social sciences, behavioral sciences, journalism and information, business, management, and law, but it does not show differences among disciplines within the same area. Generally speaking, female participation is closer to equality in life-sciences, social sciences, law, and business, and a larger gap is shown in basic sciences and engineering. However, there is no data on female participation in the academic philosophy in faculty and research positions. It is important to highlight that the reported numbers relating to different areas may not give an adequate account on gender disparities among the disciplines within them. The representation – or overrepresentation, of women in a discipline within an area may give the wrong idea about the general equality of the distribution among disciplines. For example, within the social sciences, particularly in areas such as sociology, the presence of research topics led by female academics such as critical feminist studies, gender and sexuality theories, or ethics of care can increase the percentages of women in the general area, hiding the disparities within other disciplines such as philosophy, included in it.

Studies done in the United States, Canada and Australia have shown that, contrary to what happens in humanities and social sciences such as literature, history, and sociology – and even STEM areas – gender equality among philosophy programs has not advanced at the same rate in the last four decades (see Hutchinson and Jenkins 2013; Haslanger 2008). Reports by the Australian Association of Philosophy (AAP), the American Philosophical Association (APA), and the Canadian Philosophical Association (CPA) stated a participation of women of 28%, 21%, and 21% in 2008–2009. More recent data show that the proportion of women professors in

---

[1] "Women receive more bachelors degrees than men in three of the five regions and more masters degrees in two. When it comes to Ph. D.s, however, men have an advantage in all regions. One interesting region is Latin America and the Caribbean, which is the only region where women participate at a higher rate in Ph. D. programs than in masters programs" (UNESCO 2012, 80).

philosophy in the United States is close to 24% (Schwitzgebel and Dicey 2016), along with 29% of recently graduated Ph. D.s. The 2016 report shows that, when comparing data from 1970 and 2010, an important increase in female participation can be seen; however, it also shows that growth has slowed down since the 1990s.

There are no earlier documents than this that show the gender disparity in philosophy in Colombia, nor are there any other previous studies which offer a critical approximation to the disparity in the discipline in Colombia. In other areas such as sociology and engineering (Arango 2006), there are some efforts to diagnose the issue and discuss it. The absence of such a study in philosophy, in hand with the scarce acknowledgment of the problem, has an impact toward the continuation of this disparity.

Conditions of Inequality

A frequent explanation for the low participation of women in faculty and research positions in university alludes to the relatively recent inclusion of women in academia. It would appear that the 25 centuries' inertia of masculine exclusiveness in academia takes more than a few decades to turn around. Even if it feels late and pending, equality is, without a doubt, coming, and it has already made enormous leaps.[2]

There is a alarming naivety in assuming that inequality is simply the result of a premature diagnosis of an otherwise well-driven process, and in tacitly admitting that at least 50 more years would be necessary to achieve gender equality in academic circles. A comfortable skepticism about the existence of barriers for access and permanence in academic life presented to women and other historically marginalized groups, works not only to hide the causes of historical and current inequalities, but also to uphold the conditions which perpetuate it. This attitude feeds off on the typically neoliberal ideas of academic merit and hard work as the only conditions for success. It also seems to depend on the belief – questionable and worthy of constant review – in the historical non-existence of female philosophers, and their lack of relevance in the setting of a philosophical canon.

---

[2] We have found it both surprising and worrisome that in informal conversations and in public discussion forums the question about why equality in academic philosophy would be desirable seems to arise with frequency. On more than one occasion, male colleagues have asked us if it is not too excessive to demand (or expect) 50% of women faculty and research positions. This experience suggests the necessity to design qualitative research about perceptions and representations of women, and other minority groups in academic philosophy.

Implicit Bias and Epistemic Injustice

In addition to the historical and institutional conditions that give way to gender inequality in faculty positions in philosophy programs, it is important to ask which other elements are at play in order to understand it. On one hand, the archetypal figure of the *philosopher, professor,* and *researcher,* is loaded with a masculinist bias that might have an impact on the participation of women philosophers, or discourage women from beginning or continuing an academic career in philosophy.[3] For example, if the general idea of how a philosopher should look like is the image of a mature white male, this might cause women and other people who do not fit this stereotype to find it difficult to identify or imagine themselves in that role. It might also implicitly lead to the idea that bodies and subjectivities that do not fit in must be exceptions, anomalies, or rarities. In other words, the notion that philosophy and philosophers are mostly or normally white males becomes natural and normalized. Correspondingly, this will not only discourage those who traditionally have not been part of the field from participating and demanding equality, but also this creates hostility, pressure, and unconscious threats upon non-hegemonic groups.

Gender stereotypes may also have an impact on the genderization of certain topics of research within philosophy. Schwitzgebel and Dicey's (2016) research for the Committee on the Status of Women for the APA showed that the proportion of women philosophers was larger – although still not close to equal – in areas such as ethics and value theory, whereas in other areas such as logics, metaphysics, and epistemology, the gap was wider. If curricula and research topics privilege some methods or topics where there is a lower participation of women, the gender gap can be perpetuated or even deepened. Similarly, the idea that there is a single way or a best method for doing philosophical work gives way to hostilities toward what is perceived as feminine or feminized ways of philosophizing.[4]

Some studies in the United States about representations and unconscious associations of ideas related to the words "philosopher" and "philosophy" have

---

[3] Future research will seek to determine the number of female graduate philosophers in philosophy programs who practice or take advanced studies in other disciplines or fields, as well as the number of women in graduate philosophy programs who come from other areas.

[4] Statistics from the members of the Colombian Network of Women Philosophers show that about 50% of the close to 300 members state an interest in feminist philosophy, which is considered "less philosophical" in highly conservative academies. Further research will seek the relationship between declared interests and the curricula form undergraduate and graduate programs, research projects recognized and financed by MinCiencias, and publications on specialized journals and academic publishers.

shown that both men and women associate the practice of philosophy to a male archetype (see Brownstein and Saul 2016). The construction of stereotypes regarding philosophical practice not only encourages a tendency to undermine or ignore the contributions and participation of female philosophers in highly masculine contexts, but it also encourages a form of the "stereotype threat" (Bronwstein and Saul 2016) that perpetuates the negative bias against women who produce such contributions.

In circumstances in which there is much at stake, for example, during a job interview, in public speaking, or during thesis defenses – which can be part of the process for hiring faculty –, women, as a minority, hold the additional burden of becoming unwilling spokespersons for their gender. For instance, if a candidate cries or raises her voice during a debate, she will not only be judged as hysterical-irrational person – not suited for academic discussion –, but she will be taken as proof that women, in general, are not capable of rational debate. Hiring processes generally include interviews and oral presentations, aside from a review of CV and relevant work, and in these contexts, there might be an important impact from implicit bias on part of interviewers and participants. This might account for a lower number of women being hired in faculty positions.

Research on structural oppression (Young 1990), epistemic injustice (Fricker 2007; Brownstein and Saul 2016; Cely 2019), and sociolinguistics (Coates 2004) reveal that women are often perceived as having less "epistemic authority" or credibility when they participate in masculinized contexts. In these contexts, discursive practices and gender performativities are established and normalized. A high-pitched voice, for example, or a lack of disposition for discussions as a type of combat, tends to be interpreted as lack of mastery of a subject, or to a poor handling of the classroom.[5] Additionally, negative bias relating to class, race, sexual orientation, or functional diversity might decrease the chances that interlocution by members of marginalized groups are considered as valid or of the same quality as those from hegemonic voices.

Imagining the possibilities of philosophy only through the lens of the masculinist hegemony regarding methods and ways to practice and teach philosophy can also make interdisciplinary, non-Western, or just non-canonical proposals be undervalued or disregarded in competitive settings, such as grant proposals, and hiring processes.

---

5 In addition, there is a gendered double standard for performing a debate, so that different adjectives describe the same action in men and women: when a man raises his voice in the middle of a discussion, he is regarded as vehement and deliberate, but when a woman raises her voice, she is irritable and irrational. This also applies to what is considered a sign of a good disposition for debate (see Coates 2004).

At the core of the matter is the use of merit as a supreme standard for evaluation, and understood as a neutral category, impervious to the structural conditions of inequality and the subjective conditions of evaluation which inevitably make part of hiring processes. Although merit as criterion for selection stems from an interest to counteract unfair systems for distributing benefits and honors – in which arbitrariness such as family, or friendship would give an unfair advantage –, a meritocracy that barely sees oppressive structures becomes, at best, insufficient in terms of justice. In addition, insisting that unconsciously biased evaluations are objective and neutral also gives way to a decrease in the epistemic confidence of women participate on selection and hiring processes, thus, and can prevent their further participation on future evaluation scenarios.

To analyze gender disparity in academic philosophy is relevant not only as a resource for wider discussions on the global status of philosophical education, but also because it raises questions about equality and inclusion in higher education in Colombia and Latin America. This is important because, as Luz Gabriela Arango puts it: "in contemporary societies, the distribution of educational oportunities is one of the most significant manifestations of the state of social and gender inequalities" (Arango 2006, 13, Translation DMAZ & MLRS). As part of the humanities, philosophy has traditionally held a privileged place in the construction of critical reflections and conceptual frameworks to address issues such as justice, power relations, the protection of democracy, and the defense of human rights. From this privileged standpoint, it is important that contributions to the construction of a fair society include a constant and thorough exercise of self-reflection. It also needs to include questions about gender equality in the field, the real possibilities for women of access to a disciplinary education, the conditions for their permanence and academic success, and participation in positions of power, recognition, and decision-making.

It is fundamental to diagnose and characterize the Colombian philosophical community, to evaluate the status of the discipline in terms of gender equality and set inclusive guidelines on the different levels of philosophical practice and academic life. We recognize that it is not enough to examine whether women are present in philosophy programs in some universities. It is imperative that research like this give way to studies on feminine representation and academic women, and on gender relations in academic spaces from an intersectional perspective, considering not only gender, but also race, class, sexual orientation, functional diversity, among others. As stated by Buquet, "one of the most efficient ways of building equality within institutions and combating discrimination is to study their magnitude, their insistence, their reasons, their forms, their incidence and their definitions" (Buquet, et al. 2001, 9, Translation DMAZ & MLRS).

This report is an initial approach to the inquiry about participation conditions, representation, gender relations, and impact on women philosophers in Colombian academy. As opening questions of a wider research, we take on the following: What is the proportion of women in faculty positions in Higher Education Institutions (HEI) that offer philosophy programs in Colombia? What is the distribution of women philosophers who work in philosophy programs in Colombia? How does academic philosophy as a field in Colombia compare to the data offered by UNESCO?

Methodology

A descriptive study based on data obtained directly from academic programs in philosophy in Colombia collected on three sources: (1) the National Information System of Higher Education (SNIES for its name in Spanish) of the National Education Department of Colombia (MEN, for its name in Spanish);[6] (2) the institutional webpages of the philosophy programs; (3) direct requests for public information via e-mail to directors and heads of departments offering philosophy programs.

To verify the information in webpages, letters were sent requesting confirmation or updates on the information available, assuring a discretionary use of data and privacy of names, contacts, and sensible information of participants. Public and private HEIs were included in the study, as well as programs in disciplinary philosophy, pedagogical philosophy, mixed programs, and interdisciplinary programs such as philosophy and arts, and philosophy and humanities.

The observation window is the second semester of 2018. The sample consists of people working in in 34 HEIs, from a total of 37 HEIs which offer philosophy programs in Colombia. This amounts to 91% of the programs in the country. A descriptive analysis was done with absolute and relative frequencies (Software: LibreOfficeCalc and Jasp) for the distribution of female and male population hired in programs, according to the following categories: City of the HEI; Type of HEI (public/private); Size of faculty (20 professors or larger, between 10 and 19 professors, 9 professors or smaller); Religious affiliation of the HEI (religious/secular); Type of undergraduate program offered (pedagogical philosophy, disciplinary philosophy, or both); Highest degree offered (Ph. D., masters, specialization, bachelors). It was not considered as variable whether the dedication of teaching hours is exclusively for philosophy programs, or professors have lectures and courses assigned

---

[6] Available online at https://www.mineducacion.gov.co/sistemasinfo/SNIES/ (last accessed 8 December 2022).

in other academic programs of the HEIs. This is because there is no available information regarding this matter that would make it possible to analyze differences between exclusivity and other types of assignment. There is also no available information regarding types of hiring (tenure, full-time, half-time, per-lecture) nor terms of hiring (regular or permanent), except for public universities.[7]

Among the considered HEIs, 15 are public institutions (44%), and 19 are private institutions (56%). 17 HEIs are based in Bogota (50%), 15 offer their programs across different regions of the country (44.2%), and 2 HEIs offer online programs (5.8%). Among HEIs based in Bogota, 2 are public, which corresponds to 11.8% of the offer in the city; whereas 15 of 17 HEIs are private, which corresponds to 88.3%. 15 public HEIs are distributed across the country in 13 departments, with 1 HEI each, except for Bogota where 2 are located (see Figure 1). The remaining public HEI offers online and distance programs. From 19 private HEIs, 15 (79%) are in Bogota, 2 in Antioquia, and 1 in Barranquilla. The remaining private HEI offers online programs.

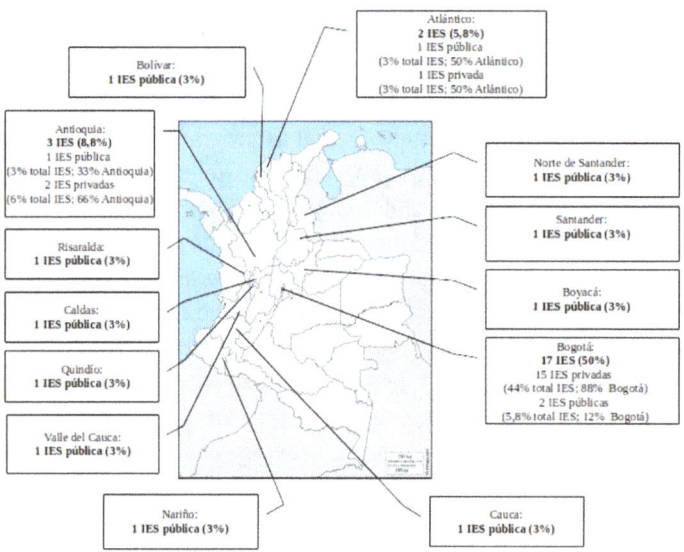

Figure 1: Distribution of HEIs in Colombia that offer philosophy programs.

---

[7] Further research will focus on hiring conditions of women philosophers, taking account of salary gap, job stability, promotion possibilities, and so forth.

Results

In 34 institutions that offer philosophy programs a total of 611 people is reported to be hired in faculty and research positions; 459 are men, and 152 are women (see Figure 2). These numbers correspond to: 75.12% of male professors, in contrast to 24.88% of female professors in philosophy programs in Colombia (see Figure 3). This indicates that the percentage of female professors hired by HEIs that offer philosophy programs in Colombia is below the global percentage of female professors and researchers in related areas (i. e., 71% men against 29% women), and also below the general percentage of hired women professors in Colombia, which fluctuates between 35% and 45% (UNESCO 2012). Compared to the numbers in the United States and Canada, the proportion of female philosophers is similar in Colombia.

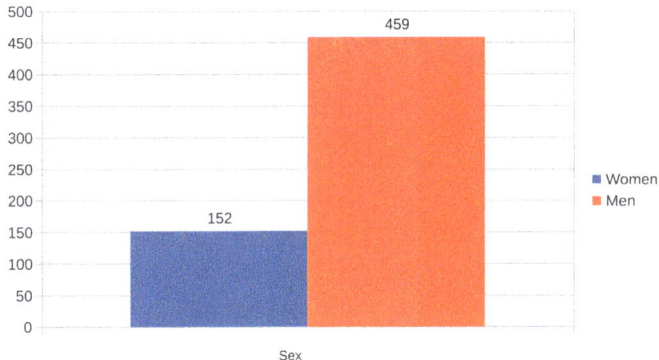

Figure 2: Total of female and male professors hired by HEIs that offer philosophy programs in Colombia.

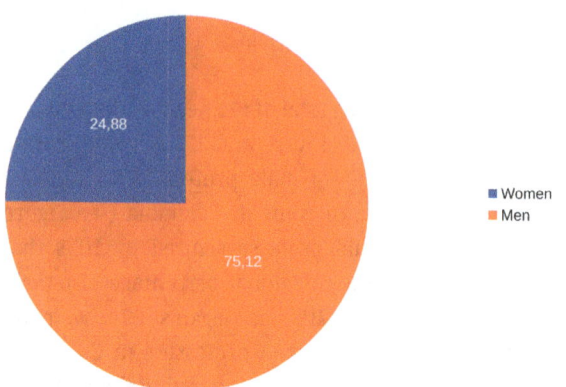

Figure 3: Percentages of female and male professors hired by HEIs that offer philosophy programs in Colombia.

It was reported that 50% of the programs are located in Bogota (17 programs) and the number of hired people in this city (279) is close to the number of hired people outside Bogota (332). This shows that 46% of the total of faculty positions are in Bogota, whereas 54% are in other cities. When considering the number of hired women according to their location, something similar can be seen: The number of hired women in Bogota (70) is closed to the total number of hired women in other cities (82). Out of 152 hired women in philosophy programs in Colombia, 46% are in Bogota, and 54% in other parts of the country. Although Bogota has a large number of programs and also a high number of hired women (46% in both cases), when percentages of women professors are displayed according to location, it can be observed that (see Figure 4) Bogota is not among the most equal averages, which happens to be occupied by HEIs located in Rionegro, Barranquilla and Bucaramanga.

Out of 611 people working on philosophy programs in Colombia, 325 (53.2%) work in public HEIs and 286 (46.8%) work in private HEIs. In public HEIs there are 254 male professors (78.15%), in contrast to 71 female professors (21.85%), while in private HEIs there are 205 male professors (71.68%), and 81 female professors (28.32%) (see Figures 6, 7 and 8).

In terms of female distribution according to the type of HEI (see Figure 5), data show that out of 152 hired women in philosophy programs in Colombia, 81 (53.29%) work in private HEIs, in contrast to 71 women (46.71%) who work in public HEIs.

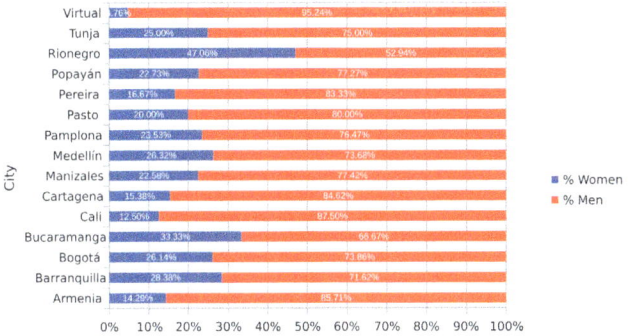

Figure 4: Female and male professors' percentage according to HEI's cities.

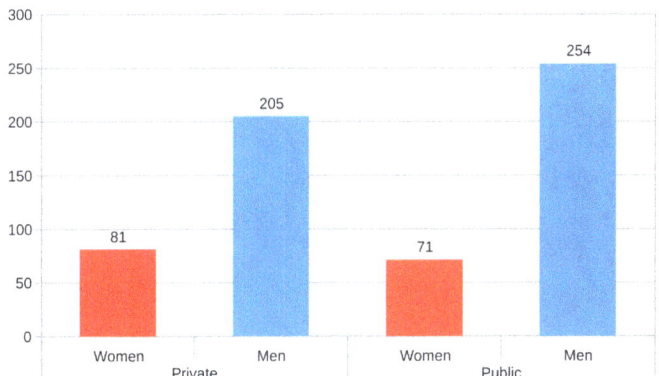

Figure 5: Number of female and male professors in philosophy programs according to the type of HEIs.

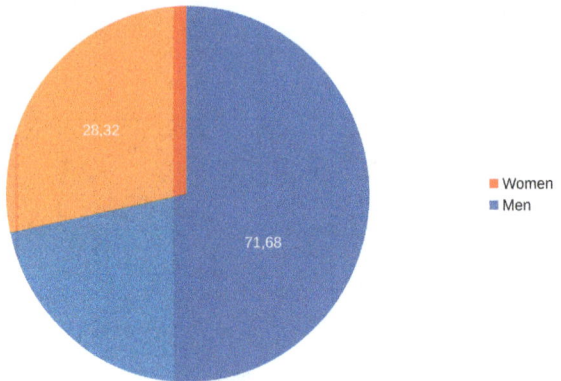

Figure 6: Percentage of female and male professors in private HEIs.

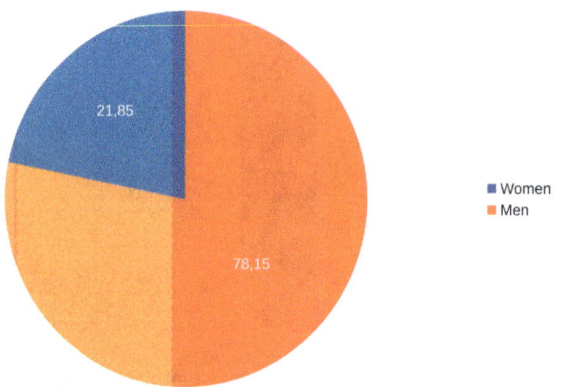

Figure 7: Percentage of female and male professors in public HEIs.

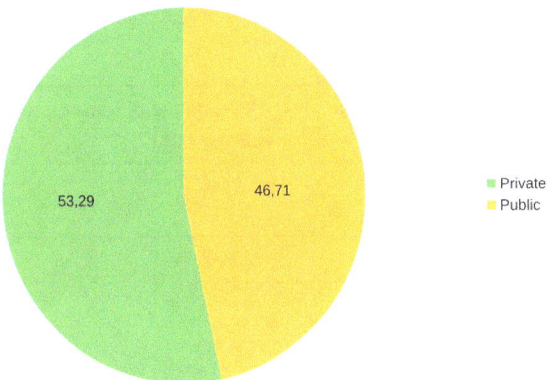

Figure 8: Distribution of female professors according to the type of HEI (public/private).

In order to organize the data according to the hired female professors' percentages in HEIs we set up the following Table 1.

Table 1: Percentages of male and female professors in HEIs offering philosophy programs in Colombia

HEI	Percentage of male professors (%)	Percentage of female professors (%)
Universidad Católica del Oriente	52.94	47.06
Universidad del Norte	53.33	46.67
Universidad Pedagógica Nacional	54.17	45.83
Uniagustiniana	57.14	42.86
Universidad del Rosario	58.33	41.67
Universidad de San Buenaventura	60.00	40.00
Universidad de la Sabana	62.50	37.50
Universidad Industrial de Santander	66.67	33.33
Universidad Santo Tomás	69.23	30.77
Universidad El Bosque	69.23	30.77
Universidad de la Salle	69.57	30.43
Universidad de Antioquia	71.43	28.57
Universidad de los Andes	71.43	28.57

Table 1: Percentages of male and female professors in HEIs offering philosophy programs in Colombia *(Continued)*

HEI	Percentage of male professors (%)	Percentage of female professors (%)
Universidad Tecnológica y Pedagógica de Colombia	75.00	25.00
Universidad Externado de Colombia	75.00	25.00
Universidad de Pamplona	76.47	23.53
Universidad del Cauca	77.27	22.73
Pontificia Universidad Javeriana	77.27	22.73
Universidad de Caldas	77.42	22.58
Universidad de Nariño	80.00	20.00
Universidad Pontificia Bolivariana	80.00	20.00
Universidad Católica Luis Amigó	81.82	18.18
Universidad del Atlántico	82.61	17.39
Universidad Sergio Arboleda	83.33	16.67
Universidad Tecnológica de Pereira	83.33	16.67
Fundación Universitaria Autónoma de Colombia	83.33	16.67
Uniminuto	84.21	15.79
Universidad de Cartagena	84.62	15.38
Universidad de Quindío	85.71	14.29
Universidad del Valle	87.50	12.50
Universidad Libre	92.86	7.14
Universidad Nacional Abierta y a Distancia	93.33	6.67
Universidad Nacional de Colombia	94.12	5.88
Fundación Universitaria Católica del Norte	100.00	0.00

Table 1 shows that 15 HEIs are above the global average (24.88%), 11 HEIs (32% of 34 HEIs that report data) have a percentage of hired women above 30%; whereas 6 universities (17%) are above 40%, and the 3 universities closest to gender equality (8%) are above 45%.

Out of 34 HEIs, 12 are religious institutions (35%), and 22 are secular institutions (65%), which include all public HEIs.

Out of 152 people that teach in religious HEIs, 47 are women, which corresponds to a proportion of 30.92%. Out of 459 people hired to teach in secular HEIs, 105 are women, which corresponds to 22.88% (see Figure 9).

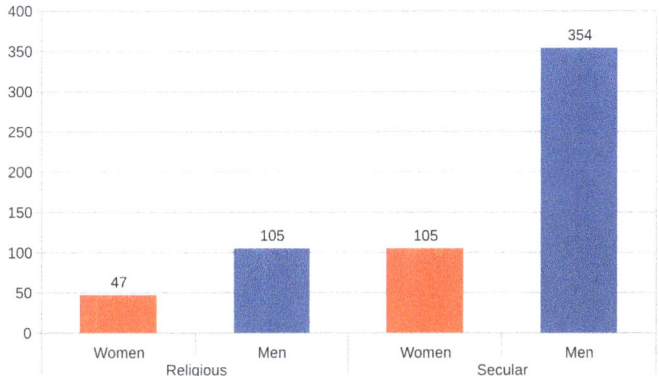

Figure 9: Number of female and male professors in HEIs according to its religious affiliation.

While 75% of religious-driven HEIs (9 out of 12) surpass 20% of women in their faculties, only 54% in secular HEIs (12 out of 22) surpass this percentage.

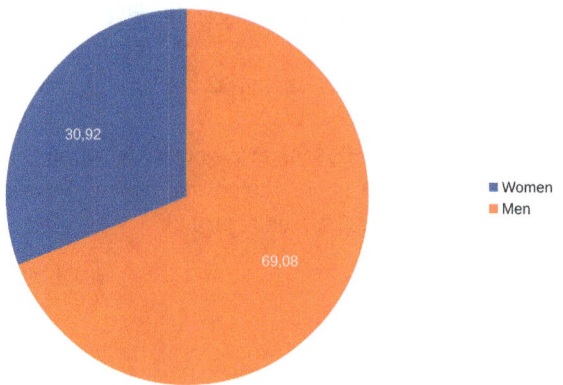

Figure 10: Percentage of male and female professors in religious HEIs.

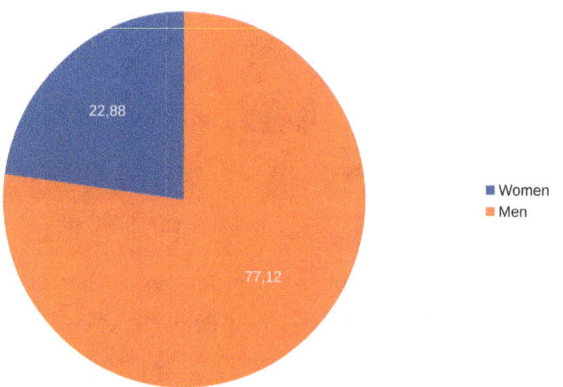

Figure 11: Percentage of male and female professors in secular HEIs.

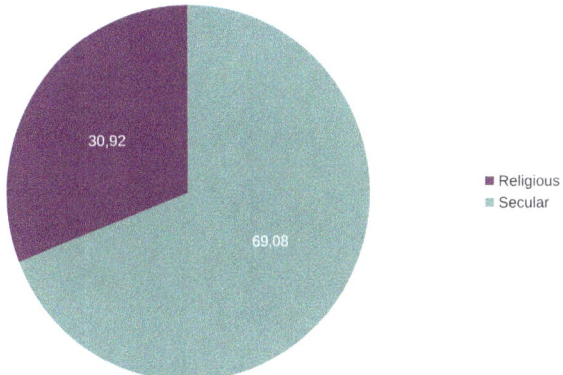

Figure 12: Distribution of female professors in religious and secular HEIs.

In general terms, religious HEIs have a superior percentage of female professors (30.92%) in contrast to the secular HEIs' percentage (22.88%). Religious HEIs are also above the global average of women in philosophy programs (24.88%) (see Figures 10, 11 and 12).

The χ^2 test (p= 0.047) indicates that it is probable that religious filiation in HEIs is related to the number of hired women. Further research is required to determine the causes of such co-relation.

According to SNIES, the country has 48 active undergraduate programs and 32 graduate programs. The offered undergraduate degrees can be divided into two general categories: pedagogical philosophy and disciplinary philosophy. Some universities offer both undergraduate degrees.

According to the offered academic program, the 34 HEIs are distributed as follows: 15 (44%) offer philosophy undergraduate studies, 8 (23%) offer pedagogical philosophy undergraduate studies, and 11 (33%) offer both.

Out of 12 HEIs that declared themselves religious, 4 (33%) offer undergraduate programs in philosophy, 4 (33%) offer pedagogical philosophy, and 4 (33%) offer both. Among 22 HEIs that declared themselves secular, 11 (50%) offer undergraduate philosophy, 4 (18%) offer pedagogical philosophy, and 7 (32%) offer both (see Figure 13).

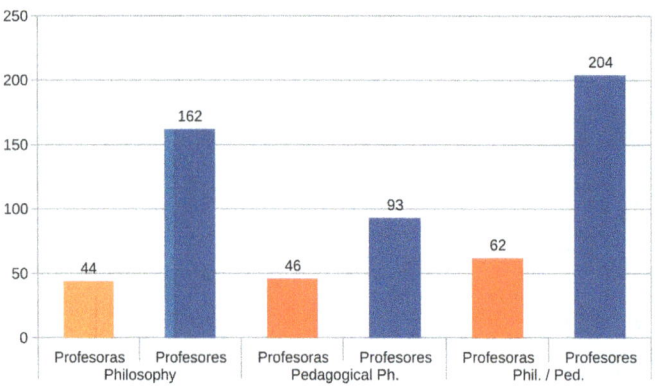

Figure 13: Number of hired female and male professors according to the type of undergraduate program (philosophy, pedagogical philosophy, both programs).

Out of 15 HEIs which offer undergraduate philosophy programs, only 1 offers an interdisciplinary program in philosophy and arts (Universidad de la Salle). Out of 206 people hired in disciplinary philosophy programs, 44 are women, and the average of female participation in faculties of HEIs that offer undergraduate philosophy programs is 21.36% (see Figure 14). Not a single university in this group surpasses 40% of female participation, only 4 (26%) HEIs surpass 30% of female participation in faculties, and 53% have a participation inferior to 20%.

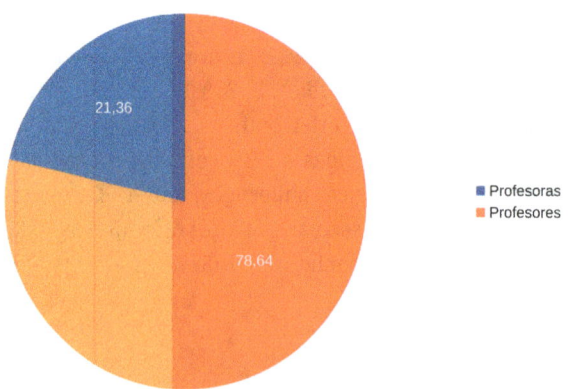

Figure 14: Percentages of male and female professors in HEIs offering only disciplinary philosophy.

Out of 8 HEIs that offer undergraduate pedagogical philosophy programs, 2 offer pedagogical philosophy and arts (Universidad Santo Tomás and Universidad de Nariño). 4 of these HEIs (50%) are public institutions, and 4 (50%) private. 50% (4) of these programs are offered by religious HEIs, and 50% (4) by secular HEIs. Out of 139 people hired in HEIs that offer pedagogical philosophy as bachelor's degree, 46 are women, which is an equivalent of 33.09% of female participation ratio (see Figure 15). 50% of these universities surpass 40% of female participation, and only 1 university (12%) has a participation ratio inferior to 20%.

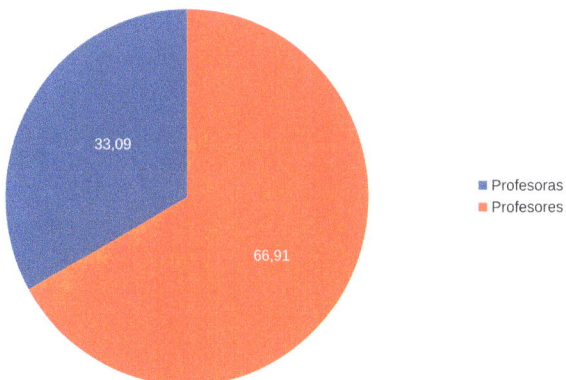

Figure 15: Percentages of male and female professors in HEIs offering only pedagogical philosophy.

11 HEIs that offer undergraduate programs in both philosophy and pedagogical philosophy are classified as follows: 8 offer philosophy degrees, 2 offer philosophy and humanities degrees, and 1 offers philosophy and arts. The majority (9 HEIs) offer pedagogical studies on the same degree as a disciplinary career, except Universidad Sergio Arboleda, which offers philosophy and humanities separate from pedagogical philosophy and arts; and Universidad Pontificia Bolivariana, which offers undergraduate studies in philosophy and pedagogical philosophy and arts. 4 (36%) HEIs that offer both undergraduate programs are public institutions, and 7 (64%) are private institutions. 63% (7) of the HEIs that offer both undergraduate programs are secular, and 37% (4) are religious HEIs. 266 people work as professors in HEIs that offer both undergraduate programs, from which 62 are women, this corresponds to 23.31% (see Figure 16). 2 HEIs (18%) surpass 40% of female participation, 5 HEIs (45%) surpass 20% of female participation in faculties, and 3 HEIs (27%) have a participation inferior to 20%.

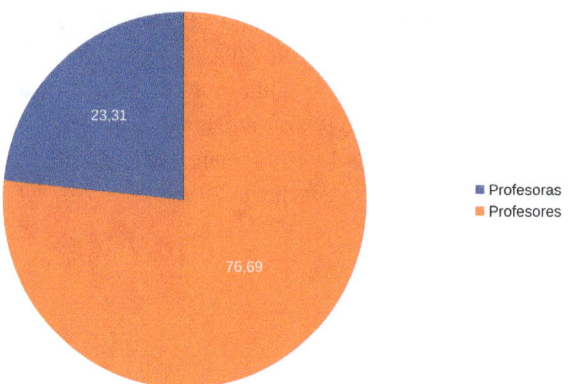

Figure 16: Percentage of male and female professors in HEIs that offer both disciplinary philosophy and pedagogical philosophy programs.

The χ^2 test (p= 0.034) indicates that it is probable that the type of undergraduate program offered by the HEIs is related to the number of hired women. Further research is required to determine the causes of its co-relation.

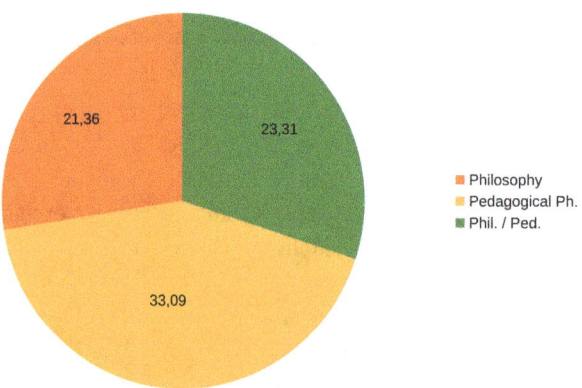

Figure 17: Distribution of female professors according to the type of undergraduate program (philosophy, pedagogical philosophy, both programs).

Geographical distribution by type of program does not vary in terms of offer quantity in the city of Bogota, which is always close to 50%. The ratios between public and private HEIs vary according to the type of offer, and HEIs that offer both disciplinary and pedagogical programs are in their majority public institutions (64%), in contrast to those which offer only disciplinary programs (50%), and those who offer exclusively pedagogical programs (40%). In terms of size of faculty, HEIs that offer both programs tend to be larger faculties (56%), whereas HEIs that offer only pedagogical programs (37%), or only disciplinary programs (26%), tend to be medium-sized and small-sized faculties (between 10 to 19 professors, and less than 9 professors). In terms of female participation in faculties, we highlight that HEIs that offer only pedagogical programs have an outstanding average (33.09%), in contrast to the HEIs that offer only disciplinary programs (21.33%) or both (23.31%). This percentage is almost 10 points above the global of female participation (24.88%) in faculty positions of HEIs that offer philosophy programs in Colombia.

The distribution of hired women in philosophy programs in Colombia according to the highest degree offered is the following. Out of 239 people hired by HEIs that offer only undergraduate programs, 57 are women (23.85%); out of 13 people hired in the only HEI that offers a specialization degree (Universidad El Bosque), 4 are women (30.77%); out of 183 people hired in HEIs which offer masters degrees, 50 are women (27.32%); out of 176 people hired in HEIs that offer Ph. D. degrees, 41 are women (23.30%) (see Figure 18).

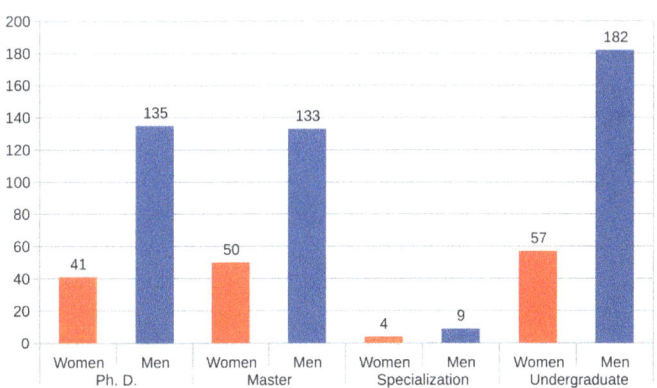

Figure 18: Number of female and male professors according to the highest degree offered by HEIs.

Out of 15 HEIs that offer only undergraduate studies, 3 (20%) have a female participation above 40%; 4 (26%) have female participation between 20% to 30%; 7 (46%) have participation inferior to 20%. The percentage of hired women in these HEIs (23.85%) is very close to the national average (24.88%) (see Figure 19).

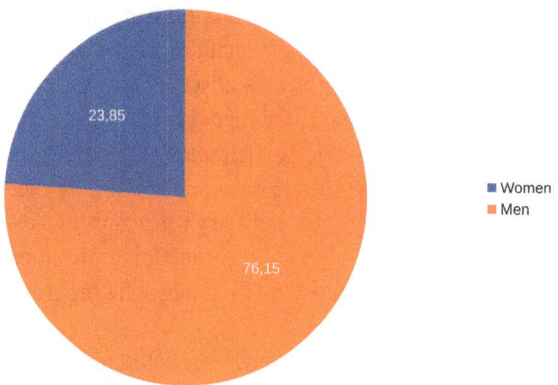

Figure 19: Percentage of male and female professors in HEIs that offer bachelors as highest degree.

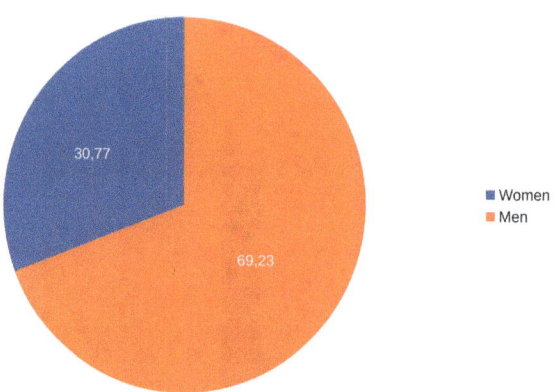

Figure 20: Percentage of male and female professors in HEIs that offer specialization as highest degree.

Out of 10 HEIs that offer the master degree as the highest degree, 3 (30%) have a female participation above 40%; 2 (20%) have a female participation between 20% to 30%; 4 (40%) have a female participation inferior to 20%. The percentage of hired women in these HEIs (27.32%) is above the national average (24.88%) (see Figure 21).

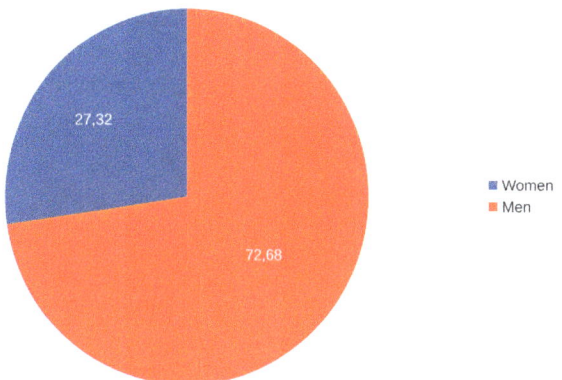

Figure 21: Percentage of male and female professors in HEIs that offer masters as highest degree.

Out of 8 HEIs that offer Ph. D. as the highest degree, none surpasses 40%; 2 HEIs (25%) have female participation above 30%; 4 HEIs (50%) have female participation between 20% to 30%; 2 HEIs (25%) are below 20% in female participation. The percentage of hired women in these HEIs (23.30%) is very close to the national average (24.88%) (see Figure 22).

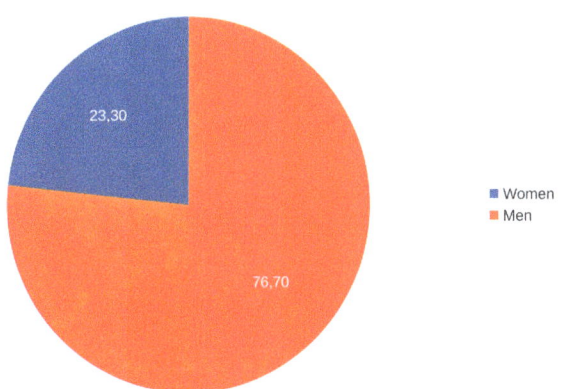

Figure 22: Percentage of male and female professors in HEIs that offer Ph. D. as highest degree.

Out of 378 people hired in faculties within HEIs that offer graduate education in philosophy, 94 are women, with a ratio of 28.57%. This percentage is slightly higher than the global percentage of women participation (24.88%). Compared to HEIs that do not offer graduate education: out of 235 hired people, 59 are women, which corresponds to 25%, which is closer to the global percentage. Female participation is slightly higher in HEIs that offer graduate programs. 152 female professors are distributed according to the highest degree offered as seen in Figure 23.

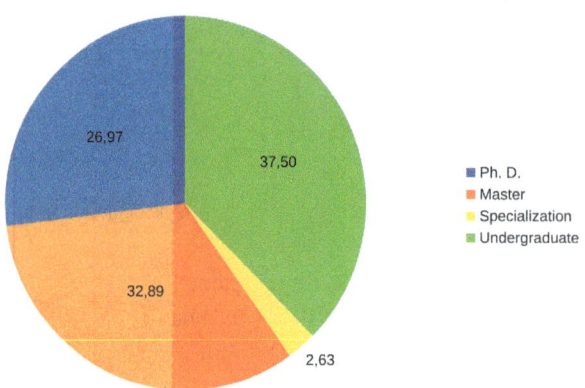

Figure 23: Female professors' distribution according to the highest degree offered by the HEIs in which they work.

Figure 24 illustrates that out of 152 female professors working in HEIs that offer philosophy programs, most (62.5%) work in HEIs that, in addition to undergraduate education, offer specialization, masters, and Ph. D. programs.

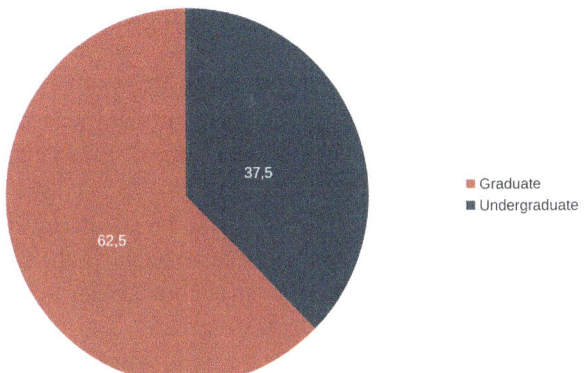

Figure 24: Distribution of female professors in HEIs offering graduate or only undergraduate degrees.

Discussion

Many elements emerge when analyzing the data. First, the gender proportion in faculties of philosophy programs in Colombia is still very far from equality, according to the considered variables above. This is a reason to examine the conditions for access and permanence in faculty positions of women philosophers, considering that universities should prevent and correct any exclusion towards women (and other marginalized groups) in the production of knowledge (CRES 2018). To comprehend such inequality, we found a few important points.

First, the difference between pedagogical and disciplinary programs in terms of female participation stands out: 33.09% women in pedagogical philosophy programs vs. 21.36% women in disciplinary philosophy programs. The χ^2 test outcome indicates that the type of program is a variable that might be related to a difference in participation of women. A possible explanation of this co-relation is a feminization of pedagogical work, in contrast to a masculinization of the "pure" disciplinary philosophy. Pedagogical programs, by principle, include within their curricular structure pedagogy, and education courses, as well as pedagogical practices. If it is considered that pedagogy is a care-related occupation, particularly in relation to children and youth, pedagogical occupations are related to an hegemonically feminine role in society.

Given the above, female philosophers might have found less hostilities or less obstacles to access a faculty and research career in HEIs that offer pedagogical philosophy programs. This might be caused by the "sexual division of intellectual work" in which women find more space in educational and pedagogical programs, and less space in exclusive disciplinary contexts. Even so, it would require further research to support that statement. According to this argumentative route, a higher female participation in pedagogy programs does not necessarily imply a more inclusive and equalitarian understanding of philosophy, because the very inclusion of women in these programs may be the outcome of a gender bias. It is essential to carry out qualitative research on the subject in order to confirm this hypothesis or to identify alternative explanations. For example, it would be significant to make research on perception about teaching and practice of philosophy in the Colombian academic community, as well as research on proportion of gender in admission and graduation from students across philosophy programs.

Second, differences between men and women's distribution among private HEIs (71.68 % and 28.32 %, respectively) and public HEIs (78.15 % and 21.85 %, respectively) indicate that there are better conditions to gender equality in private HEIs. A hypothesis that supports this tendency is that private HEIs have more flexibility in hiring processes, hence, it is possible – when institutional willingness allows it – to generate vacancies and open competitions that prioritize female hiring. Either way, internal management of resources and budgets to hire faculty members may indicate that private HEIs offer vacancies more often than public HEIs. It also may indicate a wider mobility and staff rotation on faculties that provide more opportunities to women when it comes to hiring.

Third, to consider the faculty size variable, it is important to highlight that the fragility of gender equality manifests itself differently in larger and smaller faculties. This indicates the need of inclusive and permanence policies that would be differentiated according to this criterion. A relatively good gender proportion, without explicit policies tied to a thorough disciplinary self-reflection, is rather fragile, particularly in small and medium-sized faculties. As a result, when 30 % of faculty correspond to two women, an instance of firing, quitting, or retiring will dramatically alter gender equality in the program. The bright side to this is that, in terms of hiring, small and medium-sized faculties have a better chance of bridging the gender gap.

Fourth, the results show a centralization of philosophy programs in Bogota, particularly in programs offered by private institutions (there are only two HEIs that offer philosophy programs outside this city). This implies that for some women with philosophy degrees, the access to a teaching and researching career in philosophy might involve moving away from their home.

Conclusions and Recommendations

Gender disparity in faculty positions in philosophy programs in Colombia is a problem, not only because it is a symptom of structural and systematic inequality at every level of society. For philosophy as a discipline, it raises questions pertaining to the representation of women and of femininity, to job access and security, to the recognition of works by women philosophers, and self-reflection about the contents, methods, and conditions in the field. If philosophy seeks to assume a relevant place in the production of knowledge, the decrease of the gender gap can promote not only a greater number of voices, proposals, and research horizons, but can also deepen and improve the quality of current knowledge and teaching. Finally, the participation of an equal number of women in faculty positions implies the promotion of participation and progress of female students in the area. Having role models not only leads to imagine a better future in the field – reconstruct the imaginary of who makes philosophy, and therefore, who aspires to be a philosopher –, but also shows a commitment with equality and justice ideas into wider levels of society. If philosophy claims to be a self-reflective field that has an impact on social structures, teaching practices, the protection of democracy, and well-living development, it must address its own problems, as well as structural, and systematic issues that affect gender disparity in academia.

References

Arango, L. G. (2006). *Jóvenes en la universidad: género, clase e identidad profesional.* Bogota: Siglo del Hombre Editores; Universidad Nacional de Colombia.
Brownstein, M. and Saul, J. (Eds.) (2016). *Implicit Bias and Philosophy.* Vol. 2. Oxford: Oxford University Press.
Buquet, A., et al. (2013). *Intrusas en la universidad.* Ciudad de México: UNAM.
Cely, F. E. (2019). "Reconstrucción de autoridad epistémica de las mujeres a través del autonocimiento y transformación hábitos corporizados". *Humanitas Hodie* 2(1), 1–23.
Coates, J. (2004). *Women, Men and Language. A Sociolinguistic Account of Gender Differences in Language.* New York: Routledge.
CRES (2018). "Declaración de la III Conferencia Regional de Educación Superior en América Latina y el Caribe". Córdoba, Argentina, 14 June 2018.
Fricker, M. (2007). *Epistemic Injustice. Power and the Ethics of Knowing.* Oxford: Oxford University Press.
Haslanger, S. (2008). "Changing the Ideology and Culture of Philosophy: Not by Reason (Alone)". *Hypatia* 23(2), 210–223.
Hutchinson, K. and Jenkins, F. (2013). *Women in Philosophy. What Needs to Change?* Oxford: Oxford University Press.

Schwitzgebel, E. and Dicey, C. (2016). "Women in Philosophy: Quantitative Analyses of Specialization, Prevalence, Visibility, and Generational Change". *Public Affairs Quarterly* 31, 83–105.

UNESCO (2012). *World Atlas of Gender Equality in Education.* Paris: Author.

Young, I. M. (1990). "Five Faces of Oppression". In Young, I. M., *Justice and the Politics of Difference.* New Jersey: Princeton University Press.

Tzitzi Janik Rojas Torres

Teaching Islamic Feminisms in the History of Philosophy in Mexico: A Decolonial and Feminist Effort

Abstract: The institutional teaching of philosophy in Mexico has traditionally been historicist and Eurocentric. The intellectual wealth of peripheral cultures and peoples does not appear in the universal history of philosophy taught in Mexico. Specifically, Islamic philosophy and the Islamic intellectual universe barely appear, and if so, just as mere translators of the Hellenistic tradition. Therefore, I propose Islamic philosophy, but specifically Islamic feminisms, as a subject that needs to be introduced into the courses of philosophical history in Mexico: I suggest that the Eurocentric and patriarchal paradigms can only be questioned when the silenced alterity is made visible and a space for dialogue with it is constructed.

The main goal of this paper is to argue in favor of teaching Islamic feminisms as part of the history of philosophy segment of the Philosophy degree, at the Autonomous National University of Mexico (UNAM), the biggest university in the country. Mexico is a mostly Catholic, Spanish-speaking country that is geographically distant from Muslim countries and possesses a very small Muslim population. About 0.01 % of the total Mexican population is Muslim according to the last estimation of the Pew Research Center. Mexico also has own painful problems – such a high rate of feminicides and discrimination towards the native inhabitants of our country, and a systemic corruption issue to mention just some –: so, why should Mexico, and we Mexicans, study Islamic feminisms and Islamic philosophy?[1]

Presented this way, the inclusion of Islamic philosophy, let alone Islamic feminisms, could appear as an "exotic" interest: the intrusion of a new orientalism on a country that has its own dilemmas to analyze before gazing away to "Arabesque stories". However, let's not fool ourselves: behind the question of whether to teach Islamic philosophy is hidden a question about whether it is important to teach phi-

---

[1] It is important to point out that when we speak of Islam, we are in fact speaking of a plural, diverse, complex, and historical universe. There is therefore no single Islam, no single religious or intellectual expression that we can call "genuine and unique" Islam. In this sense, we align ourselves with the position of the French Islamologist Henry Corbin: rather than speaking of Arab philosophy, we should speak of philosophy in the lands of Islam, or, failing that, Islamic philosophy, understanding the plurality that such an expression implies.

losophies and philosophers other than euro-centrical or Western ones. In fact, the question challenges the foundations of philosophy itself as a neutral objective discipline grounded on a supposedly unbiased and impartial human being. Since its historical foundations as a discipline – localized, of course, in Greece, as if before the Greeks no humans asked themselves the perennial questions about their own existence –, philosophy has pretended to be a kind of neutral and universal knowledge; however, at the same time, that universal knowledge seems to be produced just for a very restricted group of human beings – the canon: male, white, heterosexual and Christian Europeans – within an also very limited geographical area – the Northern hemisphere, specifically Europe and the United States. The Cartesian subject is not just expressed by "I think, therefore I am", but rather, as Ramon Grosfoguel noted, by "I think – from a certain white male heterosexual Christian horizon on an European context – then I exist" (2008). We need to question how this very narrow horizon of human existence became synonymous with "Universal" and "Classical" thinkers and ideas.

When we ask about whether or not teaching Islamic philosophy, and specifically Islamic feminisms, we are asking a question the answer of which will also affect whether we teach Asian philosophy, African philosophy, non-white Feminism and all the philosophy and dialogues produced between and from human beings who do not belong to the ideal individual of the canon. We may even question why to teach those philosophies in the reverse: why do we teach just Western or Eurocentric philosophy? Answering one of these questions answers the others as well.

In order to arrive at those answers, this essay will: 1) appreciate the little-known work of the Mexican-Costa Rican philosopher Vera Yamuni as a primordial antecedent to the topic and put her ideas into dialogue with contemporary Islamic feminisms, and 2) expose from an intersectional and decolonial feminism why the study of Muslim feminist philosophers is important to the history of philosophy taught in Mexico, and, as a conclusion, propose strategies for how to develop a set of transferable skills through the study of alterity.

From Vera Yamuni to Our Days

Compared to academic events and programs centered on European authors and schools of thought, currently there are few academic endeavors focused on Islamic humanities within Latin-American academia, and when there are, they revolve around historical and geopolitical issues brushing aside the deepness of Islamic culture, literature, arts, and, of course, philosophy. Specifically, in our university, the National Autonomous Mexican University, the curricula of the Philosophy degree, besides just one course about Mexican philosophy, does not include any compulsory course centered on non-Western philosophies. The few Muslim authors included during the degree owe their presence to their direct link to Aristotle and Greek philosophy (Al Farabi as a reader of Plato's *Republic*, and Ibn Sina and Ibn Rush as mere translators of Aristotle's work). When included, those philosophers' names are Latinized, their roots invisibilized and their religion muted, as if they were merely translators, empty bridges for Greek philosophy. As if their lives, personal contexts, beliefs and cultures were not important at all, when at the same time, while studying European authors we are taught to understand some of their "problematic arguments" in context. Needless to say, those philosophers are exclusively men: under the Western prejudices about Islam, women are not even considered intellectual agents capable of philosophy and academic work.

Not being the goal of this paper to examine in detail the different efforts focused on Islam in Mexico – among which should be mentioned the activities of the Colegio de México, the University Program for Studies of Asia and Africa, and the work of doctor Luis Xavier López Farjat, to mention a few –, I have focused my exposition on teaching practices of the Faculty of Philosophy and Literature at UNAM, in Mexico. During the 60s, the Mexican-Costa Rican philosopher Vera Yamuni Tabush, fulltime professor at the faculty, was a pioneer in feminism and Islamic philosophical studies in Mexico. Her contribution, very important at the time, has gone almost unnoticed by new generations: the study and re-evaluation of her thought may represent a door to enter into dialogue with great feminist philosophers from the Middle East.

Part of the Middle Eastern diaspora in Latin America, Doctor Vera Yamuni, deceased in 2003, was a feminist translator, writer and philosopher from Lebanese origins, her father was from Sardal, Lebanon, and her mother was a Costa Rican whose parents emigrated to Costa Rica from the Lebanese city of Hasrun. She was multicultural and polyglot: speaking English, French, Arabic and of course Spanish, she acknowledged her identity as a carrefour of cultures and worlds. All her academic career was developed in Mexico at the Faculty of Philosophy and Literature of the National Autonomous Mexican University. She was deeply aware – to say the least – of the marginalized situation of women in her own family, in the societies where she had lived, and around the world in general. Maybe that's why she became a pioneer of feminism in Mexico. According to Grace Prada Ortiz in her book *El ensayo feminista en Costa Rica* (2005, 74), in an interviewed made to Graciela Hierro, known as the establisher of feminism in Mexico, it was not Hierro who introduced feminism but Vera Yamuni, who was her mentor and the one who first taught her about feminism. At the time she focused her studies on some of the most iconic feminist figures such a Virginia Woolf, Sappho from Lesbos and Simone de Beauvoir, on which she had written several articles, and also incorporated Muslim female figures such as Scherezade, as will be outlined below. She was also known as a great disciple of the exiled Spanish philosopher Jose Gaos: her story with him is an example of the efforts of female scholars in Latin America around relevant intellectual figures whose machismo was hardly questionable. Yamuni struggled to disprove his misogyny for a long time. A lot of Yamuni's most extensive work revolves around the systematization and analysis of his thought, as Gaos was also her doctoral thesis director. However, it is important to say that the support of Gaos and other main intellectual figures in the Mexican academy at the time such as Jaime Torres Bodet and Alfonso Reyes was substantial to her development in Mexico (Prada 2005, 70–76).

Yamuni was deeply sensitive to the dynamics of power, marginalization and exclusion: regarding Sappho, she was sure that the poor recognition of her poetry was due to fear of facing a strong-willed, liberated woman (Prada 2005, 76). This empathy towards the excluded and repressed is important when we come to the subject of Islamic studies. Long before the concept of epistemic injustice was proposed, Yamuni was well aware of the epistemic injustice Islamic culture and Islamic philosophy suffered compared to European philosophy, the importance of which she never denied and which she had long studied.

She identified the importance of Islamic philosophers on the development of medieval scholarship and emphasized their role as readers and active interpreters of Greek philosophy, leading to their preservation and inheritance by the medieval and latter Western philosophy. Her interpretation of the classical Middle East work *One Thousand and One Nights* (1961, 130–131) is in fact surprisingly close to what years later the important Moroccan feminist philosopher Fatima Mernissi would declare: Scheherazade is seen as a symbol of women, as a link between intelligence, language and communication in contraposition to the barbaric and violent world of men, represented by the Shahryar, the king of the story (2001, 53–72).

Yamuni's interpretations of the Islamic world were all sensible to the situation of women and her systematized study of Islamic thought must be reviewed. Without imposing on her anachronisms – since we should not consider Yamuni's work is decolonial – we can affirm that she set up a very important precedent for Islamic studies but, most importantly, for the study of Islamic feminisms and feminisms of the Middle East.

Returning to the aim of this paper, throwing back a glance at her works lets us realize that important efforts have been made to introduce the formal study of Islamic philosophy in our faculty. We should not just let time bury those precedents to a point where we forget them. To this end, I propose Islamic feminisms – and Islamic philosophy in general – as a subject that needs to be properly introduced into the courses of philosophical history in Mexico: I suggest that the Eurocentric and patriarchal paradigms can only be questioned when the silenced alterity is made visible and a space for dialogue with it is constructed.

The dialogue between Latin-American and Middle-Eastern women implies a recognition of the links that unite otherness and the construction of an enriching dialogue addressing resistance against religious and social structures of domination. This is framed in an even wider effort to build intersectional bridges between decolonial feminisms from Latin America and those enunciated in other peripheral spaces, carving out the possibility for identity creating that is relational and situational as opposed to self-contained and closed.

Philosophy as a Warden of Exclusion: The Construction and Exclusion of the Othernesses

The institutional teaching of philosophy in Mexico has traditionally been historicist and Eurocentric: usually, philosophy has been taught and thought in chronological order and articulated around European intellectual movements and philosophers. The above implies that non-Eurocentric othernesses are made invisible: the intellectual wealth of peripheral cultures and peoples does not appear in the "universal" history of philosophy taught in Mexico, in a clear example of what sociologist Boaventura Sousa de Santos would call *epistemicide* (2010, 7–8). An *epistemicide* is the systematic extermination of the systems of knowledge of certain communities through European colonialism, and the prolongation of this violence even after the ending of colonial political and geographical control. Meaning that, even when European colonialism seems to have ended and political control "handed" to the locals, the epistemological-existential structure that was laid as the basis for colonialism as a political-economical practice of oppression and violence remains inside the subjectivities constructed through it – and that remaining oppressive structure is what the decolonial Latin-American modernity/coloniality group has called "coloniality" in opposition to "colonialism". This structure, considered by the Muslim scholar Sirin Adlbi a prison (2016, 72–73), continues modeling and creating a world as the colonialists would have wanted, even when they are not there anymore, even when we have thought colonialism has historically ended; through this mechanism colonialism persists as coloniality, modeling subjectivities and societies. Tied to the concept of *epistemicide*, we find another important one: that of epistemic injustice. *Epistemic injustice*, a concept first introduced by English philosopher Miranda Fricker, has long evolved from the hermeneutical and testimonial injustices proposed by Fricker to a broader complex concept including the systematic epistemic oppression and violence, and the exclusion, invisibilization, undervaluing, and misrepresentation that certain communities face from those more privileged. The subject to discuss here is how *epistemicide* and epistemic injustices are enabled by a certain way to understand, do and teach philosophy – and, of course, humanities as well.

Edward Said's main postcolonialism proposition was precisely that humanities, social sciences and sciences in general have been accomplices in the process: they specifically have helped create an idea of "other" as a complete alterity (1979, 31–90). A dichotomic dynamic where either you belong to the canon of culture and civilization (the idealistic European white male) or you are in some degrees savage, barbaric and so on. In this system, from white heterosexual men to Muslim women, passing through all spectrums of human experience and identity, there exist degrees of importance, degrees of rationality and civilization, and degrees of abilities to create knowledge and culture. On this hierarchy racism can't be understood, as Ramon Grosfoguel says, as mere ignorance and prejudices (2013). Racism is a dynamic deeply embedded in the hierarchy (maybe even the praxis of the hierarchy itself): you must disregard others "below" you because the scale implies a moral lecture of the alterity. As a perverted *kalokagathia*: the good, beautiful and truthful can only be the idealistic canon of human being, while all the others participate in some degree of evilness. Within this paradigm of world, Muslim culture is presented as barbaric, exotic and incapable of deeply spiritual and philosophical experiences. According to Sirin Adlbi, the lowest point on the scale is the Muslim woman (2016, 128): always represented as a passive, submissive, voiceless being, left to the mercy of Muslim men and thought to be waiting for a Western savior. The above position intentionally ignores the fact that in the history of the Middle East, as well as in the history of Islam and in the intellectual history of Islam, the role of women has not been that of mere passive spectators, submissive and distant from the discussions that have shaped the various Islamic disciplines. Since this is not the place (although we would desire it so) to make an intellectual history of Muslim women, we have to be content with mentioning some iconic examples from the classical period of Islam, such as the active role played by women like Aishah bint Abu Bakr, who played an important role in the formation of the body of hadith and the shaping of early Islam, or as one of the first Sufis, Rabia Al Adawiya, whose thought resonated and resonates throughout the history of Tasawwuf, Sufism or Islamic mysticism, among many other women such as, for example, scholastics of the Middle Ages as Nashwan, Hajar or Bayram whose names and work are concealed in simple mentions within the history written by men.[2]

---

[2] A more in-depth account of the history of these women can be found in the work of Leila Ahmed, *Women and Gender in Islam* (Ahmed 1992, 103–123) which relates how, thanks to works

Unfortunately, philosophy has been the warden of this ontological colonialist human hierarchy: enshrining the ideas of European philosophers and dismissing those of anyone else. Beneath the sole inclusion of Western thought in supposedly objective curricula lies the assumption that only some human knowledge is worthy based on its provenance and producer, while other knowledge can be dismissed and ignored. Discounting the knowledge produced by a group makes invisible the individuals and communities who produce it. The other does not exist then, or exists, as Edward Said wrote, just as a mere object of my production, malleable and disposable like an object of study but never as a worthy human being (1979, 31–48). Production of knowledge is an abyss between who exists and who can't exist; between who can produce knowledge, culture, art and all the range of humans systematically denied that right.

In accordance with the above, introducing Islamic philosophy to a Philosophy degree curriculum in Latin America is not trivial: it is not just an "exotic" interest and it should be taken seriously while we ask ourselves the same questions about other non-Western and non-male philosophies. But the goal is not just the sudden insertion of a miscellany of authors and backgrounds: diversifying the curriculum is far from being really inclusive if we do not focus on tackling the structure that systematically excludes the other. The mere incorporation of authors from several backgrounds different from the Western one would be just a strategy of distraction if we do not criticize the ontological hierarchy, or in words of Sirin Adlbi, if we do not break out of the epistemological-existential prison (2016, 9) which rules out some human existences, condemning them to lower ranks of an artificial ontological scale.

Epistemic injustice also plays an important role: Islamic philosophers and Islamic feminist women philosophers are not granted what Fricker calls hermeneutical justice neither testimonial injustice (2007, 9–17, 147–175). In other words, in the first case, experiences, expressions and knowledge produced by Muslims are systematically obscured and interpreted from prejudiced perspective, and in the second case, especially for Muslim women, and based on the hermeneutical injustice they suffer, their voices receive unfair treatment and are considered lacking in credibility.

To face those injustices perpetuated by philosophy, philosophy needs to examine itself and criticize and abandon its obsolete roll as warden of a violent, repressive and discriminating colonialist system: even if that means demystifying its sacred classical authors and school of thoughts. As we have come to accept that

---

such as the biographical dictionary of women scholars by the cairene Al Sakhawi, we could know an extensive list of scholastic women involved in Islamic disciplines.

science is not objective but subject to history, culture, and social context, philosophy must be examined with the same scrutiny. With no intention to discard European classical philosophy – after all, no one seeks to reproduce the same practices of invisibilization and violence –, the time has come to talk about Aristotle and Plato's misogyny, for example, or Kant's sexism and discrimination, and also to discuss, revendicate, and recognize those whose voices have been stolen and muted. That does not mean that Islam and Islamic philosophy itself are clean of violent and repressive practices, but it means that instead of judging from an authoritarian perspective, we should listen to their voices first and validate their identities before drawing final conclusions – a benefit more privileged individuals have long received –, especially when it comes to the subject of Muslim women.

The epistemological-existential prison is a restrictive and excluding mechanism/ structure supported by philosophy and implies specific social practices including certain teaching methodology and agenda.

Changing that structure requires criticizing and questioning the structure of philosophy but also its most basic tenets, questions like who can think, from which places of enunciation and on what concepts. In order to achieve those goals, decolonialism and feminisms can provide methodological and theoretical tools to deconstruct the paradigm of philosophy and eliminate epistemic and social injustices enabled by it. A common objective between decolonialism and feminism is the denunciation of structures of power and domination in order to situate the individual in a resistance with peripheral links.

Conclusion

Now, we can give an answer to our initial question: why teach Islamic philosophy and Islamic feminisms within a Mexican philosophy curriculum. Well, the dialogue with those excluded communities – of which, we should not forget, we as Mexicans are also a part – is a way of resistance to coloniality and its mechanism of epistemic violence and injustices. Although we cannot erase and reverse centuries of erasure of systems of knowledge, we may act towards a fairer epistemic philosophy. This resistance must work towards a dialogue with several other philosophies and widen its scoop as much as possible without confusing mere diversity with the decolonial effort. This fight for epistemic justice must be accompanied by a systematic critique of the colonialist fundaments of humanities.

Let us not deceive ourselves: the exclusion of Islamic feminisms from our academic sphere makes us accomplices in our own exclusion. By participating in the exercise of discrimination, Latin America does not realize that it is wearing the mask of the Catholic, of the Spanish-speaker, the disguise of being European without being so, like the slave who is allowed to dress like the master and serve in the house, and so believes himself to be better than the other slaves. It is therefore a question of solidarity. The rejection of portrayals of the Muslim woman as total otherness is an act of resistance against the epistemic-existential prison constructed by the Westerner, and that also exerts her yoke, perhaps in a more veiled way, on us. The dialogue with Muslim feminisms is an act of solidarity, of resistance and of freedom, in the face of an imposed identity as another" of which we are also victims.

The struggle for the recognition of identities as dynamic, intersectional and open processes also implies the recognition of the dynamicity of Islamic identity and its exercises. Perhaps the careful reader has noticed that throughout the text we have avoided speaking of "Islamic feminism" and have opted for the plural "Islamic feminisms". The decision was made consciously: just as we cannot speak of a single Islam, we cannot speak of a single Islamic feminism. Islamic feminisms are plural and their places of enunciation are diverse: secular feminisms of secular activists, secular feminisms of religious activists, Islamic feminisms of religious activists, and anti-patriarchal struggles of religious activists who refuse to call themselves feminists as a political act of rejection against the discrimination they themselves have experienced at the hands of white feminisms that seek to "save" them and label them as victims. The study of this diversity of interactions between women and their feminist-political-philosophical positions within the lands of Islam can result in, by analogy, the recognition also of the plurality of trenches from which we struggle in our own context.

In this sense, it is important to trace the genealogy of these resistances. Acknowledging Vera Yamuni's work implies recognizing the isolated efforts that have been made to reach a dialogue among the peripheries, to revalue and re-signify those who have been made invisible. It is important to recognize the isolated efforts in order to link them in such a way that we realize that silently there have been many attempts to dialogue with otherness *from* otherness. Those of us who are interested in Islamic philosophy in Mexico should recognize and thank those who preceded us and find strength and inspiration in their struggles. Perhaps in the flashes of parallels that we find between some of Vera Yamuni's ideas and some ideas of more contemporary Muslim feminists, such as Fatima Mernissi, we can deduce that, from two different spaces, from two different times, cultures and countries, it is possible to reach common analyses; timeless and important bridges in the construction of new Mutually-Supportive identities.

The introduction of Islamic feminisms as a subject in the university curriculum is a first step towards its decolonization. It will not be just a matter of randomly including Muslim women authors – as if it were just a matter of fulfilling a quota. It will be necessary: understand basic notions of Islamic history and how

Islamic disciplines themselves have been constructed from patriarchal dynamics, explain the different roles of women throughout Islamic history, enhance the dialogue that secular and religious women have had in their own contexts, contextualize secular efforts for gender equality, to understand how some currents that are vital to Islam (such as Tasawwuf or Sufism) have introduced strategies used by Muslim feminists in their efforts to reject sexist interpretations and practices, and also to understand in their own context the gender violence within Islam and the struggles and resistance of Muslim women as active agents of change. It is not an easy task, but at each point there is an opportunity for analogy with our own experiences: each topic contains the seed of a fruitful dialogue in which our Latin-American reality enhances understanding and allows us to re-examine ourselves with insightful similes.

Finally, we must say that studying Islamic philosophy and Islamic feminisms also serves to develop intellectual virtues such as empathy, open-mindedness, fair-mindedness and epistemic fairness. These abilities can be transferable to our own surroundings and may help us identify systematical violence that we may find hard to see because we are immersed in it. This transferability matters vis-à-vis the objection that we should be studying otherness within our own country before studying otherness outside it; in order to better understand the moments of otherizing that happens within our own context, we need to study the way parallel otherizing happens in the cultural or religious alterity. It is when listening to those voices from far away that we may better hear the voices muted from within.

References

Adlbi Sibai, S. (2017). *La cárcel del feminismo. Hacia un pensamiento islámico* decolonial. Mexico City: Akal.

Adlbi Sibai, S. and Garcés, H. F. (2019). "El pensamiento islámico decolonial, una herramienta contra la islamofobia de género". In *Tabula Rasa*. DOI: 10.25058/20112742.n30.11.

Afnan, S. F. (1965). *El pensamiento de Avicena*. Ed. by Vera Yamuni Tabush. Mexico: Fondo de Cultura Económica.

Ahmed, L. (1992). *Women and Gender in Islam*. New Haven and London: Yale University Press.

De Sousa Santos, B. (2010). *Descolonizar el saber, reinventar el poder.* Montevideo: Ediciones Trilce.

Fricker, M. (2007). *Epistemic Injustice: Power and the Ethics of Knowing*. New York: Oxford University Press.

Grosfoguel, R. (2008). "Hacia un pluri-versalismo transmoderno decolonial". *Tabula Rasa* 9. URL: https://www.redalyc.org/pdf/396/39600911.pdf (last accessed 22 November 2022).

Grosfoguel, R. (2012). "El concepto de 'racismo' en Michel Foucault y Frantz Fanon: ¿Teorizar desde la zona del ser o desde la zona del no-ser?" *Revista Tabula Rasa* 16, 79–102.

Grosfoguel, R. (2013). "The Structure of Knowledge in Westernized Universities: Epistemic Racism/Sexism and the Four Genocides/Epistemicides of the Long 16th Century". *Human Architecture* 11(1). URL: https://www.okcir.com/product/journal-article-the-structure-of-knowledge-in-westernized-universities-epistemic-racism-sexism-and-the-four-genocides-epistemicides-of-the-long-16th-century-by-ramon-grosfoguel (last accessed 22 November 2022).

Horneffer, R. (1994). "Vera Yamuni". In: Universidad Nacional Autónoma de México (Eds.), *Setenta años de la Facultad de Filosofía y Letras*, Mexico: FFyL/UNAM, 553–554.

Mernissi, F. (2001). *El harén en occidente.* Madrid: Espasa.

Pew Research Center (n. d.). "Religions in Mexico: PEW-GRF". Pew-Templeton Global Religious Future Project. URL: http://www.globalreligiousfutures.org/countries/mexico#/?affiliations_religion_id=16&affiliations_year=2020&region_name=All%20Countries&restrictions_year=2016 (last accessed 22 November 2022).

Prada Ortiz, G. (2005). "Vera Yamuni. Pensadora Latinoamericana". In Prada Ortiz, G., *El Ensayo Feminista en Costa Rica.* Costa Rica: Universidad Nacional de Costa Rica, 54–95.

Said, E. (1979). *Orientalism.* New York: Random House.

Verges, F. (2019). *Un féminisme décolonial.* Paris: La Fabrique éditions.

Yamuni Tabush, V. (1965). "Filosofía y religión en el islam". In *Revista de la Universidad de México* 12–14, 2. URL: https://www.revistadelauniversidad.mx/articles/f5f9bffc-0e9b-4b68-9978-d397b9cf52db/filosofia-y-religion-en-el-islam (last accessed 22 November 2022).

Yamuni Tabush, V. (1961). "El mundo de las mil y una noches". In *Anuario de Filosofía, Año 1.* Mexico: UNAM.

Yamuni Tabush, V. (1966–1967). La mujer en el pensamiento filosófico y literario. In: *Anuario de Letras, vol. 6.* Mexico: UNAM, 179–200. URL: https://filosofiamexicana.files.wordpress.com/2012/11/yamuni-tabush-vera-la-mujer-en-el-pensamiento-filosc3b3fico-y-literario.pdf (last accessed 22 November 2022).

Yamuni Tabush, V. (1993). "El feminismo y el neofeminismo de Simone de Beauvoir". In Hierro, G. (Ed.), *Antología, Perspectivas feministas.* Mexico: Benemérita Universidad de Puebla, 13–32.

Ingrid Alloni
From Self-awareness to Political and Social Improvement: A Feminist Identitarian Path

Abstract: The theme of identity is present in different feminist currents, both in Western tradition and in Black thought. In fact, it is argued that identity can be claimed as an instrument of emancipation both from the recognition of personal history and biographical bearing, but also as a request for affirmation of the self in collective political and social struggles. Both sides must be considered: the feminist subject and the colonial subject are products of systems of domination, oppression and lack of recognition. The body becomes the terrain from which it is possible to rethink the self, starting from the experience of being a plural, relational and contextual subject.

The theme of identity is one of the greatest topics of the last century, mostly in the second half of the 20th century in the West, particularly with regard to gender, racial and generational dimensions. These terms can be considered on the one hand as terms of identity and on the other as an element that determines social and political possibilities.

The first interesting distinction concerns the fact that both categories can be clearly distinguished into two currents, consisting of essentialism and constructivism. In this case, naturalness is the main characteristic in the constitution of the subject. The differences are not confined to the phenotype only, but they also extend into the moral and spiritual domain and describe political and social possibilities. The constructivist counterpart rejects the naturalness of ontological differentiation and argues, instead, that the distinctions are the result of various kinds of impositions, such as political, economic and epistemic, which are affirmed by the necessity to create a worldwide taxonomic order and global cartographies in modern times.

In this sense, race and gender must not be understood as an eternal identity trait, inscribed in a deterministic framework in the definition of the human, but as a contingent system, which, however, profoundly influence the political structures of the relational and social universe. In fact, prejudices and stereotypes are used to classify humans. The identity, on the other side, is composed by personal history and collective memory, experience and self-awareness influenced by the gaze of the other, heritage and cultural production.

In the public space, race and gender represent one of the main references for the basis of a political and economic system of domination, which is determined by social ontological discrimination.

From Dual to Multiple Perspective

After the deconstruction of the affirmative Cartesian subject and the resulting identity crisis, the strategies of constructing an identity process concern the use of the narration of one's own singular life history and participation in the social movements of claiming rights.

Feminist philosophies show how it is possible to represent the self in a different and polyvalent way: the subject described in its attributes by Descartes and Kant (self-centered, solipsistic, autonomous and man) can have stable characteristics or fit into a permanent non-definition. For this reason, it is possible to support the overcoming of identity, because, in addition to the possibility of continuous redefinition of the particular, the most important elements in the definition of identity are a personal history and the series of actions arising from adherence to social movements that do not necessarily claim rights for themselves.

In this sense, the construction of the feminist subject shows that identity is not based only on the recognition of one's own individual biographical positioning, but also on a project built collectively.

The claim of the existence of infinite existential postures and subjectivation allows to break the symbolic patriarchal, hierarchical, normative, heterosexual and phallocentric order. In different currents of feminist philosophy the subject is represented in the multiplicity: Adriana Cavarero proposes an inclined and relational subject, Judith Butler a performative and multiple subject, Angela Davis a subversion of the role of woman's subjectivity starting from the awareness of the past, bell hooks a transgression of the pedagogy in the process of identity's construction. The multiplicity and the possibility of constant change show the unpredictability and the impossibility to insert identity it in a classification.

What feminism has shown is that new subjects are no longer definable through a universal positioning that does not consider the singular history of life. The subjects presented by feminist currents show a remarkable distance towards the neutral and universal subject which modern philosophy is used to: Cartesian rationalism, human solipsism, Kantian autonomy are traits that can be maintained by some subjects, but that no longer represent the totality of the human race.

It is no longer possible to present descriptions of humanity using universally valid characteristics: the element that characterizes everyone is one's own life history, mostly in the practical domain.

The main point of tangency between the category of the modern subject and that of metaphysics is an antithetical and dichotomous principle: since the Greeks, they think of being and not being, and all categories concerning living beings are articulated and cataloged on this dual division.

The ontology of feminist subjects is presented as a range of possibilities so varied and multiform that it is no longer possible to establish a static and immutable logic in which there is a hegemonic pole. The main constituent aspect of the modern subject was rationality, for feminist subjects it is represented by relationality. The subject is also defined through clear and stable characteristics. But the young generation has begun to think itself as being in an immersion of a continuous flow of changes.

Defining Identities: The Role of the Narration

Adriana Cavarero and Judith Butler fit into the thought of sexual difference and gender binarism. Although the strategies they adopt are different, for both identity remains a constant and consistent element in the life of each individual.

Adriana Cavarero, an Italian philosopher belonging to the current of the theory of sexual difference, proposes a relational and autobiographical model, based on three key concepts to define the subject: plurality, storytelling and inclination.

In *Nonostante Platone*, Cavarero takes up figures lacking in the literary and mythological tradition, including Penelope, Demeter and Diotima, using them as archetypes to show the relational and constitutively dialectical attitude of identity. Cavarero contests the view that male-female differentiations have a natural matrix, arguing instead that such dichotomies are derived from socio-cultural structures. Referring to the heroes of the Homeric poems, first of all Ulysses, who represent the individual in his solitary position, Cavarero proposes groups of women that are presented in the different works of antiquity, imagining scenarios of daily and domestic life that no one has ever told.

The "narrative's who" is the mode through which Cavarero explains the construction of the process of identification of the self. In this case the central element is the narration of the self to the Other. In the gaze of the Other and in the narrative restitution that the Other implements, the subject builds and (re-)finds itself in a path of meaning and significance. The mutual story of the story of life highlights the uniqueness of the Other.

The third category she explains is a critique of the most important philosophers of all time and their fear of the emotional and biographical components of the individual. Those philosophers emphasize the centrality of these components in the constitution of identity. The erotic and instinctual experience are confined in the female sphere. On the other hand, the subject of tradition is free and rational, balanced and static, coherent, controlled and above all is a man. The existential conditions of care, motherhood and birth are characterized by gender. The weight of irrationality, emotions and attention to the Other is just the responsibility of women. Through this binary division, philosophy has forgotten the meaning of inclination, relationship, and protection towards the other, the stranger. And it is precisely the stranger that allows us to explore territories of unknown self-knowledge.

If the subject of the tradition is characterized by the statute of self-sufficiency, freedom, autonomy and independence, the subject of Cavarero is established in relations with others.

The geometric verticality is contrasted with an inclined *ego* to the advantage of a subject that is formed in a plural and relational context. Relationality therefore ontologically marks a deep dependence and a continuous tension towards the Other.

Cavarero concludes her work focusing on the validity of the ontological condition of vulnerability that characterizes the human: the recognition of error, imperfection and dependence opens new horizons for subjects in which the paradigm of the free and rational individual can be reformulated through the categories of interdependence and reciprocity. Euclidean geometry is replaced by a geometry of postural variables in which each inclination towards the Other assumes a role of redefinition of the subject.

The Queer Model and the Role of Games

Judith Butler reproposes a feminist theoretical debate on the path of identity constitution: her version of the performative self, immersed in constant change, takes its distance from the thought of sexual difference and also from the French stream of materialism. Gender is part of a process of continuous construction and deconstruction of the subjects ego: each subject is in fact in a repetitive rhythm of doing and undoing in a practical way. The definition of identity is never an exclusively personal or social process, but it is always a cross between the two dimensions that are in a constant continuum. Butler's goal is to challenge the idealized limits of the body (physical and mental), to replace the supposed immobility of them with the conception of an incessant weaving practice.

For this reason, the American philosopher uses the category of performativity: gender is performative in the first place because it is the result of a practice, a path of actions that each subject has the opportunity to perform in a voluntary framework; secondly, it is performative because, since it is never given, it is unique. The desire to recreate one's own identity must not be interpreted as a postmodern substitution of individual Cartesian and Kantian autonomy. In fact, everyone is characterized by a story inscribed in the body, but also by the faculty of transformation and the game of his own self.[1]

Two key concepts of Butlerian reflection are *body* and *agency*. In relation to these concepts, Butler argues that accepting the fact of being socially constructed opens the possibility of contesting the ego's supra-determining rules (for example the heteropatriarchal regime, which imposes mandatory heterosexuality and places individuals in a naturally hierarchical context). Recognizing the potential for body change is a revolutionary act also in relation to the political and social world.

As regards agency, Butler uses a theatrical context as a descriptive panorama of her theory: each subject improvises itself on a stage, without knowing the script by heart of its role (against the corporeal mechanism), but always with the other and for the other. In this sense, gender is never made in a solitary dimension, because it demands recognition. The collective dimension is therefore also functional to the construction of an alternative vision.

With regard to this political dimension, Butler also emphasizes the policy of alliance of bodies: a feminism that wants to be consistent in practice with the theoretical conception of plurality and the elimination of any symbolic order must accept its contradictions, implementing coalition strategies that recognize the differences and the possibility of confrontation between them.

Cavarero and Butler show that identity has a polyvalent nature and that the meaning attributed to each subject is related to the context within which the subject acts, relates and is recognized and appointed. The identity criteria are therefore modified because of the addiction of metamorphosis. The third criterion concerns the porosity of identity, related to the openness to the future.

On the other side, post-colonial and trans-feminist movements have taught the recognition of the meaning of which everybody is the bearer. For this reason, identity is also recognized not only as a present temporality, but also as a past, which is often represented by prejudices and stereotypes deriving from a system of domination and oppression of which the body is the carrier.

---

[1] A similar reasoning may refer to intersex persons, for example to the violent physical and symbolic imposition on the bodies of intersex newborns.

To put this in a wider temporal framework, body construction also allows to recognize the existence of a past of domination and oppression and to appeal to individual and collective responsibilities in the future perspective.

The Centrality of the Body in Stereotypes: The Myths of the Black Woman

The most emblematic position to demonstrate the centrality attributed to the role of the body, both in an ontological and epistemic position, but also in the political and social domain, is the black body.

The body is the bearer of cultural signs and is therefore historically constructed. For this reason, fantasy and eccentric expression play a politically revolutionary role: subtracting the body from the dichotomously sexualized economy allows to take part in a policy of openness and acceptance of contradiction and diversity.

An example of narration of the self as instrument of reshaping is present in black feminism. As Angela Davis shows, the history of feminism is populated not only by the bodies of white and *bourgeois* women, but it is found, perhaps in its most resistant version, in the history of the bodies of black slave women. Davis proposes a non-traditional interpretation of the slave who, far from being a symbol of oppression and compliance, emerges as an example of moral and physical resistance. The bodies of black slave women are in contrast within the female norm. Black women are categorized as male bodies when their strength and resistance is to be employed for profit in the great plantations of the South. The slave's body, however, is also the body that does not break under the weight of fatigue, which shows with evidence its strength.

The stereotype that derives from the two binomials refers to the sphere of morality and also to the aesthetic one: the myth of the beautiful white, which is made to coincide with the right and the moral good, is not declined in modern times only with regard to pigmentation, but it is extended to the whole phenotype, which is canonized in art. Stereotypes related to white beauty and the good are particularly evident in the way black beauty is presented, especially of the female body.

The black slave's body is a synthesis of the two oppressions, race-related and gender-related. The myths in which the black woman is the protagonist in fact show the intersectional nature of oppression experienced by black women: they represent such women through a series of racist and sexist cultural stereotypes that have been assimilated as the ontological archetypes of the black body.

As George Mosse argues that the stereotype of the body is born in modern times, so black feminists trace the stereotypes of black women's bodies back to the age of slavery, arguing that such myths still conditioned the Western imagery and the relationship between black and white. The three myths arising are today a justification for the racist attitude, for example, towards unpaid work allocation. Sex and assisted reproduction work, domestic work, care work and jobs requiring unskilled work in the economic and political order of capitalist societies are carried out by subjects who are included in a historical scope of exploitation and racism.

The first myth that is considered refers to the animal construction of the body of the black woman. The myths that see the black woman's body as the protagonist are characterized primarily by their historical nature. As reported by Angela Davis and bell hooks, the black woman's narratives fit into a historical and relational framework built during the 18th- and 19th-century slavery experience in the southern United States. During the experience of slavery, women work as slaves in the fields of the landowners next to black men and at the same time they have sexual and reproductive relations with the white master. They are doing domestic work and care at the house of the white settler in the service of the wife.[2]

The two contrasting representations of black women depend on the Other with whom they have relations. Michele Wallace highlights the process of virilization of the female body during working time. The process of equality between the black male and the female body removes the woman's body from the dynamic of protection, which is a peculiarity of the white woman. The instrumentality of the elimination of gender relationships is therefore at first functional, it aims at preventing the creation of relational alliances. Wallace argues that assigning the black woman the attribute of power means referring to her historical self. This creates a comparison and a consequent oppressive dynamic with respect to the female alterego: compared to white women, in fact, black women are beasts of burden.

The animal trait with which they are described also falls within the dynamics of sexual relations: unlike white women, black women lack the virginal aspect that leads the illiterate white girls to the altar. The animalistic connotation is a further justification for the possibility of sexual abuse by the colonist: he is master both as a man and as a white man. For these reasons, the sexual act is considered as a more legitimate practice because it is inserted within a process of domestication.

---

[2] In the word of bell hooks: "Black female slaves had shown that they were capable of performing so-called 'manly' labour, that they were able to endure hardship, pain and privation, but could also perform those so-called 'womanly' tasks of housekeeping, cooking and child rearing".

The animalistic construction of the representation of the black body and the alleged equality between men and women with respect to labor exploitation in the fields feed two other cultural stereotypes: the black woman is at the same time a superwoman and a prostitute. The myth of the superwoman, declined in the meaning of the matriarchy, concerns the family context both with respect to the children and with respect to the partner/husband and the work context.

The sexual aspect is a source of stereotypes for both the woman and the black man, whose bodies are both hypersexualized. Although the bodies are subject to the same representative dynamic, the rhetoric that is used towards the man is different from that adopted for the woman: on the one hand, the accentuation of the black man's sexuality is often used to legitimize violence against non-white communities, in the name of defending their own women. On the other hand, black women are credited with sexual promiscuity to justify acts of violence and rape.[3]

The sexual dynamic between the black woman and the white man is relevant in two aspects: first, the body object of the black slave is a guarantee compared to the production of labor power and a certainty of sexual enjoyment for the colonist. Secondly, this dynamic also affects the relationship with the white woman, which guarantees the colonist the birth of children, allowing the hereditary succession of the large estate.

According to Collins, the black prostitute should not only be considered as an object to satisfy sexual pleasure, but also as Jézabel: the body of the black woman is tempting and the sexuality she proposes is deviant and therefore the man has no chance to resist it. The specific trait of Jézabel concerns the insatiability of her sexual appetites and for this reason she is often presented as a monster.[4] The white body and the black body of the woman are carriers of two different sexual approaches: the first is subjected to a passive dynamic, the second is instead active and enforceable. The black man's sexuality and the role played by the Jézabel are therefore a danger to the purity of the white race and for this reason it is necessary to adopt a monstrous rhetoric towards their inhuman bodies.

In addition to being presented as an animal body subjected to labor fatigue and as a monstrous body and tempter from a sexual point of view, the body of the black woman is also inserted within relational contexts of care. The figure of the nanny is the other aspect in which the motherhood of black women is de-

---

3 As Davis argues, "The right to dispose of slave bodies claimed by the owners was a direct expression of their presupposed right owned by the entire black population", *Women, Race and Class*.
4 The Western counterpart is represented by the Sirens in Greek mythology, hypersexualized monsters that tempt men through singing, as Cavarero (1997) shows in *Tu che mi guardi, tu che mi racconti*.

clined alongside the figure of the matriarch. This role is determined according to the relationship that the slave woman entertains with the wife of the colonist.

Moreover, just as matriarchs represent a bad version of motherhood, the nannies under the control and orders of the colonist and his wife realize the ideal of the good mother, obedient and devoid of sexual impulses.

A second fundamental characteristic of the nanny concerns the sexual aspect: in total contrast to the Jézabel, the body of the nanny is depicted as asexual and missing any attribute that can cause sexual attraction to the male gaze. The representation of the fatty body of the nanny plays the allegorical function inherent to fertility: it is not the reproductive fertility, but productive fertility.

The functionality of myths and stereotypes used to describe the black woman as a workable and sexually exploitable body, in addition to having a specific historical and cultural matrix, shows that these representations have their roots in a sexist and racist mythology. The process of recognition of the mythological transformation in an ontological archetype is therefore necessary to make explicit the modalities through which the identity construction can be determined by domination relations linked to race and sex. The female body, in fact, in each of its roles, can be declined according to a sexual meaning compared to a male counterpart. The slave working in the fields, the matriarch and the nanny share with white women the sexual attribute: in this sense the category of the "woman" is built in that it is inserted within a biological determinism related to reproduction and in a heterosexual relational paradigm, in which rape as a tool of systematic domination and sexual enjoyment explicitly indicates the position of male domination.

Conclusion: A Post-identity Perspective

In this paper I tried to problematize and link the dichotomy between the abstraction of theoretical reflection on the constitution of the subject with the dimension of lived, emotional past. I recognized the existence of an "I" which is characterized by a biographical terrain. It is not confined to individual experience, but it is shared in a collective dimension.

Although I focused mainly on the constitutive dimension of the female and the black self, my interest was directed by the intention of overcoming the identity paradigm itself. For this reason, I have progressively shifted the attention from the singular aspect to the plural one, taking into consideration both the constitutive dimension of the process of subjection within an ecological and intra-relational framework and the social dimension of identities.

Recognizing one's own formation as a result of belonging to multiple social groups is the first fundamental step to undermine the conception of identity as a defined, stable and fixed dimension. By giving experience a central role in the process of shaping identity, I underscored the unpredictable aspect of the self, which undermines the notions of racial definition, including ethnic belonging and origin (both national and phenotypic).

A relevant aspect is the investigation of the social component in the creation of the plurality of the self of which everyone is the bearer: membership of multiple groups determines a variety of aspects and attitudes that undermine the very foundations of the notion of identity. In addition to this functionality, the notion of social identity also makes it easier to undertake paths of politicization.

Considering, for example, racism as the institutionalization of the hierarchy involved in global labor inequality and exploitation, social identity plays a fundamental role in the organization of political resistance.

The use of an identity policy is functional only when it is not considered as particularism of a minority, but, on the contrary, when the aim is to implement an overall different paradigm. At the same time, an identity policy is only functional until it translates into a political ideological universalism. This risk can be avoided if identity is investigated on the basis of social relations and if an analysis of the same conditions is undertaken by adopting a materialistic prospective.

The continuous interaction with the other and the constitution of a subject that is defined starting from human, non-human and environmental relations represents the emblem of the anti-essentialism. It also makes it possible to demonstrate the role played by the social component in the formation of the self and the adoption of the whole as the only possibility of identity definition.

An appeal to identity is useful only as an act of claim for the improvement of conditions on a global scale.

At an individual level, the identity must be considered both with respect to a horizontal dimension and to a vertical dimension, that is temporal, with regard to the process of change and transformation that characterize the same. In this sense, identity must be considered as an element inserted in a dialectic path. If at first the construction of one's own identity facilitates the political act of claiming improvement or emancipation, once such positioning is obtained it is necessary to abandon the identity attribute.

Within a historical perspective, identity has represented an excellent category of description and reorganization of the world for the 20th century, a criterion around which people have created a sense of belonging, civil struggles and communities, but today, within the global paradigm, it is a reactionary approach. Identity, in fact, is no longer called into question, in the Western context, as a possibility of openness for political participation and for a real implementation of representative democracy, but is presented as a strategy of defense and exclusion of the other.

For this reason, the 21st century is a chance to embark on a post-identity policy, in which identity as a strategy of "oppression-of-the-self" is replaced by the post-identity practice of "self-inventing", in imagining new postures based on relationships and no longer based on the classification distinction of humans, but also between non-humans.

In this sense, overcoming identity means abandoning the politics of singularity and recognizing the existence of a subject starting from the relationships that it entertains and that form it, as the different currents of feminism have demonstrated.

References

Appiah, K. A. (2005). *The Ethics of Identity*. Princeton: Princeton University Press.
Butler, J. (1990). *Gender Trouble. Feminism and the Subversion of Identity*. London: Routledge.
Cavarero, A. (1987). "Per una teoria della differenza sessuale". In: Cavarero, A. et al. (Eds.), *Diotima. Il pensiero della differenza sessuale*. Milan: La Tartaruga, 41–79.
Cavarero, A. (1990). *Nonostante Platone. Figure femminili nella filosofia antica*. Rome: Editori Riuniti.
Cavarero, A. (1997). *Tu che mi guardi, tu che mi racconti. Filosofia della narrazione*. Milan: Feltrinelli.
Collins, P. H. (2018 [1990]). *Black Feminist Thought. Knowledge, Consciousness and the Politics of Empowerment*. Montreal: Les éditions de remue-ménage.
Davis, A. (2005). *Beyond the Frame: Women of Color and Visual Representation*. New York: Palgrave Macmillan.
Davis, A. (2018 [1983]). *Women, Race and Class*, tr. By A. Prunetti. Rome: Alegre.
Hamrouni, N. and Maillé, C. (2016). *Le sujet du féminisme est-il blanc? Femmes racisées et recherche féministe*. Montreal: Les éditions du remue-ménage.
Mosse, G. (1978). *Il razzismo in Europa. Dalle origini all'Olocausto*. Rome: Edizioni Laterza.
Wallace, M. (1979). *Black Macho and the Myth of Superwoman*. London: Verso.

Ariadni Polychroniou
"*Je me* révolte, donc *nous* sommes": Reconceptualizing Contemporary Refugee Resistances through the Butlerian Reconstruction of Hannah Arendt's Public Sphere

Abstract: The present article critically investigates Judith Butler's feminist reconstruction of the Arendtian public sphere in terms of a novel theoretical framework for the illustration of contemporary refugee mobilizations. The first sub-section introduces the reader to the tumultuous historical reception of Hannah Arendt's political thought within feminist philosophy. In the second sub-section, the article explores the Butlerian re-interpretation of the performative character of the Arendtian public sphere within the context of contemporary collective struggles against neoliberal governmentality. In the third sub-chapter, the article illuminates Butler's feminist problematization of the core Arendtian distinction between the public and the private, by tracing four different, yet interrelating, pillars of Butlerian critique. In the final sub-chapter, the author argues that the radical Butlerian reconceptualization of the Arendtian public sphere provides a more coherent epistemological approach to the critical depiction of contemporary refugee resistances than the direct application of the Arendtian political philosophy to the social phenomenon in question.

Hannah Arendt' s Nebulous Reception within the Realm of Feminist Philosophy

Arendt's reception within the realm of feminist theory is characterized by a turbulent history of confrontational interpretations, critical confutations and productive resignalizations. Therefore, the historical periodization of the interaction between the Arendtian oeuvre and feminist thought does not possess a clear, homogeneous or linear texture. Following significant theoretical contributions of prominent feminist scholars (Young-Bruehl 1982; Dietz 1995; Honig 1995), we could taxonomize the feminist responses to the polysemous Arendtian legacy in a threefold historical schema. Interestingly, the mutable theoretical interplay between the Arendtian political theory and feminist critique is crucially influenced by the evolution of feminist thought itself: From the radical feminism of the 1970s to the post-structuralist redefinitions of gender, sexuality and embodiment in the beginning of the 21st century, Arendtian philosophy is drastically reconstructed in multiple and unanticipated modalities with the realm of feminist theory.

The echoing absence of a gendered perspective in Arendt's political theory,[1] as well as her troubling reluctance to actively support her time's women struggles, led the first feminist theoreticians that systematically studied her legacy (Rich 1979; Pitkin 1981; Hertz 1984; O'Brien 1981) to categorically label Arendtian political philosophy as profoundly anti-feminist. According to these early feminist evaluations, Arendtian thought is infiltrated by a problematic male-oriented discursive economy. In particular, feminist critique focused on the core Arendtian distinction between the lucid public sphere of political action and the hidden a-political private sphere of need, as well as on Arendt's problematization of the pure political's submersion in the social. Some feminist school further designated the Arendtian subject's construction in terms of an abstract, rational and immaterial entity. Along with other early feminist confutations of Arendt's legacy, these critical insights contributed to the early stigmatization of the Arendtian corpus as a representative illustration of "the tragedy of a female brain nourished on male ideologies" (Rich 1979, 211–212).

Contrary to this first Arendtian renunciation in the realm of the 1970s–1980s feminist tradition, feminist thinkers such as Julia Kristeva (2001) and Adriana Cavarero (1995, 2002, 2005) attempted, since the beginning of the 1990s, to re-read Arendtian theory under a renewed prismatic. By illuminating the crucial conceptualization of *natality* as a constitutive nucleus of Arendtian thought, and by further tracing liberating and empowering female qualities within her numerous writings, these feminist scholars re-establish the figure of Hannah Arendt within feminist politics in terms of a highly influential 'female genius' ('la genie feminine') and a 'philosopher of birth', respectively. Under this prism, feminist reconceptualizations of the Arendtian notions of embodied action, narrative, critique, uniqueness, plurality and reflexivity, forged unprecedented communicative channels between the Arendtian corpus and feminist theory, leading to the development of new social ontologies and gendered redefinitions of political action.[2]

---

[1] For a critical contemporary refutation of Arendt's indifference towards gendered issues, see Maslin 2013.

[2] By critically evaluating early feminist responses to the Arendtian scholarship, Honkasalo (2014) interestingly argues that both the first hostile interpretations of Arendt in terms of a 'masculine philosopher' and the second "gynocentric" feminist re-explorations of the Arendtian corpus reproduce normative patriarchal limitations of gender bipolarity, while essentializing the notions of masculinity and femininity.

Through the ground-breaking retheorization of Arendtian theory by the feminist philosopher Bonnie Honig, Arendt's philosophical work is re-introduced to feminist critique in terms of a performative, agonistic and democratic political theory of difference and plurality. By systematizing Arendt's theoretical convergence with Nietzsche, Foucault, Derrida and Butler, numerous recent scholars (Dietz 1995, 2002; Ring 1991; Zerilli 1995; Cutting-Gray 1993; Adams 2002; Allen 1999; Kramer 1989; Kaplan 1997; Eribon 1999; Feit 2011; Honkasalo 2014) revitalize the Arendtian conceptions of political action, identity, distinctiveness, collectivity, resistance and the notion of the pariah. Drawing upon Arendt's emblematic works *The Human Condition* and the *Origins of Totalitarism*, as well as her less studied oeuvre, such as her biographies of Rosa Luxemburg (Arendt 1966) and Rahel Varnhagen (Arendt 1957), current feminist and queer scholars have redefined the Arendtian corpus as a fertile breeding ground for the theoretical reconstruction of sexuality, subjectivity, citizenship, recognition, coalition strategy and non-identitarian solidarity.

The above overview of Arendt's adventurous reception within the realm of feminist theory foreshadows the equally hybrid and contested philosophical relationship between Hannah Arendt and Judith Butler. We believe that the complex theoretical dialogue between these two prominent women philosophers could be systematized through four distinct modalities: Contemporary Butlerian re-interpretations of central Arendtian notions (e. g. the Butlerian codification of the Arendtian 'right to have rights' as a performative collective enactment on behalf of precarious subjectivities[3]), direct theoretical influences of the Arendtian political thought on the reformulation of significant Butlerian conceptualizations (e. g. the Arendtian public sphere of appearance as a theoretical platform for the Butlerian transition from gender performativity to the sociopolitical notion of collective performativity), polemic Butlerian critiques of anti-feminist Arendtian axioms (e. g. the Butlerian deconstruction of the Arendtian distinctions between the private and the public), as well as unexpected points of theoretical convergence, that do not derive from a traceable Arendtian influence on Butlerian philosophical reflections.[4]

---

3 *Contra* Benhabib (2004), Butler reinterprets the Arendtian 'right to have rights' in terms of an agonistic collective performative enactment of freedom (Butler 2007, 2015). However, Butler is neither the first philosopher to trace performative features in the Arendtian scholarship (Honig 1992, 1993, 1995), nor the only postmodern thinker to designate the inherent contingency and constitutive non-foundationalism of the Arendtian notion of the 'right to have rights' (Balibar 2014, 165–186).
4 Ingala (2017) argues, for instance, that both female philosophers construct their notion of the political in anti-essentialist and relational terms. According to Ingala, both Arendt and Butler conceptualize the public topology of the political as a multi-prismatic, plural and constitutively heter-

Contrary to other feminist theorists and male philosophers (Rancière 2004) Butler does not perfunctorily reject Arendt's political legacy by virtue of its phenomenally essentialist, elitist or depoliticizing character. In fact, Butler retrogressively dwells upon the Arendtian oeuvre, chiseling crucial conceptual tools that both elucidate and fertilize her own poststructural ethico-political theory. Butler's ambivalent interaction with the Arendtian universe, constitutes, in reality, a profoundly complex philosophical osmosis, the theoretical unraveling of which could dynamically lead to radical reconceptualizations of our contemporary sociopolitical condition.

The Public Sphere as a Relational Topology of Contemporary Political Struggles

In her emblematic work *The Human Condition* (1958b), Arendt conceptualizes the public sphere as a lively political topology. Within the public sphere, openly visible and widely recognizable acts of political significance take place in the presence of others and compose, together with the equally public and influential performances of other co-actors, a common political reality. According to Arendt, the public sphere does not encapsulate a static, natural, a-chronical or apriorical substance of the political. On the contrary, the political emerges *performatively* through the concerted action and mutual recognition of plural and heterogeneous actors that publicly circulate their political ideas and openly pursue their political attainments. Hence, the construction, development and preservation of this Arendtian spatiality of political co-existence depends on the disparity, fluidity and heterogeneity of its political actors and devitalizes itself, respectively, under a regime of enforced uniformity or an authoritarian status of unilateral political decision-making.

As Arendt uniquely argues, the public sphere constructs an *in-between*, which, similar to a table, both unites and separates distinct political members. By emphatically establishing the radical alterity and indomitable multiplicity of world-views

---

ogeneous nexus of constantly renegotiated and variable bonds. Moreover, in both theoretical frameworks, the subject is constructed within a relational social ontology, by acquiring fluid, non-identitarian and relational conceptual features. However, Butlerian subjectivity is not forged through a theoretical osmosis with the Arendtian heritage. Butler's account of subjectivity conceptually emerges as relational, fluid and vulnerable through a heterogeneous and constantly re-articuled amalgam of post-structuralist feminist theory, Althusserian structuralism, Foucauldian philosophy, Levinasian ethics and psychoanalytical theories of Freud, Lacan and Klein.

as quasi-normative sources of the political, Arendt discerns that both autocratic regimes and capitalist consumerist societies suppress, through differentiated power mechanisms, the vital political parameters of difference and plurality. As she eloquently observes, "The end of the common world has come when it is seen only under one aspect and is permitted to present itself in only one perspective" (Arendt 1958, 57).

Partially echoing the ancient Greek conception of the *polis*, the limpid public sphere of the political constructs itself dialectically with the dark, unseen and propolitical realm of the private, the "kingdom of life and death", which is deprived of an estuary to both the worldly community and the others. In this private topology, biological, embodied and material needs are satisfied away from the public eye, reproduction takes place, manual activities are carried out, personal and familial bonds are forged, interiority is explored, the household is ruled and property is organized. According to Arendt, the historical transition to modernity blurs the strict archaic divisions between the private and the public through the ardent surface of pressing social issues, such as financial distribution, labor organization, material sustainment, house economics, reproductive and bodily concerns, within the heart of politics.

Prominent feminist thinkers adopt a selective approach towards the Arendtian conceptualization of the public sphere (Zerilli 1995; Honig 1992, 1995; Cavarero 2005; Benhabib 1993; Butler 2015).The majority of them heavily criticize the public/private division as inherently anti-feminist, while positively acknowledging the performative and relational structure of Arendtian politics as an innovative theoretical framework for the current re-interpretation of feminist, anti-racist, immigrant, LGBTQ+ and widely democratic political struggles.

As Taylor (2017) interestingly claims, Butler facilitates the crucial transition from her early theory of gender performativity to her latest ethico-political account of precarious subjects' collective performativity via the reconceptualization of the Arendtian public sphere. By reinterpreting the sphere of appearance in terms of a formerly non-existent, but *ad hoc* emerging, political topology of multiple agonistic struggles, Butler indeed theorizes contemporary social mobilizations and political assemblies as radical expressions of *collective embodied performances* (Butler 2013, 2015, 2020). Under this prism, the heterogeneous and plural agonized resistances of institutionally invisibilized *abjects* penetrate the normative frames of recognizability and the dominant schemas of intelligibility (Butler 2004, 2009), by dynamically re-introducing alternative modalities of being within the public sphere of appearance. This collective political enactment performatively abrogates certain social categories and populations' legally dictated or socioculturally embedded *prohibition to appear* – or license to appear in restrictively validated tropes – in the sphere of the public. Therefore, for Butler, these subversive collective appearances radically re-establish discoursively expelled and hegemonically depoliticized social subjectivities as *par excellence* political actors. Hence, the fragile enactment of the right to appear on behalf of precaritized populations performatively constructs the realm of the political itself as a not pre-defined, yet incandescent, fluid and tumultuous, spatiality of constant translocations, conceptual recodifications, unexpected coalitions and inherent power struggles.

By re-theorizing the non-reductive, pluralistic and disperse political mobilizations of our time as enfleshed depictions of the performative surfacing of the public, Butler masterfully intertwines two core Arendtian conceptualizations, namely the relational emergence of the public sphere and the ambivalent enactment of the 'right to have rights'. Interestingly, she interprets the right to publicly appear as an actual manifestation of the latter and claims that its agonistic vindication on behalf of dispossessed subjectivities opens up and transforms the public sphere of appearance:

> In Arendtian terms, we can say that to be precluded from the space of appearance, to be precluded from being part of the plurality that brings the space of appearance into being, is to be deprived of the right to have rights. Plural and public action is the exercise of the right to place and belonging, and this exercise is the means by which the space of appearance is presupposed and brought into being. (Butler 2015, 59–60)

Under this Arendtian influence, Butler further accomplishes to theoretically re-approach the hybrid post-identitarian texture of sociopolitical bonds between distinctively precaritized subjects. Contemporary revolting subjectivities function, at the moment of their multi-participatory mobilizations, neither individualistic, autonomous and self-centered, nor as a uniform collective body with pre-fixed essentialized qualities and identical political aspirations. On the contrary, an ephemeral, interdependent and spontaneous 'we' emerges performatively during the climactic temporality of collective political struggle in terms of "a collective acting without a preestablished collective subject" (Butler 2015, 59). Through an aspiring analogy, we could trace the core of this Butlerian conception in the emblematic Camusean paraphrase of the Cartesian cogito, "*Je* me révolte, donc *nous* sommes" (Camus 1951).

Towards a Radical Reconstruction of the Limits of the Political

Based on the above observations, Butler vividly endorses the performative emergence of the Arendtian public sphere. Nevertheless, Butler emphatically argues that the capacity to performatively enact these constitutive political actions is not equally allocated to all social actors, given that the fulfillment of this potential extensively depends on complex gendered, racialized and class-based hierarchizations. In particular, Butler focuses on the synthetic plexus of sociopolitical, cultural and discursive power mechanisms which enable, undermine or pulverize each social subject's access to the realm of the political. She, therefore, claims that precarious political struggles and subversive social protests cannot apriorically transmute themselves into revolutionary spikes, adept at perforating the exclusionary limitations of the public sphere.

Under this prism, Butler problematizes the rigid Arendtian dichotomy between the public and the private on the grounds that it normatively constructs two hierarchically structured and strictly non-interchangeable subject-positions: On the one hand, the political subjects of the public realm, which only resort to the hidden domain of the private for the satisfaction of – politically indifferent and hierarchically subordinate – biological-material necessities. On the other, the depoliticized embodied subjects of the private sphere, which reside in obscurity, burdening themselves, through their unpaid or low-paid domestic care work, with the invisible *reproduction* of the former. According to Butler, this Arendtian polarization dominantly articulates certain – masculine, heterosexual, rational, white, assertive – subjects as ideotypically appropriate for political action and public appearance, by ostracizing the sexualized, feminized, racialized, foreign Other within an unseen pro-political or a-political territory.

Highlighting the profoundly *phallogocentric* texture of this Arendtian distinction, Butler designates the Arendtian political theory's incapacity to codify the political struggles of those social subjects, which typically "belong" to the private sphere and dynamically assert their access to the prohibited realm of the political. Hence, according to Butler, the emergence of the public sphere does not solely require performing political acts in concert with other equal and free social actors. More importantly, the radical construction of the realm of the political burrows through the *critique* of the power differentials, that dominantly regulate the exclusionary boundaries of the public sphere, as well as through the formation of non-identitarian *solidarity alliances* among the multiple social categories of the excluded:

> There can be no entry into the sphere of appearance without a critique of the differential forms of power by which that sphere is constituted, and without a critical alliance formed among the discounted, the ineligible-the precarious-to establish new forms of appearance that seek to overcome that differential form of power. It may well be that every form of appearance is constituted by its "outside," but that is no reason not to continue the struggle. Indeed, that is only a reason to insist upon the struggle as ongoing. (Butler 2015, 50–51)

Based on the Butlerian critique, the Arendtian dichotomy *depoliticizes* in advance certain social subjectivities, by naturalizing their entrapment in the private and by further invisibilizing the dominant sociopolitical processes that lead to their violent exclusion from the vibrant political arena:

> Can the public ever be constituted as such without some population relegated to the private and, hence, the pre-political, and isn't this radically unacceptable for any radical democratic political vision? Is this very distinction evidence of an anti-democratic ethos in Arendt, one we would have to overcome if we were to extend her reflections on the stateless more radically and in ways that speak to contemporary global conditions? (Butler and Spivak 2007, 22–23)

The Butlerian re-reading of *Arendt contra Arendt* (Beltrán 2009) radically transforms the performative texture of Arendtian political action into a struggling political endeavor of the dispossessed (Butler and Athanasiou 2013). The multifaceted agonistic mobilizations of contemporary precarious subjects are, therefore, reconstructed as a performative force capable of blurring and deconstructing the boundaries between the private and the public through the accomplishment of a drastic rift in the sphere of appearance.

Moreover, the Arendtian exclusion of *necessity* from the sphere of the political obscures the theoretical reflection on the contemporary political struggles against neoliberal precarity. As Butler claims, collective mobilizations against precarity shall not be perceived as less political or evaluatively inferior to the 'pure' Arendtian fights for freedom. The political character of these struggles emerges precisely from the decomposition and re-assemblage of both the symbolic and the material public topology of the political. Within this theoretical horizon, the Arendtian polarization between freedom and necessity denotes, according to Butler, an inmost Cartesian-inspired dualism between the mind and the body. As other feminist scholars have already noticed (e. g. Zerilli 1995), the Arendtian body is dichotomized and depoliticized through the expulsion of biological processes, material necessities and reproductive activities from the political realm. The Arendtian confinement of both materiality and vulnerability within the domain of domesticity constructs an abstract, immaterial and bodiless entity as the subject of politics, while privatizing embodiment as a natural and unavoidable, yet profoundly a-political, condition of the human. Butler, on the contrary, claims that the multitudinous assembly of vulnerable bodies in the public sphere of appearance debunks the Arendtian exclusion of the body from politics and re-establishes contemporary political struggles in terms of primarily embodied collective performances.

Moreover, Butler alleges that the Arendtian dichotomy between the private and the public obfuscates the inexorably *intersubjective and interdependent relations* that are developed among social subjects, living beings, biological processes, institutional procedures and socio-economic structures at the interplay of these illusively oppositional realms. At a first level, Butler critically notices that

> the foreign, unskilled, feminized body that belongs to the private sphere is the condition of possibility for the speaking male citizen (who is presumably fed by someone and sheltered somewhere, and whose nourishment and shelter are tended to in some regular ways by some disenfranchised population or another). (Butler 2015, 45)

Therefore, the normative distinction between the public and the private invisibilizes the constitutive dependence of the luminous topology of politics, civilization and action on the unseen strenuous physical-material activities of the private. Moreover, this Arendtian polarization largely ignores every living being's unexceptional and indivisible dependence on both political enshrinements, democratic processes and institutionalized societal structures, *as well as* on material infrastructures, intersubjective relationships, financial systems, natural environments and biological processes. Hence, according to Butler, vulnerable life's apriorical exposure to a conjoint nexus of personal relationships, materialities and structures shall be emphatically recognized as a core axis for a drastic reconceptualization of social subjectivity, as well as for a radical re-articulation of heterogeneous contemporary political struggles against institutionalized precarity. Under this prism, collective mobilizations opposed to the asymmetrical withdrawal of a liminal life-sustaining plexus are resignified as constitutively political and expansionary of the normative limitations of what is seen and what is expressed within the public sphere.

Butler's Re-articulation of the Arendtian Public Sphere in Practice

In the last decade, numerous refugee and migration scholars have extensively utilized the Arendtian political theory for the interpretation of multiple aspects of the contemporary refugee crisis (Berstein 2005; Franke 2008; Agier 2011; Adelman and Barkan 2011; Krause 2008; Oudejans 2014; Osso 2019). Among them, Patrick Hayden and Natasha Saunders (2019) and Ayten Gündoğdu (2015) develop two of most systematic epistemological analyses of modern refugee resistances through the Arendtian conceptual framework. Within this context, the relational articulation of the Arendtian public sphere, as well as the performative character of the Arendtian 'right to have rights' have been intensively retheorized for the conceptualization of refugee and migrant political struggles in terms of *alternative political practices of citizenship* (see also DeGooyer et at. 2018).

However, based on the above reflections, we believe that the Butlerian reconstruction of the Arendtian public sphere provides a more nuanced epistemological, theoretical and methodological framework for the critical illustration of contemporary refugee political struggles. In particular, we claim that even if we re-introduce Arendt's polysemous conceptual universe in agonistic, performative and relational terms, the pressing question remains: *Where* is the contemporary refugee subject located within the Arendtian public-private axis, and, subsequently, *how* can refugee struggles be interpreted as political under these strict Arendtian distinctions?

As Bradley (2014) interestingly argues, the refugee subject is passivitized in the Arendtian thought, in that she lacks political agency and co-constructing political capacity. Although Arendt theorizes the "talented refugee" as an exceptional personality that individually overcomes the grave calamity of the refugee condition (1958), and despite the fact that she further traces, in the examples of Franz Kafka or Bernard Lazare, the illuminated refugee figure of the 'conscious pariah', to whom "history is no longer a closed book and politics is no longer the privilege of the gentiles" (Arendt 1943, 274), the above refugee subjects reflect strikingly notable *singular exceptions*. They do not illustrate generalized processes of mass politicization or subversive collective actions, adept at re-establishing a morally diminished and juridopolitically deprived population in the center of the public topology of political contest.

As we have observed above, the more mature Arendt of the *Human Condition* makes the direct implementation of her political theory in the modern retheorization of refugee political struggles even harder. Given that the subject of the current refugee crisis resides at the margins of the political community and survives, moves, works and struggles within a restrictive *extrapolitical* field beyond the eyes of the public, she would be reasonably taxonomized, in Arendtian terms, as a modern *animal laborans* or as a shadowy figure within the expelled territory of the private. As Judith Butler eloquently argues, the radical precaritization of the modern refugee subject derives from this very subject's uncontested positioning in the depoliticized realm of the private before the emergence of any possibility for equalized interaction, political recognition or solidarity building with other social subjectivities (Butler and Spivak 2007, 14–16).

In reality, contemporary refugee resistance oscillates between the public and the private, the luminous and the dark, the legal and the illegal, the city and the camp, by drastically de-constructing and re-articulating all the above normative polarizations. Such phenomenally imperceptible and largely unrecognized acts of political resistance are manifested through the refugees' activism and mutual assistance, collective protests, public mobilizations, cultural interchanges, embodied vindications, networking and communication practices, solidarity alliances, hunger strikes and other self-destructive acts with apparent political signalization. As many significant scholars of refugee resistance critically observe (Nyers 2006, 2019; Tyler and Marciniak 2015; Sager 2015), current refugee vindications are characterized by unbridgeable plurality, polyvocality and heterogeneity, and are visibilized through the close examination of non-typical political actions, everyday practices, linguistic utterances and embodied interactions.

Contrarily to the Arendtian conceptualization of political action as apriorically public, free and unadulterated from economic, social and material concerns, contemporary refugee resistance emerges as a hybrid amalgam of simultaneous rabid struggles for actual survival, legal recognition, material support, educational and working opportunities, political co-existence, cultural osmosis, intentional mobilization and meaningful self-representation. Multifaceted refugee resistances cannot be categorized in advance either as belonging to the public sphere of conjoint political action or as encapsulated within the private realm of naked existence, since, as both Butler and Rancière highlight, such precarious struggles *constitute* the very mutable border of the political. As an interstice between the external and the internal, modern refugee resistance is, therefore, re-articulated as infinitely *performative:* It performs, disassembles and recreates the limits of the public sphere, the notion of the political, the definition of citizenship, the texture of political subjectivity and the context of participatory democratic struggles.

Conclusion

In a different paper, we have argued that the Butlerian constellation between vulnerability and resistance theorizes modern refugee subjectivity in the most luminous way by overcoming the dominant representational threat-victim bipolarity (Polychroniou 2021). In this theoretical contribution, we endeavored to illustrate that the Butlerian reconstruction of the Arendtian public sphere provides the most nuanced epistemological framework for the re-conceptualization of modern refugee struggles in terms of radical perforations of the political sphere and autopoietic deconstructions of the normative distinctions between the private and the public. For us, the Butlerian reconstruction of the Arendtian public sphere functions as illustrating evidence of the fascinating theoretical entanglement between the Arendtian heritage and contemporary post-structuralist feminist theory. Moreover, the socio-historical contextualization of this theoretical osmosis within the ongoing refugee crisis introduces critical analytical tools for the comprehension of the political character of formally not recognized collective struggles. Finally, we believe that through this theoretical re-articulation of the political, Butler accomplishes, in her latest work, to directly theorize contemporary refugee protests as embodied performative exercises of non-violent agonistic action (Butler 2020). Thus, the public refugee protests that took place in 2012 in Würzburg, Germany and in 2017 in Calais, France were interpreted, in Butlerian terms, as alternative embodied, wordless, theatrical-like incarnations of political action and collective resistance, which drastically re-established the limits of the Western public sphere by the agonistic invasion of normatively depoliticized and structurally invisibilized social subjects within the heart of the political.

References

Adams, K. (2002). "At the Table with Arendt: Towards a Self-Interested Practice of Coalition Discourse". *Hypatia* 17(1), 1–33.
Allen, A. (1999). "Solidarity After Identity Politics: Hannah Arendt and the Power of Feminist Theory". *Philosophy & Social Criticism* 25(1), 97–118.
Arendt, H. (1943). "We Refugees". *The Menorah Journal* 31(1), 69–77.
Arendt, H. (1957). *Rahel Varnhagen: The Life of a Jewess.* London: Institute by the East and West Library.
Arendt, H. (1958a). *The Origins of Totalitarianism.* New York: Harcourt Brace.
Arendt, H. (1958b). *The Human Condition.* New York: Harcourt Brace.
Arendt, H (1968). "Rosa Luxemburg 1871–1919". In Arendt, H., *Men in Dark Times.* New York: Harcourt Brace Jovanovich.
Balibar, E. (2014). *Equaliberty: Political Essays.* Durham: Duke University Press.
Beltrán, C. (2009). "Going Public: Hannah Arendt, Immigrant Action, and the Space of Appearance". *Political Theory* 37(5), 595–622.
Benhabib, S. (1993). "Feminist Theory and Hannah Arendt's Concept of Public Space". *History of the Human Sciences* 6(2), 97–114.
Benhabib, S. (2004). *The Rights of Others: Aliens, Residents, and Citizens.* New York: Cambridge University Press.
Bradley, M. (2014). "Rethinking Refugeehood: Statelessness, Repatriation, and Refugee Agency". *Review of International Studies* 40(1), 101–123.
Butler, J. (2004). *Precarious Life: The Powers of Mourning and Violence.* New York: Verso.
Butler, J. (2009). *Frames of War: When Is Life Grievable?* London and New York: Verso.
Butler, J. (2015). *Notes Towards a Performative Theory of Assembly.* Cambridge, MA: Harvard University Press.
Butler, J. (2020). *The Force of Nonviolence: An Ethico-Political Bind.* London and New York: Verso.
Butler, J. and Athanasiou, A. (2013). *Dispossession: The Performative in the Political.* Cambridge: Polity Press.
Butler, J. and Spivak, G. Ch. (2007). *Who Sings the Nation State? Language, Politics, Belonging.* Calcutta, New York and London: Seagull.
Camus, A. (1951). *L'Homme révolté.* Paris: Gallimard.
Cavarero, A. (1995). *In Spite of Plato: A Feminist Rewriting of Ancient Philosophy.* Oxfordshire: Taylor and Francis.
Cavarero, A. (2005). *For More than One Voice: Towards a Philosophy of the Vocal Expression.* Palo Alto, CA: Stanford University Press.

Cutting-Gray, J. (1993). "Hannah Arendt, Feminism, and the Politics of Alterity: 'What Will We Lose If We Win?'" *Hypatia* 8(1), 35–54.
DeGooyer, S. et al. (2018). *The Right to Have Rights.* New York: Verso.
Dietz, M. (1995). "Feminist Receptions of Hannah Arendt". In Honig, B. (Ed.), *Feminist Interpretations of Hannah Arendt.* University Park: Pennsylvania State University Press, 17–50.
Gündoğdu, A. (2015). *Rightlessness in an Age of Rights: Hannah Arendt and the Contemporary Struggles of Migrants.* Oxford: Oxford University Press.
Hertz, D. (1984). "Hannah Arendt's Rahel Varnhagen". In Fout, J. C. (Ed.), *German Women in the Nineteenth Century: A Social History.* New York: Holmes and Meier.
Honig, B. (1995). "Towards an Agonistic Feminism: Hannah Arendt and the Politics of Identity". In Honig, B. (Ed.), *Feminist Interpretations of Hannah Arendt.* University Park: Pennsylvania State University Press, 135–166.
Honkasalo, J. (2014). "Hannah Arendt as an Ally for Queer Politics?" *Redescriptions: Political Thought, Conceptual History and Feminist Theory.* DOI: 10.7227/R.17.2.5.
Ingala, E. (2018). "From Hannah Arendt to Judith Butler: The Condition of the Political". In Rae, G. and Ingala, E. (Eds.), *Subjectivity and the Political: Contemporary Perspectives.* New York and London: Routledge, 35–53.
Kristeva, J. (2003). *Hannah Arendt.* New York: Columbia University Press.
Maslin, K. (2013). "The Gender-neutral Feminism of Hannah Arendt". *Hypatia* 28(3), 585–601.
Nyers, P. (2006). *Rethinking Refugees: Beyond State of Emergency.* New York: Routledge.
Nyers, P. (2019). *Irregular Citizenship, Immigration, and Deportation.* New York: Routledge.
O'Brien, M. (1981). *The Politics of Reproduction.* Boston: Routledge and Kegan Paul.
Pitkin, H. F. (1981). "Justice: On Relating Private and Public". *Political Theory* 9(2), 327–352.
Pitkin, H. F. (1998). *The Attack of the Blob: Hannah Arendt's Concept of the Social.* Chicago: Chicago University Press.
Polychroniou, A. (2021). "Towards a Critical Reconstruction of Modern Refugee Subjectivity: Overcoming the Threat-Victim Bipolarity with Judith Butler and Giorgio Agamben". *Open Philosophy* 4(1), 252–268.
Rancière, R. (2004). *The Politics of Aesthetics: The Distribution of the Sensible.* London and New York: Continuum.
Rich, A. (1979). *On Lies, Secrets, and Silence: Selected Prose, 1966–1978.* New York: Norton.
Ring, J. (1991). "The Pariah as Hero: Hannah Arendt's Political Actor". *Political Theory* 19(3), 433–452.
Saunders, N. and Hayden, P. (2019). "Solidarity at the Margins: Arendt, Refugees, and the Inclusive Politics of World-Making". In Hiruta, K. (Ed.), *Arendt on Freedom, Liberation, and Revolution.* Cham: Palgrave Macmillan, 171–199.
Taylor, D. (2017). "Butler and Arendt on Appearance, Performativity, and Collective Political Action". *Arendt Studies* 1, 171–176.
Tyler, I. and Marciniak, K. (2014). *Immigrant Protest: Politics, Aesthetics, and Everyday Dissent.* New York: SUNY Press.
Young-Bruehl, E. (1982). *Hannah Arendt, for Love of the World.* New Haven: Yale University Press.
Zerilli, L. (1995). "The Arendtian Body". In Honig, B. (Ed.), *Feminist Interpretations of Hannah Arendt.* University Park: Pennsylvania State University, 167–194.

Rosaura Martínez Ruiz
Covid-19 and "Stay at Home": A Contrast Dye That Highlights Gender Violence and the Violence of Inequity

Abstract: In this paper I argue that the Covid-19 pandemic has been a sort of magnifying glass or perhaps a contrast dye that renders already glaring inequities even more visible by shedding light on their pressing consequences, now showcased in all their cruelty and immediacy. I also claim that the "Stay at home" Mexican social distancing campaign had glaring blind spots, such as the foreseeable increase in domestic violence against women and children, as well as the lack of decent or sufficient shelters for migrants, homeless and sexual dissidents expelled from home. These observations lead me to advocate, first, a critique of the family household as the shelter par excellence; and second, a feminism that stems from a logic of intersectionality.

The Covid-19 pandemic has been a sort of magnifying glass or perhaps a contrast dye that renders already glaring inequities even more visible by shedding light on their pressing consequences, now showcased in all their cruelty and immediacy. If we are to resist a future that has long been shaping itself up as a dire fate, this health, economic and social crisis must get us to think long and hard about the state and government policies that ought to outline our immediate political agenda.

Key national projects – such as free, public, scientific-humanist, quality education, as well as free, quality public health services, and welfare projects for the care and protection of vulnerable sectors of the population – have been historically neglected by Mexican governments (although this seems to be a global phenomenon that pertains to so-called developed countries too), and this disregard has exacerbated the effects of the epidemic to a frightening magnitude that I believe was wholly avoidable. In short, the sheer extent of this health, economic and social crisis cannot be understood without a careful regard of the sociopolitical conditions under which the SARS-CoV-2 virus broke out. For these conditions of worldwide negligence and inequity have turned this pandemic into the story of tragedy upon tragedy that we are all too familiar with – a story which, I insist, must not be naturalized, taken for inevitable or explained away.

The lockdown in Mexico began merely a few weeks after the enormous and unprecedented women's march in Mexico City that took place on 8 March 2020. And when social distancing came about soon after, the questions with regard to political agendas were many: what can be done from lockdown? How to keep feminist thought and struggle alive from home? This is precisely where I wish to address feminism from – that is, from lockdown, at home – but, above all, I want to take on the household itself as a unit of analysis.

"Stay at home" has been at the heart of the Mexican Jornada Nacional de Sana Distancia (National Campaign for Social Distancing). And we cannot turn a blind eye to the fact that social distancing as a policy can only be enforced amongst the most privileged, who can actually take on this mandate to protect themselves and others from the virus. But this policy has also had a glaring blind spot – a form of violence that has been chillingly regarded as collateral damage – which is domestic violence towards women, and physical and sexual abuse of kids at home; a phenomenon that has increased dramatically during lockdowns.

In one of the video ads for the Mexican National Campaign for Social Distancing, the SARS-CoV-2 virus was depicted as a hungry monster roaming the streets of a neighborhood, devouring anyone who was not locked away at home (Roque 2020). Then, once every human was safely indoors, wisely weary of venturing outside, the monstrous virus died of starvation. This didactic cartoon was a good way of conveying the merits of social distancing when it came to preventing the massive spread of the virus. But watching the animation made another reality quite difficult to turn away from: that of the many women and children for whom confinement with their families would translate into exacerbated, relentless intrafamily violence. And a further frowning dimension of this monster-metaphor is that the vulnerability and helplessness of women and children is a social failure that stems from negligent policies that have excluded them from public spaces, from equal salaries, from patrimony, from purchasing power. Women in Mexico own merely 35% of the homes and earn 25% less than their male counterparts, but their unpaid care-work makes for 23% of the GDP. Women also suffer from time poverty, which means that we work double and triple shifts, and even in the cases where the resources for recreation are available, what is lacking is the time – which has health repercussions. Social policies that favor the creation and upkeep of day care centers, nursing homes and residences for the elderly have been few and far between, and the resources allocated to these institutions have been too scarce to yield decent spaces where one would feel happy entrusting the care of one's relatives. Thus, care-work falls on women. Furthermore, the very short schedules of primary and secondary schools in Mexico have also impacted women's lives negatively. Back in April 2020, one could sense that perhaps the monster was not only roaming the outsides of homes – and we now have data to back up that, indeed, it was not. During the first weeks of the pandemic in Mexico, that is, from the months from March to June 2020 – when confinement was more pressingly recommended and taken up because the vast majority of confluent or public spaces were closed – femicides increased by 8% compared to the first quarter of 2019, and 911 calls from women asking for help skyrocketed by 80%. According to an article by *Aristegui Noticias:* "2020 closed as the year with the highest number of femicides on record. Family violence also reached an all-time high. It went from 210,158 complaints registered in 2019, to 220,028 in 2020, which represents an increase of 5%, the highest number of registrations in the last five years" (Aristegui 2021, Translation RMR).

The National Campaign for Social Distancing uncritically portrayed the household as a refuge, but for many women and minors, home became the scene of physical and sexual abuse and in some cases the lockdown turned into a death sentence. It is true that some governments launched initiatives for the protection of women and girls during lockdown, particularly in Mexico City, but my critique is not aimed so much at this specific social distancing campaign as at the universal, taken-for-granted notion that home is the ideal shelter. Some of the initiatives that were supposedly rendered necessary by the emergency (as for instance the set-up of emergency numbers, or the code of requesting a "purple facemask" at the drugstore to set a domestic violence protocol in motion) are a mere band aid; the reality is they became urgent because we have failed as a society and were a far-cry from prepared. There are no good enough or sufficient shelters for women and children victimized by domestic abuse, nor for migrants, for the homeless, for those who are not welcome at their family home because of their gender and sexual identity, and so on. These amendments are meager attempts to patch up our social debt to all the abject bodies of these households; and this patchwork is itself complicit in perpetuating the fiction of the family and the household as the normative horizon, which merely needs be de-pathologized and for which we must fight at all costs. There is an urgent need for a critique of the family, of the home-as-shelter and of the parental and consanguineous bond, which have been culturally romanticized but are often actually a monster of a thousand heads.

It has been empirically demonstrated that "home" is the location where the physical and sexual abuse of children most often takes place, and that a high number of femicides are perpetrated by someone who lives in the same house as the victim. In socio-political terms, the feminist project cannot be limited to de-pathologizing household by household, or to restoring the well-being of each victim; the program must be far broader, and it must stem from a critique of the units of analysis of household and family that are so often regarded as the space-time of shelter. When taken as the design, aspiration and regulative idea of social order, the traditional heterosexual home and family prove untenable. In other words, if empirical data points to the family household as the space where gender violence and physical and sexual abuse occur most, then this space can certainly *not* be regarded as the shelter sine qua non. Moreover, this much longed-for household – by which I mean the place where a nuclear heterosexual family resides and which is not synonymous with refuge – is inhabited only by a minority with specific characteristics of ethnicity, citizenship, gender and social class – albeit a minority that is perceived and acts as a majority. Therefore, the project of merely de-pathologizing these spaces loses all meaning, since any one-size-fits-all approach is violently false.

As we approach the frightful "new normal", it has become increasingly clear that our political agenda must prioritize the demand for shelters that do not stem from and are materialized according to this notion of "family" which operates within heteronormative, racist, classist, misogynist, homophobic, transphobic and consanguinity logics, but according to other ways of fostering community – chosen families, which is how the LGTB+ community calls these non-consanguineous communities and support networks that share everything from a physical space of cohabitation to the ebb and flow of day-to-day life, in all its fun and all its pain. Kinship, as Butler rightly points out, is not a matter of consanguinity, but is rather the set of practices that sustain affective bonds while *negotiating the reproduction of life and the demands of death.* It is, then, about relationships that go beyond biological reproduction and that resolve our radical ontological dependence. In her words: "... kinship practices will be those that emerge to address fundamental forms of human dependency, which may include birth, child-rearing, relations of emotional dependency and support, generational ties, illness, dying, and death (to name a few)" (Butler 2002, 14–15). Kinship, then, is performative and is not underpinned by a symbolic or biological structure that precedes its exertion.

Thus, I would like to emphasize that one of the many phenomena that this pandemic has shed light on is the sheer urgency of shelters for all the bodies abject from the heteronormed and supposedly nuclear family home. The feminist social project cannot merely aim to reintegrate abused women and minors, or people victimized and displaced for their sexual dissidence, or homeless people into a family. Instead, it must aim to build other spaces, collective shelters where walls are distributed differently, in arrangements no longer reminiscent of the Oedipal triangle. We must deconstruct this insidious fantasy of the traditional/heterosexual family-home-as-shelter if we are to denounce and transform a super-egoistic mandate that, on the one hand, oppresses and abuses women's labor force as the exploited underpinning of the domestic sphere and, on the other, excludes alternative forms of love and care. The heteroparental home as a normative aspiration of the State is nothing more than an oppressive fantasy that has already been, de facto, irreversibly disputed and threatened by a reality that increasingly recognizes other forms of families and parental bonds that are neither heterosexual nor consanguineous. And although the Mexican State has somewhat maintained its social housing program, we ought to demand access for other types of families or communities and, consequently, we must deconstruct these units' architectural design in order to better respond to the needs of these other modes of cohabitation. Along with other demands for radical equity, our immediate political agenda must showcase the call for shelters other than the Holy-Family-household, with its monster lurking in the closet or under the bed.

We must reflect on kinship relations that are not based on blood ties, but on communal ties of closeness, shared history, friendship, neighborhood, and a long etcetera; these must be render intelligible because they are already here and because they have always been here, albeit denied by and excluded from the legal order. Following Butler, a revolution in this symbolic order will have "clearly salutary consequences [...] since kinship ties that bind persons to one another may well be no more or less than the intensification of community ties, may or may not be based on enduring or exclusive sexual relations, and may well consist of ex-lovers, non-lovers, friends, community members" (Butler 2002, 37). Butler goes on:

> In this sense, then, the relations of kinship arrive at boundaries that call into question the distinguishability of kinship from community, or that call for a different conception of friendship. These constitute a "breakdown" of traditional kinship that not only displaces the central place of biological and sexual relations from its definition, but gives sexuality a separate domain from that of kinship, allowing as well for the durable tie to be thought outside of the conjugal frame, and opening kinship to a set of community ties that are irreducible to family. (Butler 2002, 37–38)

Although feminism as a movement that fights for equity in human and political rights, as well as for the uprooting and the eradication of practices and discourses of oppression and domination against women, I believe that this movement must be thought of as a struggle for equity and against violence more broadly precisely because women and the feminine are not fixed categories with a given essence, but a heterogeneous unit of analysis populated by difference. In other words, "woman" is always in the plural and the category encompasses bodies already crossed by any number of forms and means of oppression as well as of privilege: ethnicity, citizenship, social class, sexual preference. Feminism must therefore be a battle against inequity in a broad sense, since the fights against violence and inequity are linked from the get-go and lie at the root of what the determination of woman implies.

In keeping with this perspective, feminism must be part of a struggle *from* and *for* intersectionality, that is, an expanded movement in solidarity with every minority and every abject body and subjectivity. The instances of expulsion, disavowal, dispossession and disregard by and within the family household during this pandemic have also been a magnifying glass pointed towards the impossibility of many different bodies, not just of women, to take shelter at home; therefore, they shed light on the battles that must be lead, yes, from feminism, but within an intersectional logic.

The notion of subject always refers to a hybrid, to a unity that answers to an array of natures. It also refers to hubris as excess, to that which cannot be contained within anything. In each and every instance, every subjectivity responds to multiple and contradictory calls, since both subjectivation and subjection are movements or journeys *from* more than one place of interpellation *to* more than one place of interpellation. In short, the subject is always and has always been the effect of interpellations, identifications and mixed determinations. No subject is wholly female, wholly male, or wholly generically non-binary. Neither is one fully X or Y, and not even XX and XY are indistinct, universal data for all bodies – which is to say that, genetically, one is also XX and XY in different ways. Every subject is populated by more than one identification and disidentification. We are, as José Muñoz rightly argues (1999), migrant souls, not in the sense of a displacement proper to immigration, but in the sense of a coming and going from one vector of subjectivation to another; and these coordinates are spaces and times of both oppression and of agency. Hybridized identificatory positions, Muñoz adds, are always in transit, traversing lines of identification that are multiple and distinct (1999, 32). Thus, the radical feminist struggle must be in solidarity with other battles against inequity and it must be unconditional, for women are always determined by other oppressions or privileges in terms of ethnicity, class, sexual preference, migratory status, and so on.

In ontological terms, I would like to refer to Butler's ideas on the constitutive fact of our interconnectedness and our deep dependence on others. Following Butler, feminism must work from the idea of relationality to show not only how our lives are interdependent, but also how our ethical obligations to protect and sustain our lives derive precisely from this interdependence (Butler 2019) – a radical dependence of the living on other forms of the living, as well as on the inert nature and infrastructure that sustain human life. We need each other to live in physiological as well as psychic and sociopolitical terms. In other words, the human being is not a self-sustaining being. The pandemic we are living through has presented us with something that used to be looked over: our radical dependence on the peasant who works the land to produce food, the farmer who raises the animals we eat, the baker, the seamstress, the teacher, the artist, the scientist who has devoted her energy and time to crafting the vaccine and now the treatment, the nurse and the doctor and her aides (and I am speaking in the feminine only for political reasons, not because we can do without men). We need these people to sustain our literal physiological survival, but today, more than ever, we have also experienced how indispensable tactility is, how bad we feel without the caress and embrace of others, and how the lack of caress or mere contact could lead us to melancholy and even death. Rejecting violence and affirming radical equity makes no sense without fully grasping that whenever the lives of women and minorities of all kinds are mistreated or annihilated, it is a sign that those lives are not being regarded as equally valuable. Then, it becomes quite clear that a feminist political agenda cannot be limited to the fight for women's rights and to the dismantling of sexist practices and discourses, but must fight for radical and global equity. We need each other in order to live, and this fact goes well beyond ties of family and kinship – it crosses borders and is a transnational and global reality.

Stating that the feminist struggle must follow an intersectional logic also means acknowledging that an individualist, capitalist model denies, on the one hand, that other modes of subjection and domination are as pernicious as sexism and, on the other, that emancipation for the majority will remain a mere fiction until these modes are dismantled. This is because, firstly, different forms of oppression are compounded upon many feminine or feminized bodies and, secondly, because our life and our world also depend on the livability and habitability of the worlds of others. What would women's emancipation mean without ethnic equity, without the rights of migrants or without addressing exploitative labor? The struggle against violence is a way of acknowledging and honoring the bond that stems from the equal value of all lives. Nonetheless, this is not an abstract or formal principle; it is a call. An eloquent illustration can be found in the points of contrast between the feminist movements #MeToo and #NiUnaMenos (#NotOneLess). The #MeToo movement implies an individualistic notion of the experience of violence because it is based on the rights of the individual subject and on a conception of freedom as a personal rather than a social good. #NiUnaMenos, on the other hand, is itself a sentence with a collective subject; that is, the agency of the demand is a "we" rather than an "I". As Butler has described it (2019), #NiUnaMenos is a movement that fights for equity at work, in the neighborhood, for the freedom to make choices on one's own body, for the right to abortion, the right to equal pay and against the neoliberal economy that has intensified precariousness, especially for women, indigenous and poor people. #MeToo – as well as #MiPrimerAcoso in the case of Mexico, although this hashtag was more local and did not transcend in time – has been key in shedding light on the abuse and harassment of women at work and in their homes. But this movement operates by compounding individual stories – which is not to say that listening to and building testimonies or calling for the restoration of damage is not important. However, the demand here is not so much one of worldwide transformation as a specific call for punishment. I do wish to stress how important this has all been for feminism, but I also want to argue that punishment will not lead to a transformation of the world we inhabit, and that sexual harassment and violence are only one of the many forms of oppression that women suffer. Therefore, if the feminist struggle does not embrace the call to end all forms of violence, full emancipation will never come. The solidarity whereby collective action is grounded must then abandon the assumption of individualism and reject the idea that bodies have a single determination from which abuse or privilege is experienced.

The subject of radical feminism is collective. It encompasses all feminized and oppressed bodies in as much as they are historically and culturally vulnerable and precarious. It is our responsibility, as subjects who identify as women (but of course, not just ours, I merely say women thinking of the "us" within the feminist struggle), it is our obligation, then, to ask ourselves how it is we are living, reproducing or resisting these structures. As housewives, how do we deal with the historical abuse of women in care-work or with the exploitation of domestic workers? As academics, where do we acknowledge the space of indigenous, sexual dissident, transsexual colleagues or students? As Mexican citizens, what agenda do we regard as urgent on our southern border? As mothers, what patriarchal and sexist practices and discourses do we reinstate with our offspring? As professionals, what rights do we demand for working men and women? As inhabitants of planet earth, what is our agenda to stop climate change?

Believing that our subjectivation is completely defined by being a woman is a fiction. Being a woman means being a woman in many different bodies, in diverse forms, and with very dissimilar histories and life projects. Change cannot really take place on a personal level. In sociopolitical terms, we know that the revolution is not the sum of individual liberations because even if, hypothetically, all individuals were to suddenly turn feminist, institutions would still implement different modes of sexist oppression. An ethical project of non-violent cohabitation must be conceived in stark contrast: on the basis of the transformation of collectivities, of modes of solidarity that truly resonate with our interdependence. No project based on individual transformation can actually achieve the radical dismantling of modes of violence against vulnerable groups.

Let us go back to the Covid-19 epidemic and what it has so blatantly laid bare. What this highly contagious virus for which there is still no cure or universal inoculation has aired with clarity, is that our life is literally in the hands of others, and that the lives of others rest in ours. But the pandemic has also unveiled, in an irrefutable way, something less immediate and perhaps less evident: that care for an-other is care for oneself, that when the other does not have access to health, education and a universal minimum income, then she must go to work, or denies the existence of the epidemic because she has no concept of virus. As I said some lines back, this pandemic has been a magnifying glass that has rendered something visible, a something that has always been here, but that privilege – and, also, pathological but comfortable disavowal – had until now allowed us to deny while leading our lives as if reality were different. The dilemma of having to either stay home or leave the house and be exposed to the virus has been a slap in the face, an urgent call to take charge – collectively, in solidarity and transnationally – of all inequity, misogyny, racism, nationalism, classism, and so on. This call that is so pressing now has, of course, been urgent for a long time, but the crisis specifically calls for immediate decision-making; we must address and disarm the violence brought about by the neglect of social policies meant to fulfill the very basic needs of a population: free, good-quality public education and healthcare; a universal basic income; the protection and guarantee of physical and psychological integrity; decent housing; among others. The pandemic shows us that while caring for others is caring for oneself, it is our moral duty to ensure that all human beings in the world have access to every basic need, which encompasses access to culture and art, to the enjoyment of nature, to a life worth living. These demands are longstanding and must be heeded. We can unequivocally say that the world has built a violent differential allocation of value on some lives over others, and this statement is not merely a diagnosis, but an ethical vehicle that allows us to craft a political imaginary of equity. It is thus a normative aspiration.

We must take our efforts to dismantle the forms of knowledge, the epistemological frameworks linked to the reproduction of objectionable practices of power and tie them together with projects of social transformation that seek to achieve substantial democratic goals, such as freedom, equity and justice. How this will be achieved remains unclear, but everything points to how this project relates to the ability to, on the one hand, tell and study the history of events and, on the other, imagine a better future. Critique must be an intervention in the course of history, one that has the capacity to effectively fracture history itself so the horizon of a better future, of a future to come, springs forth from that rupture.

Many have chosen to believe that we are experiencing a specific period of abnormality and upheaval, when instead we are living through a critical reckoning in terms of our biological, political, ethical and ontological interdependence. It is imperative to recognize our ontological quality of interdependence and act accordingly.

References

Aristegui (2021). "2020 fue el año con más feminicidios desde que existen registros de este delito: Causa en Común | Documento". *Aristegui noticias*, 25 January. URL: https://aristeguinoticias.com/2501/mexico/2020-fue-el-ano-con-mas-feminicidios-desde-que-existen-registros-de-este-delito-causa-en-comun-documento/ (last accessed 22 November 2022).

Butler, J. (2002). "Is Kinship Always Already Heterosexual?" *Differences: A Journal of Feminist Cultural Studies* 13(1), 14–44.
Butler, J. (2019). "When Killing Women Isn't a Crime". *The New York Times*, 10 July. URL: https://www.nytimes.com/2019/07/10/opinion/judith-butler-gender.html (last accessed 22 November 2022).
Muñoz, J. (1999). *Disidentifications. Queers of Color and the Performance of Politics.* Minneapolis: University of Minnesota Press.
Roque, V. (2020). *Monstruo de COVID 19 – quedate en casa* [Video]. YouTube, 8 August. URL: https://www.youtube.com/watch?v=aLgZi-NR1Nk (last accessed 22 November 2022).

Valentina Gaudiano
A New-old Topos for the Future. Rethinking and Rediscovering Oneself as Human

Abstract: The consequences of the pandemic, especially the relational ones, are so many and so intertwined that a new focus on the question of the human being by philosophers becomes necessary. Despite the experienced physical limitation of proximity and sharing of emotions, it seems fundamental to rethink the human under these aspects. Giving back to love an ontological value and reaffirming its absolute essentiality to understand the human being and his relationships, we could trace a new-old *topos* for the future, something as the relationship expressed through the image of the embrace – as a plastic image of me, of each of us, who welcomes and holds in his/her arms another person and doing so says: I love you, you belong to me, I'm *with* you, I'm *by* you, *I'm you.*

Living Bodies Not Androids

Almost a century ago Martin Heidegger had spoken of "ours" as a "time of the night of the world", meaning not so much the death of God or the experience of a lack of it by human beings, but just the lack of any experience at all! Later Bruno Forte, an Italian theologian, affirmed that "what we are especially sick of, in the time of so-called postmodernity, is the absence of real reasons to live and live together, the lack of horizons of hope and common hope" (Forte and Natoli 1997, 29, Translation VG).

And yet, the degree of coexistence and interdependence has reached levels that were certainly unthinkable in the not too distant past. An example is the fact that something infinitely small – called Cov-Sars 19 – has crept into a human body and from there into many human bodies generating on one side, disease, suffering, death – the common and regrettable experiences that mark the limited dimension of the human body – and on the other, deprivation of those common bodily expressions that enrich personal and community life. The reality in which we have been living worldwide for more than two years (isolation and "social distance") has obviously changed our daily life at all levels, first of all the relational one: uncertainty and unpredictability of events have made us experience not only the transience of our lives, experienced firsthand through the deaths of relatives and friends, but also through the death of many other people we have heard of. In this sense, the international community created by the new media

https://doi.org/10.1515/9783111051802-032

played a great role, because from the beginning of the pandemic event most of the people were involved only through the media. We also experienced the physical limitation of proximity. Our interpersonal relationships were cut short on the spot because from one day to the next we were no longer allowed to express affections and emotions with our whole body and we could not even share the most crucial moments of human existence, those moments that mark the passage between life and death; we were asked to suffer and even die without hugs or caresses, without the human warmth of those who love us.

"Do not touch me" could be the summary expression of all this and of a new form of social regulation of cohabitation, and it is no coincidence that I chose that expression which, as the French philosopher Jean-Luc Nancy carefully highlights in a brief essay, has a very clear and socially shared meaning. "'Do not touch me' is in the register of a warning in front of a danger ('you will hurt me' or 'I will hurt you', 'you will endanger my integrity' or 'I will defend')" (Nancy 2015, 28, Translation VG).[1]

Love as a Concrete Expression of the Human Being

Probably the distance and the inability to reach loved ones has stimulated the search for ways and forms that could make love flourish or increase, putting it back at the center of our existence, purified of the burrs that had met the time of postmodernity, as liquid love (Bauman 2003) – to take up the well-known definition of the sociologist Zygmund Bauman. It is an unexpected response to this

---

[1] The context in which Nancy uses this expression is that of his reading of Jesus of Nazareth's *"noli me tangere"* towards Mary Magdalene who sees him risen from the dead in the garden where he was buried. In interpreting this expression and its meaning, Nancy emphasizes how, in fact, this expression has lost its link and, therefore, its theological value, to maintain a purely sociological meaning of a prohibition of contact. At the center of the reflection, however, is the body itself – specifically the body of Jesus – which cannot be touched because touching expresses an alteration that occurs simultaneously in the one who touches and in the one who is touched. It is primarily the hands that are touched, the extreme extension of the human body that is the first to reach where the head and the back do not reach. The hands brush, touch, press, squeeze, slap the surface of things, but can also intertwine with other hands or wrap them around: always, however, in an encounter between human beings they generate the double experience of feeling touched and at the same time of the other person feeling touched. This touching always also implies a desire to possess, which is at the same time a reassuring sign. However, the most interesting aspect of Nancy's analysis is that "only a body can touch or not touch" (Nancy 2015, 72, Translation VG) (we mean here the body as a living body, not only a material one).

passing time, in which we are all involved, beyond cultures and religious beliefs, ethnic affiliations and political structures of government, rich and poor. The fragility and vanity of many structures and idols built over time – from economic to technological, political and of welfare – comes out stronger as in the past. Moreover, we find us sharing the same needs of closeness and proximity with our loved ones. What we are experiencing seems to me an extraordinary opportunity to rethink love in its ontological value and its absolute essentiality when it comes to understanding the human being and his relationships.

In fact, as Maria Zambrano stated as early as the 1980s, "one of the deprivations of our time is that which relates to love [...]. In the limitless space that the mind apparently opens up to every reality today, love comes up against infinite barriers" (Zambrano 2012, 51, Translation VG). Love can return, silently, but powerfully, to reclaim its place in human existence, to inhabit it with full dignity and recognition. Because love discovers the misery and ephemeral aspect of things and reality and perhaps, as De Luca states, because love has always to coexist with the possibility to loose someone (De Luca 2014, 450). In the growing confrontation with the suffering, loss and death that the pandemic has forced upon us, the urge to love and not just to care and look after those in need has re-emerged. Loving and encountering a "you", as Stein rightly points out, are in encounters that take place within the person. This is what the many gestures and glances of those who are in the front-line of an emergency as the pandemic show. In the secret of a daily work, they were giving all they had to make themselves close and to bring to others a charge of life, physically and spiritually; many others were finding the most original and creative ways to generate in virtual reality deeply human spaces of sharing. The many words that travel the ether – the only space that in recent months we have been allowed to live in[2] without restrictions, at least for the lucky ones – are no longer carrying only useless fragments of selfishness, but pieces of fraternity that are lived and felt.

A whole history of reflections and in-depth analysis has shown the complexity of human love[3] and its inextricable link with corporeity: certainly one can love

---

[2] We can say that we are really and completely "on-life", as Luciano Floridi remarks in his book *The Fourth Revolution: How the Infosphere Is Reshaping Human Reality* (Floridi 2014).

[3] The first well-known text is Plato's *Symposium*, followed by a large number of dialogues, treatises and aphorisms that have highlighted various aspects and dimensions attributable to this human experience. For some, it is fundamentally linked to the will, for others to the sphere of the emotions. Especially in the 20th century the phenomenologists gave to love a new interpretation as an act or "movement", which involves all the person in the different aspects of the living body and of the spirit. I gave a brief overview on the history of love in the European philosophy in the first chapter of my book on Dietrich von Hildebrand (Gaudiano 2013 and 2021).

with the will alone, through an inner decision, however, even such a decision is not an expression of love if it does not imply at the same time the heart – that is, the affectivity linked to the senses – and therefore the intimate need to reach out to those who one loves with the entire person, in flesh and blood, in gestures of manifestation that make the other aware of being loved. In this sense, the domination of sight, as the par excellence sense of an entire Western philosophical tradition, has in a certain way debased and overcome love in its radical nature: human experience requiring co-implication of all human plans and all senses of which it has faculties.

In this sense, it seems to me that a certain human dimension regains new dignity, namely tenderness; something, which wasn't really studied until our days, perhaps because it was not completely understood[4] even if it is deeply linked to love. It can, in fact, be understood as what "makes us flexible and open to encounter: it is the *clinamen* of our hardness, able to bend us in the direction of the other" (Guanzini 2017, 71, Translation VG). Making room for tenderness means, therefore, making room for a slowed down time, in which the efficiency of production and performance is not worth it, but what is of worth is being what you are, with all the fragility that implies. Thus, tenderness

> cannot be understood except through the caresses, gestures and glances that a subject feels on its own living body [...]. For example, in the hand that passes slowly in the epidermis it inscribes in the living body of the new-born the being-received, tenderness bursts into its body, an idea that inhabits its body in a silent or mute way, like a tacit language. (Costa 2009, 93, Translation VG)

This kind of experience is absolutely free for those who receive looks or gestures of tenderness from others, but radically intentional for those who actively practice it. This double dimension of tenderness requires a brief pause for reflection.

In the movement of tenderness that appears in human interiority, as an intentional response to a certain something or someone, there is no physical contact, but exclusively a spiritual one. It is then in expressing the tenderness that a physical "touch" comes into play: something touches the organic surface by creating immediate experiences in the psychic-spiritual sphere and at the same time something/someone touches the psychic-spiritual space generating organic reactions. We can, therefore, be touched inwardly and outwardly, but it is always our whole person to be touched or to touch. Now, are we all capable of that specific touch that comes

---

[4] Tenderness is treated especially by psychologists and psychoanalysts in their clinical analyses of trauma and of the development of the person. A recent example in this direction is Paul Williams' book *The Authority of Tenderness: Dignity and the true Self in Psychoanalysis* (Williams 2021).

from the perception of vulnerability and finitude of existence called tenderness? Structurally, recalling the Steinian analyses[5] on the human person, we can only answer affirmatively: if the human being is a sentient – in the double meaning of inward and outward –, then he/she must be capable of any form of feeling. However, Stein herself does not hide the fact that the sphere of feeling is stratified and differentiated and that it must be developed, cultivated, expanded in the course of its existence. If someone does not make any experience – direct or indirect, or by empathy – of a certain feeling, this feeling will not exist for this person, in the sense that it will not be present in its explicitness until it will become in some way manifest; but it may also happen that it becomes forgotten or lost.[6]

The Embrace: Bodily Expression of Our Being of/in Relation

A creative rethinking of love, and this is also true for its expression of tenderness, can make us glimpse proposals and answers to the questions that today we are asking ourselves with new strength. It is putting love back on its own and deep language, which is not that of the head nor of the hands alone, but which needs both, because it is only in the dynamics of the indwelling of these forms to which is added that between person and person, we can give sense and meaning to ourselves.

Yes, because it is we – human beings – that the pandemic, like any other borderline situation, lets us focus with all the force of the question about who we are. That is also the central question that innervates the philosophical path in its history. As Edith Stein wisely affirmed, you cannot educate unless you know who is in front of you (Stein 2004); that is, the educational action is always moved by some form or image of man and woman who wants to help to come out and realize. We can enlarge this statement of Stein saying that this image is also important for the politicians in front of their citizens, for the doctors in relationship to the patients and so on.

---

5 See Stein 2000 and 2004.
6 Ágnes Heller has also devoted a great deal of space to the analysis of feelings, emphasizing the importance of their formation and development. In particular, she points out that the emotions are subject to flowering or impoverishment, unlike the feelings-drive or the affects themselves. Among the feelings are those of character that most constitute the personality of each person and "any emotion, assuming it becomes an emotional habit, becomes part of the personality and is, of course, subject to development" (Heller 2017, 130, Translation VG).

As the creative process of the artist is such, if and when he/she pursues a certain image that he/she wants to make it alive and present to the material eye, so that it is already alive and throbbing before his/her own spiritual eye. This is how each of us can develop oneself when one is similarly moved by an image of man and woman – which evidently does not mean only the single, personal image, but the one shared by a community of intent.

Then the image that could be offered to our future socio-political and educational paths is that of the "embrace" – plastic image of me, of each of us, who welcomes and holds in his/her arms another person and doing so says: "I love you, you belong to me, I'm with you, I'm by you, I'm you". This is an expression of the human that the pandemic has taken away from us, thus also taking away a piece of us, of our own identity. The embrace localizes us in a different manner because it makes us explicitly alter-centered – men, women, children centered in the others and not in itself and as others, because they are related. It is, in fact, in the care and custody of others that our very personality is guarded and safeguarded: closing oneself in one's ego and from there looking at the world no longer works, the pandemic has evidently unmasked what has always been an illusion of the human being and in particular of the human being in the Western world.[7] We are always in relationships, of esteem, of respect, of sympathy, of love..., and when it is love that directs us towards others – the arms that open to meet and welcome – we affirm them in their being-so and being-precious (Hildebrand 2009) and we unite spiritually with them; we give ourselves and, getting lost in them, we receive again. The experience of the embrace is, therefore, an experience of the extension of one's own world that takes place in a double movement: embracing what is different to me, I do it in some way myself, while not swallowing it because the distinction still remains, and at the same time, I do something else. On closer inspection, in fact, the dynamic of embracing is commonly aimed at expressing a range of feelings, which, despite their different shades, indicate a sense of protection, belonging, identification, solidarity, love, sharing.

No More "Studios", But "Family Homes"

This discourse requires, however, to point out something that perhaps a pandemic, like any other borderline situation, strongly focuses, that is, the question about our

---

[7] We can look, as an example of this, at Günter Anders work *Die Antiquiertheit des Menschen*, a sort of prophesy, in which he spoke of many aspects of nowadays, but more than 50 years ago (Anders 1980).

relational identity. To recover mutual transcendence, which means the fact that each of us is beyond-self in the other – that neighbor that we do not choose, but who is close to us – and just so is much more himself/herself, means looking at each person as someone that must be loved because he/she is lovable in himself/herself. The claim of acceptance that inhabits us and the promise that such acceptance, reserved to every human being, fully realizes the human side of each of us, mark and characterize human coexistence as an interweaving of relationships.

These already unfold in the simple and daily experience of communicating; in fact, as Adriano Fabris, an Italian philosopher, points out, our saying is relational because it involves others and being practiced leads to generate new relationships (Fabris 2006, 36 ff.). It therefore has a reciprocal character. We could, then, say that we not only communicate, but we are even language, we are a continuous wanting-to-be-understood and re-telling what someone has already communicated.[8] In fact, the words we say have sense and meaning if there is another who listens to them and reacts to them. We want to understand and communicate: this pushes us beyond any personal boundary – that of the other personality, that of the language unknown to me, that of a surface that encloses and holds something more – towards an agreement that is much more than just understanding and tolerating each other. After all, when we communicate, according to Hemmerle – a German philosopher and theologian of the last century –, "Understanding wants to become agreement, the different words seek consonance from the freedom of the many partners who speak them, in the one 'word' that grants them everything – and also their diversity" (Hemmerle 1972, 25, Translation VG).

The word, however, has gradually undergone a process of impoverishment, becoming a sterile production of sounds that we use like any other goods, to meet our needs or to extend our dominion over what surrounds us – an incapable word, therefore, to allow true communication with others as human.[9] Where the bounds of the sharing of meaning have been broken or failed, the quantitative desire of a communication that occupies spaces and times wins, so as not to make us think of the void of meaning. Just think of all the social media channels that overwhelm our attention, thus becoming privileged spaces of interaction and often not letting us look at those who are close to us or around us anymore. We thus pass from indifference to confrontation with the limits of our existence, of the existence of others,

---

8 Klaus Hemmerle explains this in a short text about the specific character of the human being. He speaks about communication and conversation among people as something which differentiates the human person from other living beings (Hemmerle 1972).
9 Maria Zambrano underlines this problem of language and especially of words in *De la aurora* (1986).

of the surrounding world, a culturally more varied world than before and therefore elusive and disturbing.

And yet even all this continues to express our being in relationships and does so, to take up again Fabris, in expressing precisely the movement inherent in the verb "to relate" and not so much in the noun "relationship"; "just because the relationship is a relate to, its structure is dynamic, its dynamics is that of an action, then it can be carried out, it can be put into operation, it can be activated" (Fabris 2006, 163, Translation VG), making the reciprocal gift of recognizing each other. The relational structure in which we are woven expresses a multiform space in which we can move in the continuous "tension to the other one" (Fabris 2006, 163).

The relationship with others creates a space between us that the German phenomenologist Dietrich von Hildebrand defines as "interpersonal space" (Hildebrand 1955, 181–195; Gaudiano 2018, 238–243). Since we are in contact with the different "you", each of us is a place of different and multiple interpersonal spaces, of which some intertwine with each other, others are side by side, without ways of reciprocal communication, and others still intersect a space minimally, perhaps entering it only temporally in contact. We are, therefore, not only *alter-centered* – the embrace unbalances us – but by virtue of this also *inter-located* – the embrace intertwines us. The place of the future is therefore a "commonplace", a land of coexistence and sharing, individually characterized, but commonly inhabited, a place, which expresses and realizes our humanity.

Then the commonplace of human living is the community in the deepest sense, the one that expresses the original meaning of community that means the essential and all too often hurtful fact that what concerns me as a human being also concerns other human beings, in virtue of a common humanity.[10] This common place is, therefore, the one inhabited by people capable of calling themselves "you", neighbors who know how to embrace each other because they know how to recognize and give each other back their dignity. In this common space each one is origin and goal, receiving and giving.

This community, as Klaus Hemmerle states, recalls another dimension of transcendence: to be in and for the neighbor, which "takes place where the totality in the individual and the individual on the totality go on stage" (Hemmerle 1995, 284, Translation VG). That means something "plastic" or a performative event because if it is true that the totality is made present in the individual, this one realizes total-

---

10 In this regard, it is very interesting to look at Gerda Walther's study on the community, in which she also speaks about the oneness among members of a community. The principle of her analysis is that human people are naturally related from the beginning, so that community comes before the individuals (Walther 1923).
Note: In general, about community and individuals, see: Gaudiano 2023

ity, however, not alone, but precisely with others, thanks to which he/she is able to assume responsibility for the whole.

This, in the actuality that we walk through, has become not only necessary, but indispensable: to look at every human being as bearer and representative of the totality means to invest him/her with the greatest dignity – and this in an indiscriminate way, because every human being is, without distinction. And how does that happen? Through love. Love turns with creativity and responsibility to the individual – who in this way emerges on the totality – making him/her discover that he/she is the most important being in the world precisely in his/her connection with the community, with which he/she can fully realize that totality that he/she would have in him/herself already present. As Hildebrand explains, it is love that discovers the value of the individual (Hildebrand 2009) – of the one who loves as well as of the one who is loved – as the unique one for which it is worth dropping everything (being alter-centered). At the same time making one aware of one's own responsibility in constructing totality by placing oneself in relation with others, or by recognizing in each that same totality (being inter-located).[11]

If one reduces or marginalizes the other – meaning not only the other person directly, but also his/her works and activities – for the realization of his/her own interests, or if one becomes deaf in front of him/her, one destroys the whole and with it oneself. "Only when we accept in the part the model of totality, with radical responsibility for totality, do we open our society to the future" (Hemmerle 1995, 289, Translation VG). This implies inner and physical spaces in which we recognize and educate[12] ourselves to become what we are: relational human beings.

References

Anders, G. (1980). *"Die Antiquiertheit des Menschen I: Über die Seele im Zeitalter der zweiten industriellen Revolution"*. Munich: C. H. Beck.
Bauman, Z. (2003). *"Liquid Love: On the Frailty of the Human Bonds"*. Cambridge: Polity Press.
Costa, V. (2009). *"I modi del sentire. Un percorso nella tradizione fenomenologica"*. Macerata: Quodlibet Studio.

---

11 In other words, it is a question of recognizing the full responsibility of love, as Stein also points out, and the fact that love never concerns only an I and a You, but always a surrounding world, a "between-us". This space can be reflected in the image of the embrace that places us in the position between of the relationship and simultaneously in the one in the other position of the circular reciprocity (De Luca 2014).
12 Edith Stein remarks how the human person has not only the possibility to form or educate him/herself, but the need to do this (Stein 2004).

Fabris, A. (2016). *"RelAzione. Una filosofia performativa"*. Brescia: Morcelliana.
Floridi, L. (2014). *The Fourth Revolution: How the Infosphere Is Reshaping Human Reality.* Oxford: Oxford University Press.
Forte, B. and Natoli, S. (1997). *Delle cose ultime e penultime. Un dialogo.* Milan: Mondadori.
Gaudiano, V. (2013). *"Die Liebesphilosophie Dietrich von Hildebrand. Ansätze einer Ontologie der Liebe".* Freiburg: Alber.
Gaudiano, V. (2018). "The Interpersonal Space between Gift and Annihilation". In *Aemet Wissenschaftliche Zeitschrift für Philosophie und Theologie* 7(1), 223–248. URL: https://www.aemaet.de/wp-content/uploads/2018/09/The-interpersonal-space.html (last accessed 22 November 2022).
Gaudiano, V. (2021) "La filosofia dell'amore in Dietrich von Hildebrand. Spunti per una ontologia dell'amore". Rome: Inschibboleth.
Gaudiano, V. (2023), "Sense of Belonging and Disillusionment: A Phenomenological Reading of Community Dynamics". In *Populism and Accountability. Interdisciplinary Researches on Active Citizenship.* Switzerland: Springer.
Guanzini, I. (2017). *Tenerezza. La rivoluzione del potere gentile.* Milan: Adriano Salani.
Heller, Á. (1981). *Theorie der Gefühle.* Hamburg: VSA.
Heller, Á. (2017). *Teoria dei sentimenti.* Milan: Lit Edizioni Srl.
Hemmerle, K. (1972). "Unterscheidung des Menschlichen". In Hemmerle, K., *Unterscheidungen. Gedanken und Entwürfe zur Sache des Christentums heute.* Freiburg, Basel and Vienna: Herder. URL: https://www.klaus-hemmerle.de/de/werk/unterscheidungen.html#/reader/0 (last accessed 22 November 2022).
Hemmerle, K. (1995). "Bildung und Bistum". In Hemmerle, K., *Ausgewählte Schriften*, vol. 4. Freiburg, Basel and Vienna: Herder.
Hildebrand, D. von (1955). *Metaphysik der Gemeinschaft. Untersuchungen über Wesen und Wert der Gemeinschaft.* Regensburg: Habbel.
Hildebrand, D. von (2009). *The Nature of Love.* South Bend: St. Augustine Press.
Nancy, J.-L. (2013). *Noli me tangere. Essai sur la levée du corps.* New edition. Montrouge: Bayard Édition.
Nancy, J.-L. (2015). *Non toccarmi. Maria Maddalena e il corpo di Gesù.* Bologna: Centro editoriale dehoniano.
Stein, E. (2000). *Philosophy of Psychology and the Humanities.* Ed. by M. Sawicki. Washington: ICS.
Stein, E. (2004). "Der Aufbau der menschlichen Person: Vorlesung zur philosophischen Anthropologie". *ESGA*, vol. 14. Freiburg: Herder.
Walther, G. (1923). "Zur Ontologie der sozialen Gemeinschaften". *Jahrbuch für Philosophie und phänomenologische Forschung* 1, 1–158.
Williams, P. (2021). *The Authority of Tenderness: Dignity and the True Self in Psychoanalysis.* London: Taylor and Francis.
Zambrano, M. (1986). *De la aurora.* Madrid: Turner.
Zambrano, M. (2012). "Due Frammenti sull'amore (1982)". In Maruzzella, S. (Ed.), *Sentimenti per un'autobiografia. Nascita, amore, pieta'.* Milan: Mimesis, 49–58.

Contributors to This Volume

Diana María Acevedo-Zapata
Diana María Acevedo-Zapata is Associate Professor in the Department of Social Sciences at Universidad Pedagógica Nacional de Colombia. She is a founding member of the Colombian Network of Women Philosophers (Red Colombiana de Mujeres Filósofas) and is a researcher with the Observatory for Gender and Philosophy in Colombia, she is part of the Latin American Network of Women Philosophers of Unesco. Recent publications include: *Filosofía como forma de vida: Laboratorio de escritura* (2019), "Letter-Writing as a Decolonial Feminist Praxis for Philosophical Writing" (2020), "Sobre la opresión de las mujeres por parte de otras mujeres: una zona gris en la relación madre e hija" (2021).

Ingrid Alloni
After graduating with honors from the University of Milan with a thesis about Adriana Cavarero's Italian thought of sexual difference and after receiving her master's degree on the genealogical reconstruction of the concept of race in the twentieth century, she now conducts various philosophy workshops in her social context (schools, anti-violence centers, prisons, philosophical cafes and cinefilos). Her research themes are identity, feminist theories, race studies, whiteness studies, postcolonial studies, critical theory, social theory and antinatalism. She is one of the founding members of CONTRA/DIZIONI, a research group on Feminist and Queerness Studies at the University of Milan. She has published an article on Charles W. Mills regarding white privilege and "race".

Shalini Attri
Shalini Attri is Assistant Professor in the Department of English at BPS Women's University, Sonipat, Haryana, India since 2007. Her doctorate is from Punjab University Chandigarh on "Politics of Representation: A Feminist Study of Vijay Tendulkar's Selected Plays". Her area of research includes Indian English Literature and Classics, Diasporic and Migration Studies, Women Studies, Theatre Studies, and Folk Literature. Being actively engaged in academic research, her publication includes 25 papers in national and international journals and books. She has co-authored and edited four books –*Effective English II, III, VI, Queens of Indian Sports* – and has presented research papers at international conferences at India, Canada, Sweden, Russia, USA, Estonia, Germany, Turkey, and England. She is currently member of the Academic Council, and has been a member of DRC, PGBOS, and the Faculty of Arts and Languages at BPSMV. She has acted as a resource person at HIPA for Comprehensive training program for school teachers on Inclusive Education; UGC HRDC, BPSMV; STRITE. She has received a JIWS fellowship from Bridgewater State University, USA and is also on the editorial board of JIWS Journal, Bridgewater State University.

Emma Baizabal
Emma Baizabal is a philosophy graduate from the School of Philosophy and Literature (FFyL), UNAM. She has participated in various lectures, reading circles, discussions, and workshops about philosophy of technology in relation to feminist epistemology and decolonial studies. She is especially interested in the relations between ontology and politics that intersect with questions of the technical and technological from situated perspectives. She collaborates with the Seminar of Philosophical Technologies (#SeminarioTF) at UNAM and is co-founder of the collective La Filosofería, dedicated to the problematization of the dissemination of philosophy from feminist and decolonial

perspectives; and with @NFTecnológica, an accelerator of philosophical projects that aims to converge blockchain and philosophy. Publications among others: "La potencia técnica de los cuerpos: sujetos vivos, sujetos metaestaestables" (2022), "La potencia inventiva en la organización de las luchas feministas y de mujeres en Abya Yala" (2022).

Sarah Bonfim
Sarah Bonfim is a graduate philosophy student at Universidade Estadual de Campinas (Unicamp) and holds a FAPESP scholarship (Process 2021/02257–5). She is part of the project Blog Mulheres na Filosofia: https://www.blogs.unicamp.br/mulheresnafilosofia/. She is also a member of the project New Voices: https://historyofwomenphilosophers.org/find-scholars-mary-wollstonecraft/. Publication among others: "Review of Mary Wollstonecraft's *Thoughts on the Education* (2021)" and "The Orientalism of Mary Wollstonecraft under Nawal El Saadawi: A Cross-cultural Dialogue" (2022).

Annabelle Bonnet
Annabelle Bonnet is associate researcher at the Raymond Aron Center for Sociological and Political Studies at the School for Advanced Studies in the Social Sciences (EHESS), Paris, France. Her research in cultural studies focuses on the socio-history of women philosophers/intellectuals and feminist thought in Europe and Latin America in the 19th and 20th centuries. She approaches gender relations through the prism of class and geographical inequalities. She is the author of a doctoral thesis about women philosophers in France (EHESS, 2020). Publications among others: *Léontine Zanta: The Forgotten History of the First French Woman to Hold a Doctorate in Philosophy* (2021, preface by Geneviève Fraisse), *Women and Philosophy in France (XIX–XX centuries)*, published in 2022 at the CNRS Editions of Paris.

Corinna Casi
Corinna Casi holds a Master in Philosophy from the University of Bologna, Italy. Currently she is a doctoral candidate in Environmental Ethics at the University of Helsinki, Finland, and a HELSUS (Helsinki Institute of Sustainability Science) member. Her doctoral research focuses on non-economic values of nature such as moral, aesthetic, ecological, and indigenous value. She is also a doctoral researcher in the ValueBioMat interdisciplinary project (STN, Academy of Finland) on bioplastics, affiliated with the University of Lapland, https://valuebiomat.fi/. She is a board member of YHYS (The Finnish Society for Environmental Social Science), https://www.yhys.net. Publications among others: "Traditional Ecological Knowledge" (2021). In 2020, her article about decolonizing food security within the Sámi community was published by Routledge as a book chapter. For the article about Sámi Food Practices and Traditional Ecological Knowledge (TEK), the EU Society for Agricultural and Food Ethics awarded her the Vonne Lund Prize in 2019.

Timothy DeGriselles
Timothy DeGriselles received his M. A. in philosophy from the University of Toledo in 2021. His thesis was on the 17th-century Mexican philosopher nun, Sor Juana Inès de la Cruz. His studies have focused on feminism with a special focus on what questions are asked and how they throw light on what was important to the thinker. Timothy's goals in philosophy are to show how these different philosophers change, broaden, and improve the current canon of philosophical discourse.

Eric Deibel
Eric Deibel is Assistant Professor of Political Science and lecturer in STS at Bilkent University. He received his Ph. D. in science and technology studies (STS) from the Vrije Universiteit Amsterdam asso-

ciated with the sociology department of Wageningen University and the department of philosophy of biology at Egenis, Exeter University. After completing his Ph. D. on "Common Genomes: Open Source and Life Sciences" he won an Andrew W. Mellon fellowship from the University of Indiana, Bloomington and an IFRIS research fellowship (Institut Francilien Recherche Innovation Société) in Paris. He is a board member of Nordic Summer University and the co-coordinator of the symposium series "Human Technology Futures". Publications among others: *Rousseau and the Future of Freedom* (forthcoming), and *Recoding Life: Information and the Biopolitical* (2018, together with S. Tamminen).

Talya Ucaryilmaz Deibel
Talya Ucaryilmaz Deibel holds the chair for Roman law at Bilkent University. She serves as a deputy board member of Nordic Summer University where she also actively contributes to the academic circle "Human Technology Futures", dedicated to philosophy and the sociology of technology. She published her book *Bona Fides (Good Faith) in Legal Theory* in 2018, based on her doctoral research which she completed *summa cum laude*. She has held post-doctoral research positions at the Unidroit Institute, La Sapienza University, Rome, at University of Oxford, the Hamburg Max Planck Institute for Comparative and International Private Law, and at the Amsterdam Centre for Transformative Private Law where she conducted an interdisciplinary project on law and technology. Her research interest lies in legal philosophy, Roman law and Roman philosophy, and law and technology. Publications among others: "Back to (for) the Future: AI and The Dualism of Persona and Res in Roman Law" (2021), "The Principle of Proportionality from Roman Law to Modern Ius Gentium" (2021).

Valentina Gaudiano
Valentina Gaudiano is Extraordinary Professor of Philosophical Anthropology at Sophia University Institute (Loppiano by Florence) and trainer of teachers and educators in philosophical dialogue. Ph. D. from the University of Munich with a study on the philosophy of love in Dietrich von Hildebrand; post-doctorate at Sophia University Institute on Trinitarian Ontology, specifically on the link between philosophy and theology in Klaus Hemmerle. She is on the editorial board of the journal *Teresianum* and collaborates with the international group *New Voices* linked to the Center for the History of Women Philosophers and Scientists. Fields of research: German phenomenology (Stein, Scheler, Husserl, Hemmerle, Conrad-Martius, Walther) and Trinitarian ontology. Publications among others: *La filosofia dell'amore in Dietrich von Hildebrand. Spunti per un'ontologia dell'amore* (2021). *Sul maschile e sul femminile. In dialogo con Klaus Hemmerle* (2021, together with A. Clemenzia).

Federica Giardini
Federica Giardini teaches Political Philosophy at Roma Tre University. She is the director of the Master in "Studies and Gender Policies" and has founded the Master degree in "Environmental Humanities". She has worked on the relational body by confronting the thought of feminist difference, Husserlian phenomenology and Lacanian psychoanalysis; on feminist genealogies; on commons; on social reproduction. Lately, her research has focused on "cosmopolitics", the space of transition that scrambles the boundaries between nature and politics.

Andrea Günter
Andrea Günter is lecturer at the University of Freiburg, author, instructor in the adult education and team coach for different organizations. Since 1996, she holds several visiting professorships and lectureships in philosophical, interdisciplinary and gender study courses, e. g. at the University of Freiburg, Klagenfurt, HU Berlin, Graz, Saarbrücken, Hamburg, Bielefeld/Bethel, Bremen and the University of Applied Police Studies of Villingen-Schwenningen. Selected publications: *Philosophie und*

Geschlechterdifferenz. Auf dem Weg eines genealogischen Geschlechterdiskurses (2022); *Wertekulturen, Fundamentalismus und Autorität. Zur Ethik des Politischen* (2017); "Can an Ethics of Justice Have Its Starting Point in a Situation of Lack? Decentering Richness along with Plato's Politeia" (2016); *Die Kultur des Ökonomischen. Gerechtigkeit, Geschlechterverhältnisse und das Primat der Politik* (2013).

Ruth E. Hagengruber
Ruth Edith Hagengruber holds a chair dedicated to the Philosophy of Economics and Information Science at Paderborn University. She is also Director of the Center for the History of Women Philosophers and Scientists. From 2011 to 2019 she served in the Advisory Board of Technology in Society for the Technical University Munich and became life-member of the International Association of Philosophy of Information Science in 2011. On 2020 she became elected member of the Leibniz-Sozietät der Wissenschaften zu Berlin. She serves as chief editor of the German Springer series *Frauen in Philosophie und Wissenschaft* and as co-editor of the International Springer series *Women in the History of Philosophy and Science*. With Mary Ellen Waithe, she co-edits the *Encyclopedia of Concise Concepts by Women Philosophers* and the *Journal for the History of Women Philosophers* at Brill's.

Toyomi Iwawaki-Riebel
Toyomi Iwawaki-Riebel is currently a lecturer at the University of Applied Sciences, Würzburg-Schweinfurt (FHWS). She is also a scholar of philosophy, comparative philosophy, and Japanology. Iwawaki-Riebel translated and published children's literature, philosophical books, and writes essays and magazine articles among others in Germany, Japan, and Korea. In 2003 she completed her doctorate with her dissertation "Philosophy of the Wanderer by Friedrich Nietzsche", in which she researched intercultural understanding with the help of the phenomenology of the body through Nietzsche's hermeneutics. Iwawaki-Riebel had been an active lecturer in Japanese language and Japanese studies at Würzburg University and Erlangen University. In Erlangen she was a research assistant and in 2016 held the translatology-related conference "Language – Translation – World(s)". The corresponding book *Sprache – Übersetzen – Welt(en)* was published in 2017. She is also a poet and published a haiku anthology, *Haiku without Title*, in 2020.

Priyanka Jha
Priyanka Jha teaches Political Science at the Department of Political Science, Banaras Hindu University, India. Her research interest lies in the domain of Political Theory, Political Science and Intellectual History of Ideas. She is particularly interested in mapping gendered thinking in modern India and South Asia, engaging with women thinkers as crucial interlocutors on normative debates and key concepts. Most recently, in 2022, she was awarded the 20th Dr. D.C Pavate fellowship at POLIS and Sidney Sussex College, University of Cambridge.

Kateryna Karpenko
Kateryna Karpenko is a Doctor of Philosophy (2007) and professor since 2008. She is Head of the Department of Philosophy at Kharkiv National Medical University and Director of the Centre for Gender Education. She took part in more than 100 international conferences in Ukraine, Germany, Great Britain, USA, China, Estonia, Hungary, Austria, Holland, Switzerland, Italy, and Macedonia. She published more than 200 works, including her monograph *Nature and Woman: Ecofeminist Perspectives in Ukraine* (2006, in Ukrainian). Publications among others: "Ecofeminist Analysis of Environmental Economics" (2020, together with I. Karpenko and O. Karpenko).

Tatiana Kolomeitceva

Tatiana Kolomeitceva is an independent researcher in Moscow, Russia. She got her Ph. D. in History of Russian Philosophy in Yekaterinburg, Russia in 2012. From 2011 to 2017 she taught philosophy in higher education institutions in Yekaterinburg and Moscow. She has also run the science blogs entitled "How to Finish Your Thesis" and "Hegel and Russia".

Rosaura Martínez Ruiz

Rosaura Martínez Ruiz is Full Professor of Philosophy at the National Autonomous University of Mexico (UNAM) and a member of the National System of Researchers, level III. She was coordinator of the research projects "Philosophers after Freud" and "Philosophy and Psychoanalysis as Critical Boarders of the Political". She is the author of *Freud y Derrida: escritura y psique* (2013) and *Eros: Más allá de la pulsión de muerte* (2018). This last book has been translated into English and published by Fordham University Press, *Eros: Beyond the Death Drive* (2021). She has coordinated several collective books and published articles on the intersections between psychoanalysis and philosophy and on the field of the psychopolitical. In 2017 she was awarded the Research Prize in Humanities by the Mexican Academy of Sciences and in 2019 she was a Fulbright Scholar. She is part of the advisory board of the "International Consortium of Critical Theory Programs" coordinated by Judith Butler.

Herta Nagl-Docekal

Herta Nagl-Docekal, Univ.-Prof. em., Department of Philosophy, University of Vienna, Austria; full member of the Austrian Academy of Sciences; membre tit. of the Institut International de Philosophie, Paris. Vice-President of FISP (2008–2013); currently, member of the FISP Gender Committee. Visiting professor: Utrecht, the Netherlands; Free University Berlin, University of Konstanz and J. W. Goethe University, Frankfurt a. M., Germany, University of St. Petersburg, Russian Federation. Recent book: *Innere Freiheit. Grenzen der nachmetaphysischen Moralkonzeptionen* (2014). Selected publications in English: *Feminist Philosophy* (2004), *Continental Philosophy in Feminist Perspective* (co-ed., 2000), "Feminist Perspectives on Kant's Conception of Autonomy" (2022). Co-editor *Deutsche Zeitschrift für Philosophie*. Further publications can be found at: https://home.phl.univie.ac.at/herta.nagl.

Julie A. Nelson

Julie A. Nelson is an American feminist economist and professor emeritus of economics at the University of Massachusetts, Boston. She is best known for her application of feminist theory to economics. Nelson is a leading researcher in the field and often regarded as a founder of the discipline. Her research interests include feminist economics, ecological economics, ethics and economics, economic methodology, and the empirical study of individual behavior. She is the author or editor of many books including *Economics for Humans* (2nd ed. 2018), *Beyond Economic Man* (1993), and *Feminism, Objectivity and Economics* (1996). She is also the author of many articles in journals including *Economics and Philosophy*, *History of Political Economy*, and *Hypatia: Journal of Feminist Philosophy*.

Andrea Pérez-Fernández

Andrea Pérez Fernández is a predoctoral researcher at the Faculty of Philosophy of the University of Barcelona. Her project, funded by a doctoral research contract of the Spanish Ministry of Universities, deals with the political dimension of German artist Hannah Höch's theory and practice of photomontage. She is a member of the Philosophy and Gender Seminar, where she has worked on Simone Weil and Rosa Luxemburg. She is also a member of ADHUC – Research Center for Theory, Gender, Sexuality. She has been a visiting researcher at the Freie Universität Berlin (2021) and at the

Institute of Advanced Studies in Loughborough University (2022). Recent publications: "Simone Weil's Critique of Marx: A Source for Ecosocialist Thought" (together with Pau Matheu, Isegoría, forthcoming), "From Compassion to Distance: Hannah Höch's 'Mother'" (2022).

Ariadni Polychroniou
Ariadni Polychroniou has studied law (LL.B) at the National and Kapodistrian University of Athens and has been working for the last five years as a lawyer specialized mainly in public and civil law. She has obtained her LL. M. in Philosophy of Law from the National and Kapodistrian University of Athens, Greece and her second Master Degree in Gender Studies from Umeå University, Sweden. She has been, since December 2018, a Ph. D. Candidate in the Department of History and Theory of Law at the Law School of Athens. For the spring semester 2021–2022, she has been selected to teach Sociology of Law, Gender and Law and Literature and Law in assistant courses for undergraduate students. Her main research and academic interests focus on critical legal theory, post-structuralist feminist theory, feminist phenomenology, as well as critical refugee studies, social movement and democratic theory. In the last four years, she has presented her original research in numerous academic conferences in Italy, Sweden, U. K., France, Germany, Austria and Greece and has published research papers in the field of feminist theory both in international and Greek academic journals. Her most recent research paper is titled "Towards a Critical Reconstruction of Modern Refugee Subjectivity: Overcoming the Threat-Victim Bipolarity with Judith Butler and Giorgio Agamben" (2021). She has also worked as an intern and an external collaborator in the National Bioethics Committee of Greece, the Greek Council for Refugees, the Hellenic Foundation for European and Foreign Policy and ActionAid.

Pedro Falcão Pricladnitzky
Pedro Pricladnitzky is a professor of philosophy at the State University of West Paraná (UNIOESTE). Between 2016–2020, he was professor of philosophy at the State University of Maringá (UEM). He graduated from the Federal University of Rio Grande do Sul (UFRGS) where he continued his studies earning his M. A. and Ph. D. in philosophy. He is one of the organizers of the international conference "Women in Modern Philosophy" in Rio de Janeiro and editors of the volume *Women in Modern Philosophy – Latin American Perspectives*. His research focuses on early modern metaphysics and natural philosophy, particularly the perspectives of Descartes and Cavendish.

María Lucía Rivera-Sanín
María Lucía Rivera-Sanín is a professor in the Department of Bioethics at Universidad El Bosque in Bogotá. She is a founding member of the Colombian Network of Women Philosophers (Red Colombiana de Mujeres Filósofas) and is a researcher with the Observatory for Gender and Philosophy in Colombia, she is part of the Consultive Committee of the Latin American Network of Women Philosophers of Unesco and part of Redbioetica Unesco. Recent publications include: *Perspectivas feministas para a bioética* (2022), *Phobos: Evil and Urgency in a Conflictive Pandemic* (2022), *Narrativas de una guerra cotidiana, o una cotidianidad en guerra* (2020), *Autonomía, agencia y autoconfianza. Reflexiones desde la bioética feminista* (2020).

Laura Roberts
Laura Roberts is a lecturer in Women's and Gender at Flinders University and received her Ph. D. in Philosophy from the University of Queensland. She is author of *Irigaray and Politics: A Critical Introduction* (2019), co-editor with Prof. Lenart Skof of a Special Issue *Irigaray and Politics* (2022) and has

published articles in edited collections and journals including *Hypatia, Feminist Review* and *Australian Feminist Studies*. Laura was co-convener of the Luce Irigaray Circle from 2018–2022.

Tzitzi Janik Rojas Torres
Tzitzi Janik Rojas Torres graduated from the UNAM with a degree in philosophy. Later she studied for a master's degree at the same institution researching Islamic mystical thought from a decolonial perspective. She has been giving workshops and courses of philosophical and cultural dissemination for a broad audience for more than ten years. Her various academic studies abroad include a stay at the University of Ankara as an international scholarship holder of the Yunus Emre program, granted by the Turkish government, and a research exchange at the Iranian Studies Department of the Sorbonne Nouvelle-Paris III. Her areas of study are aesthetics, ethics, and non-Western literature and philosophy from a post-colonial perspective. She currently teaches a Research Methodology seminar as a permanent professor at the Faculty of Music and a seminar about the Problems of Ethics in Islamic Philosophy at the Faculty of Philosophy and Arts. Her syllabus is one of the few courses at the faculty that focuses entirely on Islamic philosophy from a decolonial and south-south dialogue perspective.

Cristina Sánchez
Cristina Sánchez Muñoz is Professor of Philosophy of Law and a researcher at the Universidad Autónoma de Madrid. In her academic career, she has developed two fundamental lines of research: the study of the thought of the philosopher Hannah Arendt, and research connected with contemporary feminist theory and, more specifically, with critical theory. Among her current lines of research is the study of evil in contemporary societies, based on the ethical, political, legal and philosophical problems raised by the Holocaust, and the forms of accountability for violent traumatic pasts.

Anne Sauka
Anne Sauka is a researcher at the University of Latvia, where she also works as a lecturer in social philosophy. Anne is currently implementing the postdoctoral project "Onto-genealogies: The Body and Environmental Ethics in Latvia" (2021–2023). Anne studies materially embedded genealogies of the body and the environment. Her previous experience is related to the themes of philosophical anthropology, critical genealogy, and biopolitics of the body. Later she engaged more closely with new materialist theories, exploring processual approaches to the question of body, leading to including biophilosophy, eco-phenomenology, embodied critical thinking and environmental humanities in her areas of interest. Anne is the author of several articles, including "The Nature of Our Becoming: Genealogical Perspectives" (2020) and "A Bite of the Forbidden Fruit: The Abject of Food and Affirmative Environmental Ethics" (2022). Anne's latest publications can be found here: https://www.researchgate.net/profile/Anne-Sauka/publications Contact: anne.sauka@lu.lv.

Priyanka Singh
Priyanka Singh is Assistant Professor of English at Arya Kanya Mahavidhyalaya, Shahabad Markanda, Kurukshetra, India. Previously she worked as Associate Professor and Head of Department of English at JMIT, Radaur, Yamunanagar, India. She has a diverse experience of 17 years in professional and degree colleges. She is an alumnus of Indraprastha College for Women, Delhi University. Dr. Singh completed her Ph. D. on "From Submission to Affirmation: A Study of Women Characters in the Novels of Bapsi Sidhwa". She has remained Member, Board of Studies (English), at Kurukshetra University, Haryana, India. Her areas of research interests include feminist studies, partition studies and

postcolonial studies and Haryanvi literature. She has published 22 research papers in reputed international and national journals and books and has presented research papers in international and national conferences and has chaired sessions in international conferences. She is associated with the Department of Higher Education, Panchkula, as Resource Person and has prepared and delivered e-content telecasted on Utkarsh and YouTube channels of DHE, Haryana. She writes poems, both in English and Hindi, and has published a few of them in anthologies. Her debut collection of poems is titled *Search, Singh, Shine*.

Sabine Thürmel
Interdisciplinary work on the foundations and effects of culture changing information technologies is Sabine Thürmel's focus since the 1990s. Her background is both in computer science (Ph. D. in Computer Science) and philosophy (Ph. D. in Philosophy of Science and Technology). As a computer scientist she has first-hand experience in creating and deploying the technology she writes about from a philosophical perspective. She profits from her work in academia and industry. Currently she is an independent researcher and a lecturer at the Technical University of Munich (TUM). For details, esp. publications, see http://www.sabinethuermel.de/ where computer science meets philosophy.

Demin Xu
Demin XU is Doctor of Philosophy, post-doctoral researcher at LLCP – University of Paris VIII and teacher of Chinese language and culture at Paris Institute of Political Studies (Sciences Po). Her areas of research cover modern democracy, individual freedom and political freedom, Chinese politics and society.

Index of Names

Acevedo-Zapata, Diana María 10, 295
Adlbi, Sirin 327–329
Agarwal, Bina 100 f.
Akiko, Yosano 8, 191–199
Al Adawiya, Rabia 328
Al-Farabi 325
Alloni, Ingrid 11, 335
Amorós, Celia 290–293
Ankersmit, Frank 147–150
Apel, Karl-Otto 60–62
Arendt, Hannah 11, 173, 271 f., 277 f., 286, 289, 291, 347–351, 354, 356
Aristotle 37, 45, 48–54, 120 f., 123, 160 f., 165, 172, 325, 330
Attri, Shalini 5, 69

Baird Callicott, J. 59
Baizabal, Emma 5, 109
Baudry, Jeanne 265
Baumann, Zygmund 61
Beard, Mary 174, 176, 182
Benhabib, Seyla 286–288, 290–292, 349, 351
Bergson, Henri 266
Birulés, Fina 271, 277 f., 291
Bonfim, Sarah 9, 249
Bonnet, Annabelle 9, 261 f., 264, 266
Bordo, Susan 24
Braidotti, Rosi 36, 39, 82, 84, 91 f., 99–101, 103
Bruno, Giordano 123, 130
Butler, Judith 11, 17, 57, 63, 336–339, 347, 349–358, 364–367

Camillo, Giulio 123
Campanella, Tommaso 124 f.
Camus, Albert 352
Canguilhem, Georges 267
Carson, Rachel 71
Casi, Corinna 5, 97
Cassirer, Ernst 122
Cavarero, Adriana 336–339, 342, 348, 351
Cavendish, Henry 9, 235–247
Chakravarti, Uma 174, 176 f., 182

Cicero 158
Confucius 199, 217, 233

Darwin, Charles 85 f., 225
Davis, Angela 336, 340–342
Dawkins, Richard 147–151, 153
De Beauvoir, Simone 17, 35, 43, 53, 55, 173, 234, 261 f., 265, 267 f., 325, 333
De Gouges, Olympe 233, 286
De la Cruz, Sor Juana Inés 203 f., 206–212, 214
De Pizan, Christine 77, 79, 260
De Reina, Casidoro 208
D'Eaubonne, Françoise 99
DeGriselles, Timothy 8, 203
Deibel, Eric 7, 157, 158, 164
Deibel, Talya Ucaryilmaz 7, 157, 158, 164
Demeter 337
Derrida, Jacques 39, 63, 290, 349
Descartes, René 127, 247, 264, 336
Devi, Rassundari 177, 187
Diotima 36, 123, 337
Duxiu, Chen 8, 217 f., 230, 234

Eikjok, Jorunn 104 f.
Ernst, Waltraud 7, 147, 149, 154

Fabris, Adriano 377 f.
Fichte, Johann Gottlieb 16
Firestone, Shulamith 110
Floridi, Luciano 121–123, 125, 373
Forbes, Geraldine 177 f.
Forte, Bruno 371
Foucault, Michel 16, 39, 85 f., 349
Fox Keller, Evelyn 24
Fricker, Miranda 299, 327, 329
Friedlaender, Salomo 277
Friedman, Marilyn 287

Gandhi, Mahatma 99, 176, 186 f.
Gaudiano, Valentina 12, 371, 373, 378
Giardini, Federica 4, 35 f., 39, 41
Gilligan, Carol 64 f.
Green, Joyce 102, 272

Grosz, Elizabeth 137–140, 144f., 272, 274
Günter, Andrea 4, 45–47, 50, 54, 376

Habermas, Jürgen 29, 286
Hagengruber, Ruth E. 3, 119, 124, 127
Hanolin, Rosalin O. 177
Haraway, Donna 39, 41, 63, 83, 85, 111f.
Harding, Sandra 24
Hegel, Georg Wilhelm Friedrich 150, 165, 194
Heidegger, Martin 60, 114, 147f., 152, 371
Held, Virginia 29, 64
Heller, Ágnes 375
Hemmerle, Klaus 377–379
Hierro, Graciela 325
Hobbes, Thomas 60, 82, 138, 247, 286
Höch, Hannah 10, 271–279
Homer 337
Husserl 151, 383

Irigaray, Luce 16, 36, 40, 50f., 62f.
Iwawaki-Riebel, Toyomi 8, 191

Jain, Devaki 179
Jha, Priyanka 7, 171
Joshee, Anandibai 177, 187
Junwu, Ma 8, 217f., 222f., 225, 233

Kafka, Franz 356
Kanitkar, Kanshibai 177
Kant, Immanuel 47, 59, 82, 147f., 151, 154, 163, 198, 330, 336
Karpenko, Kateryna 4, 57
Kohlberg, Lawrence 64f.
Kolomeitceva, Tatiana 6, 147
Kosambi, Meera 176f.
Kristeva, Julia 83, 348

Lacan, Jacques 62f., 350
Lalita, K 178
Lazare, Bernard 356
Lee-Lampshire, Wendy 63
Leibniz, Gottfried Wilhelm 41, 150
Lerner, Gerda 174, 176, 182, 187
Liezi 199
Locke, John 82, 138
Longino, Helen 24
Lonzi, Carla 36

López Farjat, Luis Xavier 325
López McAlister, Linda 13
Lovelace, Ada 127
Luxembourg, Rosa 173

Macaulay, Catharine 178, 260
Majumdar, Veena 179
Marion, Henri 264
Martínez Ruiz, Rosaura 11, 361
Marx, Karl 23, 30, 150, 198
Mead, George Herbert 61
Mernissi, Fatima 326, 331
Mies, Maria 72, 100
Moller Okin, Susan 98
Moore, Thomas 70
Mosse, George 341
Muñoz, José 366
Muraro, Luisa 36

Naess, Arne 65
Nagl-Docekal, Herta 13, 15
Nancy, Jean-Luc 293, 372
Neimanis, Astrida 81, 84, 92f.
Nelson, Julie 4, 23, 58f.
Nietzsche, Friedrich 82, 85f., 197f., 349
Nussbaum, Martha 105, 288
Nzegwu, Njiru 99, 102–104

Pateman, Carole 10, 37, 285–287
Pérez-Fernández, Andrea 10, 271, 274, 279
Phillips, Anne 10, 285, 292
Phule, Savitiribai 177, 187
Piaget, Jean 54
Plato 8, 16, 48, 123, 172, 203, 205, 212–214, 325, 330, 373
Polychroniou, Ariadni 11, 347, 357
Pricladnitzky, Pedro Falcão 9, 235

Qichao, Liang 8, 217f., 220–226, 228f., 233

Ramabai, Pandita 177, 187
Ranade, Ramabai 177
Rancière, Jacques 350, 357
Rawls, John 61, 286
Raworth, Kate 60, 65f.
Reyes, Alfonso 326
Rivera-Sanín, Maria Lucía 10, 295

Roberts, Laura   6, 137
Rogers, Barbara   103, 263
Rojas Torres, Tzitzi Janik   10, 323
Rokeya Sakhawat Hossain, Begum   5, 69
Rolston, Holmes   59
Rousseau, Jean-Jacques   8f., 199, 217–222, 225f., 228f., 233, 250, 252f., 255, 260
Royer, Clémence   262, 265
Rush, Ibn   325

Said, Edward   328f.
Salleh, Ariel   40
Salomon, Mathilde   266
Sánchez, Cristina   10, 285f.
Sandel, Michael   29
Sangari, Kumkum   176
Sappho from Lesbos   325
Sarasin, Philipp   85f.
Sarkar, Lotika   175, 179
Sarkar, Tanika   175–177, 182
Sartre, Jean-Paul   267
Sauka, Anne   5, 81f., 85–87, 91, 93
Scheherazade   326
Segal, Lynne   57, 62
Sen, Amartya   98
Sen, Hemabati   98, 177
Sheikh, Fatima   177
Shi, Hu   8, 217, 220f., 230f.
Shiva, Vandana   69, 71–73, 79, 100
Simondon, Gilbert   114–116
Sina, Ibn   325
Singh, Priyanka   5, 69
Sinha, Mrinalni   176
Smith, Adam   23, 37, 102, 121, 160, 175
Socrates   8, 16, 123, 203–205, 212–215
Sousa de Santos, Boaventura   327

Starhawk   71
Stein, Edith   373, 375, 379
Stone, Alison   148, 154, 163
Stuart, Maria W.   30, 225f., 288

Tharu, Sussie   178
Thatcher, Margret   122
Thürmel, Sabine   6, 129
Tianhe, Jin   8, 217f., 223, 225–227, 233
Toledo, Gustavo Leal   8, 148–150
Tolstoy, Leo   194, 196f.
Torres Bodet, Jaime   326
Tristan, Flora   262
Turing, Alan   127, 161

Vaid, Sudesh   176
Varnhagen, Rahel   349
Von Bingen, Hildegard   16
Von Hildebrand, Dietrich   373, 376, 378–380, 383

Wallace, Michael   341
Warren, Karen   58
Weber, Max   16
Weil, Simone   261
Wittgenstein, Ludwig   60
Wollstonecraft, Mary   9, 173, 249 – 260, 286
Woolf, Virginia   325

Xu, Demin   8, 220
Xun, Lu   8, 217f., 231

Yamuni Tabushi, Vera   324 – 326, 331 – 333

Zambrano, Maria   373, 377

Index of Subjects

Activism   6, 36, 137, 179, 286, 289, 356
Ancient Rome   7, 157 f., 165
Anthropocene   39, 43
Antiquity   7, 157, 165, 174 f., 337
Art   77, 111 f., 130 f., 133, 195 f., 209 f., 265, 271–279, 301, 312 f., 324, 329, 340, 369
Artificial Intelligence   6 f., 119 f., 127, 157, 161
Authority   35, 69, 78, 82, 132 f., 208, 211 f., 254–256, 299, 374
Autonomy   4, 37, 63, 83, 105, 113, 131, 142, 164, 166, 171 f., 181, 254, 263, 287–289, 291, 336, 338 f.

Balance   28, 71, 73, 264, 277
Barcelona en Comú   6, 137 f., 141–145
Bias   25 f., 50, 66, 109, 115, 147, 174 f., 262, 298 f., 320
Binary System   6, 119, 125
Biology   81, 83, 85–88, 110, 113, 115, 149, 162
Biopolitics   83
Black Feminism   340
Body-Environment   5, 81
Brazil   12

Canada   5, 18, 97, 102, 104, 296, 303
Capitalism   5, 31, 48, 50 f., 69–72, 76, 82, 90, 109 f., 143, 198
Change   3 f., 6, 46, 49, 57, 63, 65, 71, 84, 86, 113 f., 119, 122 f., 125–127, 130, 132–134, 137, 141 f., 154, 164 f., 176 f., 181, 197, 224, 240, 242, 246 f., 276, 279, 285, 292, 332, 336–339, 344, 368
Chauvinism   273
China   9, 17 f., 217
Class   3, 12, 71, 101, 139, 166, 177, 183, 196, 198 f., 219, 224, 226, 263, 266, 287, 299 f., 342, 353, 364–366
Classical Roman Philosophy   157 f., 162, 164
Climate Change   4 f., 23, 42, 58, 66, 69, 368
Colombia   10, 295–298, 300–304, 307 f., 315, 319–321
Communication   7, 59–63, 66, 149, 163, 186, 244, 326, 356, 377 f.

Consciousness   9, 83, 85–87, 90, 160, 164–166, 173, 182, 186, 194 f., 197–199, 235 f., 238, 242
Contemporaneity   57
Contingency   271 f., 277–279, 349
Covid-19   11, 38, 142, 199, 361, 368
Cultural Criticism   8, 191
Cyberfeminism   5, 109, 111
Cybernetics   7, 157 f., 160, 162

Dadaism   272
Damage   4, 23, 40, 255, 362, 367
Data   6, 23 f., 37, 87, 121, 125, 129–134, 137, 140, 143 f., 204, 258, 296 f., 301, 304, 307 f., 319, 362 f., 366
Democracy   10, 72, 141 f., 144, 164, 191, 196, 261–264, 285–293, 300, 321, 344
Development   10, 13 f., 25, 36, 39, 42, 46, 48, 64 f., 69, 71–74, 79, 81, 86, 98, 100, 103, 112, 114, 119 f., 129 f., 132, 134, 143, 153, 163–165, 179, 182, 196 f., 237, 250, 252 f., 255, 271, 276, 278, 289 f., 321, 326, 348, 350, 374 f.
Digital Technology   7, 157
Digitization   7, 157
Diversification   13, 47
Diversity   12, 47, 73, 117, 141, 178 f., 185, 188, 258, 299 f., 330 f., 340, 377

Ecological Issues   4, 57–60
Ecology   4, 35 f., 39–42, 58 f., 69–72, 78, 89, 157, 163
Economics   3 f., 18, 23–28, 30–32, 35, 37–42, 46, 48, 50 f., 58 f., 65 f., 69, 71, 75, 351
Ecotopia   5, 69–71, 73, 75, 78 f.
Emancipation   9, 11, 16, 75, 109–111, 114, 154, 165, 177, 179, 181 f., 249–251, 259, 335, 344, 367 f.
Enlightenment   6, 24, 147 f., 150 f., 154 f., 198, 264, 286, 289–291
Enslavement   114
Environment   3–6, 18, 30 f., 59, 63–65, 71, 74, 78, 81–91, 99–101, 103, 129, 138, 355
Epistemology   6, 35, 119 f., 123–125, 127 f., 183, 298

https://doi.org/10.1515/9783111051802-035

Equality   36, 45, 49–53, 57f., 62, 105, 142, 164, 187, 196–199, 253, 263, 265, 267, 285, 288–293, 295–298, 300, 319, 321, 341f.
Ethics   15f., 23, 26, 28, 30f., 59f., 64f., 71, 81, 89, 92, 99, 127, 163f., 193, 290, 296, 298, 350
Eurocentrism   11, 100, 109, 173, 323, 324, 326, 327

Fear   111, 160, 203, 206, 210, 257, 264f., 275, 278, 326, 338
Femininity   24–26, 62, 64, 69, 89, 250, 321, 348
Feminism   11f., 16, 35, 39, 58, 62, 72, 79, 99, 102, 109, 111–114, 117, 141f., 179, 183, 285f., 288–293, 324–327, 330f., 336, 339f., 345, 348, 361f., 365–368
Feminist   4–6, 8, 10f., 14–17, 23f., 27f., 30, 35–37, 39–42, 45f., 49f., 57f., 62, 69–74, 79, 81, 84, 89, 98–102, 104, 110–112, 114, 121, 128, 137–145, 171, 173f., 176–180, 182f., 185, 217, 263, 266, 274, 285, 288–293, 296, 298, 323–326, 329, 331f., 335–339, 341, 347–351, 354, 363f., 366–368
Feminist Perspective   4, 6, 16, 35, 39, 58, 109, 117, 123, 142, 145, 292
Feminist Technology   5, 109
Feminist Theory   4, 45f., 58, 101, 286–288, 291f., 347–350, 357
Feminist Thought   3, 9, 36, 347f., 362
Fragility   83, 271, 276–279, 320, 373f.
French Philosophy   9, 261f., 264f., 268
Future   3, 7f., 12, 17f., 39, 41, 45f., 52, 69, 76f., 82, 93, 109, 113, 130f., 133, 141, 144, 158f., 163–165, 171, 182, 191, 211, 260, 263, 265, 291, 298, 300, 321, 339f., 361, 369, 371, 376, 378f.

Gender   3, 6, 10, 17f., 24f., 27f., 45–48, 50, 52f., 57–60, 63–66, 73, 90, 101–105, 110, 112–114, 128, 137, 139, 141f., 145, 147, 166, 174f., 178f., 184–186, 188, 193, 196f., 199, 209, 259f., 262–264, 267f., 274, 287f., 293, 296–301, 319–321, 328, 335–341, 348f., 351, 363f.
Gender Equality   3, 7f., 10, 57, 65, 97, 142, 198, 217, 268, 285, 295–297, 300, 309, 320, 332
Gender Inequality   5, 10, 58f., 97f., 105, 295, 298
Gender Justice   4, 57–60, 66, 142
Gender Metaphor   4, 23
Gender Studies   187
Gender Violence   11, 141, 293, 332, 361, 363
Genealogy   41, 85–87, 91f., 331
Geology   5, 69
Germany   4, 6, 13–15, 18, 26, 272f., 275, 279, 358
God   8, 46, 82, 90, 203–205, 207f., 210–213, 251f., 254, 371
Governance   6, 38, 129, 132, 144
Greek   49, 160, 162, 166, 212, 324–326, 337, 342, 351

Healthcare   6, 29, 129, 132, 369
Hierarchy   4, 37, 113, 120f., 128, 142, 153, 204, 276, 328f., 344
Higher Education   10, 191, 266, 295f., 300f.
History   3, 7, 9, 11, 13, 18, 31, 48, 50, 54, 82, 85f., 88, 97, 104, 121, 123, 149–151, 154, 158, 160, 164, 172–177, 180–182, 187f., 191, 260–263, 265, 267f., 271, 289, 296, 323, 326, 328, 330–332, 335–337, 340, 347, 356, 365, 369, 373, 375
History of Philosophy   7, 11, 14, 16, 109, 151, 250, 259, 261f., 266, 291, 323f., 327
Human Values   6, 119

International Association of Women Philosophers (IAPh)   13–18, 43
Identity   11, 57, 64, 104, 114f., 121, 141, 243, 325, 327f., 331, 335–339, 343–345, 349, 363, 376f.
Igbo   5, 97, 102f., 105
Impact   3, 5f., 9f., 38, 57, 69, 89, 102, 129f., 142, 182, 187, 245, 249f., 255, 258, 265, 275, 289, 297–299, 301, 321
Imperialism   154, 175, 195
Inclusion   14, 93, 175, 285, 287, 290, 297, 300, 320, 323, 329
India   5, 7f., 12, 71–75, 77, 91, 99f., 171–180, 182–184, 186f.
Indigenous Feminism   5, 97f., 101f.
Indigenous Women   5, 72, 97, 99, 101f., 104f., 172f.

Index of Subjects — **395**

Inequity   11 f., 361, 365 f., 369
Instrumentalism   6, 24, 77, 87, 109, 114, 177, 341
Intellectual History   7 f., 171–176, 178–184, 186–188, 328
Internationalization   8, 13, 17, 191
Intersectionality   361, 365
Islamic Feminism   11, 323 f., 326, 330–332
Islamic Philosophy   323 f., 326, 329–332

Japan   8, 191, 193–195, 197, 199
Justice   4, 30, 45–54, 57, 60, 64–66, 72, 93, 154, 175, 181, 219, 285, 300, 321, 329 f., 369

Kahnawa:kev   5, 97
Knowledge   4, 6, 8 f., 11, 23 f., 26, 36–38, 41–43, 64, 69 f., 72, 77, 79, 84 f., 89, 93 f., 101, 103, 110 f., 114, 119–129, 131–133, 150–152, 155, 161, 171, 174 f., 179–181, 187 f., 206–208, 213, 240, 242, 244–246, 249–251, 257–260, 263–265, 295, 319, 321, 324, 327–330, 338, 369

Legal Subjectivity   157 f., 160–166
LGBTQIA+   141 f., 351
Liberation   8, 73, 191, 289, 368

Machines   6, 109, 115, 119, 124, 126 f., 129 f., 132 f., 147, 154, 157, 159–162, 166
Market   4, 23–25, 29, 32, 38, 46, 48, 50 f., 53, 100, 116, 288
Masculinity   15, 25 f., 62, 287, 348
Materialism   235 f., 338
Materiality   5, 53, 81 f., 86–88, 90, 112 f., 354
Media   6, 129, 140, 144, 147, 371 f., 377
Medicine   6, 129–133, 245
Meiji Era   8, 191 f., 194
Mexico   5, 11, 113, 323–327, 331, 361–363, 367
Minority   297, 299, 344, 364 f.
Modern China   8, 217
Modernity   10, 123, 171, 285, 288 f., 291, 327, 351
Modernization   8, 74, 191 f., 289
Money   4, 24, 29, 32, 45–54, 75, 254, 265
Money Economy   45–47
Moral   4, 23, 29 f., 32, 37, 40, 61, 63–65, 98, 105, 164, 195, 197 f., 231, 250 f., 253–259, 263, 286–288, 328, 335, 340, 369
Muslim   75, 323–332

Nature   3, 5, 9, 42 f., 49, 58–63, 65, 69–79, 82 f., 86, 89 f., 97–103, 109–111, 113, 120, 124, 127 f., 149, 152, 157–160, 163, 177, 179, 182 f., 188, 204 f., 235–247, 251, 256 f., 287, 339–341, 366, 369, 374
Neocolonialism   97
Nicomachean Ethics   45, 48
Nigeria   5, 97, 99, 102 f.

Ontogeanology   5, 81, 83, 85–89, 91 f., 94
Ontology   6, 83, 88, 91 f., 116 f., 119–121, 123, 125 f., 128, 337, 350

Pandemic   10–12, 38–40, 76, 199, 293, 361 f., 364–366, 368 f., 371–373, 375 f.
Panpsychism   235, 238, 241 f., 245–247
Paradigm   5, 11, 39, 69, 81–83, 85, 90, 92, 111, 131, 137, 143, 164 f., 287, 323, 327 f., 330, 338, 343 f.
Past   3, 7, 12, 39, 48, 93, 100, 122, 133, 149–151, 166, 171, 182, 211, 260 f., 275, 291, 336, 339 f., 343, 371, 373
Patriarchy   48, 58, 149, 174, 178, 182, 292
Perception   4, 9, 39–41, 84, 119, 181 f., 219, 236, 238–241, 244 f., 258, 279, 297, 320, 375
Pharmacy   6, 129, 131
Phenomenology   81, 84 f., 92, 194
Philosophical Canon   35, 41, 291, 297
Philosophy   6–11, 13–18, 28, 31, 35 f., 42, 59 f., 63, 69 f., 74, 77, 79, 81, 85, 89, 92, 119–124, 137 f., 143, 151, 153 f., 158–160, 163 f., 166, 172, 191, 196, 199, 235, 238, 240 f., 244, 259, 261–268, 277, 285, 289–291, 295–305, 307, 311–315, 317–321, 323–330, 336, 338, 347 f., 350, 373
Plurality   16, 278, 323, 331, 337, 339, 344, 348 f., 351 f., 357
Poetry   8, 191, 193, 195, 204 f., 208–210, 212, 215, 326
Political Improvement   11, 335
Political Issues   16
Politics of Presence   10, 285, 292
Post-Colonialism   8, 43, 106, 171–173, 179 f., 188, 339, 387
Power Imbalance   7, 157
Pre-Modern Japan   191
Propaganda   8, 191

Qing Dynasty 9, 217

Race 3, 10, 32, 101, 128, 139, 166, 287, 299f., 335f., 340, 342f.
Rationality 9, 27, 29, 37, 63, 174, 235, 237f., 242f., 246, 253, 257, 259, 328, 337
Reason 7, 9, 15, 25, 31, 38, 41, 60, 72, 82, 94, 97, 101, 109, 119f., 151, 157f., 164, 172, 186, 188, 196f., 207, 211, 213, 236f., 239-243, 245f., 249-261, 264, 276, 291, 300, 319, 336, 339-343, 345, 353, 366, 371
Refugee 11, 347, 355-358
Religion 10, 82, 101, 120, 174, 183, 187, 231, 325
Remodeling 197f.
Roman Philosophy 7, 157f., 162, 164f.
Russia 6, 97, 104, 154

Sami 5, 97, 99, 104f.
Sapmi 5, 97, 102, 104
Science 4-6, 8, 15, 24, 30, 37-39, 42, 69-74, 76-79, 81-86, 90, 102, 119, 121, 123, 129, 131-134, 148f., 151-153, 162-164, 172, 184, 196, 204-207, 209f., 212, 218, 231, 262-265, 295f., 328, 330
Self-Awareness 11, 160, 164, 166, 242, 335
Self-Defense 8, 203, 206
Sensitivity 9, 65, 235, 238, 243-246
Sex 35, 52f., 57, 62, 65, 103, 110, 138, 182, 217f., 225, 229, 250-257, 341, 343
Sexual Contract 10, 285, 287
Slavery 7, 157-160, 162, 164-166, 256, 259, 341
Social Change 6, 126, 137, 264, 279, 292
Social Improvement 11, 335
Social Machines 6, 129-131, 134
Socio-Historical 147, 150, 261f., 357
Sor Filotea 8, 203f., 206, 209, 211, 214f.
Sovereignty 138, 143, 157f., 165
Spain 10, 18, 141, 204f., 285f., 289-293

Sultana's Dream 5, 69f., 73-75, 77-79
Sustainability 5, 26, 69, 71-73, 79

Teaching 10f., 104, 172, 175, 184, 188, 257, 263, 267, 295, 301, 320f., 323-325, 327, 330
Techno-feminism 110
Technology 3-7, 18, 65f., 70-72, 90, 109-115, 117, 119, 125, 129f., 134, 137, 140, 143-145, 157f., 163-166
Topos 12, 371
Trans-Feminism 339

Ukraine 4, 12
User Experience 6, 147-149, 151-155
Utopia 70f., 74, 78f., 109, 113, 115, 124f.

Value 4, 27f., 30, 39f., 42, 46, 49, 57, 59, 61f., 64, 69-71, 74, 82, 104, 143, 152, 181, 193, 197, 207, 264, 287f., 298, 367, 369, 371-373, 379
Violence 10-12, 58, 104, 112, 149, 271f., 274f., 277, 288, 293, 327, 330, 332, 342, 361-363, 365, 367-369
Visibility 73, 113
Vulnerability 271f., 274, 293, 338, 354, 357, 362, 375

Women 3-10, 12-17, 25f., 28, 32f., 35, 40, 46-54, 57f., 61-65, 69-79, 97-105, 110, 112, 114f., 120, 123, 141-143, 145, 147f., 151, 153-155, 171-188, 191-199, 204f., 209, 217, 225, 249-253, 255-257, 259-268, 271, 274-276, 285-293, 295-301, 303f., 308f., 311-321, 325-332, 337f., 340-343, 348, 361-368, 376
Women Philosopher 3, 7, 9, 13-18, 35, 147f., 151-155, 261f., 264-266, 268, 290f., 298, 301f., 319, 321, 329, 349
Women Rights 9, 97, 189, 249, 251, 367
Women's Liberation 8, 36, 191

www.ingramcontent.com/pod-product-compliance
Lightning Source LLC
Chambersburg PA
CBHW061927220426
43662CB00012B/1824